D1319806

PRAISE FOR *BLOOD WASH...*

A curious fact about the Afghan war is that many soldiers we sent to fight the Taliban — a movement whose name translates as "students" — themselves became students, educating themselves about the history and peoples of South Asia. Some of these warrior-scholars read deeply and could hold their own in any room of grey-bearded tribal leaders. Phil Halton is an exemplary part of that tradition, a careful historian who knows the facts about Afghanistan but also knows the limits of any foreigner's understanding. His sweeping narrative is foundational reading for any student of the war or anyone curious about why our armies fared no better than their predecessors.

> — Graeme Smith, Emmy-winning journalist, bestselling author of
> *The Dogs Are Eating Them Now: Our War in Afghanistan*

Rather than focusing on the more recent decades of war in Afghanistan, Halton offers an astute analysis of the deeply rooted political issues driving conflict in Afghanistan over the last century. *Blood Washing Blood* is an engaging and well-written text that will open eyes for scholars, policymakers, and general readers interested in one of the most enduring conflicts of our time.

> — James Tharin Bradford, author of *Poppies, Politics, and Power*

Through this sweeping and grand political history of Afghanistan, Halton proves himself to be one of Canada's leading warrior-scholars. *Blood Washing Blood* combines meticulous scholarly research and ground-level field experience in a compelling story about Afghanistan's enduring war.

> — Dr. Aisha Ahmad, University of Toronto, author of *Jihad & Co.:*
> *Black Markets and Islamist Power*

Phil Halton has done an impressive job of objectively chronicling and making unique sense of the devilishly complicated subject of contemporary political and social upheaval from an Afghan perspective. The conflicts between Afghanistan's strategic partners and adversaries, the international community, and the coalition and governments of the day is a backdrop to the "Afghan way" of personal, tribal, and ethnic influences and loyalties that have shaped domestic power struggles — something that is exceedingly difficult for outsiders to grasp. It is one thing to see the continuing saga as an outcome of the Great Game, but Halton nuances this by additionally portraying how Afghan leaders have consistently levered the Great Powers to their particular purposes. This is a very credible and readable work that resets the narrative around 100 years of upheaval, progress, and setback.

— Michael J. Ward, Major General (Retired), Deputy Commander
NATO Training Mission Afghanistan 2009–2010

I wish *Blood Washing Blood* had been available to read before my first deployment to Kandahar, Afghanistan, in 2007 or even my second tour to Kabul in 2012. I would have made it compulsory reading for my whole combat team or task force. It provides a detailed but easily understood analysis of the complicated, convoluted intricacies of Afghan history, politics, tribal relations, and power struggles.

— Colonel (Retired) Alex Ruff, the Royal Canadian Regiment

Halton has an easy style, which he uses to effect in this well-researched and highly readable history, while endeavouring to untangle a highly complex subject. The author wisely goes back more than a century in order to establish that the current animosities had their roots long before the Soviets or the West found themselves fighting in Afghanistan.… This book is at once both a warning and required reading for any who would insert expeditionary military forces into parts of the world that they do not fully comprehend.

— Colonel (Retired) Charles S. Oliviero, CD, PhD

Blood Washing Blood is an extremely readable account of a century of unending Afghan warfare. It provides valuable context and understanding of the human dimensions of a conflict in which the West has been mired for the last two decades.

— Dr. Howard G. Coombs, Associate Chair War Studies,
Royal Military College of Canada

Understanding Afghanistan and its evolution necessitates a grounding in its political history. In this volume, Phil Halton has taken a complex topic and woven a detailed, highly readable narrative that makes the topic easily accessible to anyone interested in the region and how it became what it is today. The events of 9/11 created a resurgence in our interest in Afghanistan. In *Blood Washing Blood*, author Phil Halton has shown that the path to 9/11, and beyond, actually began much earlier. Tracing the last century of twists and tumult in Afghan history, he has created a narrative that makes a very complicated history readily accessible to the contemporary student of the region.

— Colonel Tod Strickland, CD, Commandant, Canadian Army Command and Staff College

Afghanistan's history and evolution is often as mysterious as it is complex to many outsiders, but Halton has expertly unpacked it for the reader in this richly detailed and easily readable overview of its past hundred years. Combining extensive research and sources with first-hand experience on the ground, he has given us an invaluable primer for unlocking the reasons behind much of the recent conflict taking place there.

— Lieutenant Colonel Andrew B. Godefroy, CD, PhD, Canadian Army Command and Staff College

In *Blood Washing Blood*, Phil Halton has brilliantly captured the essence of the roots, goals, and nature of the Taliban insurgents who fought Canadian soldiers in the dusty groves and sun-baked plains of southern Afghanistan. It's a compelling, nuanced, and unflinching window into the heart and soul of the movement behind the insurgency.... *Blood Washing Blood* is essential reading for anyone who wants to understand the rivalries, hopes, hatreds, and complex motivations behind the Taliban and the men who fill its ranks.

— Chris Wattie, author of *Contact Charlie: The Canadian Army, the Taliban, and the Battle for Afghanistan*

BLOOD WASHING BLOOD

BLOOD WASHING BLOOD

Afghanistan's Hundred-Year War

PHIL HALTON

DUNDURN
PRESS

Publisher and acquiring editor: Scott Fraser | Editor: Cy Strom
Cover and interior designer: Laura Boyle
Cover image: istockphoto.com/RobinOlimb
Printer: Marquis Book Printing Inc.

Library and Archives Canada Cataloguing in Publication

Title: Blood washing blood : Afghanistan's hundred-year war / Phil Halton.
Names: Halton, Phil, author.
Description: Includes bibliographical references and index.
Identifiers: Canadiana (print) 20200272683 | Canadiana (ebook) 20200272802 | ISBN 9781459746640 (softcover) | ISBN 9781459746657 (PDF) | ISBN 9781459746664 (EPUB)
Subjects: LCSH: Afghan Wars.
Classification: LCC DS363 .H35 2020 | DDC 958.1/03—dc23

We acknowledge the support of the Canada Council for the Arts and the Ontario Arts Council for our publishing program. We also acknowledge the financial support of the Government of Ontario, through the Ontario Book Publishing Tax Credit and Ontario Creates, and the Government of Canada.

Care has been taken to trace the ownership of copyright material used in this book. The author and the publisher welcome any information enabling them to rectify any references or credits in subsequent editions.

The publisher is not responsible for websites or their content unless they are owned by the publisher.

Printed and bound in Canada.

Dundurn Press
1382 Queen Street East
Toronto, Ontario, Canada M4L 1C9
dundurn.com, @dundurnpress ✔ f ⊚

For Lily and Leif

Out beyond the ideas of wrong doing and right doing,
there is a field — I'll meet you there.
　　　　　　　— Jalaluddin Rumi, Afghan poet

CONTENTS

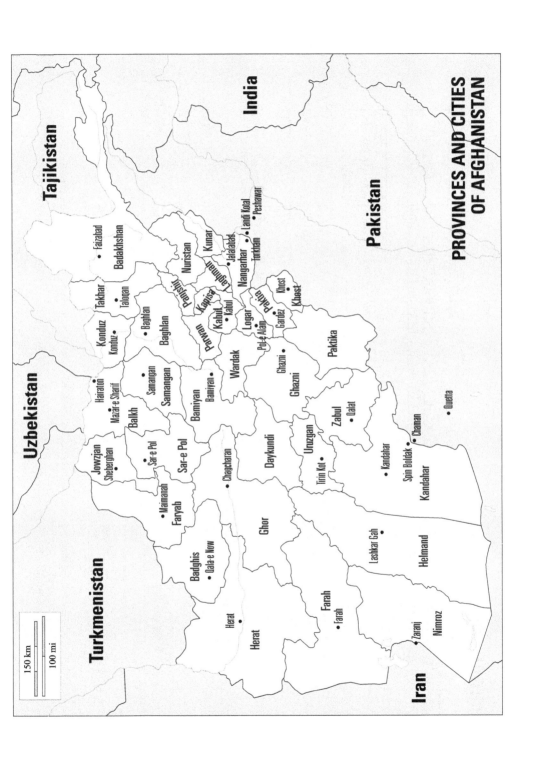

PROVINCES AND CITIES
OF AFGHANISTAN

PASHTUN TRIBES

SONS OF QAYS
ABDUR RASHID

SARBANI

DURRANI
- Barakzai — Alizai
- Popolzai — Nurzai
- Alikozai — Ishaqzai
- Achakzai — Mohammedzai

- Mohmand
- Mand
- Shinwari
- Madda Khel
- Tarkani

KARLANI
- Afridi — Banuchi
- Zadran — Daur
- Khogyani — Mehsud
- Wardak — Wazir
- Khattak — Mangal

GHURGUSHTI
- Kakar
- Musa Khel

BITANI

GHILZAI
- Ahmadzai
- Hotaki
- Ali Khel
- Suleiman Khel
- Taraki

*The relationships shown in this diagram are representative only, and will not be true in all times and places. Thousands of tribes and sub-tribes have been omitted. The Pashtun tribal structure is fluid.

**Though the Pashtuns are otherwise patrilineal, the Ghilzai claim descent from Bibi Matu, a daughter of Bitan (also known as Sheikh Bayt).

BARAKZAI DYNASTY 1826–1978

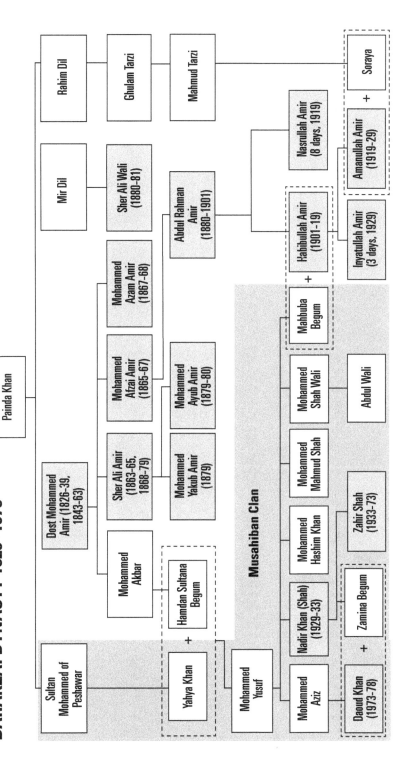

* Afghani rulers indicated by shaded boxes.
** Marriages indicated by dotted line.

Painda Khan

Sultan Mohammed of Peshawar

Dost Mohammed Amir (1826-39, 1843-63)

Mir Dil

Rahim Dil

Ghulam Tarzi

Mahmud Tarzi

Sher Ali Wali (1880-81)

Mohammed Akbar

Sher Ali Amir (1863-65, 1868-79)

Mohammed Afzai Amir (1865-67)

Mohammed Azam Amir (1867-68)

Abdul Rahman Amir (1880-1901)

Mohammed Yakub Amir (1879)

Mohammed Ayub Amir (1879-80)

Nasrullah Amir (8 days, 1919)

Habibullah Amir (1901-19)

Inyatullah Amir (3 days, 1929)

Amanullah Amir (1919-29)

+ Soraya

Yahya Khan + Hamdan Sultana Begum

Mohammed Yusuf

Mahbuba Begum

Mohammed Shah Wali

Abdul Wali

Mohammed Mahmud Shah

Mohammed Hashim Khan

Nadir Khan (Shah) (1929-33)

Mohammed Aziz

Zahir Shah (1933-73)

Daoud Khan (1973-78) + Zamina Begum

Musahiban Clan

CHAPTER 1 1919

AFGHANISTAN'S HUNDRED-YEAR conflict began on the 20th of February, 1919.

Afghanistan's ruler, Habibullah Amir, was a keen outdoorsman, and liked to hunt wild duck and other marsh fowl, as well as the country's ibex and mountain sheep. He had travelled to the mountainous province of Laghman, just east of Kabul, with his harem in tow, on a hunting expedition. On the morning of February 20, he was shot in the temple with a pistol while asleep in his tent. Although many of the seeds of the coming conflict were planted years or even decades before then, his death led to a struggle within Afghan society that continues to this day.

Habibullah had ruled Afghanistan since succeeding his father, Abdur Rahman (known as the "Iron Amir"), who had died peacefully in 1901. A hesitant modernizer, like his father he was an enthusiastic autocrat. Over decades of rule he had made no effort to change the system of power that put him in absolute control at its centre. His efforts at modernization were largely for his own prestige or benefit.

Impressed by British might and wealth during a visit to Imperial India, on his return in 1903 Habibullah set up Afghanistan's first secular school, which he modestly named Habibiya College after himself. The school taught a modified Anglo-Indian curriculum and was led by foreign professors. In part to mollify Afghanistan's religious leaders, who were alarmed by a secular school run by foreigners, he also founded three madrassas with a purely religious curriculum that became the preparatory schools for Habibiya. In 1909 he also opened a military school, where Turkish instructors taught drill and military science to prospective officers.

Outside the sphere of education, Habibullah built Afghanistan's first power station, a hydroelectric dam at Jabal-us Seraj in Parwan that supplied electricity exclusively to his palace and various government buildings. He built no other power stations that might have served the general population, perhaps because of the difficulty in building the first one: the major parts were carried to the site by elephant, taking two and a half months to arrive from Jalalabad.

Habibullah's father had instituted a system of cruel punishments in hope of stamping out crime within the kingdom. Criminals were stoned, impaled on stakes, or caged at the scene of their crimes until they starved to death. Others were thrown down the "black well," where they were left to die. Merchants who were caught cheating their customers had their ears removed and displayed above their shops. Habibullah modernized this system, replacing the punishment of mutilation with imprisonment, although the practices of stoning and execution remained unchanged.

The Iron Amir had fought and won four civil wars and defeated over one hundred rebellions during his 21-year reign, becoming progressively crueller over the years. Afghanistan had been a relatively cohesive state with a Pashtun ruler since Ahmed Shah Durrani was declared Afghanistan's amir by his fellow Pashtuns in 1747. Although descended from two generations of Afghan rulers, the Iron Amir was placed on the throne by the British in 1880, at the conclusion of the Second Anglo-Afghan War. The resulting stain on his legitimacy meant that his throne was secure only as long as he defended it by force. He was quoted as saying that he "ruled with an iron hand because he ruled an iron people." This was a lesson that his successors perhaps did not learn.

Habibullah had designated his brother Nasrullah as his successor, over his own three sons. Nasrullah, who commanded the Afghan

Army and presided over the State Council, and Habibullah's eldest son Inayatullah were both present in the hunting camp when he was killed. In accordance with the late ruler's wishes, Nasrullah declared himself the amir. Inayatullah, who as the eldest son also had a claim to the throne, immediately gave Nasrullah his support. Just as Habibullah had become amir without conflict after his father's death, it seemed at first that succession would again be without bloodshed.

But in the capital there was intrigue. Habibullah's third son, Amanullah, was the governor of Kabul Province. He claimed that he should ascend to the throne by right of being the eldest son of Habibullah's first wife, Ulya Hazrat. Succession was muddied by the fact that Habibullah had children from the four wives allowed to him under Islam, as well as 10 other women who occupied a lesser position in court. Ulya Hazrat was Pashtun, from the Loynab sub-tribe of the Barakzai, the same tribal confederacy as the amir himself, while Inyatullah's mother was not. Though Nasrullah commanded the Afghan Army, it was based in Kabul and he had no means to quickly give it orders. Amanullah had control of the treasury, and the ear of a number of the amir's advisers. Counselled by his mother, Amanullah called the senior officers of the army together, along with the members of the Council of Notables. These were the largely hereditary elite who formed the amir's court, from the foremost families within the capital.

Amanullah, only 27 years old, was well known as a reform-minded and energetic member of the royal family. There were several factions at court, all with different ideas of how Afghanistan should be run, though none were so broad-minded as to consider any system other than autocracy. Habibullah himself had been staunchly pro-British, and saw even small attempts at modernization purely as a means to increase his own wealth and prestige. He was content with the political arrangement made by his father, whereby Afghanistan was permitted to have diplomatic relations only with the British Empire. This relationship was managed through the Viceroy of India. In exchange, the British paid Habibullah a large stipend, allowed him to purchase vast quantities of arms and ammunition at cost, and promised to come to his aid should he be attacked.

Nasrullah was seen as leading a conservative, pro-British faction within the court that largely agreed with the direction taken by Habibullah.

Nasrullah was also closely allied with the religious leaders of the country, who were Sufi clerics drawn from two major families — the Gailani and Mojaddedi. Although Afghanistan is now associated with religious extremism in the minds of many, Sufism is a moderate, mystical strain within Islam that emphasizes personal and direct contact with God rather than strict regulation of outward behaviour. Sufism was so widespread in Afghanistan that it was known as the "land of the saints" for the number of its Sufi shrines. Although Nasrullah agreed with Habibullah's acceptance of his status as a client king installed by the British, it did not sit well with everyone in the amir's court.

Amanullah was a member of an opposing nationalist, pro-Turkish faction, although he was not its leader. That role was filled by his father-in-law, Mahmud Tarzi, whose daughter Soraya he had married in 1914. Tarzi's family had been exiled by the Iron Amir, and he had grown up outside of Afghanistan. His family first fled to India and then to Turkey, before settling in Damascus, then part of the Ottoman Empire. Tarzi eventually became a well-educated Ottoman bureaucrat, and was exposed to the modern political and philosophical ideas of the age. He travelled to Iraq, went on pilgrimage to Mecca, and visited Paris, engaging with intellectuals of all stripes wherever he went. In Istanbul he became a student of Jamal al din Afghani, a noted Islamic thinker and political activist. When his family, along with many other exiles, was invited to return to Afghanistan by Habibullah, he brought with him the experience gained from living for 20 years in a relatively modern Islamic state.

Tarzi's view of modernization was combined with pan-Islamic political ideas in a potent combination that appealed to both the conservative clergy and hot-headed youth. He preached a return to greatness for Islamic civilization, including in the realms of science and mathematics, under the political structure of a caliphate. His anti-colonial and anti-British views were the hardest to square with those of Habibullah, though he was careful not to provoke the amir directly. From 1911 to 1918 he was the editor of *Seraj al Akbar-e Afganiya*, Afghanistan's first newspaper, which he used to state his views. It was influential in court circles and among the capital's elite, though in a country with an approximately 2 percent literacy rate its reach was limited.

In addition to the connection with his father-in-law, Amanullah also had a connection to a more radical group of thinkers, who gave themselves an almost farcical name: the Jamiat-e Sirri-ye Melli (National Secret Party). They desired a drastic change in Afghan politics, specifically the introduction of a constitution and a truly representative national assembly that would limit the powers of the amir. For this reason, they are sometimes referred to as "Constitutionalists." Ironically led by the Indo-British principal of Habibiya College installed by Habibullah, the group was organized in a cellular structure and drew from three main elements of society: Habibiya graduates, educated members of the court, and the educated Indo-British community.

In 1909 an alleged Jamiat-e Sirri-ye Melli plot against Habibullah's life was discovered by his secret police and brutally suppressed. About four dozen people were arrested and seven were executed, though Amanullah's connection to the organization does not seem to have been publicly revealed.

The struggle between Amanullah and Nasrullah was short-lived. Amanullah quickly gained the support of the assembled notables and military officers in Kabul, and sent word to Nasrullah, then in Jalalabad, of his own claim to the throne. After a week, while the succession hung in the balance, Nasrullah and Inayatullah came to Kabul and submitted to Amanullah.

The amir's first actions as ruler were surprising. On March 3 he sent a letter to the Viceroy of India provocatively declaring himself the ruler of a "Free and Independent" Afghanistan. The viceroy did not deign to reply, as at that time there were more pressing concerns in India. Nationalist protests and rioting broke out all across the country in March and April, and much of the military that might have been used to subdue Amanullah either was still returning from the First World War in Europe or was dispersed for internal security duties. On April, 11, 1919, British troops attempting to break up a large crowd of protesters opened fire and killed an estimated 375 people in what became known as the Amritsar Massacre, creating a crisis for the colonial government as nationalist sentiment rose sharply across the country.

In mid-April the same group of notables and military leaders whom Amanullah had petitioned for support to become amir were convened again in a *darbar*, or royal court, to investigate Habibullah's murder. They quickly came to the conclusion that the murder was committed by an army colonel as part of a wider plot that also implicated Amanullah's uncle Nasrullah. The colonel was executed, and Nasrullah was imprisoned for life, dying in custody not long afterward. Other alleged conspirators were rounded up and imprisoned. Inyatullah pledged allegiance to his brother and publicly renounced his own claim to the throne. At the same time, Amanullah released all the Constitutionalists who had been imprisoned by his father.

When Amanullah realized that the British would not reply to his letter, and sensing the limited British appetite for war after four years of bloodshed in France, he took action: he decided to attack British India. On May 3 Afghan soldiers supported by tribal levies paid in plunder attacked and occupied Bagh, a village in the Khyber Pass on the Indian side of the border. They also seized the springs at Tangi, which controlled the water supply to the trading settlement of Landi Kotal. A bustling trade crossed through the Khyber Pass: cutting the route through the pass and threatening Landi Kotal choked off this trade.

A small British force was dispatched on May 9, quickly bogging down outside of Bagh, where it dug in and looked to the Royal Air Force for support. Aircraft dispersed Afghan forces concentrated nearby, causing many tribesmen to take the weapons and equipment they had been given and return home. Tribal enthusiasm for attacking the British was motivated less by patriotism or anti-colonial feelings than by the desire for personal profit. A stronger British attack on May 11 captured the Afghan artillery and caused the remaining men to retreat, harried from the air as they went.

After this attack, Amanullah called for a *loya jirga*, which roughly translates as a "grand assembly," only the third in Afghanistan's history. The jirga as a local institution is central to the Pashtunwali or "way of the Pashtun," a customary way of life whose tenets include hospitality, forgiveness, revenge, personal bravery, loyalty, honour, egalitarianism, and faith. The Pashtun tribes by tradition are egalitarian and collaborative, and their main means of dispute resolution and decision-making is the jirga. In its ideal form, no one person oversees the conduct of the jirga, and all adult members of a community are entitled to speak at it as equals. Despite this ideal, it is not uncommon for powerful or respected individuals to exert influence over the members of the jirga to obtain a decision in their favour. A jirga can be called by any member of the community, and it sits until a consensus is reached. Both customary and shari'a law will be used to reach an agreement, though in practice most Pashtuns do not differentiate between the two.

Amanullah called for a jirga of Pashtun representatives from every province of the country, as well as senior members of the clergy and his court, to discuss the war with the British. This seemed to demonstrate his willingness to consult and collaborate with his people, and was well received. He sought support for the declaration of a *jihad*, a word that can mean many things but in this case is best translated as holy war. Ignoring the fact that his forces had attacked British India in the first place, Amanullah swore that he would not only defeat the British incursion through the Khyber Pass, but he would capture the distant city of Karachi and absorb it into his kingdom. He received enthusiastic approval from the assembled group, and so from the *minbar* (similar to a pulpit) of the Eid Gah mosque in Kabul, he declared jihad. Amanullah's popularity was on the rise.

There was a further degree of duplicity to Amanullah's actions, as at the same time he was putting out feelers to the British asking for a ceasefire. He must have known that the Afghan Army was hopelessly outclassed by the British Indian Army, and it was only a matter of time before sufficient force would be rallied against him to carry the war all the way to Kabul.

The Afghan Army at this time numbered about fifty thousand conscripts in a mix of infantry and cavalry units. With no headquarters above the battalion level, operations larger than a thousand men had no effective means of being organized, though senior officers would try to do so without any staff or procedures to support them. The army had been provided with Krupp 75mm artillery pieces and modern rifles by Germany, in vain hopes of securing Afghan co-operation against the British during the world war that had just ended. But while the artillery pieces themselves were modern, all but a few were either drawn by oxen or carried by elephant. Conscripts who finished their two years of service returned to their villages to form a kind of reserve that also encompassed all the untrained tribesmen who could be raised in an emergency with the promise of weapons and plunder. All camels in the country were also required to be registered for potential conscription, which was reputed to be more effective than the system for conscripting soldiers. All things considered, the Afghan Army was much better suited to putting down rebellious tribes within the country than fighting a modern war.

To augment the army, Amanullah hoped to raise tribal levies from Pashtuns living inside India, separated from their brethren by the hated artificial border known as the "Durand Line." Agreed to in principle in 1893 by Sir Mortimer Durand, a British member of the Indian Civil Service, and the Iron Amir, it took a joint survey team until 1896 to complete the actual mapping of the boundary line. Stretching 2,200 kilometres through the heart of the traditional lands of the Pashtun, it remains contentious even today. Many Pashtuns, rejecting the authority of either state, simply ignored the border and crossed back and forth freely. At the same time, it was not unknown for tribes to seek assistance from either state against the other when it suited them. Meant to simplify relations between British India and Afghanistan, and to curb Russian ambitions by demonstrating British restraint, the border has complicated relations between the states on either side and their Pashtun subjects. As recently as 2017 former Afghan President Hamid Karzai, a political moderate (also a Ghilzai Pashtun), was quoted in the Pakistani newspaper *Dawn* that Afghanistan would never recognize the Durand Line. This refusal has dogged relations between Afghanistan and its neighbour, whether British India or Pakistan, ever since the line was first drawn.

Although Amanullah hoped to exploit and perhaps increase the unrest in India, his sudden attack had the opposite effect. As much as there was discontent with colonial rule, there was greater fear among the population of hordes of wild Afghan tribesmen looting their homes. This meant that public opinion in the country was quickly galvanized against the invaders.

The British Indian Army formed the ad hoc Trans-Indus Force to repel the Afghans, which grew in size to over 340,000 men with modern artillery, motor transport, and support from the Royal Air Force. The Afghan forces were defeated on all fronts. Most humiliatingly, the Royal Air Force bombed the cities of Jalalabad and Kabul, and the Afghans had no means to respond.

The only Afghan success in this Third Afghan War was a minor one, General Mohammed Nadir Khan's temporary capture of the fortress of Thal. Nadir Khan was a distant cousin of Amanullah whose family had been exiled to British India by the Iron Amir and permitted to return under Habibullah, who married his sister. Despite growing up outside of Afghanistan, Nadir Khan had good relations with the eastern Pashtun tribes, particularly the Mehsud and Wazir tribes, whom he led against the British.

The British were concerned that to subdue the Afghans militarily would be both costly and risky. Failure might damage British prestige in such a way that it might encourage a nationalist uprising across India. And so limited military action continued to keep the Afghan Army off balance and prevent an invasion of India, while a negotiated settlement was sought.

With both parties seeking peace, agreement to a ceasefire was quickly reached, although it was largely ignored by Amanullah's tribal levies, who continued raiding, and the Royal Air Force, which did not put a stop to its bombing. Negotiations began in earnest on July 26, and the Treaty of Rawalpindi was signed on August 8, 1919.

Although Amanullah had seen little military success, he again took to the Eid Gah mosque to declare victory. The terms of the treaty were favourable to Afghanistan, so much so that the viceroy came under heavy criticism from England for being too light handed. The right of Afghan rulers to manage their own foreign policy, bargained away by Abdur Rahman, was restored. The only gains made by the British were that they would no longer pay the Afghan amir a subsidy, and would no longer allow him to buy arms at favourable prices through India. Britain, distracted by internal issues in India and perhaps exhausted by the First World War, had lost control of what had been seen as a vital corner of the Empire's frontier.

This was a stunning achievement for Amanullah, who only six months into his reign could declare himself the liberator of Afghanistan.

CHAPTER 2 EARLY REFORMS

AMANULLAH'S VICTORY OVER the British added to his popularity and allowed him to portray himself in subtly different ways to the many parts of his diverse kingdom — as a successful military leader to the tribes of the east, as a pious warrior to the clergy, and as a reformer and modernizer to the Kabul elite. Not only was he seen as successful and dynamic, but uniquely among his dynasty he seemed to be interested in his subjects; it was rumoured that, like the storied ruler Harun al-Rashid, he wandered his capital at night in disguise, observing and questioning common people. Even during daylight he would stop to speak with commoners at length, and unlike his predecessors, he travelled without a heavy bodyguard. He saw himself as a "revolutionary king" without internal enemies.

Rhetoric aside, there was a revolutionary aspect to his plans. Political power in Afghanistan had long been held in a balance between three poles — the state, the *ulema* (literally "the learned ones," an informal body of religious scholars), and traditional leaders. Amanullah's reforms stripped the other two poles of their authority and vested it in the central state, embodied in the amir himself. This drastic change to how power was exercised in the country sparked most of the opposition he faced. The opposition to Amanullah, often violent, created cycles of revenge that continue to play out today. There is an Afghan proverb that says, "Blood cannot wash out blood," but this has been forgotten in the conflict over how to balance these three poles that has wracked the country ever since.

Early in his reign he began to undertake a series of public works to modernize the country and to cement power within the central government. He decided to build a new capital 10 kilometres south of Kabul that could contain his own residence and the public buildings he planned to house the new government bureaucracy. German and French engineers were brought to create this new city, which he named Darul Aman (translated as either the Abode of Peace and Refuge or the Abode of Aman[ullah]). He planned for the new capital to connect to Kabul by Afghanistan's first narrow-gauge railway. The most famous of the new buildings was the Darul Aman Palace, which was intended to house the court when it met. The Tajbeg Palace, built nearby on a hilltop amidst terraced gardens, was connected to the Darul Aman Palace by a cable car. Much of the rest of the planned European-style capital was never built, and the lavishness of the intended construction struck even some of the Kabul elite as excessive.

Roads in the country were poor and barely linked the capital to the second city of Kandahar and the outside world. Amanullah began to improve and extend a road network into every district. There is a common saying in Afghanistan: "The mountains are high, and the king is far away." Many remote communities, particularly the tribal ones in the mountainous east of the country, saw roads as bringing only government officials, tax collectors, and military detachments on punitive raids. Nothing good could come from roads. In many of these areas, Amanullah was obliged to protect his surveyors and construction workers with a military escort.

Amanullah also launched a series of legal, social, military, economic, and political reforms, emulating both Kemal Ataturk in Turkey and Reza Shah in Persia. His desire for change is evident in the energy he put into these projects, becoming personally involved in the creation of huge volumes of government regulation and law impacting nearly every aspect of Afghan life. But despite the early legend that grew around Amanullah as a "man of the people," he did not fully consider the differing needs and desires of his many subjects when crafting his reforms. He also did not consider the reaction that he should have expected from those disenfranchised by his plans to exercise power almost exclusively through the central state, usurping powers seen as belonging to the ulema and tribal or local leaders. Without their support, resistance was inevitable.

The urban elite in Kabul, who were literate and aware of the reforms going on in Turkey and Persia, were generally supportive. Many of the Constitutionalists who had been imprisoned or who could only act in secret under Habibullah were given important government posts. His mentor Tarzi was made foreign minister and given the important task of negotiating the formal peace treaty with Britain in the wake of the 1919 war. In the echo chamber of his court, Amanullah's plans struck all the right notes.

But Afghanistan outside of the capital was a very different place, with a diverse and independent population. Even today, Afghanistan is overwhelmingly rural, with only 25 percent of its population in urban centres; in 1919, this percentage was even less. And although Amanullah and nearly all of his inner circle were Pashtuns, this is only one of the 14 different ethnicities that make up the population of Afghanistan.

There were also major differences among the Pashtun tribes that had developed over centuries — most notably between the "settled" Pashtuns of the south and capital, the "martial" or "traditional" tribes of the east, and the nomadic *powindah* (animal herders) or Kochi. Although the Kochi are sometimes referred to as a separate ethnicity, they see themselves as the most traditional of all the Pashtun. The distinction between the groups is sometimes spoken of as between those driven by *nang,* or honour (the Kochi and eastern tribes) and those driven by *qalang* (taxation). The idea that Afghanistan as a whole is a tribal society is often used to both explain its troubled history and propose possible solutions, and so it is worthwhile to take a moment to examine the concept.

The word used in Afghanistan for tribe is *qawm*, which has a much more elastic meaning than its English translation. It can mean the same as the English word *tribe*, but might also be used much more loosely to refer to solidarity or belonging within a small group. Western analysts of tribalism in Afghanistan often default to organizational charts, of the type used to show corporate structures, to explain the relationship between the major tribes and sub-tribes. These static, linear diagrams do not give a good idea of how qawm relates to identity.

It is true that every Pashtun will be able to tell you what tribe he belongs to, at least a portion of his lineage, and how that tribe relates to others. Pashtuns recognize a common and possibly apocryphal ancestor, Qays bin Rashid, whose four sons created the four major Pashtun tribes — the Durrani, Ghilzai, Gurgushti, and Karlani — which are sometimes referred to as tribal confederacies. Each is broken down many times further into sub-tribes, usually created by the multiple sons of a patriarch each creating his own new group. This in itself should be a clue as to how Pashtun tribalism impacts identity, as with every generation there is the possibility of schism as well as belonging. Any Pashtun looking to relate to another can appeal either to their common ancestor or to a division that occurred at some point. Pashtun identity, even in its ideal form, both unites and divides communities.

Pashtun society recognizes how this way of organizing drives conflict, encompassed in the idea of *turborwali*. Meaning both enmity and cousinhood, it refers to the fact that a boy's patrilineal first cousin (the son of his father's brother) is his natural rival. This stems from the fact that inheritances in Pashtun families are divided equally between a man's sons. "Fairly" divided agricultural land quickly becomes too small to sustain a family, and while brothers are expected to work together, cousins are far enough removed from each other that they come into conflict over resources and ownership of their grandfather's property. The idea behind turborwali is that this conflict is both natural and inevitable.

In a more practical sense, a qawm should be thought of as a group of people who live in relatively close proximity, share a collective sense of identity, and assist and support each other as needed. This might be in terms of collective defence, enforcement of customary law, or the sharing of agricultural labour. Particularly in Afghanistan with its weak state presence, this kind of collective support can mean the difference between life and death. We often call this small group of people a clan (a group of related families), and it might be in conflict with another qawm of the same sub-tribe. Practicality often trumps pedigree when determining solidarity and identity.

Tribal relations are also not static, as it is possible for a weaker tribe to be absorbed by a stronger one. An example of this is the Babozai sub-tribe spread across eastern and southern Afghanistan. In Zabul Province, it is regarded as a sub-tribe of the Hotak, part of the Ghilzai tribal confederacy. But in neighbouring Uruzgan, it is considered a sub-tribe of the Nurzai, who are a part of the competing Durrani tribal confederacy. The same sub-tribe can be seen as part of two different confederacies because, at some point in history, part of the Babozai people moved from one location to another, and the practical requirements of survival caused them to be integrated into the local tribal structure. This process of change continues today, making the hundreds of tribes and sub-tribes within the "Pashtun" identity well-nigh unmappable in any detail.

Tribal leadership is also unstable, despite traditions to the contrary. Within many (but not all) Pashtun tribes there is a *khan khel*, a clan or sub-tribe from whom the traditional leaders of the tribe are drawn. This is more common in the southern tribes (such as the Durrani and Ghilzai) than the eastern ones, in part because for centuries their members have formed the core of the country's central government. The egalitarianism of Pashtun society means that both the institution of the khan khel, as well as the particular group who wield the title, are under constant pressure from other contenders. The identity of the khan khels themselves, as well as the importance of the idea, shift with time as different groups gain ascendance over others and as tribal solidarity grows or weakens.

Although the Pashtun tribes dominated Afghanistan politically from the beginning of the reign of Ahmad Shah (a Durrani) in 1747, there are also many non-tribal groups within the country. The largest of these are the Tajiks, Uzbeks, and Hazaras, all of whom have suffered varying degrees of repression at the hands of the Pashtuns. Even today there has been no comprehensive census of the people of Afghanistan to determine the size and composition of the population, but Pashtuns likely make up roughly 50–60 percent, with Tajiks and Hazaras making up much of the rest. It is these different groups and their specific interests, as well as the varying interests of the Pashtun tribes, that Amanullah did not fully consider when crafting his reforms.

The Tajiks of northern and western Afghanistan are not tribal, although their history in the region stretches at least as far back in time as the Pashtuns, if not farther. Though they see themselves as Persian, they are likely descended from the Bactrians who inhabited Central Asia more than two millennia ago, and may have inhabited most of what is now Afghanistan before waves of other peoples flowed into the country. The Tajiks who live in the remote and mountainous province of Badakhshan speak an archaic form of Persian, unlike those who inhabit Afghanistan's northern plains and speak the modern language. Tajik society in northern Afghanistan was centred around large towns surrounded by intensely cultivated land. Rather than tribal leaders selected from a khan khel, the leaders of Tajik society were the *zamindars* or landowners. Within the towns lived a well-established class of merchants and craftsmen with trade connections throughout the region. Much of the bureaucracy in Kabul at the time of Amanullah was also composed of Tajiks, as although the ruling class was Pashtun, the language of government was Persian.

The Uzbeks in Afghanistan are a Turkic people who were originally tribal and nomadic and whose wealth was based on the size of their herds. Over centuries the southern Uzbeks, particularly those in Afghanistan, have become sedentary farmers whose culture is similar to that of the Tajiks with whom they share the north of the country. Although they speak their own tongue, most Afghan Uzbeks speak either Persian or Pashto as well. Perhaps as many as half a million people, mostly Tajiks and Uzbeks, fled south into Afghanistan around the time of Amanullah's ascension, driven out of their homes by the Bolshevik consolidation of power over the Central Asian portion of the former Russian Empire. Culturally, they would have been little different from their Afghan brethren.

The Hazaras are the third largest ethnic group in Afghanistan, after the Pashtuns and Tajiks, and are concentrated in the central highlands known as the Hazarajat. Over time, these lands have been encroached on by settlers of other ethnicities, and particularly by nomadic Pashtun Kochi. It is commonly thought that the Hazaras are descended from the garrisons of Genghis Khan. Their native language is an archaic version of Persian known as Hazaragi, which is peppered with many words from the Mongol language. The Hazaras were traditionally a tribal people, but over time adopted a largely sedentary lifestyle in which the tribes were no longer political entities. Although there is a distinct Hazara culture, which has mixed with Tajik and Pashtun culture in some regions, the main thing that sets the Hazaras apart from other groups in Afghanistan is that they are predominantly Shi'a, while the rest of the country is Sunni.

This difference has been a serious one in Afghanistan, and has resulted in discrimination, exclusion, and genocide. When the Iron Amir felt secure on his throne, he targeted two groups within the country who were not Sunni. The first were the pagan inhabitants of Kafiristan, whose religion was found only in their rugged valleys. The *kafirs* (unbelievers) were forcibly converted to Islam after a short but vicious military campaign, and the name of their region was changed to Nuristan (Land of Light), which it retains to this day. The second group who were targeted in a campaign of suppression were the Shi'a Hazaras, who rose up in rebellion multiple times in response. Over a period of about five years, the Afghan Army supported by Pashtun tribal levies subjugated the communities of the Hazarajat as part of a jihad, killing or displacing a large part of the population, perhaps as large as 60 percent. The Iron Amir helped to defray the costs of the campaign by selling thousands of Hazaras into slavery, an action made possible within Islam by declaring them unbelievers. New communities of displaced Hazaras formed in northern Afghanistan, western British India (now Pakistan), and Persia, and Pashtuns were settled in the Hazarajat in their place. Large numbers of Hazaras also moved to the cities, particularly Kabul, to find work during the winter months when they could not be employed in farm labour.

Each of these different ethnic groups had a different relation to the Afghan state, and so saw the need (or not) for reform in different areas. The settled Pashtuns who had benefitted from control of the state apparatus, and particularly the well educated, were broadly in favour of modernization. Many took advantage of economic changes to become wealthy. The eastern Pashtuns, who still saw taxation and government interference in their lives as a form of humiliation, took the opposite view. The Tajik and Uzbek minorities stood generally to benefit from modernization, particularly those who as part of the capital's bureaucracy formed the lower tiers of the elite. Even those living outside the capital preferred the light rule emanating from Kabul to the heavy hand of the Soviets across the northern border. The Hazaras also stood to benefit from modernization, particularly as it included liberalization of attitudes toward slavery and increased religious tolerance, though they remained suspicious of the motives of the state itself.

An example of how this relationship played out in practice centres on the issues of corruption and nepotism, which were (and remain) endemic within the Afghan bureaucracy. Amanullah publicly took steps to combat these, as well as ending the large stipends paid to tribal leaders who did not render any service in return. These stipends were entirely given to Pashtuns, paid from the taxes of the other groups and from the money that Habibullah received from the British. While from a modern, Western point of view these allowances were little more than bribes paid to prevent (or forestall) rebellion, viewed with a tribal lens they can be seen differently.

Particularly among the egalitarian Pashtuns, the role of a tribal leader or *khan* is precarious — he needs to be seen to be benefitting the tribe or he risks being deposed. Allowances from the government, as well as the ability to appoint tribe members to salaried government positions, create a means to be beneficial. While khans certainly kept a share of this wealth for themselves, they would not have remained in power had they not shared a sizable proportion of it with their people. Public generosity was seen as the mark of a "good" leader; it is said that there can be no khan without a *dastakhan*, or tablecloth. Successful khans managed a web of influence by balancing payments and favours paid and collected among family, ulema, other tribal leaders, and government officials. They were typically surrounded by *mulgurey*, companions who were both friends and retainers, whose lives they subsidized and whose presence increased their own prestige. An effective khan is said to "tie the knot of the tribe" more tightly. When Amanullah cut tribal allowances he disenfranchised the leaders most likely to be supportive of him as a Pashtun ruler, and best able to rise against him as well.

Corruption also needs to be seen through a different lens. In order to receive many basic services from a government official, even today, *baksheesh* or a small bribe is required. The modern Western view is that this practice is a drain on the economy and unethical. In Afghanistan, where government employees were underpaid, regulations were thin, and social relationships governed nearly all transactions, baksheesh was a lubricant that kept the wheels of government slowly turning. While at the outset of the anti-corruption drive many senior officials thought that Amanullah's efforts were merely for publicity, it quickly became clear that he was serious. A senior member of the Barakzai tribe and a member of the royal court, Shahgasi Mohammed Sarwan Khan, was arrested on charges of corruption and jailed. The fact that he was a member of the king's own larger tribe (and his mother's stepfather) did not dissuade Amanullah. While some might see this as admirable, many Pashtuns saw it as a base betrayal of tribal loyalties, and it hurt Amanullah's reputation overall.

Amanullah's first reforms included a prohibition against slavery, which did much to increase his support among the Hazaras, though this law was unevenly enforced. He attempted to garner broad support for his plans by wrapping them in the language and authority of Islam. He wrote to Britain's King George V in August 1919 and again in January 1920 seeking his agreement with a remarkable request. To the modern ear the word *caliphate* would remind many of the Islamic State government in parts of Syria and Iraq, but in Amanullah's time it was linked to the recently collapsed Ottoman Empire. In pan-Islamic thought, there is an ideal of a state ruled in accordance with shari'a by a just and righteous ruler (known as a caliph) who is the de facto leader of the Muslim world. Various governments since the time of Mohammed have been given the title of the caliphate, the last being that of the Ottomans, which held it from 1517 until it was formally renounced by Kemal Ataturk in 1924. Amanullah's letter to King George asked for his support in reestablishing the caliphate in Afghanistan, with Amanullah as the Amir al-Mumineen, or Commander of the Faithful. Later that year, the highest clerical authority in Afghanistan (as quoted in R.T. Stewart's 1973 book *Fire in Afghanistan*) declared that as Amanullah was "the only independent Moslem ruler left in the world, he was now the head of Islam. The Moslem world should salute him as caliph, and the *khutba* should be read in every mosque in the name of Amanullah." The khutba, a special sermon given on Fridays at noon prayers and during certain festivals, is the traditional way for the legitimacy of an Islamic ruler to be recognized by religious authorities.

While King George's approval was clearly not required from an Islamic point of view, it was necessary from a practical one to ensure that such a declaration did not provoke a negative response. British India had millions of Muslim subjects who might wish to join the caliphate, and Afghanistan was in no position to either receive them or fight for their liberation. King George never replied to these letters, and Amanullah eventually dropped the idea when the need for good external relations exceeded the need to espouse pan-Islamic ideas.

Another early policy championed by Amanullah was the controversial Family Code of 1921. This new law prohibited both child marriage and intermarriage between close relatives, put limits on the size of dowries, enforced the requirement to register marriages with the state, and gave women the right to divorce their husbands. These changes provoked discontent from a few different quarters. Marriages had been governed by a mix of shari'a and customary law and administered by local mullahs and *qadis* (judges). Among the Pashtun, many aspects of marriage were particular to specific tribes, whose local interpretation of Pashtunwali trumped even shari'a, under the authority of often poorly educated mullahs who were beholden to tribal leaders. These mullahs would now lose that authority to the state.

The prohibition on intermarriage between close relatives was particularly controversial. Because of the size of dowries that were required to secure a marriage, many families had little wealth other than livestock or land to use to pay. This put them in a bind, as paying the dowry also threatened their ability to sustain themselves, or created small parcels of land that were essentially unfarmable. Because of this, marriages between first cousins were considered to be the optimum matches, as the wealth that was transferred remained within the extended family. This aligned with a narrow idea of what constituted a qawm, and greatly lessened the financial risk and impact of marriage.

Granting women the right to divorce their husbands was also rejected by many of the Pashtun tribes, although it is permitted in classical shari'a law. Different kinds of divorce are included within shari'a, although they are interpreted differently by the various schools of Islamic jurisprudence, but in all cases there are means for women to initiate a divorce, and even stipulations about the payment of child support. But divorces initiated by women were unheard of within Pashtun customary law, and so even though this element of the Family Code was meant to enforce existing practice within shari'a, it was rejected as "un-Islamic" by mullahs in the country's hinterland. Given the high level of illiteracy, it is not surprising that many people could not distinguish between written shari'a law and oral customary law.

Another element of this law affecting the lives of women was granting them the right to choose their own husbands, a prerogative that had previously been held by their fathers or brothers. Not only is most of traditional Afghan society patriarchal and patrilineal, it is also patrilocal — brides leave the family of their birth forever to live within their husband's extended family. Most rural families could not afford to keep women in strictly segregated *purdah*, as their labour was needed for the family to survive. In an unmechanized agricultural society where survival is not assured from season to season, and that relies on having the right ratio of useful hands to consuming mouths, this represents a transfer of labour power and responsibility, and therefore wealth, that is an important decision for a family to make. Traditionalist Afghans resented both the intrusion of the government into their family life and the change that this law implied to the power structure within communities. The state continued to have little real ability to interfere in the administration of marriages or the treatment of women within their families — the unease these laws provoked was directed less at their content than at the idea of state interference in family matters. This was particularly marked among the eastern Pashtun tribes, where customary law was strongest, as was the rejection of state authority.

Amanullah's reforms were driven in part by the counsel of his wife, Soraya. Educated in Damascus, she was an intelligent and strong-willed woman who sought to improve the lot of Afghan women through her husband's reforms. In a public speech quoted by Nancy Dupree, she made clear her feelings on the role of women in Afghanistan:

> [Independence] belongs to all of us and that is why we celebrate it. Do you think, however, that our nation from the outset needs only men to serve it? Women should also take their part as women did in the early years of our nation and Islam. From their examples we must learn that we must all contribute toward the development of our nation and that this cannot be done without being equipped with knowledge.

So we should all attempt to acquire as much knowledge as possible, in order that we may render our services to society in the manner of the women of early Islam.

Soraya was the driving force behind the formation of the Anjuman-e Himayat-e Niswan (Women's Protective Association), a government-sponsored organization headed by Amanullah's sister, Qubra Jan. The purpose of the organization was to encourage Afghan women to report any abuses they suffered, and to organize women's protests in favour of women's rights. Although it had little impact outside of the capital, this was still a step that traditional society found shocking.

Part of what society found so alarming about these reforms was that they confused gender roles that were strongly delineated in Afghan society. Particularly in rural families these interdependent spheres of work and responsibility defined how the household functioned and were seen as the foundation of a family's survival. For example, carpet weaving is a common cottage industry in Afghanistan that involves both genders. Men work outside the home, herding and shearing sheep, while women work inside to spin the wool and weave the carpet. Both roles are equally necessary and important. Within the family, women typically are responsible for managing the family's finances, and tend to wield influence that is not seen outside of the family. Representing the family and its concerns in the wider world was the responsibility of men, though ideally they were restrained by what was agreed upon within the home.

Of all the measures that Amanullah worked to implement in the first years of his reign, the most important to him was always education. He realized that the only way to modernize the country was to create an educated population, and to this end he made primary education compulsory for all boys and girls. He even attempted to hire itinerant teachers who would travel with the nomadic tribes between their summer and winter pastures. Despite his intentions, compulsory education was never enforced. Even after creating the Medal of Education as the highest military or civilian decoration that the Afghan government could bestow, and appointing his wife as the minister of education, there remained a chronic lack of schools across the country.

Given the lack of primary schools, it was exceedingly difficult for Amanullah to create any institutes of higher learning. He built technical schools to produce the teachers and skilled tradesmen that a modern economy would demand, although their output of graduates was always small. Recognizing that the establishment of a university was many years away, Amanullah instead focused on the creation of language schools that would allow students to be sent to study abroad in the great universities of the world. The wisdom of this policy was proven by the fact that the list of students who were sent abroad during this period comprises a "who's who" of later important government officials.

Recognizing that these changes were causing a stir among the populace, in 1922 Amanullah called for a loya jirga of people from every province of the country, including non-Pashtuns for whom the practice would be foreign. Held in the unofficial winter capital of Jalalabad, the gathering was intended to both reassure the population and gain approval of the country's first constitution.

The Constitutionalists who were influential in court were likely disappointed with this document, which in its 73 articles made little attempt to reform the government itself. Rather than limiting the power of the amir, as they had long demanded, the constitution entrenched it. The document created a hereditary monarchy as a permanent institution, and while it also codified the existence of bodies such as the Council of State, their role was merely advisory. Final authority in all matters remained with the amir.

One important change wrought by the constitution was the source of this authority. All the Durrani rulers since Ahmed Shah in 1747 had been chosen, or at least approved, by a jirga. This represented a transfer of a portion of the authority of tribal leaders to the central government, and created at least the theoretical possibility that the authority they granted could be withdrawn. As might be expected in an egalitarian society, the source of an amir's power was the consensus of the Pashtun tribes that he should rule. Amanullah's first constitution was instead based on a classic Islamic model of governance, where the ruler's authority came directly from Allah. This implied that anyone who opposed the amir's rule opposed the will of Allah as well, marking the rebel as an apostate, punishable by death.

At the same time that it codified despotism, the constitution also contained forward-thinking elements. Article 8 stated that all the inhabitants of the country were considered citizens, regardless of their religion or ethnicity. This was novel, as previously the terms "Pashtun" and "Afghan" had been used synonymously, and non-Muslims had been explicitly disqualified. Article 10 promised that a citizen's personal freedoms would not be infringed except through due process of law, which theoretically ended the practices of Habibullah and the Iron Amir, whose secret police arrested, tortured, and murdered anyone thought to oppose the crown. Like the abolition of slavery, these clauses were particularly welcomed by the Hazara community. Article 8 in particular was a point of heated discussion, as there was resistance to granting the rights of a citizen (limited as they were in practice) to non-Muslims, even if there were few to whom this would apply. Kabul had long had a small Jewish community, along with a cluster of Sikh and Hindu traders. At the jirga it was agreed, in the end, that citizenship would not extend outside the Islamic faith, though the Shi'a and Ismaili minorities would be included.

Amanullah hoped that the loya jirga would give the constitution legitimacy in the eyes of Afghan citizens, even though this jirga differed from the traditional concept. The Afghan hinterland is sometimes referred to as *yaghistan*, a "land of insolence" where no man rules over another. As practised in the tribal communities, jirgas could be called by any man regardless of social status, and they remained in session until a consensus was reached. They were, at least as an ideal, an egalitarian institution. Amanullah's use of the loya jirga differed from this ideal significantly. The members of the jirga were summoned from across the country on his authority, and rather than seeking consensus, he largely sought agreement with decisions he had already made. While the jirga approved the constitution, in reality it had little choice. Many members of the meeting who lived on the periphery of the government's reach left with grave concerns at the reforms that were being implemented. This might have been a warning to Amanullah, but instead he pushed onward with even greater reforms.

The Conscription and Identity Card Act of 1923 was meant to improve the effectiveness of the standing army, but it had the opposite effect. The system implemented by the amir's grandfather was called the *hasht nefari*, or "one in eight." Tribes or communities were required to provide one man in eight as a conscript for a period of two years, with the men not chosen supporting the cost of the conscript's service. Although this was meant to work as a form of lottery, with the conscript chosen randomly, this was not the case. The tribal chiefs managed this system and selected the recruits themselves. This meant that the army received a steady stream of the least intelligent, productive, or liked men in the country as conscripts. As a result the standing army was nearly always inferior to the quality of the levies that the tribes themselves could raise, tipping the balance of power from the central government to the tribes.

The hasht nefari was replaced by a "population" system that relied on centralized selection of conscripts from the pool of men who had been registered and issued identity cards. Quite a few of the Pashtun sub-tribes within the Durrani and Ghilzai confederacies had been granted exemptions from conscription in the past, and these exemptions were now revoked. The changes stripped tribal or community leaders of their power, and were badly received outside of Kabul. While this reform was intended to improve the quality of recruit that the army received, in practice it simply reduced the number of recruits, as identity cards were slow to be issued, young men paid bribes to government officials to avoid being selected, and many communities simply refused to comply. Intended to strengthen the army, the reform further undermined it.

There was a similar reaction to the issue of the country's first passports. Not only were these a mark of a modern system of national administration, they were necessary to achieve Amanullah's aspirations to send significant numbers of Afghan students to study abroad — not just in Persia and India, but in Europe as well. He believed that by living in these modern societies, the students would internalize many of the aspects of reform that their less-travelled countrymen struggled to understand or accept. Most shockingly, Amanullah planned to send women as well as men abroad, which met with resistance even among the reformers in the capital.

The groups who objected most to the passport scheme were the tribal leaders in the country's border regions, particularly in the east, and those who still lived as nomads. The passports were seen as a first step to restricting the tribes' practice of crossing unhindered to India.

It was a combination of these grievances that led to the first serious armed rebellion under Amanullah's rule.

CHAPTER 3 REBELLION ON ALL SIDES

IN LATE APRIL 1924 a small rebellion flared up around Khost, the largest settlement in the country's southeast. The rebels were from the independent and fearsome Mangal tribe initially, but the uprising quickly spread throughout the east of the country and to many other tribes as well. The central figure in the revolt was a man known as Mullah-e Lang Abdullah, or the "Lame Mullah." While there is some ambiguity in the historical record, the most detailed and compelling explanation for the rebellion is given in the writing of Fayz Mohammed Kateb, a Hazara scribe attached to Amanullah's court.

Kateb blamed the revolt on a dispute between the Lame Mullah and a government official. A Mangal tribesman, engaged to an underage girl, petitioned the Lame Mullah to allow the marriage to take place, as the betrothal predated the new law forbidding the practice. The Lame Mullah ruled in favour, but the government official was tipped off about the case by a rival suitor and overruled him. Kateb adds the detail that the Lame Mullah was particularly upset as he had accepted a bribe to rule in favour of the would-be groom.

The many laws that Amanullah passed had little impact on the lives of tribes in eastern Afghanistan, as the government had no capacity to enforce them in the face of tight-knit Pashtun tribal society. It was the idea of the new laws that created the outrage. The Mangals saw themselves as living a "true" Pashtun life marked by nang, or honour, unlike their settled and Persianized cousins in Kabul. A new law requiring all mullahs to pass a centrally administered exam in order to practise also stung, as poorly educated men such as the Lame Mullah would be stripped of their authority and livelihood.

The Mangal tribe did not rise up over a single marriage. Nor did the tribe take up arms against Amanullah's legal, social, and religious reforms, which were largely ignored outside of the capital. It was a combination of the affront to their honour caused by government interference in a family matter and their contempt for a centralized (and settled) government in any form that drove them to action.

One of the major defects of the Afghan government at this time was its inability to communicate with its citizens. The radical newspapers and written decrees that were read with interest by the elite in Kabul had no impact on the largely illiterate population of the rest of the country. The people of Khost knew of the amir's reforms largely through rumour, distorted by their own biases and the desires of local power brokers. When Amanullah passed a law that discouraged women from wearing the veil, defining it as a tribal custom rather than an Islamic requirement, this was presented as a law that banned the veil. When he encouraged men to wear Western hats rather than turbans, it was presented as an attempt to prevent Islamic prayer, allegedly because Western hats would fall off during the prostrations.

There were also attempts by the government to more efficiently collect taxes, in cash rather than in kind, which reduced the chances for graft that existed as crops or livestock passed through many hands from the point of collection to the royal treasury. Rumours that the government would prevent movement to traditional lands on the other side of the Durand Line, through the forced issue of identity cards and passports, were worrying. The law that made primary education mandatory for girls was also seen as an intrusion on family life, even though in practice there were no schools in rural areas for children of either gender to attend.

Another controversial policy of Amanullah's concerned opium and a form of Afghan hashish known as *chars*. Both opium and hashish have a long history of use in Afghanistan, which has been described as having one of the oldest continuous cannabis cultures in the world. Afghan folk-lore includes a figure known as Baba Ku, a mystic who roamed the mountains and cured different ailments by prescribing hashish. Cannabis was grown all across the country, and was either smoked as hashish or mixed with tea, or made into a hard candy known as *mofarah*, mixed with poppy seeds, sugar, honey, almonds, and pistachios. Mofarah was seen as both an intoxicant and an aphrodisiac, and is still available in bazaars throughout the country. Hashish use was widespread among the lower and middle classes, both in urban and rural areas.

Opium cultivation was encouraged by Afghan rulers from the 16th century onward, and the legal sale of opium and cannabis in British India drew Afghan producers into that market. Persia also had a long history of opium use, providing a second market for Afghan producers. Opium use in Afghanistan, other than as a medicine, was largely a practice of the lower classes. Opium was too valuable an export to be widely used outside of small pockets of opium culture, such as are found in Badakhshan, or among urbanites influenced by Persian drug culture.

Western governments only began to collectively control opium production with the International Opium Convention signed at the Hague in 1912, although it had been made illegal in the United States in 1909. Like his father, Amanullah encouraged the production of hashish and opium as export products. There were laxly enforced laws against the use of drugs, but Amanullah enshrined heavy penalties against opium use through a *nezam-nama*, meaning "decree." (The term was chosen by Amanullah over the more common *qanun*, or law, as *nezam-nama* implied a lesser authority than shari'a.) He also imposed a lucrative 100 percent tax on opium and 50 percent tax on hashish produced for export. Both the heavy Afghan government taxes on opium and hashish and the import taxes imposed by British India meant that many producers turned to smuggling to get their product to market. The porous border between the two countries, and the links between Pashtuns on both sides, flooded the market in British India with low-priced Afghan opium and hashish. A single *seer* (about seven kilograms) of opium produced legally and exported to India cost 151 rupees, while a seer of smuggled opium sold for 65. While Mangal farmers did not produce opium, they did profit from its transit across the border, and Amanullah's tax was seen as excessive.

A reform that struck the Mangals directly was the conscription law. The Mangals were one of the Pashtun tribes that had been exempt from conscription for many decades. Amanullah's reforms centralizing the selection of conscripts prevented tribal leaders from controlling who was chosen and using it as a source of graft and a demonstration of their power. When the sons of prominent families who would never have served under the old system were conscripted by lottery, this was seen as another insult.

There is an Afghan proverb that at the root of all conflicts are three things: *zar, zan,* and *zamin* (gold, women, and land). In the eyes of the Mangals, Amanullah's reforms and attempts to centralize government threatened all three. The rebellion spread from the Mangals to the neighbouring Zadran tribe as well, incited by a widening number of minor religious and tribal leaders who preached against reform. Amanullah, once seen as a candidate to rule the caliphate, was now being described by the rebels as an apostate, and his laws as contrary to Islam. The many concerns of the tribal leaders, largely to do with wealth and power, were fused with the concerns of the mullahs, whose power was threatened, and wrapped in a cloak of religious indignation and propaganda. A contemporary British report said: "With the new [legal] code in one hand and the Koran in the other, they called the tribes to choose between the word of God and that of man, and adjured them to resist demands, the acceptance of which would reduce their sons to slavery in the Afghan Army and their daughters to the degrading influence of Western education." Yet what was truly threatened was the balance of local power.

Early in the rebellion Mangal and Zadran tribesmen attacked a military garrison at Matun, routing the soldiers and creating a sense that the government was weak. The model battalions of the Afghan Army were dispatched with their Turkish trainers, but they did not acquit themselves well in battle, and many conscripts deserted at the first opportunity, either joining the rebels or slipping over the border into India. Disgusted with how badly Amanullah was handling the conflict with the tribes, Nadir Khan, the minister of war and hero of the Third Afghan War, refused to lead the troops in battle. He instead requested an overseas post, and was sent to be the ambassador to France. Two years later, still unimpressed by Amanullah's reforms, he resigned and remained in France as an exile.

Amanullah's forebears knew well how to deal with rebellion — in particular the cruel Iron Amir. But the revolutionary amir was different, and he sought to rule by persuasion. He sent a group of respected religious leaders from the capital to meet with the Lame Mullah and others, to persuade them that the recently enacted laws were in fact in accordance with shari'a. The meeting took place at Baidak in the Logar Valley, and lasted several days. During this time the Lame Mullah did not argue the religious merits of the rebels' case, but merely tried to convince the opposing clergy to withdraw their support for the amir and throw in with the Mangals. The meeting ended without either side convincing the other of anything.

When the delegation returned to Kabul, it reported that it did not believe there was a religious basis to the rebellion, but it was important to reconsider the new laws to ensure that they conformed with shari'a and were more widely accepted. Amanullah agreed, and as the revolt gained support from even more tribes he convened another loya jirga, this time in Paghman, the traditional summer residence of the amir. This was a larger jirga than the last, with over a thousand delegates, including all the major tribal leaders not in open rebellion, members of the court, military officers and state bureaucrats, and the leaders of the ulema, or body of religious scholars. For the entire duration of the jirga, they were treated lavishly. Every delegate was greeted personally by Amanullah on his arrival, embraced, and presented with gifts, as well as access to free medical care and tickets to Afghanistan's only cinema. They were then billeted in one of the royal residences or with a member of the court, at Amanullah's expense. At the conclusion of the 18-day meeting, Amanullah again received every attendee at a personal audience and gave them commemorative medals. A jirga is not a democratic institution, although in its ideal form it is an egalitarian one. Amanullah's treatment of the delegates made it clear that although he was benevolent, he was also their superior.

To Amanullah's surprise nearly all of the ulema argued in favour of repealing many of his reforms. These were the same men who had grudgingly accepted the constitution at the previous loya jirga, but perhaps emboldened by Amanullah's apparent weakness in the face of the Mangal and other tribes, this time they spoke up. Recognizing that he needed their support to defeat the growing rebellion, Amanullah gave in and accepted a number of changes.

Five articles of the constitution were amended, drastically changing the tone of Amanullah's document. The basic rights of non-Muslims were rescinded, and Jews and Hindus were required to pay a special tax and wear distinctive clothing. The Hanafi rite was enshrined as the official religious rite in Afghanistan, excluding those who followed other schools of Islamic thought, especially the Shi'a. An article that guaranteed individual rights was amended to read: "All Afghan citizens enjoy freedom subject to strict observance of religious duties as imposed by the shari'at and the state penal codes." In practice, this bound all subjects to the rules of the Hanafi rite, further disenfranchising religious minorities. An article precluding torture was also amended to allow punishments that were in accordance with shari'a law, which include amputation, mutilation, and stoning.

Amanullah also rescinded a number of the offensive nezam-namas that had been implemented since he took the throne, particularly the requirements for all Afghans to have identity cards and for compulsory girls' education. The laws against child marriage and discouraging polygamy were repealed. Although conscription was not repealed, it was agreed that it would be largely relaxed in the tribal areas. These changes were enough to satisfy all present that the government's actions were in accordance with shari'a, and that there was no religious basis to the rebels' demands. The ulema present at the jirga then issued a *fatwa* (a nonbinding religious opinion on a point of Islamic law), condemning the rebels as un-Islamic. It read, in part: "We declare that the ruler has the right … to impose any type of punitive measure which he feels appropriate upon whomever [*sic*] either by personal choice or encouragement of others would rise up against the state." This gave Amanullah religious sanction to use force to put down the rebellion with impunity.

Many of the changes made by the 1924 loya jirga were concerned with the laws that limited the powers of the ulema. One nezam-nama in particular, "The Guide for Religious Judges," was controversial, as it prescribed set punishments for a number of crimes, essentially codifying these aspects of shari'a into secular law. The Hanafi school recognizes no central religious authority, leaving religious judges with wide discretion when sentencing. This was necessary for the uneducated mullahs who doubled as judges in rural areas and applied customary law as often as they did shari'a, without differentiating between the two. Set punishments also reduced the benefit of bribing judges to impose lighter sentences. Although Amanullah won a victory of sorts through the loya jirga, he had to cede a large degree of power to the ulema, and reverse reforms that were dear to him, in order to do so.

By the end of July the rebels had transformed themselves into a more serious threat. Abdul Karim, a notable Barakzai and illegitimate son of former Afghan ruler Yakub Amir, had emerged from exile in British India. With the backing of the eastern tribes, he made a claim for the throne. He appointed the Lame Mullah as his senior religious official and advanced his forces up the Logar Valley toward the capital. Amanullah persuaded the previously neutral Khogyani and Shinwari tribes to back him and purchased two aircraft from Britain for use by the nascent Afghan Air Force. The weight of the tribal levies, whose enthusiasm was high given that the fatwa against the rebels allowed them to loot at will, turned the tide of battle and in early 1925 the rebellion was crushed.

Although Amanullah was unquestionably a modernizer, he retained more than a small degree of absolutist thinking. He made no attempt to bring the defeated Mangals back into the fold of his rule. The Lame Mullah and dozens of other rebel leaders were captured and executed without trial. Thousands of prisoners were paraded through the streets of Kabul, separated by tribe to increase the shame and humiliation. Thirty-five hundred homes belonging to the Mangal tribe were burned and six thousand head of cattle were seized by the Khogyani and Shinwari tribesmen. In all, contemporary reports suggest that as many as fourteen thousand people were killed in the conflict, and many more were displaced, a cost that the Afghan state could ill afford.

Ever willing to make grand gestures, Amanullah built a monument in Kabul to his victory, grandly named the Minaret of the Triumph of Knowledge over Ignorance. His rule remained in a fragile state, however. Amanullah's mentor Mahmud Tarzi was said to have lamented, "Amanullah has built a beautiful monument without a foundation. Take out one brick and it will tumble down." Amanullah must have realized that his hold on the country was tenuous, because from this point he dramatically slowed the process of modernization. Throughout his reign he issued 76 nezam-namas, though all but 19 preceded the Khost rebellion.

In 1927 Amanullah and his entourage embarked on a grand tour of the Middle East and Europe. They were greeted with pomp and ceremony, even in their first stop in British India. This was the first foreign tour by a reigning Afghan monarch, and Amanullah expressed his intentions directly in a speech that was quoted in the *New Statesman:* "I want to show Europe that Afghanistan has its place on the map of the world."

While visiting Egypt he was not shy with his criticism of the country, specifically cultural practices, such as dress, that were more restrictive than was required by Islam. He was critical of anything that he perceived to be "backward," even as his own country outside of Kabul was resisting nearly every aspect of modernity that he introduced.

In Italy, France, Britain, and Germany he sought to understand the best examples of everything — from government to education to industry — that could be integrated into his vision of a new Afghanistan. Amanullah received many honours from governments trying to court him, including honorary degrees from Oxford University for both him and his wife. He also signed treaties of friendship and co-operation with a number of countries with which Afghanistan had previously not had formal relations. The governments of Europe were seeking opportunities for joint ventures where their country's industries could capitalize on the untapped resources of Afghanistan. Large deposits of copper and the gemstone spinel were known to exist, and much of the country had not been thoroughly explored to determine what wealth was available. They also signed lucrative contracts to provide experts to build railroads, bridges, and factories. Amanullah was particularly well treated in Britain, where he was given a ride in a submarine and allowed to fire a torpedo.

Returning to Afghanistan via the USSR and Persia in July 1928, Amanullah drove a Rolls Royce from Persia to Kabul, his vision for the future of the country reinvigorated. The slow pace of progress since the Khost rebellion no longer satisfied him, and he undertook another round of reforms. He sequestered himself with like-reminded members of the royal court, working on his plans. He allegedly said of his trip: "Paris filled me with joy, Berlin astounded me, London caught my imagination, but it was my homeland which ignited fire in me." Just over a month after his return home, he called for another loya jirga.

This grand assembly was held again in Paghman, although in this case there was less discussion and more opportunity for Amanullah to lecture the jirga. For four days he spoke to the assembled group, laying out the case for modernization, and blaming previous failures on "ignorant" members of the ulema who were "corrupt, hypocritical, restrictive, and narrow-minded." He also outlawed *purdah*, the common practice of segregating unrelated men and women, both at home and in public. Most shockingly, he repeated that wearing the veil (which is a public aspect of purdah) is not a requirement of Islam; to underline the point, his wife tore hers off her head in front of the assembly. He insisted that in order to progress, they would have to root out the superstition and customary beliefs that corrupted true Islam.

A further attack on the ulema was the renewal of government-sanctioned exams for all clergy, even at the lowest level, and a ban on all foreign-trained ulema. Given the lack of schools in Afghanistan, many Afghan clerics had been trained in India in *madrassas* established by the Deobandi movement, and they would now be prevented from practising. The Deobandis were a conservative Sunni movement that sought to instill orthodoxy of religious thought, taking a more rigid approach than the Sufi. But he also banned a key element of Sufi practice, the formal relationship between master and student (or *pir* and *murtad*) that underpinned the structure of the movement. Amanullah also created a new political party that was meant to support his reforms, called the Ferqaye Esteqlal wa Tajaddod (Party of Independence and Modernity). A key element of the party's official platform was to "remove from religion the superstitious and heretical beliefs which do not conform with Islam." His desire to reform and modernize Afghanistan now seemingly extended to improving its religion as well, an affront to the conservative religious scholars who had previously supported him.

Unlike the earlier jirga where the delegates had been treated as honoured guests, this time they were lectured like school children. As the *Contemporary Review* quoted Amanullah saying that same year: "An Afghan boy is worth ten Afghan men, because a boy can be trained, but a grown [Afghan] man is mostly fit for the scrap heap." A hastily passed law written by Amanullah on his return from overseas decreed that everyone in the capital must wear European dress. This meant that most of the delegates, some very far from home, had to scramble to find European clothing when they arrived for the jirga. Sitting in ill-fitting borrowed clothes for days on end likely only added to the feeling of insult.

The first signs of major discontent arose shortly after the jirga's conclusion. The most prominent Sufi religious leader in Afghanistan was called the the Hazrat of Shor Bazaar, a title typically held by the patriarch of the Mojaddedi family. This family, although Ghilzai rather than Durrani, claimed the hereditary right to crown amirs of Afghanistan, and had supported Amanullah's claim to the throne in 1919. The Hazrat now declared that he opposed Amanullah's reforms and had the support of over four hundred clerics.

When Amanullah demanded that they reverse their opposition, the Hazrat fled the capital. He and his followers were quickly captured by government troops and dragged back to face the amir. Amanullah had a half dozen of the ringleaders executed, and the remainder, including the aged and venerable Hazrat, imprisoned. This created a serious gulf between the monarchy and religious leaders across the country.

A few weeks later, on November 12, a relatively small uprising unsettled the Khyber Pass. Around 30 tribesmen from the Sanghu Khel and Alicher Khel sub-tribes of the Shinwari attacked two villages and an army post. The army detachment surrendered without a shot being fired, and the Shinwari returned to their homes burdened with loot. The governor in Jalalabad vacillated, requesting direction from Kabul rather than responding decisively. The weak government response emboldened the Shinwari as a whole, and the rebellion quickly spread to other parts of the tribe. Two leaders emerged, Mohammed Alam and Mohammed Afzal, supported by a tribal mullah known as Hafiz Sahib of Faqirabad.

The exact reasons for this uprising are obscure, and various authors have suggested different causes. A contemporary writer suggests a member of Amanullah's court, jealous of a rival's promotion, instigated the raids in order to gain favour by persuading the rebels to stand down. An alternative is that Ghilzai tribesmen may have attacked the Shinwari, only to be arrested and later freed by the army without punishment, giving the Shinwari a reason to seek revenge. Amanullah himself blamed the British for inciting the revolt, claiming as proof that the famous British insurgent leader T.E. Lawrence was at that time in Miranshah in Waziristan. This was true, but when Amanullah issued a standing order for Lawrence's arrest, the British Foreign Office ordered that he return to England.

The most convincing argument, however, is somewhat tangled, and relates to the government's role in a tribal dispute. Both the Shinwari and their principal rivals, the Mohmand tribe, were involved in the lucrative *badraga* business. All caravans travelling into or out of Afghanistan through the Khyber Pass, the principal gateway for trade, were obliged to hire escorts from one of the two tribes. If they did not, they were attacked by the very men who had offered them protection. If they did hire protection, they were often attacked by the opposing tribe, creating a cycle of grievance and revenge between the two groups that was nonetheless lucrative.

Upon his return from Europe, Amanullah had instructed the governor of Jalalabad to end the practice of badraga, in order to encourage trade. The governor did not want to take on both tribes at once, and so chose to first outlaw the practice by the weaker of the two, the Shinwari. The loss of their way of life, and the insult they sustained when the Mohmand continued the practice while they were forbidden to, caused the Shinwari to attack the local symbols of government.

No contemporary explanation of the uprising suggests that the tribesmen were responding to the reforms proposed at the loya jirga. As has been discussed, for the most part these did not impact the very independent eastern tribes, as the reach of government was limited in their lands. Some of the reforms were also not contentious — Shinwari women were largely unveiled even before Amanullah's reforms.

The common picture of women in Afghanistan today is of them wearing the head-to-toe covering known as a *burkha* (or *burqa*). This is a relatively recent phenomenon, although similar garments were known in Persia and Arabia, and among the Pashtuns, even in pre-Islamic times. In rural areas where the Shinwari lived, women were needed for agricultural work. It was impractical for them to wear restrictive burkhas while working, and so the only families whose women were veiled were those who could afford for them not to work. In essence, the veil was a middle- and upper-class affectation. Most women in the countryside wore a scarf over their hair, but were not otherwise covered. Amanullah's reforms regarding the veiling of women only truly shocked the families who could afford to veil them in the first place.

As the rebellion grew in size, and the Shinwari were joined first by the Khogyani and then by nearly all the tribes of Nangarhar, Laghman, Kunar, Paktia, and Paktika regions, a list of grievances began to form, many religious but some also social. Taxes had risen dramatically during Amanullah's reign, fourfold in the case of land taxes and fivefold in the case of livestock. But the mullahs who were appalled at the imprisonment of the Hazrat of Shor Bazaar gave the opportunistic rebellion a gloss of legitimacy by claiming that Amanullah was again an apostate and an enemy of Islam. Many wild rumours circulated, including that Amanullah had imported machinery from Germany that would be used to turn the corpses of Muslims into soap to be sold in Europe. Photographs of Queen Soraya, bare-armed and mingling with foreign men, also circulated, suggesting wanton impropriety. The rebels used religious language to describe their uprising, seizing the moral high ground from the government. Whatever their true motivation, by the end of November nearly every tribe in the east was in open rebellion, and the city of Jalalabad was under siege.

Amanullah had to respond, but his options were limited. His military reforms had meant that the army had dwindled from around sixty thousand men to just over ten thousand. Amanullah had also "reformed" salaries in the army in a manner that badly affected morale. His intention was to cut pay but provide the men with better lodgings as well as free food and uniforms. Corruption and lack of industry among the officers meant that in practice the soldiers' pay was reduced without any of the improvements being implemented. Consequently, many soldiers deserted at the first opportunity. In the end, Amanullah did send the army to fight the rebels, but its performance was stunningly poor.

The strategy used by many previous amirs was to bribe rival tribes to fight the rebellious ones. This option was also unavailable to Amanullah, as he had alienated many of the tribal leaders he could have relied upon. His reduction or elimination of tribal stipends had also weakened the power of the tribal leaders, making it more difficult for them to provide support even if they were inclined to do so. And so in this situation, Amanullah took the only other course open to him and sent a delegation of representatives, headed by his brother-in-law Ali Ahmed Jan, to negotiate with the rebels.

The delegation returned to the capital in early December after having convinced the Mohmand tribe to return to their homes, although all the others remained in rebellion. The delegates presented a list of demands from the remaining rebels that Amanullah could not reasonably fulfill: he was to reverse all social reforms, reduce taxation, and divorce and exile his wife and her family. Amanullah flatly refused.

In December 1928 a potential solution emerged in the north. A famous Tajik bandit, named Habibullah Kalakani but better known as Bacha-e Saqqao ("son of a water carrier," so named after his father's low-prestige profession), approached the amir through the local governor. Habibullah Kalakani had made his living for many years by raiding caravans traversing the Shomali (Northern) Plain just outside of the capital, but now he offered his services to Amanullah.

Desperate, Amanullah agreed to hire Habibullah Kalakani to fight against the rebels in the east, though he extracted an oath of allegiance from him before providing arms and ammunition. Famously wily, Habibullah Kalakani checked Amanullah's loyalty as well. He allegedly telephoned Amanullah and impersonated a local government official, telling the amir that Habibullah Kalakani's men were surrounded and asking for instructions. Amanullah replied, "Shoot the scoundrel like the dog that he is!" and Habibullah Kalakani revealed himself. Telling the amir that he would have to catch him first, he ended their short-lived alliance.

On December 10 Habibullah Kalakani led his bandits in an attack on the garrison at Jabal-us Seraj, capturing all nine hundred men without a shot being fired. Four days later he attacked the capital itself. Although Habibullah Kalakani's men were quickly repulsed and forced to retreat, they led their pursuers into a series of costly ambushes. The army garrison of the capital now either destroyed or deployed in the east, there remained only the amir's small personal guard to defend him.

Amanullah's desperation showed again when he was approached by an Ahmedzai khan known as Ghaus ud-Din, who offered to lead his tribe against Habibullah Kalakani and the eastern rebels. Although the Ahmedzai, as Ghilzai Pashtuns, were ancient enemies of Amanullah's family, he provided them with arms and money in exchange for their loyalty. But no sooner had he armed them than Ghaus ud-Din led his men back to their tribal stronghold in Ghazni and declared himself amir.

Amanullah had well and truly run out of supporters, and consequently out of options as well.

On December 21 Amanullah sent his wife and family to Kandahar on a Russian-crewed airplane, where they could be better protected by the surrounding Durrani tribes. On January 7 he released the Hazrat and his co-signers from prison, and the following day announced that he would reverse all of his previous reforms. None of this was enough to sway the eastern tribes or Habibullah Kalakani, who attacked again from the north. On January 14, with the capital about to fall to the Tajik rebels, Amanullah announced his abdication in favour of his elder brother Inyatullah, and drove south to Kandahar to join his wife.

An epitaph to Amanullah's reign appeared a week later in the *Spectator*, a London newspaper: it said that in terms of the amir's efforts at reform, "it would have been wise to hasten slowly." This only tells part of the story. Opposition to his rule was not universal, as there were no uprisings in the south or west during this period, or within the Hazarajat. And many of those who rose against his rule were the least affected by the comprehensive reforms that he had decreed. It was not haste that undid Amanullah's reign.

Amanullah was too focused on the outward appearance of reform rather than on substantive changes. In many ways, he was more concerned with raising the status of Afghanistan in the world, and consequently his own status as well, than improving the condition of the average Afghan citizen. He rightly put an emphasis on education, but one wonders what an educated class of Afghans would do with themselves given the lack of effective economic reforms.

He did not recognize that there was a need to find a balance between the centralization and decentralization of power, and that unless he co-opted the existing power structures — tribal leaders and the ulema — his efforts would be for naught. Not only did he need these structures to enact his reforms, he also needed them to explain the reforms and their benefits to the common person. Written laws and decrees are an ineffective means of communicating in a country with single-digit literacy rates.

His focus on the need to provide equal rights to women was done so ineptly that it gave his opponents a rallying cry against him. Queen Soraya is notable as the first identifiable Afghan feminist, but her efforts had little regard for the reality of all Afghan women, urban and rural, pastoral and nomadic. Her work best reflected the needs and desires of the educated Kabul elite. The very idea of these feminist reforms provided the substantiation for the uprisings that overthrew the regime, even though the rebels were actually concerned with the power of men.

Operating in the echo chamber of the royal court, Amanullah and his close associates assumed that it was obvious for all to see that reform would have a positive effect on the country, even in the face of clear evidence to the contrary. His country paid the price for both his optimism and his naïveté.

CHAPTER 4 THE WATER CARRIER'S BOY

HABIBULLAH KALAKANI WAS a character one might expect to find in a 1930s dime novel. Little has been written about him in academic circles other than to note that his reign was an aberration from centuries of Durrani Pashtun rule. Much of what is known about his early life comes from his supposed autobiography published many years after his death by a reputed member of his bandit gang.

Born in a rural Tajik village north of Kabul, he left home as a teenager after burning down the home of a hated teacher and assisting an older brigand, Nur Khan, in the murder of a Hindu jeweller. Illiterate, he drifted into a life of thievery and gambling in Peshawar. A soothsayer there gave him an amulet that protected against bullets and told him that one day he would be king. The old wise man also prophesied that Habibullah Kalakani's life would only last two moons longer than his own. When Habibullah lost everything gambling, he returned to Afghanistan and enlisted in the army. Ill-suited to the discipline, he soon deserted and returned home to resume a life of brigandry.

At that time there were three main routes from the capital that connected the centre of the country with the north, all passing over high mountain ranges. One of these routes crossed the Shomali Plain, dotted with many narrow passes, making it rich ground for bandits. Habibullah Kalakani's reputation grew, as did the size of his band, eventually numbering in the hundreds. Although not exactly respectable, he was both respected and feared. His chief rival in the region was a man named Sharfuddin, known as the "King of the Passes." Habibullah Kalakani established his primacy by conducting a sneak attack on Sharfuddin's village, killing all the male inhabitants and parading Sharfuddin's head on a stake.

Amanullah had sent the army to kill or capture Habibullah Kalakani numerous times, but in every case he humiliated the army instead. During one of the last expeditions he captured two machine guns and over forty thousand rounds of ammunition, which fuelled his campaign against the capital.

Attacking with a band that had grown to two thousand men, though only three hundred with modern weapons, he outmatched the weakened army and was in a position to seize the capital when others who opposed Amanullah were not. He did his best to spread terror and confusion by cutting all the telegraph cables that led out of the city and damaging the power plant at Jabal-us Seraj. He received information about the army's movements from high-level government officials whom he regularly bribed. Despite being wounded during the offensive on the capital, he maintained tight control over his forces and their morale remained high.

When Inyatullah ascended the throne and word of his brother Amanullah's flight reached the army, it began to evaporate, its soldiers either joining the rebels or simply returning home. And even though Amanullah had distributed fifty thousand rifles to the citizens of Kabul, few were willing to fight for his brother. Inyatullah quickly sent the Hazrat of Shor Bazaar to negotiate an end to the fighting with Habibullah Kalakani. With neither an army nor a treasury to support him, Inyatullah offered the only thing he could: the throne. Habibullah Kalakani accepted, giving Inyatullah a promise of safety.

With the amir's emissaries as his honoured guests, Habibullah Kalakani entered the city on January 16, 1929. His troops, looking like savages to the genteel Kabulis, marched through the city shouting *"Ya chahar ya!"* — a Sunni war cry that likely caused shivers in the Shi'ite Hazara and Qizilbashi communities. He immediately took up residence in the Arg, a combination of fortress and palace in the middle of the city. The same courtiers who had just pledged allegiance to Inyatullah only days before now did the same to "Habibullah Amir," their new ruler. He was the first non-Pashtun to claim the Afghan throne since the start of the Durrani Empire in 1747.

Apparently Habibullah Kalakani and his men were overwhelmed with the luxury to be had in the Arg, where they saw their first bathtubs and European furniture. Their first night, Habibullah Kalakani tricked his deputy Malik Mohsin into sleeping on a billiard table, convincing him that it was a special bed for distinguished guests. Fayz Mohammed Kateb, the court scribe, recounts a story that Habibullah Kalakani was so out of his element that when he invited his father to join him for a meal in the palace, they mistook a water closet for the dining room, and ate soup out of Amanullah's porcelain chamber pot.

Habibullah Kalakani's first order of business was to reward his followers. Although he was not a member of a tribe such as the Pashtuns, as a Tajik he belonged to an informal social structure based on influence and the ownership of land. All the men he led against the capital were from Kohistan district, and the large majority of them had not been part of his band of brigands. They joined him largely to gain riches. The presence of major *zamindars* such as Malik Mohsin gives a good sense of the amount of influence Habibullah Kalakani wielded, though it would dissipate quickly once he failed to provide for his followers. Although he never said so explicitly, Habibullah Kalakani's effect on how power was wielded in Afghanistan was to negate the central government, reverting to a form of society that predates the organized state. This reflected the reality in many corners of the country where the state's influence was weak to begin with, but it did not create a stable system that could last for long.

Habibullah Kalakani claims in his autobiography that when he took the capital he found the treasury empty. He immediately rounded up all the capital's moneylenders, and extorted an exorbitant amount of money from them by cutting off the thumb of one of their leaders. He claims to have received 100 million rupees from them, but even this was insufficient. Habibullah Kalakani also closed all schools, libraries, and the Royal Museum, and sold every piece of property he could, trying to cut costs and raise funds at the same time. He also allowed his troops to loot the capital, focusing on the merchant class and the homes of prominent government officials they perceived to be corrupt. Habibullah Kalakani's arrival brought nothing but chaos and fear.

The British disapproved but declared their strict neutrality. Nonetheless, a massive air operation known as the "Kabul Airlift" was undertaken by the Royal Air Force to fly internationals out of the capital, taking almost a month to remove nearly six hundred people. It was the first large-scale air evacuation in history, and given both the limitations of aircraft of the time and the cold, mountainous terrain, it was remarkable. The British minister to the Amir of Afghanistan, Francis Humphrys, was knighted for his role in organizing the evacuation.

Habibullah Kalakani then organized his administration of the country, later explaining his philosophy as follows: "I had seen too much of Amanullah's court to have any respect for too much learning or for courtly manners.... I distrusted those who were learned of the arts. I could neither read nor write, and I had found it no handicap. I could hire for a few rupees those who had assimilated the ways of the pen, and I determined that my Cabinet should be one of action." He immediately abolished the Ministries of Trade, Health, Education, and Justice, and simply ignored the reforms put in place by Amanullah. His court became one of personality and discussion, a much older system of governance that Afghanistan had only recently escaped. Malik Mohsin was appointed governor of Kabul, although he seems to have focused largely on organizing the systematic looting of the city. Among the changes was the return of judicial authority to the qadis, as there were no longer any secular laws to enforce.

Amanullah, safe among his tribesmen in Kandahar, became aware of his brother's flight from the capital and announced that he was rescinding his abdication. He held a durbar to try to build support among the Barakzai settled around the city, but they had little interest in fighting both Habibullah Kalakani in Kabul and the eastern Pashtun tribes that had risen against Amanullah in the first place.

One of the courtiers whom Amanullah had sent to negotiate with those tribes was a cousin and brother-in-law named Ali Ahmed Jan. After news reached him of Habibullah Kalakani's victory in Kabul, he held a loya jirga in Jalalabad, and with the support of the ulema who had accompanied him had himself declared amir. Ali Ahmed Jan was a famous *bon vivant*, tremendously fat and known to be fond of alcohol. It is unclear how he gained the support of the eastern tribes. There is a Pashto proverb: "You may try gently for hundreds of years, but it is impossible to make scorpions, snakes, or Shinwari into friends." Even as the jirga was ongoing, treachery was afoot; before it ended, the Shinwari and Khogyani tribes had negotiated a secret deal with Habibullah Kalakani in exchange for a large payment.

In early February Ali Ahmed Jan advanced toward Kabul at the head of a *lashkar*, roughly equivalent to a posse formed to enforce the decision of a jirga. The route from Jalalabad to Kabul passes through a number of narrow mountain passes. One, known as Jagdalak, was the site of a massacre of British and Indian troops as they retreated from Kabul during the First Anglo-Afghan War in 1842. In this same narrow pass, the Khogyani attacked the other members of the lashkar, scattering them and nearly capturing Ali Ahmed Jan, who barely escaped with his life. The remnants of the lashkar retreated back up the road to Jalalabad, which they sacked before returning to their homes throughout the region. As many as one thousand civilians were killed during the attack on the town, many when the garrison's powder magazine blew up. Ali Ahmed Jan fled all the way to Peshawar, where he was picked up by the British authorities and sent to face his brother-in-law in Kandahar. Amanullah first imprisoned him, but was eventually persuaded by Amanullah's mother to forgive him.

Amanullah was continuing to try to build enough support to retake his throne. On February 24 he gave a speech at the Mosque of the Cloak of the Prophet in Kandahar. After the speech, he made a grand gesture. One of the holiest relics in Islam, a cloak reputed to have belonged to the Prophet Mohammed, is housed there, and Amanullah took it out and draped it over his own shoulders. He did so, he claimed, to prove that he was not an apostate or an unbeliever. Whether through this act of propaganda or because a Tajik sitting on the throne wounded Durrani pride, he began to gain support from the Barakzai.

He next reached out to the Durranis' arch-nemesis the Ghilzai tribe to seek their support. A large part of the tribe was outside Afghanistan at that time, as their migration took them annually from winter pastures in India to summer pastures in the Hazarajat. They rejected his entreaties outright, and would prove to be very troublesome when they returned to Afghanistan in the spring, when the mountain passes were clear of snow — the traditional start of the "fighting season."

On February 25 another player arrived on the scene. Nadir Khan, former minister of war and hero of the Third Anglo-Afghan War, had been living in exile on the French Riviera after falling out with Amanullah. He now appeared in Peshawar, along with two of his brothers, claiming his only wish was to bring peace to the countryside. Both Habibullah Kalakani and Amanullah summoned him to their courts, but he refused both invitations. Nadir Khan joined a third brother at Khost where he tried to convoke another loya jirga to select a new Pashtun amir.

In March Nadir Khan wrote a letter to Habibullah Kalakani, which read in part:

> I have no doubt of your courage and I admire the fact that you have succeeded in driving Amanullah Khan from Kabul and occupying the throne yourself. What concerns me is Afghan honour and so I have arrived on this soil to put out the flames of rebellion. The thought of occupying the throne or any other high post has never occurred to me.... I have no wish to live in Afghanistan with its savage and ignorant people where presently there is nothing but killing and destruction of property. As for now, O victorious brother, I express only feelings of goodwill, but do not depend on these lasting. I advise you to end the bloodshed among Muslims and the destruction of Afghanistan.... [T]he illustrious Pashtun tribes ... will not leave the reins of government in the hands of our brother. We propose therefore that he leave the throne to someone who enjoys influence amongst the Pashtuns. If our brother wishes to continue to have some power then I would guarantee him the post of caravan leader and will do my best to help him achieve success.

Habibullah Kalakani first wrote a temperate reply to the insulting letter, claiming to agree to bend to the will of shari'a, but was convinced by the ulema and courtiers who were advising him to take a different tack. They had several members of Nadir Khan's family, who were still resident in Kabul, summoned to the palace. These family members were then forced to write a letter that read:

> We, both men and women, know the respect that Amir Habibullah Khan feels for you. We enjoy full health and peace of mind now, but if you refuse the honour of being received by him then we face destruction.

This letter was entrusted to the Hazrat of Shor Bazaar and his brother, who were instructed to deliver it personally. To be ready to make good on the threat, Habibullah Kalakani confined Nadir Khan's wife and the wives of his brothers (all of whom were sisters of Amanullah) to the Hazrat's house.

Habibullah Kalakani's grip on the capital was tightening, but repeated episodes of looting and arbitrary arrests created an atmosphere of anarchy. The looting got so out of hand that Habibullah Kalakani even had the city's governor Malik Mohsin twice publicly caned for theft. Price controls the amir put in place only worsened the availability of food, which was already scarce, as merchants would not sell at a loss. The register of pack animals created under Amanullah was used to appropriate many camels, horses, and donkeys for use by Habibullah Kalakani's men, forcing citizens to hide their animals rather than lose them.

Habibullah Kalakani's brother, Hamidullah, became infamous as the "King's Helper." A former wedding dancer and bandit, he led much of the looting in the city, raping and killing with impunity. When butchers were caught selling cuts of meat with too much bone, Hamidullah selected six of them to be publicly caned and then nailed through their ears to stakes in the market. Unsurprisingly, this did nothing to improve the city's economy.

Habibullah Kalakani tried printing money as well as stamping coins in leather to create the cash he needed to pay his soldiers, but public confidence was so low that both currencies were rejected. He had exempted many of his supporters from paying taxes as a means to gain their support, and without expanding his control of the country beyond the capital and his own homeland to the north, he was forced into an endless cycle of looting to make ends meet.

When spring arrived military operations began in earnest. Habibullah Kalakani struck southward to Ghazni, while Amanullah advanced northward toward the same goal. Nadir Khan had convinced the eastern tribes to adopt a six-month truce between themselves, which was deemed long enough to depose Habibullah Kalakani and put a Pashtun on the throne instead. Many of the tribes were suspicious that Nadir Khan was in league with Amanullah, and forced him to swear an oath to deny it before they would agree to the truce. Demanding an oath is tantamount to calling a Pashtun a liar, underlining the seriousness of their concern. Nadir Khan led his force westward toward the capital, having also secured the support of Ghaus ud-Din, now known as the Amir of Ghazni.

All the contenders for the throne made efforts to use propaganda to build their case and undercut the legitimacy of their rivals. As before, the arguments they used were largely religious, couching their rejection of each other in the language of jihad. Each accused the others of being apostates or unbelievers, while claiming that they themselves were *ghazis,* or holy warriors.

Each created newspapers to carry his message. Habibullah Kalakani produced *Habib al-Islam* (Beloved of Islam, also one of his royal titles), written by his supporters among the ulema. Nadir Khan created *Islah* (Reform), a word common both in the Quran and in modern Islamic politics; the paper continues to be published in Afghanistan to this day. Even Ali Ahmed Jan printed one edition of *Ghairat al-Islam* (Islamic zeal) before he was forced to retreat to Peshawar. The most effective propaganda was likely spread orally, either through the networks of village mullahs or through rumours in the bazaar. One of the most widespread rumours was directed at Amanullah's wife, who was said to have travelled naked in a motor car through Europe. It was claimed that photographs of her were circulating among the population. No one had actually seen any, but the rumour was believed by many, furthering the idea that Amanullah and his family were not true Muslims.

Habibullah Kalakani also used aircraft captured from Amanullah to drop leaflets over the tribal areas. A copy of one of the leaflets, dropped on April 16, reads in part:

> In the name of God, the Merciful, the Compassionate! A government proclamation. May it be known to brother Muslims in the Eastern and Southern Provinces! Information about the cowardly and treacherous activity of Field Marshal Nadir proves that he has shown himself to be an infidel ... trying to divide Muslim from Muslim.... Anyone who brings Nadir in alive will be paid forty thousand rupees. Thirty thousand rupees, a rifle and ammunition will go to anyone who brings in his head.

The pamphlet also accused Nadir Khan of having been complicit in the assassination of Habibullah Amir in 1919, the first of a litany of sins that made him unworthy of being followed.

Habibullah Kalakani's troops had some success against the Wardak and Tagari tribes south of the capital, which opened up the road for him to attack the fortress held by Ghaus ud-Din in Ghazni. Both Amanullah and Nadir Khan also advanced in that direction, though not in coordination with each other, and without the support of the Ghilzai tribes whose land they passed through.

Amanullah's supply lines back to Kandahar were harassed by Ghilzai tribesmen, some of whom had fought against him during the Khost rebellion. They took this opportunity to exact *badal* (revenge) for their humiliating defeat. This was significant, as revenge is one of the tenets of the Pashtunwali. A Pashtun is required to avenge himself when his honour is slighted.

Habibullah Kalakani first defeated Amanullah's army, forcing him to retreat southward, and then turned on Nadir Khan who had advanced to Logar. At a battle near Baraki, Ghaus ud-Din's men forced Nadir Khan to withdraw eastward. Habibullah Kalakani then faced new opposition elsewhere. Ghulam Nabi Charki, the son of a famous Afghan general who had been Amanullah's ambassador to the Soviet Union, raised a force with the consent of the Soviet government, which also provided him with arms and ammunition. Still loyal to Amanullah, he led this force southward and seized the principal town of Mazar-e Sharif. This was troubling, but an even greater threat against Habibullah Kalakani emerged at the same time in the Hazarajat. Amanullah's policies that had offended many were popular among the Hazaras, who had long been discriminated against both as Shi'ites and as an ethnic underclass. Because Amanullah had put laws in place to eliminate slavery (which affected the Hazaras more than any other group) and calling for the protection of Shi'ites, and because of the rapacious policies of Habibullah Kalakani, they took up arms against the new regime. Although they did not advance far from their homeland, they were a threat close to the capital that Habibullah Kalakani could not ignore.

On May 23, in despair after his military defeat, Amanullah fled in secret with his family into British India, reaching the border town of Chaman in a convoy of cars led by Amanullah driving a Rolls Royce. From there they travelled to Bombay and sailed into exile, never to return. Amanullah lived in Italy until his death in 1960, and his wife until her death in 1968. Both were then repatriated and buried in a royal mausoleum in Jalalabad.

When word began to circulate of Amanullah's flight, his Pashtun followers despaired. Habibullah Kalakani captured Kandahar at the end of May and arrested Ali Ahmed Jan, taking him back to the capital, where he was strapped over the muzzle of a cannon and executed in front of his family. Ghulam Nabi Charki's forces evaporated, likely crossing back into the Soviet Union and safety. Ghulam Nabi himself was arrested in Paris for possession of 250 kilograms of heroin and a large quantity of cocaine, which he was trying to sell to raise money — either for Amanullah or for himself, it was unclear. The Hazaras, with nowhere to flee, continued to fight.

Habibullah Kalakani was increasingly frustrated with the refusal of the Hazara to submit to his rule. Many of the mid-level court scribes and bureaucrats were drawn from a group known as the Qizilbashi, Shi'a of Persian descent who had settled in Kabul in the 18th century. He sent a delegation of Qizilbashi, and also the noted Hazara scribe Fayz Mohammed Kateb, to negotiate with the Hazara leaders on his behalf. He assumed that their religious affinity would have a positive effect, but he did not understand the enmity between the groups. The Qizilbashi were relatively high status, compared to the Hazara who formed the underclass of Afghan society, particularly in the capital where most performed menial labour.

He sent a message with the delegation that read:

> Beginning with the reign of Abdul Rahman down to the day of Amanullah's abdication from the throne, Pashtuns have oppressed Hazaras. They have robbed, murdered, arrested, enslaved, immolated and disposed you. Nonetheless, those rulers not only did not punish the Pashtuns, on the contrary they incited them to murder, plunder, and enslave you. These same rulers also forcibly exiled the Hazaras to other countries. By your failure to recognize the authority of Amir Habibullah [as Habibullah Kalakani was formally known], you condemn yourselves to death. You should submit, put an end to the bloodshed, and save yourselves.

After long negotiations, the delegation failed to reach an agreement with the Hazaras. Perhaps suspecting treachery, Habibullah Kalakani had his delegates tortured upon their return.

He then took a different tack, demanding religious sanction for a war against the Hazaras. The Hazrat of Shor Bazaar obliged, issuing a fatwa authorizing the murder of all Hazaras as unbelievers. This was an extension of the arguments long made against their opponents by Afghan rulers and usurpers alike, who exploited ethnic, cultural, and religious identities to create in-groups and out-groups, and to justify atrocities. Habibullah Kalakani also invited Ghilzai tribesmen to attack the Hazaras, in Kabul and in the Hazarajat, enticing them with loot and the promise of his support. These kinds of raids appealed to the tribesmen, as unlike the outcome when they raided among themselves, there was little chance of setting off cycles of revenge.

In the east Nadir Khan's situation worsened in May when the truce among the eastern tribes fell apart due to a dispute about who could practise badraga along the border. This largely neutralized Nadir Khan as a military threat. But while Habibullah Kalakani was focused on the Hazara threat, Nadir Khan used the influence that he had first built in 1919, as well as his deep knowledge of the tribes, to rebuild his coalition. He won an important diplomatic victory at a jirga convened near Gardez by the Hazrat of Shor Bazaar, who was playing all sides in hopes of having supported the eventual victor. At this jirga he was able to regain consensus for a truce, in order to focus on their common enemy in Kabul.

Indecisive fighting throughout the summer led Nadir Khan to seek new resources. First he sought the support of the colonial authorities in British India to recruit among the Pashtun tribes on the other side of the Durand Line. The British response was subtle — they would neither support nor prevent such an action. Soon Nadir Khan had recruited huge lashkars from the Mehsud and Wazir tribes, much as he had done in 1919. Through the brother of the Hazrat of Shor Bazaar, he also negotiated with the Ghilzai, gaining the support of a few sub-tribes and, most importantly, the neutrality of the rest.

Habibullah Kalakani's second attempt to reach an agreement with the Hazara was successful, but shortly thereafter he faced another uprising. When he had captured Kandahar, he appointed Abdul Qadir, a Ghilzai of the Taraki sub-tribe, as the governor. This caused resentment among the Durrani who dominate the lands around Kandahar, which eventually bubbled over into a full-scale revolt. This time they did not fight in favour of Amanullah, but simply against Habibullah Kalakani and his loathed appointee. The loss of Kandahar, one of the great food-producing regions of Afghanistan, caused a massive rise in the price of bread in the capital, where most food staples were already unaffordable.

In September Nadir Khan and his brothers advanced on Kabul along multiple fronts, splitting Habibullah Kalakani's attention and straining his dwindling resources. Isolated in the centre of the country, by early October he was pushed back to the outskirts of Kabul. Soon the entire city was under siege.

Habibullah Kalakani and his closest followers took refuge in the Arg, bringing hostages with them to try to bargain for their lives. To prove his intent, he murdered two half-brothers of Amanullah, and threatened to do the same with the members of Nadir Khan's family who were within his grasp. Allegedly, the hostages smuggled a letter out of the Arg to Nadir Khan, begging him not to bargain for their lives, but instead to defeat Habibullah Kalakani decisively.

Nadir Khan's troops bombarded the Arg for several days. One night Habibullah Kalakani and Malik Mohsin slipped over the walls and escaped on stolen camels, back to Kohistan where they hoped their kinsmen would shelter and protect them. Nadir Khan sent a communiqué to the Kohistanis telling them that to aid Habibullah Kalakani in any way would invite retribution. In his autobiography, Habibullah Kalakani relates that his people instead left food and water out in the hills every night, "for anyone to partake of." After only four days on the run, both men surrendered to Nadir Khan in return for a guarantee of safety from him.

The following day Nadir Khan made a formal entry into the capital, and called another loya jirga, ostensibly to thank the tribal leaders for their support. He continued to claim that he had no desire to become the amir, citing his poor health. It was thought that he might propose his nephew Asadullah for the role, who was Amanullah's half-brother and son of the former amir's junior wife Ulya Janab. But he did not make the proposal, and allowed the the jirga to "persuade" him to accept the crown. On October 16 he was no long Nadir Khan, but Nadir Shah.

The ascension of Nadir Shah put another member of the Mohammedzai sub-tribe of the Barakzai on the throne, albeit from a different branch of the family. Nadir Shah's clan within the sub-tribe was known as the Musahiban, which means "courtier." Although his ancestors had been close to the throne for generations, he was the first Musahiban to sit upon it. Even though succession in Afghanistan had often been contested, all of the rulers of Afghanistan (save Habibullah Kalakani) had come from a narrow set of relations since 1826, a pattern that continued until 1978.

The jirga also considered the fate of Habibullah Kalakani and his men, even though they had surrendered with a promise of safe conduct. After heated discussion, Nadir Shah made one of his first decisions as a ruler. He claimed that he personally forgave his captive for his actions, but the demands of the leaders of the Hazaras and the eastern tribes had to be respected. Habibullah Kalakani, several members of his family, Malik Mohsin, and nine other rebels were executed by firing squad on November 1.

Just as when Habibullah Kalakani took the capital, Nadir Shah now had to pay his victorious troops. He also found that the treasury was empty, and he had no wealth of his own to distribute. Andrée Viollis, a foreign correspondent in Kabul, observed the eastern tribes as they entered the city and wrote that "the tribesmen considered Kabul as an enemy capital." Even in its dilapidated state, "modern" Kabul was alien to these men from the countryside. Nadir Shah paid the tribes by allowing them to sack the city, after which he dissolved the lashkar and encouraged them to return to their homes. He began his rule presiding over a capital his own men had destroyed. More than 150,000 people had been killed since the fighting began in January. In just nine months' time, nearly all of Amanullah's efforts at modernization achieved over 10 years had been undone.

CHAPTER 5 THE SHADOW OF GOD

NADIR SHAH'S POSITION as king was precarious indeed. He immediately took what steps he could to consolidate power and remove any reason for further opposition to his rule. Even though he had been acclaimed as the amir by a hastily convened jirga of the tribes that had swept him to power, much of the country lay outside of his immediate control. Although he retained power to be exercised by the central state, he was careful not to overplay his hand, leaving many issues to tribal leaders and ensuring that the ulema exercised authority over issues seen as within their sphere. He recognized that, in the situation, the most effective government would be one that ruled lightly, and in some areas not at all.

At his formal coronation at the end of November 1929, he issued a royal proclamation that summed up his policies in 10 points. Among these were the repeal of Amanullah's constitution and a return to the Hanafi interpretation of shari'a as the basis of law and administration, the total prohibition of alcohol, the closure of all girls' schools, and the compulsory veiling of all women. These measures were meant to ensure the support of the ulema, who were incorporated into state structure in a new organization called the Jamiat-e Ulema (Assembly of Muslim

Scholars). This organization was to ensure that all government policy was in line with shari'a, and to act as the sole interpreters of law. He also took modest steps to improve the administration of the country, by creating a new army of only twelve thousand men with conscription run by tribal leaders, as it had been before Amanullah, and a military school and arsenal for manufacturing weapons and ammunition. He was conservative in everything that he did, and in a manner both pious and threatening he styled himself "the shadow of God."

Fighting against rebels continued in the country for the next few years. Even though Habibullah Kalakani was now dead, his fellow tribesmen in Kohistan continued to oppose Nadir Shah and the government in Kabul. Herat, which had been taken by one of Habibullah Kalakani's generals in 1929, also opposed Nadir Shah. The ancient city, already old when it was captured by Alexander the Great in 330 BCE, had never been more than nominally part of Afghanistan. No paved roads connected it with any other major city in Afghanistan; instead it looked westward, seeing itself as a Persian city, both culturally and historically. The Iron Amir had secured it in 1881 in his campaigns to consolidate the political power of the throne, but it retained its independent spirit.

Nadir Shah was also concerned with external threats. Almost immediately after seizing the throne, he sent a message to the European powers through a foreign correspondent who was in Kabul to cover the civil war. His message to Europe differed from his internal one, as he portrayed himself as a reformer intent on reopening schools, building infrastructure, and re-establishing friendly relations with other nations, particularly France where he had lived in exile. He also sought to deepen relations with European powers that had no immediate interest in the region, such as Germany, and to establish formal relations with Islamic states such as Saudi Arabia and Iraq.

He recognized the need to establish a balanced relationship with Britain and the Soviet Union, letting neither country dominate Afghanistan or obtain a position that threatened the other. His relationship with the British, who preferred his rule to that of Amanullah, was already good. To establish better relations with the Soviets, he reversed one of Amanullah's policies. Amanullah had tolerated, and at times supported, the presence in the north of the country of Basmachi (a derogatory term for "bandit" taken from Turkish), who had been pushed out of their Central Asian homelands in the former Russian Empire by the Red Army. They shared ethnic connections with the population of northern Afghanistan, and easily assimilated themselves within the existing population. Nadir Shah allowed their political leader, the exiled Emir of Bokhara, to continue to live in Kabul, but he ordered the expulsion of the armed elements of the group back into the Soviet Union. He lacked the military resources to make good on his decision, however, and nothing was done.

Shortly after taking the throne, Nadir Shah received a congratulatory telegram from Amanullah, then in Italy with his family. According to the *Daily Telegraph,* it read: "As a patriotic Afghan I congratulate you and your companions on your epoch-making victory," to which Nadir Shah replied, "The era of [the] government of Amanullah will be inscribed in letters of gold in the history of Afghanistan and I will follow the road traced by you." Despite the exchange of compliments, the détente between the two men did not last. Nadir Shah suspected, and with good reason, that there were still people inside Afghanistan who wished to put Amanullah back on the throne.

The "Young Afghans," mentored by Mahmud Tarzi and empowered by Amanullah, still occupied positions within the court and bureaucracy. They opposed Nadir Shah's cautious approach to reform, and although they never posed a serious military threat to his rule, it was clear to him that his hold on power was not absolute. Much like earlier rulers, he carefully selected family members and close friends to fill all the key roles in government, leaning heavily on his brothers. Mohammed Hashim was appointed prime minister, and Shah Mahmud was appointed minister of war. State power was exercised by a narrow selection of men from the Musahiban clan.

Nadir Shah was also careful not to alienate any of the eastern tribes on either side of the Durand Line. He recognized that just as easily as they had swept him into power, they could topple him. He continued to strengthen his relationships with individual tribes, and ensured that the power of their khans was supported, so that he could use the levers of traditional tribal politics to keep them in check. Nadir Shah paid particular attention to the powerful tribes within British India that had been critical to his own military campaign, giving them money, minor (salaried) government positions, and promises of support should they be repressed by the British authorities.

Nonetheless, he was faced with instability in many parts of the country in 1930. A portion of the Shinwari tribe and Habibullah Kalakani's kinsmen in Kohistan rose up in revolt, and the USSR's Red Army penetrated 60 kilometres across the border in pursuit of Basmachi. Nadir Shah's hold on power was still tenuous, and the army was too fragile, to easily deal with all of these issues at once. But much as Amanullah was toppled by the relatively small forces of Habibullah Kalakani while wrestling with the larger rebellion in the east, Nadir Shah could not afford to ignore any of threats lest they get out of hand.

Nadir Shah dispatched the army to face the Basmachi, and worked together with the Soviets to deny them sanctuary on either side of the border. He suppressed the Shinwari by co-opting the remainder of their own tribe, and he defeated the Kohistanis by raising a tribal lashkar of over twenty thousand tribesmen, mostly Ghilzai, in exchange for a free hand to loot the region. A final threat was averted through negotiation: when the victorious Ghilzai surrounded the capital and demanded further payment, they were dispersed by the threat to raise an even larger Durrani lashkar against them.

The situation in Afghanistan was turbulent enough that the British minister to Afghanistan secured the transfer of fifteen thousand modern rifles, five hundred thousand cartridges, and a grant of £175,000 to help prevent the government from falling. This was not from a sense of goodwill, but because there were serious problems in British India's tribal areas that also required extraordinary measures to manage. In April 1930 non-violent protesters from the pacifist Pashtun movement known as the Khudai Khidmatgar (Servants of God), popularly called the Surkh Posh (Red Shirts), were killed in the Qissa Khwani Bazaar Massacre — one of the early defining moments of the independence movement in India. This led to thousands of Afridi tribesmen seizing the important city of Peshawar the following summer in retaliation. While the colonial administration in British India argued for a military response against the Afridis, this would further undermine the stability of the regime in Afghanistan.

Even though the Afridis had supported Amanullah in 1929, and so had a poor relationship with Nadir Shah, if they appealed to him for assistance against British repression he would be forced to act or lose a tremendous amount of face. Either action could easily lead to consequences that threatened the survival of the Afghan regime. The British minister to Afghanistan, Sir Richard Maconachie, was astute enough to point this issue out to the authorities in British India, preventing the military there from executing their plan to occupy and annex parts of the Afridi tribal lands. The matter was instead handled diplomatically, and the crisis for Nadir Shah was averted.

In an effort to consolidate his power, Nadir Shah called for another loya jirga in September 1930, to be presided over by his brother Mohammed Hashim. As it was much smaller than past jirgas, with only 286 attendees, he likely hoped to constrain the wide-ranging discussion that had characterized previous meetings, while still including representatives from every tribe and province. The group discussed a number of topics: regulations for a national assembly and provincial councils, the design of a new flag, a system of medals and titles, and a personal request by Nadir Shah for the state to confiscate Amanullah's royal properties.

The new structure of government was relatively simple. From the members present, 105 were selected to form a National Council, the lower house of a bicameral system. The upper house, an "Assembly of Nobles," was formed from 45 "intelligent and farseeing men." A key criterion for selection for both houses was loyalty to the regime, even if neither body had any power beyond advising the prime minister and king. To secure the support of the ulema, Nadir Shah also revised the curriculum of madrassas, creating an 11-year program based on Deobandi teachings. Although thorough in terms of Islamic thought, the program was weak in mathematics and science.

The loya jirga was broadly considered a success, but not all of the notable families agreed with the consensus. Ghulam Nabi Charki, in hiding in Soviet Central Asia after the failure of his invasion in support of Amanullah, and Mahmud Tarzi, also in exile, denounced the gathering as unrepresentative. Ghulam Nabi Charki proposed that there be a nationwide vote to select a leader, a recommendation ignored by Nadir Shah. Tarzi remained influential among the Kabul elite, though he did not have a tribal backing within the country to take up his cause. The Charki family, from Logar, were descended from a number of famous Islamic scholars, and had greater influence outside the capital.

Both men raised a point about the kinds of loya jirga that had been held since Amanullah came to power in 1919. At a low level, where all the individuals affected by an issue are present and can speak their mind, the system is effective: even though the decision of the group is often influenced by the desires of the powerful, the need to form a consensus leads to a degree of give-and-take that forms lasting agreements. Although imperfect, local jirgas were not just decision-making bodies, but a means to resolve conflict as well. But as can be seen from the examples spanning the years from 1919 to 1930, the concept does not scale up well, for a number of reasons. Although the other ethnic groups in Afghanistan had become accustomed to the jirga, it was a part of Pashtun culture that was an alien imposition. Tajiks, Uzbeks, Hazaras, and Turkmens did not see the jirga as a traditional means to achieve legitimate decisions in the same way that a Pashtun might. And with a small number of representatives speaking for the entire country, many of the subtle differences of opinion that might exist at the local level were lost. Afghan kings had already come to see the loya jirga as a rubber stamp, lending legitimacy to decisions that had already been made, and only to a much lesser extent as a means to test the response to those decisions. Under these conditions, the need for the jirga to reach a consensus when deciding for the whole nation meant that a further degree of dissent needed to be stifled if it was ever to reach a a conclusion. Finally, as difficult as it was to reach a true consensus, maintaining consensus after the jirga dissolved often proved even harder.

In 1931 Nadir Shah created the Anjuman-e Adabi (Literary Society), a core of Afghan intellectuals whose work was supervised by the king's secretariat, and who were housed in the northern tower of the Arg. The aim of the group was to "improve and promote the literature of the country and to adopt fine methods." The group had 13 charter members, who began to publish a monthly magazine, *Kabul*. Their work was focused on reinforcing the legitimacy of the monarchy and of ancient Pashtun customs such as the loya jirga, and supporting the slow pace of modernization set by Nadir Shah. At the same time the king also made Pashto the official language of Afghanistan, and established an academy to replace Persian loan words that had become part of the language. This was a major shift, as much of the country spoke only Persian, which had been the court language for centuries. The reasoning behind this seems to have been to appease the Pashtun tribes; Nadir Shah and his brothers preferred to speak Urdu among themselves, having been raised in exile in British India.

The Kohistan revolt had been put down the previous year, and Herat was brought to heel in 1931, leaving only the Basmachi in armed opposition to the government. Shah Mahmud led a large portion of the reorganized army into the north in a campaign to destroy or expel them, but the operation devolved into a series of fruitless chases. Over time these exiles from Soviet Central Asia had drawn increasing numbers of Afghans into their ranks. Espousing a pan-Islamic and pan-Turkic philosophy, the Basmachi offered a chance at a more representative form of government than either the Soviets or Nadir Shah. As his enemies were assisted by the local population and numbered in the thousands, Shah Mahmud had little chance of running them to ground.

And so in March 1931 he sent Basmachi leader Ibrahim Beg a letter offering amnesty, promising to incorporate his troops into the Afghan Army. Beg refused, and in April he made a fatal mistake. Leading eight hundred men, he crossed back into the Soviet Union to conduct a series of brutal raids, raising new troops as he went, but also spreading terror as he destroyed infrastructure and executed collaborators. The professional Red Army was much more effective at counterinsurgency than Shah Mahmud's forces, and inflicted a number of defeats on the Basmachi, who also lost momentum as a rift emerged between them and the peasants they ostensibly fought for. On June 31 Ibrahim Beg and two followers were captured by the Red Army as they attempted to cross back into Afghanistan. They were put on trial in Tashkent and later executed. With the loss of its charismatic leader, the Basmachi movement quickly died out. The final major threat to Nadir Shah's rule was extinguished, though not through his own efforts. The exiled Emir of Bokhara remained in Kabul, but harboured no further political ambitions.

In late 1931 Nadir Shah also promulgated a new constitution that formalized many of the elements of governance that had been agreed upon at the loya jirga the previous year. Containing 110 articles within 16 sections, it followed a similar structure to the document produced under

Amanullah. No loya jirga was called to approve the constitution, as much of what it contained had already been implemented.

The constitution enshrined the monarchy as the country's system of government, and explicitly made it hereditary with successors chosen by the amir from within his family. The ruler had to be a Muslim of the Hanafi sect, and while the roles of the upper and lower houses were defined, so was the amir's right to overrule them on any issue. Ministers were given the same privilege on matters within their portfolio.

There was no need to produce a body of written law beyond stating that shari'a, as interpreted by the Hanafi school, applied. This meant in practice that the law would be interpreted and applied at the lowest level, by individual mullahs. A system of appeals was put in place, with the amir at the apex. This structure empowered the ulema, thus guaranteeing their support.

Primary education was made compulsory, but no effort was made to provide secular schooling. Education was left to the madrassas, whose curriculum was decided by the mullahs who ran them, focusing as it had for generations on the *panj kitab,* or "five books" of classic Persian literature. The constitution also enshrined Pashto as the country's official language, though the impact of this was little more than symbolic.

There is no mention of women in the constitution, and while they could claim rights as "Afghan nationals," they were denied the same rights as men. While not specifically disenfranchised, they were not included in the loose voting practices that led to the election of members of the National Council. While Amanullah's stance on women's rights did not precipitate the revolt against him, it did give the rebels a means to justify it. Nadir Shah was careful not to provide future rebels any means to establish their legitimacy in opposing him.

As had been the practice before, Nadir Shah appointed all of the provincial governors personally, drawn almost entirely from the settled Pashtuns of Kabul or Jalalabad, even in areas like the Hazarajat. The governors had little personal connection with the areas they ruled, and little power to make decisions in any case. Telephone lines ran from the capital to all the major cities, allowing the king to manage provincial affairs directly. The governors themselves communicated his decisions by word of mouth, relying on jirgas and other gatherings to promulgate them.

With the situation stabilizing, Nadir Shah was able to turn to economic development, the area where he was most innovative. In 1932 the first bank in Afghanistan was founded, as well as the first import-export companies. The entire country's foreign trade was estimated to be worth about £5 million ($305 million today), a paltry amount driven by the lack of exportable goods and the lack of wealth to purchase imports. An estimated 60 percent of the population at this time still wore clothing made by their family in the home; many of their other needs were met by cottage industries as well. Nadir Shah oversaw the establishment of small factories, meant largely to replace imports rather than create exports. A raw sugar factory was planned in Jalalabad, and the machinery procured, as sugar cane could be cultivated there. A factory for weaving shawls was built in Kandahar, and factories for weaving cloth and manufacturing clothing were built in Kabul and Badakhshan. Ownership of these factories was given to prominent families in the capital.

A program of improving roads was instituted, and surveying was conducted for the creation of railroads, both to extend government influence and to stimulate an internal economy. At this time, the major cities of the country existed as "oasis economies," with little trade between them. Communications between each of these cities and neighbouring countries were substantially better than with the capital, and so trade was aligned externally rather than internally. It is estimated that in 1929 there were only 350 cars in the entire country, and so transport of goods remained largely by pack animal, limiting the amount of trade that was possible.

Taxation remained a major problem for the government, for a number of reasons. The eastern tribes in particular still expected to be exempt from taxes as a condition of their support for the government. In addition, their practice of badraga made it difficult for the government to tax imports. Widespread resistance to registering citizens, as well as the fact that a third of the population at this time were nomadic, roaming as far as British India in the winter, made personal taxes nearly impossible to collect. This left taxation of land and agricultural produce as the most practical solution to increasing the government's revenues. The majority of the peasantry, however, were sharecroppers working for a small number of powerful landowners. Taxing the landowners would also be politically difficult, as these were the same khans and zamindars on whose support the monarchy relied. Nadir Shah decided to focus his efforts on imposing heavy import taxes for two reasons. He hoped that doing so would stimulate the domestic production of staple items, although this mostly did not come to pass. He also recognized that the merchant class, many of whom were Sikh or Hindu, did not have the political clout to oppose him.

Education had suffered badly since Amanullah was deposed, by design under Habibullah Kalakani, and due to the slow pace of change under Nadir Shah. Whereas in 1928 Afghanistan had 300 schools in operation with 50,000 pupils enrolled, by 1932 this had dropped to 22 schools and 1,300 students. The creation of the country's first modern educational institution in 1931, the Kabul Medical School, had limited immediate impact, as there were few students suitable to enroll in it. Nadir Shah's plans to industrialize the Afghan economy did not have a foundation of educated workers to build upon, meaning that it progressed slowly.

Although the armed opposition had been defeated by the end of 1931, elements of Afghan society continued to oppose Nadir Shah as a usurper. The Hazaras who had supported Amanullah throughout the period of Habibullah Kalakani's rule did not transfer their loyalty to Nadir Shah. Through the Pashtun governor he appointed, he implemented a program of "Pashtunization," expunging Hazara place names in favour of Pashtun ones, enforcing the use of Pashto where possible, and suppressing expressions of Hazara culture. He also imprisoned and harassed Hazara intellectuals who might be able to articulate the reasons to oppose his regime. The long-standing feud between the Hazaras and nomadic Pashtuns over grazing land continued to fester, as Nadir Shah continued to grant the tribes additional rights to land occupied by Hazaras.

In the south, Ghulam Nabi Charki returned from exile in 1931. By 1932 he had begun to foment rebellion among the Dar-e Khel and Mangal tribes in an attempt to put Amanullah back on the throne. Nadir Shah was forewarned and the uprising was suppressed. A large number of Mangal tribesmen and their families escaped across the Durand Line into Waziristan, where they tried, at first with little success, to form a lashkar with the Wazir and Mehsud tribes.

Ghulam Nabi Charki was arrested, and along with a number of co-conspirators was executed on Nazir Shah's orders. This was the typical fate of those who rose against the amir, and so perhaps should not have created any particular enmity. But even erstwhile supporters of Nadir Shah felt that the execution was poorly handled. The public perception of the matter was that the execution had no legal basis, as it had not been ordered after a trial in a shari'a court. This made it a personal matter between Nadir Shah and the Charki family, and, as expected under the Pashtunwali, it started a blood feud.

In early 1933 a man called the Lewanai Faqir (a Sufi ascetic, the "Crazy Faqir") emerged in the tribal areas of British India, claiming that Amanullah would soon return. In pursuit of this aim, he raised a lashkar of ten thousand men from the Mehsud and Wazir tribes and led them across the border into Khost. They meant to march on Kabul, but were met near Matun by the Afghan Army, and heavy fighting ensued for over two months. This uprising was only subdued when British political officers persuaded tribal elders to recall the men who formed the lashkar. The main ringleaders were executed. The Lewanai Faqir, who had fled into British India to avoid capture, was pardoned on account of his advanced age and allowed to return to Afghanistan.

That ten thousand tribesmen could so easily cross out of British India to conduct a revolution in Afghanistan incensed Nadir Shah. It was all the more infuriating since, once across the border, they were able to maintain lines of communication into the tribal areas for support. Nadir Shah summoned Maconachie and expressed his anger, and in truth, the British were embarrassed by the situation as well. Their earlier policy of treating the Pashtun tribes lightly, for fear that they would ask Nadir Shah for support, had backfired. While ruling the tribal areas with a light touch through political officers and small army garrisons suited the cash-strapped colonial government, it was not enough. Spurred by Nadir Shah's protests and their own embarrassment, British policy shifted to what was known as "peaceful penetration," attempting to extend the government's reach through the construction of roads and the slow integration of the Pashtuns into civil society.

In the summer, one of Nadir Shah's brothers, Mohammed Aziz, who had been appointed as Afghanistan's envoy to Germany, was assassinated. The killer was an Afghan graduate of the Najat *lycée* in Kabul, now in Berlin for advanced studies. When captured he claimed to have murdered the man because of Nadir Shah's abandonment of the Pashtun tribes. The fact that Mohammed Aziz had replaced one of Ghulam Nabi Charki's brothers as ambassador may have also played a part. At around the same time the British minister in Kabul was also the victim of an assassination attempt by a Najat student.

On November 8, 1933, Nadir Shah was attending an awards ceremony for Kabul high-school students in the courtyard of the palace when he was shot and killed. The assassin, a young Hazara man named Abdul Khaliq, also a student at Najat, had been a household servant of Ghulam Nabi Charki, and may have become his adoptive son. Both Abdul Khaliq and his father had been convicted of involvement in the abortive 1932 rebellion. The assassination occurred on the one-year anniversary of Ghulam Nabi Charki's execution; Khaliq's motives were likely both political and personal.

Justice was swiftly administered by Nadir Shah's surviving brothers, who arrested many members of Abdul Khaliq's family as well. They were tortured and dismembered before being executed, as a stark warning to others.

Although Nadir Shah had been careful not to create any fresh reasons for rebellion through his policies, his short reign was still a turbulent one. By strengthening the crown's relationship with the ulema and the traditional khans, he retained the levers of power that Afghan rulers before Amanullah had traditionally used to play the tribes off against each other. But he could not avoid the reality that politics in the kingdom was invariably a family affair, and even if the bulk of the tribes could be placated, he could not escape the call for revenge from a family he had wronged.

He is buried in a royal mausoleum on Tepe Maranjan in Kabul.

CHAPTER 6 THE BOY KING

IN THE HOURS after Nadir Shah's death, there was a scramble to ensure an orderly succession. Of his three surviving brothers, only Shah Mahmud, the minister of war, was in Kabul at the time. Even in exile Amanullah learned quickly of the ruler's death, releasing a statement on the same day: "Today's event is the result of the anxieties among the Afghan people, provoked by the policy of Nadir. This policy has resulted in assassinations and imprisonment…. If the Afghan people invite me to return and put into action my program for progress, I shall be ready to serve my country." Before the leading pro-Amanullah families, the Charki and Tarzi, could act, Shah Mahmud had Nadir Shah's only son, Zahir, acclaimed as amir, ensuring that power was retained by the Musahiban. Despite the dreams of a section of the capital's elite, there was no real constituency in the country that supported the former amir's return.

Zahir Shah was 19 when he took the throne, and was the first Afghan ruler to have a Western education. After attending the Habibiya and Istiklal schools in Kabul, he went on to study at the Pasteur Institute and the University of Montpellier while his father was in exile. Returning to

Afghanistan in 1930, he received some training as a military officer before being appointed the minister of war and later the minister of education.

The real power behind the throne was an alliance of his three paternal uncles, all of whom had supported Nadir Shah during the campaign against Habibullah Kalakani. The eldest, Mohammed Hashim Khan, was named prime minister and became ruler of Afghanistan in everything but name. The other two uncles, Shah Mahmud and Shah Wali, held other senior posts in the government and ensured that the reins of power remained centralized within the family. It is a testament to their skill at wielding that power that no serious internal challenge to the young amir's rule emerged.

Tribal representatives from across the country sent messages of allegiance to the capital, including the Ghilzai who were wintering in British India. A man claiming to be related to Amanullah did appear among the Madda Khel tribe on the other side of the Durand Line, inciting the tribes to rise up in favour of the deposed amir. Swift intervention by the British Indian authorities ensured that no tribes gave him any support, and the threat quickly evaporated. Early in 1934 the ulema published a statement thanking the nation for accepting the son of the amir as amir, as was expected in their interpretation of shari'a. In contrast to past practice, no loya jirga was held for tribal leaders to agree on Zahir Shah as their choice for amir.

Early in his reign Zahir Shah undertook to build relationships with other countries beyond the region, ending his father's de facto policy of isolation. In September 1934 Afghanistan applied to join the League of Nations and was accepted, along with the Soviet Union. He also sponsored a trade exhibition in Kabul that drew exhibitors from around the world, eager to gain access to the Afghan market. In the same year the United States gave official recognition to Afghanistan, although they would not exchange ambassadors until 1942.

Hashim Khan guided the young amir in a policy of "positive neutrality," refusing to become dependent on or hostile to any state in the world. This was an expanded version of the balancing act that previous rulers had been forced to follow in order to nullify the dual threats of Britain and Russia. While Nadir Shah had been quietly pro-British, Hashim Khan instead sought assistance from powers without a direct stake in the region — the United States, France, Germany, and Japan. The Afghan economy would need their help to modernize.

The largest donor in the 1930s was Germany. Not only did it provide cash loans, but a number of joint Afghan-German companies were created, and advisers were sent by the German government to assist with education, particularly technical training, and to provide expertise within various government departments. Lufthansa Airlines established flights between Berlin and Kabul, an amazing feat at the time that required stops in Tirana, Athens, Rhodes, Damascus, Baghdad, and Tehran. A German civil servant was hired by the Afghan government to conduct the ambitious project of surveying the entire country to inform future plans for improved telegraph, telephone, and road networks. From Hashim Khan's perspective, German assistance came with few political strings.

The heavy presence of experts provided by the German government brought an element of ideology with it. Governing Afghanistan had always been difficult in part because of the lack of a common sense of belonging among the different ethnic groups in the country. Hashim Khan sought to create this common mythology, uniting the country under a revisionist version of Pashtun history, infusing elements of Nazi racial theory as he did so.

French archaeologists had been working in the country since the 1920s, and had made remarkable discoveries that uncovered Afghanistan's rich Bactrian and Kushan heritage. The Bactrians were cast as ancient Aryans, from whom the Nazis also claimed descent for the "pure" German people. The existence of a sophisticated Bactrian civilization was used as proof that Afghanistan had long been a centre of learning and a global exporter of culture. An example of the breadth of these claims can be found in the writing of scholar Mir Ghulam Mohammed Ghubar:

> The country of the Ancient Aryans … that is the Afghanistan of today presented the Islamic world with as many men of science and letters as any single constituent of the Islamic world has…. The contribution of the people of Afghanistan to the civilization and culture of the Islamic world is outstanding and significant. The Afghans introduced the Arabs to the philosophy and religion of the people of India long

before the Arabs had even made the slightest infiltration in to the land of the Indians. The contribution of the Afghans to astronomy, geometry, mathematics, philosophy and theology of that time is admitted by all the Muslim historians.

Government-sponsored scholars in Afghanistan published histories of the Pashtun people (claiming that the word *Pashtun* is derived from the ancient name for Bactria) that distorted actual events in order to create a simplified narrative of a continuous Pashtun culture. To create this history, a number of historical figures had to be co-opted into the Pashtun tribe, such as Avicenna (Ibn Sina) and Jalal ad-Din Rumi.

Although within these circles it was a given that *Afghan* and *Pashtun* were synonymous, there remained many other ethnicities within the country that did not subscribe to this idea. Influenced again by Nazi theory, government policy in the 1930s changed to explicitly exclude people of the "Asiatic races" from positions in the government bureaucracy and the officer corps. In practice, this meant discriminating against 25 percent of the population — Hazaras, Uzbeks, Turkmens, and Aimaqs. The small Jewish community in Afghanistan was also singled out. Already required to wear distinctive clothing under the constitution of Amanullah, many were forced to leave the country altogether. The chief administrator for the northern provinces, Mohammed Gul Mohmand, told the British minister in Kabul that removing them was necessary, as "the Jews had been the principal channels of Communist intrigue in the Northern Provinces; and so long as they remained in the neighbourhood of the Russian frontier, there was a constant danger of their acting as agents provocateurs."

The lack of a homogenous ethnic culture was seen as a weakness that could be corrected by government intervention, and so in 1936 Hashim convinced the amir to decree that all government officials had to learn Pashto, which was to become the language of bureaucracy within two years. This was at odds with the fact that Persian had been the language of government for centuries, and that the body of writing in Pashto was minuscule in comparison to that in Persian.

The effort continued to "Pashtunize" areas with a strong minority culture such as the Hazarajat. Land rights of Pashtun pastoral nomads were recognized over those of the settled farmers in the region, displacing parts of the community to less arable lands in the north. Hazara place names were "corrected" to similar-sounding Pashtun ones as well, erasing evidence of the Hazara from the landscape.

Education was seen as a prime means of indoctrination, creating a homogenous and loyal population. State textbooks produced in the 1930s and 1940s were focused on creating a sense of reverence for the royal family and for a selection of national heroes. A severe lack of resources meant that the roll-out of state-run schools was slow. By 1940 there were only 324 primary schools in the entire country, serving about sixty thousand students, and none at all for girls. The vast majority of these schools were in the capital or the districts immediately surrounding it, leaving education in the vast majority of the country to the village mullahs. This meant that by the end of the 1940s, less than 8 percent of the total population was considered literate, and only 4.5 percent of school-age children were enrolled in a school of any kind. Although this was a poor basis on which to modernize the country, there was little incentive for individuals to pursue anything beyond the basic schooling available through the madrassas, as there was nowhere to apply the skills obtained outside of service in the government bureaucracy. Even the government itself saw education as a means of indoctrination rather than providing useful vocational skills.

In contrast to the hundreds of schools in Afghanistan were the approximately fifteen thousand mosques. Although the government tried many times to regulate these, insisting on centralized training and testing and even paying salaries to mullahs, the vast majority of the country's mosques stayed outside of government control. Largely supported by contributions from the population they served, local religious leaders were both beholden to those communities and part of their power structure. Well-regarded mullahs were often as influential as the tribal leaders themselves and were able to provide a veneer of religion over the tribes' political machinations.

Hashim Khan's policy toward religion differed from that of Amanullah, who laid blame for the country's "backwardness" on the "ignorant" ulema. Senior members of the ulema were included in the cabinet and consulted on major issues, but no efforts were made to exert control over the lower ranks of clergy directly. Instead, the focus was on producing religious tracts that argued for the compatibility of Islam and modernization, effectively co-opting the vehicle of religion to support government aims. Islam was cast as a faith of reform and progress, whose guiding principles were best achieved through the acquisition of scientific knowledge. From the duty to help the poor, to the promotion of hygiene, and even to the creation of military strength to defend the faith, the argument was made that all aspects of Islam were best achieved through modernization.

There was also an effort to co-opt religious leaders to speak and write in support of girls' education, which continued to lag far behind that of boys. In an interesting twist, it was said that women, as future mothers, needed an education in order to be a positive influence when raising future generations. The government also noted that women were not accorded within customary law the full rights they were entitled to under shari'a, and that the best remedy to this situation was to educate women about their rights. In both cases it was religious education that was seen as most suitable for women, rather than modern academic or vocational training. And despite this attempt to slowly sway public opinion, Hashim Khan was careful not to enact any reforms that might be used as an excuse for an uprising or threaten any of the interest groups whose support the government needed. This cautious approach meant that the first girls' schools since Amanullah's time did not reopen until 1943.

Part of the reason that education received so little attention during this period was the need to fund reform of the army. Until the late 1930s fully 50 percent of all national expenditures were on the military, which was seen as necessary to protect the regime from overthrow by the eastern tribes. When Hashim Khan became prime minister, the army was in disarray, having suffered heavily during the war against Habibullah Kalakani and receiving little attention since. Most of the cavalry units had withered away due to the cost of their upkeep, and the army's artillery was locked in the Sherpur cantonment in Kabul. The remaining army was a collection of small infantry units, poorly equipped and ill led.

Hashim Khan invited a Turkish military mission to help revitalize the armed forces. It reorganized the army into brigades and static divisions, building for the first time staff structures to conduct planning and support commanders. It also re-established the military academy to train professional officers. Efforts were made to recruit officers among the sons of prominent tribal leaders, in hopes that the positions would become prestigious, as well as tying the families (and their success) to the regime.

Hashim Khan's greatest efforts were made to modernize the economy, which if the country was to remain independent, would have to be both the target and engine of reform. Nearly the only export goods produced by Afghanistan at this time were karakul (sheep) skins, which made up 50 percent of exports, and dried fruit and nuts, which made up another 25 percent. The foreign currency needed to buy all forms of modern machinery or consumer goods came from these agricultural exports, or loans and grants from foreign governments.

Despite the heavy reliance on agriculture in Afghanistan's economy, the actual productivity of farming was low. Even as late as the 1970s, 70 percent of all arable land was owned by a small number of local leaders, leaving the vast majority of farmers as sharecroppers. The typical arrangement was that they were given land, seeds, basic equipment, and perhaps a draught animal as well, and in return provided all the labour needed to farm their allotted land. They also were liable to provide labour to the landowner, repairing roads or clearing irrigation ditches, or even serving in the landlord's home. In return, they kept 20 percent of the crop they grew, barely enough to maintain a subsistence diet.

Where farmers did own the land they worked, their plots were often quite small, and they still were not free of the major landowners. They often were required to take loans from the landowners to purchase seeds, repaying the debt at the end of the season with a fixed amount of produce. If the crop failed they were still responsible to pay the full amount of the loan, creating a cycle of debt that often led to the loss of their land.

This system of sharecroppers and small, precarious landowners meant that little effort was made to modernize the system of agriculture or to improve the land. Little agricultural land was irrigated in any part of the country, and there was no system that allowed portions of it to remain fallow or for crops to rotate. Even as tractors and other modern equipment became available, there was little incentive for the landowners to invest in them, and they were economically out of reach for individual farmers as well. One area for improvement that the government saw was in the use of fertilizers, which Zahir Shah encouraged, including for farmers who grew cash crops such as opium and marijuana.

The production of opium had continued to be a massive source of revenue for British India until international pressure forced its suppression for domestic use and led to limits on its export. It was only in 1935 that the export of opium was banned outright, so that smuggled Afghan opium was needed to fill the still significant demand from Indian users. A legal market for Afghan opium also developed in the Soviet Union and Japan, which imported it for medical use, providing much-needed tax revenues for the government and a livelihood for those farmers who knew how to grow it. Despite its profitability, opium production was not widespread in Afghanistan, being carried out only in small pockets, notably Badakhshan in the far north.

The government attempted to create a light industrial base in the country to supply basic commodities that would otherwise have to be imported and paid for with foreign currency, such as sugar, shoes, cloth, and matches. Germany was an enthusiastic provider of machinery to outfit these factories and to train the employees. Although the government had allowed for the creation of corporations as a means to encourage private enterprise, most of the industrial initiatives, as well as ventures such as coal mines, remained state controlled and inefficient. One of the most profitable private corporations was set up in 1935 for the export of opium. Conditions in Afghanistan's factories were poor, and in 1949 the first labour strike occurred, at a textile factory in Jabal-us Seraj. Demanding a pay raise and better access to subsidized goods for their families, the strikers stayed out for four days before ending their action unsuccessfully. Future strikes were also broken, either through mass firings or violence. Although the contribution of industry to the economy as a whole was minuscule when compared to agriculture, one important aspect of manufacturing from the government's perspective was that it was easily taxed.

With little ability to manufacture the goods needed by the population, there remained a heavy reliance on foreign trade. Still, the trade networks remained antiquated. Decades of road building had not yet connected the capital with the country's major cities over four-season roads. The majority of trade goods continued to be carried by caravans of horses, mules, or camels until the late 1940s. But, like industry, trade was easy to tax, even though this drove some merchants to smuggling. Given the sensitivity and difficulty of taxing individuals engaged in agriculture or their land, the collection of duties from industry and trade provided the government with much of its income in this period.

Hashim Khan and his brothers pushed their program of gradual modernization elegantly enough that through the first five years of their rule there were no uprisings in the tribal areas of the sort that had plagued earlier rulers. The same could not be said of the other side of the Durand Line. The Faqir of Ipi, described in contemporary British newspapers as a Pashtun nationalist, led an uprising in Waziristan that quickly took on major proportions. The reported issue at the heart of the rebellion, known as the "Islam Bibi" case, was the intervention of British Indian courts to prevent the marriage of a Hindu girl to a Muslim man after reports emerged that she had been abducted and forcibly converted to Islam. The courts ordered her to be housed with a neutral party until she reached the age of majority and could choose a religion and husband for herself, which the tribes saw as tantamount to a government kidnapping of the bride.

Fighting between the Waziris and the British Indian government lasted from 1936 to 1939, and eventually involved over forty thousand government troops. A small number of tribesmen crossed the border from Afghanistan to aid the Waziris, and the Faqir often took shelter in Afghanistan when the British intensified efforts to capture him, leading to British protests. By allowing these small elements of support, the Afghan government was able to resist pressure to provide major assistance and potentially precipitate a fourth Anglo-Afghan war it could ill afford.

Afghanistan was not completely immune to this upsurge of violence, as in 1938 a Waziri lashkar crossed into Afghanistan led by Syed Mohammed Sadi al Keilani, known as the Shami Pir. Originally from Damascus, the Shami Pir was a cousin of Queen Soraya, and claimed to be fighting for Amanullah's restoration. His major activity, however, was looting, and he garnered little support from the tribes for his professed political aims. After months of agitation he was joined by the Suleiman Khel, a Ghilzai sub-tribe spread across southeastern Afghanistan that had fought against Amanullah in concert with the Mangal tribe in 1924. The two thousand tribesmen of the Suleiman Khel, joined by at least as many under Shami Pir, represented a serious threat to the stability of the Afghan government. Uprisings of this size, when seen to be successful, had quickly snowballed into much larger ones.

The government response was to send two newly trained infantry brigades, advised by Turkish officers, and 10 obsolescent airplanes to meet the threat. Defeating the rebels decisively in two battles in late June ended the revolt within Afghanistan, but Shami Pir escaped back into Waziristan. The Afghan government lodged a protest with the British for allowing him to agitate the tribes. The governor of the North West Frontier Province, Sir George Cunningham, acted decisively. He negotiated with the Pir directly and persuaded him to be flown back to his home in Syria. Cunningham wrote him a personal cheque for £25,000 to sweeten the deal, although he allegedly stopped the cheque before it could be cashed.

There was a further tribal disturbance in September 1939, when an Afridi war band crossed into Afghanistan, again with the aim of overthrowing the government. The Faqir of Ipi, still at large, was blamed for the disturbance. Despite the overwhelming forces arrayed against him, he continued to evade capture and attract more tribes to his cause. As the Faqir's fame grew, so too did stories of his mystical powers. He could turn sticks into rifles, multiply a few loaves of bread to feed the masses, and even turn aircraft bombs into paper (perhaps "proven" by the common British tactic of dropping propaganda leaflets by aircraft).

The Afridi rebels were quickly defeated by the Afghan Army. Their homelands on the other side of the border were blockaded by British Indian troops, who forced the tribesmen to hand over the Afghan refugees. This was a rare example of co-operation between the governments in Kabul and Delhi, spurred in part by the fact that the British could not afford the tribal areas to become any more unstable or to antagonize the Afghan government, given the outbreak of war in Europe.

The Second World War impacted Afghanistan only indirectly, as the country remained neutral throughout. Given the numbers of German, Italian, and Japanese technical advisers in the country, however, it is not surprising that there was intrigue. As early as the mid-1930s, both the Italian and German governments saw an opportunity to create trouble for Britain by either convincing Hashim Khan to turn against the British, or having failed at that, to find willing proxies among the tribes. The Shami Pir was approached by German intelligence a number of times to this end, but refused to return to Afghanistan. Once Syria was captured by Free French forces, he chose to live in exile in Germany, but not to do Germany's political bidding.

Lack of coordination between the Germans and Italians regarding a political plan for Afghanistan and India led to duplication of effort. With Britain seemingly about to fall in 1940, the Italian foreign office prepared a plan to replace the British in India with a government headed by one of Gandhi's political rivals, Subhesh Chandra Bose. He would eventually form the "Indian National Army," largely from captured Indian soldiers, which fought in support of the Japanese in Burma. The Italians also planned to reintroduce Amanullah, then living in Rome in exile, as a more pliant leader in Afghanistan. A key player in their plan was the Faqir of Ipi. He was willing to continue to stir up the tribes, but demanded £25,000 a month, and double that if he spread the rebellion out of its present region, and triple if he sparked a general uprising across the whole frontier. This money was in addition to a supply of weapons and ammunition. This was beyond the means of the Italian legation in Kabul.

German policy on Afghanistan was incoherent. At the highest levels, the hope was to channel the territorial ambitions of the Soviet Union (an ally under the short-lived Molotov-Ribbentrop agreement) toward South Asia, leaving Afghanistan out of the German sphere of influence. Political representatives in Afghanistan told Hashim Khan that Germany would defeat Britain in short order, and offered to create a "Greater Afghanistan" that included not only the traditional Pashtun lands but also Baluchistan, Sind, Kashmir, and western Punjab in exchange for Afghan support. This offer was declined by Hashim Khan, who stuck to the policy of strict neutrality and independence. At the same time, German intelligence was thinking along the lines of the Italians, also meeting with Amanullah and even discussing setting up an Afghan government-in-exile, which the former amir declined. Its agents also tried to contact the Faqir, who had lived in Germany and married a German woman. This was to be grandly named Operation Feuerfresser (Fire Eater), to be followed by Operation Tiger, a full-scale uprising planned for September 1941, when the invasion of the Soviet Union was expected to be successfully completed.

The Abwehr agents dispatched to find the Faqir in July 1941 were killed in an ambush by an Afghan Army patrol near the border in Logar

Province. In their car were money and ammunition intended for the Faqir. In public Hashim Khan displayed outrage, but in private he merely asked the Germans to commit no further intrigues that might attract a military response from Britain. The Anglo-Soviet invasion of Iran in September 1941 that deposed Reza Shah made clear what the consequences for Afghanistan might be. Iran had also declared its neutrality in the war, but its oil fields and strategic location as a route for sending U.S. lend-lease equipment to the USSR made the invasion necessary. In October 1941 both Britain and the Soviet Union sent an ultimatum: Afghanistan must immediately expel all German and Italian nationals. It was not lost on Hashim Khan that Iran had refused a similar ultimatum just before it was invaded.

Conscious that his countrymen might easily accuse him of being pro-British if he complied, Hashim Khan made an astute move: he summoned a loya jirga to consider the demand, placing the burden of the decision on others. The assembly quickly agreed that there was no choice but to submit; Hashim Khan complied, but saved face by reaffirming Afghanistan's neutrality and independence. About two hundred people were expelled and given safe passage to India, leaving many development projects sponsored by the German government unfinished, and the finished ones unmanaged.

The war was a difficult time for Afghanistan's economy. Global trade fell off, and demand for the country's principal export, karakul hides, vanished. By 1945, millions of unsold hides were stockpiled in Kabul and in the United States. The only new market opened by the war resulted from the disruption of the global pharmaceutical trade. The United States had previously purchased morphine from Germany, manufactured from opium grown in Turkey and Iran. In 1941 the United States began buying opium from Afghanistan. Hashim Khan attempted to kickstart the private economy by handing over many state enterprises to entrepreneurs, many of whom were wealthy traders with political connections. Without exception, the new owners failed to invest in their businesses, and particularly to maintain or replace expensive foreign machinery. One by one the businesses failed and shuttered their doors.

CHAPTER 7 PASHTUNISTAN

IN 17 YEARS as prime minister, Hashim Khan had failed to bring about significant economic or social change to Afghanistan, though he had managed to maintain social order and his family's grip on power. With the economy in shambles after the disruption of the Second World War, however, by 1946 there was increasing unrest both in the countryside and in the capital. Inflation had outstripped salaries, and with trade disrupted, the vast majority of Afghans employed in agriculture had no market for their cash crops. A family that could subsist comfortably in 1938 on about 300 afghanis a month required 1,600 afghanis a month by the late 1940s. At that time, a novice teacher received a salary of 150 afghanis a month, and a university professor 700 afghanis.

In 1945 and 1946 Hashim Khan ordered the arrest of a number of journalists and writers who were accused of plotting against the government. He even ordered the arrest of the deputy prime minister. His increasingly autocratic rule did not sit well with other members of the Musahiban family, or with the wider elite. Ostensibly for health reasons, Hashim Khan was forced by his family to resign in May 1946. He was succeeded by his brother Shah Mahmud. The amir, now 32 years old, remained subordinate to his uncles.

Shah Mahmud immediately released a number of political prisoners who had been arrested for advocating reform. Opposition to the government remained small and disorganized, mostly confined to intellectual circles in the capital. And rather than promoting a change in the form of government, their interest lay in lobbying the amir to enact reform willingly. Shah Mahmud also released a small number of Amanullah's supporters, as it appeared that the former amir's opportunity to return had passed. He announced that mayors of the major cities, who previously had been appointed by the amir, would instead for the first time be selected in direct elections to be held the following year. Pressing forward with reforms at a controlled pace, he combined existing medical, legal, and science faculties into Kabul University in 1946.

Afghanistan had been receiving aid from the Soviet Union, but during the war it had dried to a trickle. Now the focus for foreign aid was countries where communist parties had begun to rule. Shah Mahmud did settle a long-standing border dispute with the Soviets, agreeing on a boundary that ran down the middle of the navigable channel in the Amu Darya River. The Soviets, eager to appear generous and fair to smaller nations, surrendered control of a number of mid-stream islands.

Shah Mahmud also began to forge a tighter relationship with the United States, signing contracts with American engineering firms for a series of major projects, including roads, bridges, and irrigation canals. Cementing this relationship required Afghanistan to prohibit the production of opium by anyone other than state-controlled farms. Hashim Khan had already announced this prohibition in 1945, although no effort was made to enforce the directive, which in any case did not have the force of law. Still, at the end of 1949, a deal was reached where the U.S. Export-Import Bank provided the Afghan government with a $21 million loan for agricultural development, to be repaid over 15 years.

The largest American-led initiative was the Helmand Valley Authority project (now the Helmand and Arghandab Valley Authority, or HAVA), for which surveying began in 1946. The Helmand River Valley in southern Afghanistan had long been considered the breadbasket of the country, even though large areas were desert. The loss of trade and the shrinking market for karakul skins during the Second World War had lessened the economic importance of pastoralism. Repeated epidemics among the sheep herds in the early 1940s and a shortage of fodder had also caused the herds to go into steep decline, further increasing the economic importance of settled agriculture.

The American company engaged to manage the project was Morrison-Knudsen, famous for building mega-projects such as the Hoover Dam and the locks on the Saint Lawrence Seaway. The scope of the project it devised was massive. The completed irrigation canals would convert 345,000 acres of desert into arable land, improve the condition of the land that was already being used for agriculture, and generate electricity from the Kajaki hydroelectric dam to be built on the Helmand River. The project would later expand to include the Arghandab River, with its own new hydroelectric dam. The capital of Helmand, Lashkar Gah, expanded to house the many foreign workers brought in to manage the project, becoming a pocket of American suburbia in the Afghan desert with rows of bungalows on wide streets, a movie theatre, and an ice cream shop. The initiation of this project seemed to signal a decades-long commitment to developing Afghanistan. Seemingly without territorial interests in the region, and ascendant on the global stage, the United States appeared to be the perfect development partner for a neutral country.

Shifts in the political climate in British India soon complicated this relationship. The long campaign for Indian independence was finally closing in on its objective. Within the foremost pro-independence party, the Indian National Congress Party, and moving in Mahatma Gandhi's inner circle, was a prominent Pashtun leader.

Abdul Ghaffar Khan, sometimes known as the Faqir-e Afghan or Bacha Khan, was born in the village of Utmanzai in the Peshawar Valley in British India. He was a close friend and political ally of Gandhi, whom he had met in 1919 during protests against the Rowlatt Act, which indefinitely extended the emergency measures enacted during the First World War. Pashtun culture is often portrayed as warlike, but like Gandhi, Bacha Khan was a pacifist who followed a philosophy of non-violent opposition to colonial rule.

Although unable to obtain a formal education himself, Bacha Khan was responsible for opening schools across the tribal areas, making him a well-known and respected tribal figure. In 1930 he had founded the pacifist Surkh Posh. Many of the first recruits were graduates from the schools he founded, although in time the movement grew to over one hundred thousand members. Organized along paramilitary lines, with simple uniforms and drill, the Surkh Posh came to be the dominant political party in British India's Pashtun tribal lands. The organization included women, who were seen as particularly effective non-violent protesters. In a culture where public violence against women was taboo, the authorities could not strong-arm non-compliant women protesters. This was a major step forward for women within Pashtun culture.

As the Indian National Congress was an umbrella group of many parties, Hindu and Muslim, Bacha Khan's Surkh Posh fit easily within it until the question of partition forced a schism. Bacha Khan opposed partitioning British India into two new states, as demanded by Muslim political leaders such as Mohammed Ali Jinnah. When the Congress Party made it its policy to support partition without fully consulting Bacha Khan, he felt betrayed and withdrew his support.

In June 1947 Bacha Khan held a loya jirga in the town of Bannu, bringing together leaders of the Surkh Posh movement as well as Pashtun tribal and religious leaders from across the frontier region, including the Faqir of Ipi. The decision of the jirga, which became known as the Bannu Resolution, was to agitate for the inclusion of a third state in the region's referendum on partition, allowing voters to choose to become part of an independent "Pashtunistan" as well. The Afghan government also took up this cause, adding a demand for a fourth option that would have the tribal areas join Afghanistan. Britain ignored Bacha Khan, but replied to Afghanistan that its proposal was not practicable, citing as its reason the long-term recognition of the Durand Line as an international border. An official visit by Shah Mahmud to Britain was unable to sway Clement Atlee's Labour government.

When the Atlee government passed the Indian Independence Act in July 1947, it declared that British India would be divided into two states — India and Pakistan — and that no other choices would be given to voters. Afghanistan was incensed but powerless to change the decision. Bacha Khan and his followers boycotted the referendum, and although voter turnout was low in the areas where he was influential, the votes that were cast overwhelmingly favoured joining Pakistan.

Shah Mahmud, through the amir, called another loya jirga to discuss the Pashtunistan issue, again trying to build a broad consensus for his contentious foreign policy. The Pashtun leaders called to the jirga overwhelmingly supported the creation of Pashtunistan or the absorption of the tribal areas into Afghanistan. The Durand Line was seen as an ongoing insult that needed to be erased. Representatives of other ethnic groups were more circumspect. The inclusion of a greater number of Pashtun tribes and citizens would only increase the already overwhelming power of that group within the country. They also thought it unlikely that either Britain or Pakistan would give away such a large portion of territory and population.

The Afghan government's desire to pursue the Pashtunistan issue likely had two motives. The dire economic situation, and the government's failure to improve it, called for an external distraction. Whether or not it was successful at liberating the Pashtuns on the other side of the Durand Line, this was an issue that was easy to rally the Afghan tribes around. Secondly, absorbing the tribes and their territory would remove a potential threat to the crown, as numerous times in the past, tribes that were out of reach of the Afghan government had sought the role of kingmaker during a rebellion. The opportunity to more directly control these tribes would allow the government to nullify their power.

The Pashtun tribes in Pakistan themselves were more cautious. Once the referendum was over, there did not seem to be a means to pursue the idea further. The Pakistani government, much like the British, largely left the tribes to themselves, although the new nation of Pakistan did invite Pashtuns to take senior government posts. Given a choice between remaining in Pakistan, which had modernized much more effectively than Afghanistan, or joining Afghanistan, most of the tribes were content with the current situation. Nonetheless, Zahir Shah declared his support for the creation of Pashtunistan, and argued that the Durand agreement was null and void. Afghanistan was the only country to vote against Pakistan's application to join the United Nations in September 1947.

Tensions remained high between Afghanistan and Pakistan into the early 1950s, with the government in Kabul producing a steady stream of propaganda in favour of an independent Pashtunistan. Mahmud Shah claimed that while Afghanistan did not wish to annex any part of Pakistan, it also did not recognize the tribal areas as part of Pakistan, or the Durand Line as the two countries' border. In the summer of 1949 the Pakistan Air Force bombed a village within Afghanistan where it believed the Faqir of Ipi to be hiding. The Faqir was not in the village, but 24 people were killed, and the Afghan chargé d'affaires was recalled from Pakistan in protest. Zahir Shah again convened a loya jirga to discuss the matter, and a debate was held in the National Assembly. A proposal was discussed to repudiate all previous treaties with Britain, which Pakistan had inherited as a successor state. Not only would this likely lead to war, it might also invite attempts by the Soviet Union and Iran to annex Afghan territories they coveted. The final decision was to do nothing, made easier once Pakistan admitted its mistake, claiming to have been targeting a village within its own borders, and paid compensation to the families.

Worsening relations led to tightened controls at the border, which quickly came to haunt the government of Afghanistan. With Pakistan unwilling to even discuss Pashtunistan, and with Britain resolutely against the idea as well, there was nothing short of war that Afghanistan could do to advance the issue. The Pashtuns inside Pakistan sent a delegation to Kabul asking the amir to settle with Pakistan. There was no way for Shah Mahmud to resolve the matter without losing face.

At the same time, the dispute hurt Afghanistan, as a large majority of its trade either was conducted with Pakistan or flowed through its port of Karachi to the rest of the world. With this border closed, systems of trade already weakened by the impact of the Second World War were now broken. The country's poor road network did not easily support a change in the direction of trade to either the Soviet Union in the north or Iran in the west.

The gradual tightening of the border after 1929, when in the aftermath of Nadir Shah's ascension authorities in British India had begun to restrict the movement of lashkars to fight in Afghanistan, also had a major impact on the Kochi. These nomads traditionally led their flocks to winter pastures along the Indus River in what was now Pakistan. Although some Kochi adapted their migration pattern to remain within the borders of Afghanistan, others gave up their nomadic lifestyle altogether.

Whereas in the 1920s fully one-third of the Afghan population were no-mads, by the late 1940s this had dwindled to less than one-fifth.

This disruption highlighted a number of structural problems in the Afghan economy that hampered its development. The production of raw materials was limited by both a lack of internal demand and an inability to easily transport the material either internally or to foreign markets. At the same time, light industry lacked a steady supply of good-quality raw material, and even with protective tariffs had difficulty competing with higher-quality foreign goods. It was often more lucrative for farmers to grow cash crops for sale to foreign markets than to produce food for the domestic market, meaning that basic staples were often imported, and at times there were acute shortages even while export levels were high. After decades of infrastructure projects and attempts to integrate the economy, Afghanistan still functioned as a series of loosely associated "oasis economies."

The hope that major projects such as that in the Helmand Valley would greatly increase production proved to be false. As newly arable land became available, the government resettled three thousand families of landless Pashtuns from Paktia Province and 1,200 Kochi who wished to give up their nomadic lifestyle in Nadi Ali district in 1952. The set-tlers were to pay for the land that they were granted over a period of 20 years, but few remained that long. The land that they were allotted was not well suited for agriculture even when irrigated; the topsoil quickly eroded and blew away as dust. The plots given to families were not large enough to support them, and areas designated for housing were as far as 4 kilometres from the farmland, making for a difficult life. Many of these settlers simply abandoned their plots in search of better land elsewhere.

The country's development was also hampered by a lack of foreign currency. The lost opportunities for trade owing to the closed border with Pakistan, and the requirement to pay Morrison-Knudsen for the Helmand Valley Authority project, drained the available reserves. For an economy dependent on foreign goods bought with hard currency, this was a major concern.

A few industries that had been first set up in the 1940s managed to flourish, particularly those that could rely on raw materials produced in Afghanistan and a domestic market for the finished goods. Afghan wool, cotton, and silk were processed by looms owned by several private corporations, producing hundreds of thousands of yards of material a year. Similar successes were experienced by factories producing soap and ceramic tiles. Most other industries were hindered by infighting between government ministries and the ministers themselves. In general, the administration of government projects was loose, with few accurate statistics available to guide decision-making or measure outcomes. Many of the initiatives taken were driven by self-interested government officials, who stood to make personal fortunes by directing contracts to businesses they or their families owned. In 1949 several proposals for industrial development made by the minister of national economy were turned down by the cabinet. Rather than rework the proposals for approval, he resigned from his position and took up the role of president of the Bank-e Melli, the country's government-controlled commercial bank, and created the businesses directly from there. Although the number of entrepreneurs, capitalists, and major traders in Afghanistan remained small, they were becoming an increasingly powerful constituency who were both disliked and distrusted by the traditional influencers — tribal leaders and the ulema.

In addition to these three economic groups, a loosening of government control of the press in the late 1940s and Shah Mahmud's decision to release political prisoners led to the emergence of a new potential source of political power, organized parties. Although not legally permitted at that time, they were tolerated, even though they were seen as potential threats to the Musahiban clan's hold on power. The first parties that were formed were amalgamations of the political "circles" that existed before, linking politically minded people together to discuss policy and lobby the government for change. Rather than seeking to become mass movements, their intention was to become influential within the halls of power.

One of the first of these parties, Wish Zalmiyan (Awakened Youth) was formed in 1948. Focused on advocating for liberal reform, it soon began to fragment, with some elements wishing to continue lobbying the government, while others took the more radical approach of creating a larger movement to put pressure on the monarchy. As the group was originally based on a coalition of smaller groups formed through personal networks, when it fragmented it devolved back to these groups, largely based along ethnic and family lines. The Tajik intellectuals within the group formed Hezb-e Watan (the Homeland Party) and the Shi'ite members formed Hezb-e Khalq (the People's Party), both of which were committed to lobbying. Watan even went as far as to ask the amir's permission to form, although its members did not receive a reply.

Watan was perhaps the least ethnocentric of these groups, as by the early 1950s it counted Tajiks, Pashtuns, and Hazaras among its members, even within the central committee. Wish Zalmiyan was also a multiethnic party, but the Uzbek members split off and formed Ittihad wa Taraqi (Unity and Progress), which flirted with the idea of an armed uprising to drive change. The core of the party that remained transformed it into a Pashtun nationalist group, a far cry from what it had started as. Its influence was limited, as even when it was a coherent group Wish Zalmiyan never counted more than eight hundred members, with branches in just nine towns across the country.

The potential power of political parties was seen early on by one particular member of the Musahiban clan, Mohammed Daoud Khan, son of the elder brother of Nadir Shah who had been murdered in Berlin, and husband to Zahir Shah's sister. He and his brother Naim Khan had been proteges of Hashim Khan when he was prime minister. Daoud Khan, educated in France, had served as a provincial governor, cabinet minister, ambassador, and senior army officer from the time his uncle Nadir Shah had taken power. Daoud Khan tried to insert himself as the leader of Wish Zalmiyan but was rebuffed. He instead formed his own party, the Hezb-e Demokrati-e Melli (National Democratic Party), universally known as the Klup-e Melli (National Club). The membership of Daoud Khan's party was almost entirely government officials. In some circles, it was derisively known as the "Minister's Party" for its support of the current establishment. The party was Daoud Khan's tool to increase and solidify his own influence and power, rather than to seek reform.

The country's first formal Islamic parties also arose in the 1940s, largely as extensions of the personal networks that already existed between religious scholars. The first Sunni party formed was Hezb-e Tawheed (the Party of [God's] Oneness), while the equivalent Shi'a party was Irshad (Exhortation, or Guidance). Neither sought political power at this time, and so they could not be described as "Islamist"; rather, they existed to share ideas and potentially to lobby government officials. Their lack of interest in political power is perhaps a good indicator of how effectively the governments of Hashim Khan and Shah Mahmud were in integrating the ulema and slowing the pace of reform so as not to offend religious sensibilities.

The 1949 election for the Majlis-e Shura-ye Melli (National Consultative Assembly) is widely seen as the first fair and free election in Afghanistan. All Afghan males over the age of 20 who "possessed sound moral character, who were neither bankrupt, nor convicted of criminal offences, nor legally incapable of managing their own affairs, and who had resided within the respective constituencies for one year" were allowed to cast a ballot. As before, outside the major cities the system of voting was loose, without a census to determine a list of eligible voters, letting local power brokers "deliver" the votes of their constituents. Of the 116 delegates elected, 50 were considered to be liberals. Five candidates from Wish Zalmiyan were elected, and they formed a "National Front" with 11 other liberal reformist candidates. Three seats went to Hezb-e Watan. Although the National Assembly was a largely toothless organization that could be dissolved by the amir at will, this result still spooked the government of Shah Mahmud.

Without support from a mass of voters, these liberal candidates had been elected through the use of personal connections to gain support from power brokers in the provinces. Yet the government, which in practical terms was still little more than the shah and his cabinet and had functioned for 20 years with power firmly held within a small family circle, still found them threatening. The government had no experience of managing a "loyal opposition" and was unsettled by even the desire for mild reform expressed by the new parties. Having successfully managed tribal leaders and the ulema for this whole period, whose support had been necessary for the survival of the regime, it appeared to the Musahiban that the parties themselves were becoming a third locus of competing power.

In 1950 a student union was formed at Kabul University with the assistance of Daoud Khan's Klup-e Melli, in hopes of inculcating the students with a pro-establishment philosophy. The union elected as its first president a charismatic young Tajik named Sultan Hussein, who was studying in the Faculty of Law and Political Science. The son of an army major general, Sultan Hussein had first become involved in politics in high school. In addition to leading the student union, he also participated in the leftist politics of Wish Zalmiyan.

Under Sultan Hussein's leadership, the student union quickly became radicalized. When the students began to travel to other provinces to present stage plays with strong political messages, it was too much for the government. After only a few months of existence, the student union was banned. A number of prominent members fled to Pakistan, where they were initially welcomed by the government and used as a propaganda tool against Afghanistan. Sultan Hussein remained at the university and completed his studies, although eventually his political activities led to his arrest and sentencing to five years in prison. He was introduced to Marxism by other political prisoners, becoming even more radicalized and changing his name to Babrak Karmal, which means "Comrade of the Workers" in Pashto.

In this same period, a secretive political party was founded, known as Hezb-e Seri Itehad (the Secret Unity Party). Unusually for Afghanistan at the time, its two leaders came from very different social groups who would not normally have found common cause. Sayyed Ismail Balkhi was a Hazara Shi'ite leader from the country's north, and was one of the country's earliest practitioners of political Islam. Educated in Iran and Iraq, he was a strong advocate of political reform within an Islamist framework. He had earlier founded the public party Irshad, but had lost faith in the potential for reform within the current system. Khwaja Mohammed Naim, the group's co-founder, was a Sunni who occupied the powerful position of police commissioner for Kabul, as well as private secretary to Prime Minister Hashim Khan. He participated in the meetings of the royal family, where unlike meetings of cabinet or other formal government bodies, important decisions were made. He watched first-hand how the ruling Musahiban exercised power. He met Balkhi in Mazar-e Sharif when he was sent there in 1946 after being demoted. Mazar-e Sharif had been the scene of heavy-handed government actions to "Pashtunize" the country, affecting the Hazaras, Uzbeks, and Tajiks, as well as minor groups such as the Jewish community. The focus of the central government on the Pashtunistan issue gave another swell of support to Pashtun nationalism, and promised that the condition of non-Pashtun groups would worsen if a large number of Pashtuns were absorbed into the nation.

Hezb-e Seri Ite had had as its main goal the replacement of Musahiban family rule with a more open, democratic system that did not include a monarchy at all. This it intended to achieve through force. No other political party in Afghanistan at the time advocated the creation of a republic, or working outside the existing political system to achieve change. Carefully gathering followers from across the country, including army officers, it soon was in a position to attempt a coup during the Nawroz (New Year) celebration in 1950. The plan was to execute the prime minister and other senior members of the Musahiban family, including Daoud Khan (the king was travelling in Europe at the time), arm its supporters with guns seized from the military, release all political prisoners, and seize the capital's radio station to announce the coup. Betrayed by a member of the party, its leaders were arrested on the morning of the coup and sentenced to either long periods of imprisonment or exile.

While 1949–52 is sometimes referred to as the "Liberal Parliament" period, the government ensured that elections for the National Consultative Assembly in 1952 unfolded differently than the previous ones. Whereas the government did not interfere in 1949, the thwarted 1950 coup motivated it to use its influence to ensure that no opposition party candidates were elected at all. It also cracked down on many of the opposition publications, closing them down and arresting those involved. Hezb-e Watan was singled out in particular, as the party whose popular appeal was growing the fastest.

The government's attempt to suppress the opposition parties had the opposite effect. The first mass demonstration in Kabul was the response, with thousands of participants taking to the streets to demand greater political freedoms. This greatly concerned Shah Mahmud, who took the further precaution of arresting the organizers of the protest and the leaders of nearly all the political parties. Even Klup-e Melli, which was entirely pro-establishment, was targeted for suppression.

Shah Mahmud, then in his mid-sixties, was seen by the governing elite as soft and out of touch with the political reality in the capital. He was failing at delivering a workable foreign policy or effective economic reforms at home. Daoud Khan had for several years been positioning himself as a replacement for the prime minister. In September 1953 Zahir Shah persuaded his uncle to resign, replacing him with his cousin Daoud Khan. Naim Khan, Daoud's brother, was appointed deputy prime minister.

All three of the men at the pinnacle of the Afghan government were relatively young, educated in Western Europe, and ostensibly shared a vision of a modern Afghanistan. Zahir Shah, 20 years into his reign without ever having ruled, hoped that by sidelining the last of his uncles while still awarding key positions to members of the Musahiban family, he could begin to wield power himself.

CHAPTER 8 THE STRONG HAND OF THE PRIME MINISTER

ANY HOPES THAT Zahir Shah would exert more influence over the government than before were quickly dashed. Daoud Khan had a strong vision for how the country was to be modernized, and had built enough support in the bureaucracy and within the army to be able to enact it. Zahir Shah remained on the sidelines, outshone and outmanoeuvred by his cousin.

Daoud Khan did not believe that the country could develop politically while advancing socially and economically at the same time, and so he chose to keep the political system fundamentally unchanged, albeit with a much tighter rein on the opposition. Over time, this opened him to criticism as a dictator running a police state. The experiment with liberalism from 1949 to 1952 was branded a failure not to be repeated. The three main newspapers in the country, which sold on average no more than 1,500 copies of each edition, were closed. Political parties continued to be suppressed, including Daoud Khan's own party, Klup-e Melli.

In foreign affairs Daoud Khan had two priorities. The first was maintaining a neutral stance between the West and the Soviet Union. He famously quipped, "I feel the happiest when I can light my American cigarettes with Soviet matches." The second was pursuing the creation of Pashtunistan. Daoud Khan was a staunch Pashtun nationalist, which made leaders of the country's other ethnic groups wary of his rule. Whether he truly expected to precipitate the creation of an independent Pashtun state or merely hoped to exploit the issue for domestic popularity and legitimacy is unclear. The majority within the Pashtun tribes in Pakistan remained content with the current arrangement. In any case, the heightened ethnic tensions within Afghanistan led to serious fighting between Hazaras and Pashtuns over pastures in the Hazarajat in late 1954, requiring Daoud Khan himself to intervene.

The previous leadership had grown close to the United States. A strong nationalist, Daoud Khan saw this as an unbalanced approach. Reliance on any one power would undermine Afghanistan's sovereignty and independence. The Cold War provided a ready-made counterbalance to American influence, which Daoud Khan hoped to manipulate to his country's advantage.

American policy in the region at the time was focused on containing the Soviet Union. To this end, the United States formed the Baghdad Pact, a defensive alliance meant to be analogous to NATO comprising Turkey, Iraq, Iran, Afghanistan, Pakistan, and Britain. While all the other countries agreed to join, Afghanistan hesitated due to its policy of neutrality. Its previous requests for military assistance had either been declined or saddled with conditions such as dropping the Pashtunistan issue. At the same time, it saw Pakistan's growing military power as a threat.

Daoud Khan's second foreign policy goal was to create the conditions whereby the Pashtuns residing within Pakistan would be allowed a vote on their independence. This, he believed, would lead to their eventual political union with Afghanistan. He aimed a steady stream of propaganda at Pakistan, as well as keeping up the age-old tradition of payments to tribal leaders, to ensure that the Pashtun tribes remained a thorn in the side of the Pakistani government. The Faqir of Ipi had transferred his hatred of the British authorities to the Pakistani ones and continued his low-level insurgency, now paid for by authorities in Kabul, who sometimes referred to him as the "President of the National Assembly for Pashtunistan."

The problem of Pashtunistan came to a head in 1955, when Pakistan decided to merge the four provinces of western Pakistan into a single one. This initiative was known as the One Unit Plan, and meant that the North West Frontier Province, home to many Pashtuns, would disappear as a political entity, although the tribal regions would remain. Daoud Khan's reaction to this announcement was dramatic. He made a radio broadcast stating that the results of the One Unit Plan would never be recognized by the "Pashtun nation" or by his government. He again demanded a vote on Pashtun self-determination and was rebuffed by the Pakistani government.

In March 1955 violent protests in support of Pashtunistan broke out in Kabul, Kandahar, and Jalalabad. The Pakistani embassy and consulates were attacked and overrun. Equally violent counter-protests erupted in Karachi and Peshawar. Pakistan issued an ultimatum on May 4, and Afghanistan replied by ordering a general mobilization and moving its army to defensive positions along the border. For five months the border remained closed, seriously disrupting trade and the movement of the Kochi. Although the issue was of interest only to the nationalist segment of the Pashtun population, all ethnic groups suffered from the interruption of trade.

By September the two countries had reached an agreement and the border was reopened. But the détente was short-lived, as in October the Pakistan Constituent Assembly voted to enact the One Unit Plan. Daoud Khan saw that the opportunity for a vote on Pashtunistan had passed. He informed the Pakistani government that there was no chance of settling the One Unit and Pashtunistan issues, and therefore there was no need for an Afghan ambassador in Karachi. Pakistan responded by recalling its own ambassador from Kabul.

With Afghanistan at loggerheads with its neighbour, which was becoming a key American ally, Zahir Shah called a loya jirga in December 1955 to discuss the invitation to join the Baghdad Pact. Afghanistan would demand American support on Pashtunistan and a guarantee of protection should the Soviets invade. For its part, the United States was willing to grant neither demand. Daoud Khan deftly manipulated the discussion in the jirga to ensure the outcome that he sought. Afghanistan would not join the Baghdad Pact, but would instead continue its policy of neutrality. But in the absence of military aid from the United States, it was agreed that Daoud Khan would seek it from the USSR.

The Soviet response was swift and enthusiastic. The following month the First Secretary of the Communist Party, Nikita Khrushchev, and Chairman of the Council of Ministers, Nikolai Bulganin, made a state visit to Kabul. They declared that Pashtuns living in Pakistan should have the right to self-determination, making the USSR the only country to support Afghanistan's point of view on Pashtunistan. They also committed $100 million in credit for development, with a joint Afghan-Soviet committee formed to determine how to spend it. An increase in trade was also negotiated, providing a much-needed alternative to the routes that ran through Pakistan. These agreements were a major coup for Daoud Khan.

The Soviet approach to Afghanistan had changed under Khrushchev, who had no objection to providing aid to a religious monarchy as long as it was anti-Western. Guided by Soviet advisers, the Afghan government instituted a series of "five-year plans" for economic development on the Soviet model. The fact that Afghanistan was wedged in between American allies Iran and Pakistan was also a natural reason for the USSR to build a relationship with its neighbour. In his memoirs, Khrushchev wrote:

> It was clear to us that the Americans were penetrating Afghanistan with the obvious purpose of setting up a military base…. The amount of money we spent in gratuitous assistance to Afghanistan is a drop in the ocean compared to the price we would have had to pay in order to counter the threat of an American military base on Afghan territory.

Although hindsight suggests otherwise, the original Soviet interest in Afghanistan was defensive rather than expansionist, seeking just enough involvement to keep the country neutral and American influence limited. And although most Afghans had long been wary of the "godless communists" to the north, many social conservatives under Daoud Khan were persuaded to see Soviet aid positively. Bureaucrats and government officials, industrialists, royalists, and military officers saw that Soviet assistance bolstered the government's power, and by extension their own. Even though many of these people never became avowed communists ideologically, they accepted and assisted Soviet involvement in their government.

The Afghan military underwent a dramatic change as a result of Soviet assistance. As early as 1956 small quantities of hitherto unseen modern weapons began to appear, such as T-34 tanks and MiG-15 fighter jets, along with a small number of advisers, technicians, and instructors. Over time, this equipment was supplemented by even more modern models such as the T-54 tank and the MiG-17. By 1960 there were five hundred Soviet advisers assisting the Afghan military, and the Afghan Air Force had grown to over a hundred relatively modern Soviet fighters and helicopters.

Even though the government accepted what American military training assistance was available, over time the technical language of the Afghan Army became Russian. By the end of the 1960s about seven thousand Afghan soldiers, mostly officers, had been to the Soviet Union for training. In some cases officers trained there for years, transforming the leadership of the army from a collection of conservative second sons of tribal leaders into a much more educated and worldly group of people.

Development of the army into a modern military force also wrought a major change in the relationship between the Afghan government and society. Previously, the combined lashkar of the Pashtun tribes was substantially more powerful than the army. Although the army could be used to suppress a single tribe at a time, more often than not it needed to be reinforced by tribal levies. This gave the Pashtun tribes an outsized influence over the government, both in that they could threaten to topple it nearly at will, and also because they commanded many privileges in order to remain loyal. These included being informally excused from conscription and from paying many taxes. As much as the state had been dependent on their goodwill, they existed apart from it.

The new army changed this paradigm. Although it shifted a little with the first acquisition of aircraft under Amanullah, the introduction of modern weaponry in large numbers meant that now the army far outclassed the traditional military capabilities of the tribes.

This allowed the government to be bolder with its program of reform and modernization, as the displeasure of the Pashtun tribes no longer posed an existential threat.

Even with its position more secure militarily, the government continued to struggle financially. One of the means that it tried to use to increase revenues also increased tensions with the West: opium. Daoud Khan, mindful of the need to maintain America's goodwill, but equally mindful of the need for government revenues, hoped that Afghanistan would join the world's legal producers of opium for medicinal purposes. The 1953 Opium Protocol provided the framework for this, and countries such as India and Turkey were already included as legal producers. Initially with American support, Afghanistan applied to be included within the protocol, passing its own Opium Act in 1956 to become compliant. This act placed all production under government control, and again made recreational use illegal.

Afghanistan's position was undercut by problems in neighbouring Iran, at this time a key American ally. Iran, which had a long-standing culture of opium smoking, and an estimated 2.8 million addicts, imposed a total ban on production and consumption in 1955. When demand was quickly met by imports from Afghanistan, United States officials began to sour on the idea of Afghanistan becoming a legal producer. Their opinion was further worsened by Afghan officials trying to sell illegal opium to legal purchasers such as pharmaceutical companies in the United States and France. Coupled with reporting shared by the Swiss ambassador to Afghanistan, who witnessed open opium bazaars in Herat that catered to Iranian buyers, as well as evidence that government officials were involved in production, the United States decided that Afghanistan could not be trusted to enforce its own laws.

Eager to prove the Americans wrong, Daoud Khan announced a total prohibition on opium production and consumption in December 1957. In order to demonstrate that Afghanistan could control production, he chose to conduct an eradication campaign in Badakhshan, a significant region for opium growth and consumption, and one occupied by isolated non-Pashtun ethnic groups he felt he could afford to alienate. The government did not enforce the prohibition in any other area of the country, where many of those involved in the trade were Pashtun.

Badakhshan is in the extreme northeast of the country, a mountainous strip of land situated between the Soviet Union (now Tajikistan), China, and Pakistan. Only one road connects it to the rest of Afghanistan, with most of the population living in remote villages. The only cash crop produced by farmers in the region was opium, and because its harvest is so labour intensive, even those who did not grow it themselves were often involved as day labourers in March and April of each year. While assistance to transition to wheat or barley was promised to the nearly three thousand farmers identified as opium growers (some of whom were licensed by the government), nothing was promised to the rest of the population who also relied on opium growing for income.

Government officials, with American representatives as guests, met with local leaders in March 1958 to explain how the ban and transition would work. The Americans present thought that most of the farmers accepted the ban, and were willing to work with the government to plant new crops. They reported the success back to the United States, and coverage of the Afghan initiative in the international press was positive. The *London Times* wrote:

> The Afghan Government has boldly decided to ban the cultivation and export of opium. It will not be an easy decision to implement in such a country, where it is not the population's addiction to the drug that it is the problem so much as the livelihood of those who grow poppy in places where few other crops are possible. But the intention must be welcomed and aided.

The immediate effect of the ban was a total eradication of production throughout the province. This was a blow to about 10 percent of the province's population, migrant harvest workers and their families who would be unable to survive without this income. In April, Afghan officials asked the United States and the United Nations to provide aid, but it was not until a few weeks before the beginning of winter that the urgency of the matter was recognized. By the end of the year, food aid from the United States was distributed, along with some wheat from Afghan government stocks, and disaster was averted.

But the following year, when further assistance from the government failed to arrive, and the government's enthusiasm for eradication waned as well, opium production flourished again. As well as being the only cash crop in the province, opium was also engrained in local culture. Used as a medicine in the absence of modern doctors, its seeds were also used for baking and to produce oil for cooking, as well as to make soap. The perception of opium differed greatly between the United States, where it was a social vice, Kabul, where it was a source of tax revenue and a foreign affairs concern, and Badakhshan, where it was an ancient way of life.

The resurgence of opium production meant that Afghanistan would not be allowed to join the world's group of licit producers, robbing it of a major source of tax income. And so while the official ban on opium production remained in place across the country, it was ignored by the farmers and government alike, allowing a local trade to markets in Pakistan and Iran to continue.

Economic development and growth continued to be a focus for Daoud Khan, though direct investment in industry and the creation of infrastructure to support both manufacture and trade were having only limited effects. By the late 1950s the perception in Kabul was growing that there was a need to better integrate women into the economy, as they were an underused resource. Although women had gained access to education that allowed them into certain professions, becoming doctors, nurses, and teachers, they had little presence in the rest of the formal economy. In an attempt to correct this, without creating the kind of backlash experienced by Amanullah, Daoud Khan announced that the wearing of the veil was to be a "voluntary option." As before, the impact of this announcement was limited to the capital, and it was largely the wives of government officials who took the option. Daoud Khan had religious leaders who protested jailed.

Even so, making the hijab or burkha "optional" created unrest in other parts of the country. Serious riots took place in Kandahar. Mass protests were organized in Kabul by university students, led by Afghan graduates of Cairo's Al-Azhar University who had formed an underground Islamic organization. The protests were crushed through mass arrests, sending a chill through opposition groups of all stripes.

The Mangal tribe in Khost also rebelled, though its list of complaints was longer than just the challenge to purdah: its members also denounced the construction of a road linking their region to the city of Gardez, continued insistence that their children attend school, curbs on their lucrative lumber smuggling trade with Pakistan, and the imposition of conscription. Whereas in the past the discontent of the Mangal tribe had quickly spread and threatened the government, the modern Afghan Army had little difficulty in defeating the tribesmen and re-establishing order.

A state visit by President Eisenhower marked a high point for Daoud Khan's foreign policy of neutrality, and made it clear that both the Americans and the Soviets had high-level interests in Afghanistan. Eisenhower's visit was brief, and his concern was a simple one: the Soviets were outspending America in Afghanistan. From 1954 to 1959, the Soviets had provided $159 million in aid, while the United States had provided only $101 million. The resulting difference in influence was obvious, and Eisenhower committed to correcting this imbalance. Daoud Khan's hope of playing the two world powers off against each other for the betterment of his own country seemed to be working. Rivalry between the superpowers, and a desire to equal or better each other's work, nearly created a form of co-operation as potential projects were divided between them.

The signature American project in Afghanistan was still the irrigation of the Helmand River Valley. Despite initial setbacks, salinity in the soil was being overcome and unusable land reclaimed for agriculture. The government also had greater success in settling Kochi, though this was likely also influenced by their increasing inability to migrate across the Pakistani border to their traditional winter pastures. There were also marginal increases in farming productivity, even though farming practice remained rooted in ancient technology across most of the country.

After his success at enticing the two global superpowers, Daoud Khan moved to push forward his other foreign policy goal, the creation of Pashtunistan. His main agent in the tribal areas, the Faqir of Ipi, had died in April, still carrying on his guerrilla war to the very end. In an attempt to foment a popular uprising, in September 1960 over a thousand Afghan soldiers infiltrated from Kunar into the Bajaur District of Pakistan. A remote part of the frontier, this district was inhabited by Tarkani Pashtuns, and was notable for containing the now unused road between Kabul and Pakistan that had preceded the Khyber Pass route. The Afghan Army massed along the border, ready to intercede if the Tarkani rose up.

Daoud Khan's attempt to incite a popular revolt failed badly. The Tarkani tribe rose up, not against the Pakistani government, but to fight the Afghan invasion. Facing both the Pakistan Air Force and the highly effective Pashtun lashkar that formed to repel it, the lightly equipped and poorly supplied Afghan Army was forced to retreat.

Afghanistan's action was supported by India, who encouraged it to raise the Pashtunistan issue at the United Nations, and by the Soviets. Emboldened by international support, Afghanistan attempted a larger infiltration into neighbouring Dir district in May the following year. Dir was ruled by a traditional leader, Nawab Jahan Khan, who was rumoured to be partial to Afghanistan. Afghan troops entered Dir in order to support him in a conflict against the Khan of Khar, and again to incite a mass revolt.

The Pakistani government acted swiftly, removing Nawab Jahan Khan from power. It also sent its own army, equipped with American-supplied M-48 tanks and modern artillery, to fight the incursion. Remarkably, the involvement of the Pakistan Army was resisted by the Pashtuns as fiercely as they resisted the presence of the Afghan Army. The Pakistan Army was forced to withdraw and allow the local Pashtun tribes to oppose the Afghans on their own, which they did remarkably well. This informed future Pakistani policy, as it realized that it could rely on the tribes, if funded and given autonomy, to effectively resist invasion and defend the border. The second Afghan incursion was also defeated, although skirmishes within Pakistan all along the frontier continued into 1963. The issue continued to attract international attention as well. Bacha Khan, still advocating peacefully for the creation of Pashtunistan, had been jailed in Pakistan, and was Amnesty International's "Prisoner of the Year" in 1962.

Attempts by the United States and the Shah of Iran to mediate were unsuccessful, as there was no solution that would allow both parties to save face. The president of Pakistan, Ayub Khan, had gained power in a 1958 coup d'état and was focused on resisting the potential loss of territory to India, in the Kashmir or elsewhere. Even though he was a Pashtun himself, and had grown up in North West Frontier Province, he had no sympathy for the Pashtunistan cause.

Added to the risk of war that these skirmishes created were their economic consequences. The fighting had caused Afghanistan and Pakistan to break off diplomatic relations in 1961. Although Pakistan was willing to continue to allow goods to flow in and out of Afghanistan to the port of Karachi, its only real outlet to the outside world, Daoud Khan unilaterally closed the border. What effect this was meant to have on Pakistan was unclear, but the effect on Afghanistan was almost immediate — it had imposed an economic blockade on itself. Twenty-five thousand tonnes of aid and materiel, much of it donated by the United States, piled up at the port in Karachi, unable to move and creating a tremendous amount of congestion.

The ongoing closure of the border also meant that there was no means to move the Afghan harvest to market, as much of it was sold in India. Daoud Khan worked to access alternative markets in Iran and the Soviet Union, but the infrastructure leading in these directions was not as well developed. A request to the United States for funding to improve routes into Iran was denied, leaving the Soviet Union as the only other option. Leonid Brezhnev, a member of the Politburo who would later replace Khrushchev, made a state visit to Afghanistan in July 1962, demonstrating his support. Remarkably, the Soviet Union also assisted with a massive airlift of produce to market in India, which saved the harvest and provided much-needed income. Even with this dramatic intervention, the Afghan economy suffered because of the disruption.

Daoud Khan's failed military policy in Pashtunistan was humiliating enough, but the economic damage it caused had the potential to undermine support for the government entirely. As long as two intransigent leaders were facing off across the border, there appeared to be no solution. Zahir Shah and his uncle Shah Wali pressured Daoud Khan into stepping down from his post as prime minister. Perhaps Daoud Khan could not see a way forward either, as in March 1963 he willingly resigned.

CHAPTER 9 THE LAST AMIR

ZAHIR SHAH BELIEVED that he would now be able to rule the country directly, after 30 years on the throne. To replace Daoud Khan he appointed Dr. Mohammed Yusuf Khan, a government technocrat who had previously been the minister of mines and industries. Most importantly, he was a commoner, with no connections to the Musahiban.

As his first order of business, Zahir Shah resolved the crippling dispute with Pakistan, aided by the Shah of Iran as a mediator. While not renouncing the idea of Pashtunistan or reaffirming recognition of the Durand Line, he created a working relationship with President Ayub Khan, and trade resumed across the shared border. Zahir Shah accepted an invitation from Pakistan to tour the North West Frontier Province and tribal areas to see with his own eyes that Pashtuns were not being oppressed. He also accepted an invitation to make a state visit to the United States, where he met with President John F. Kennedy, who reaffirmed the United States' commitment to co-operate in Afghan economic development.

Zahir Shah used his new direct influence over government to push hard on the issue of education, which like many of his forebears he saw as critical to modernizing the country. Throughout the 1960s schools began to be established in nearly every corner of the country, though this remained contentious. The rural population, particularly among the Pashtun tribes, saw this as an unwanted government imposition. They were right in the sense that education is not neutral, and the purpose of education in the eyes of Zahir Shah was indoctrination of the population and the creation of a national identity embodied by the amir.

At this time, schools were almost the only permanent presence of the central government in rural areas, and given that primary education was compulsory, to some it might have seemed that the state was trying to acquire ownership of their children. State schools were seen as places built to mislead children rather than teach them. In many villages, only the poorest and least influential families sent their children to state schools because they did not have the wherewithal to avoid doing so. Families with greater means would either pay bribes so that their children did not have to attend, or send the children of poorer families to impersonate their own children on the school rolls. Many attacks were recorded against schools throughout the 1950s and 1960s, with the intent of driving them out of communities that did not welcome the presence of the government.

The introduction of teachers into small communities was also controversial from the point of view of local power structures. One of the roles of traditional khans was to mediate with the government on behalf of their tribe, particularly when the government was a distant entity. Some teachers attempted to position themselves as influential members of the community in their own right, challenging traditional leaders and taking a role that would previously have been the right of religious teachers. Sometimes the challenge was aimed at the teacher, as when the child of an influential person failed an exam and threats or actual violence resulted.

Not surprisingly, it was difficult to persuade trained teachers to accept posts in remote villages. As a lack of teachers would scupper the government's education plan, teachers needed to be found locally. In these cases, mullahs who were already running religious schools were co-opted by the government and paid a salary to become government teachers. They were also given a centrally devised curriculum to teach from, though it is unlikely that it was closely followed. The mullahs not only would have kept their attachment to the traditional curriculum, but they also would have lacked knowledge of the new subjects, such as science or mathematics, that they were expected to teach.

The new curriculum was dauntingly comprehensive. Even at the primary level, students were expected to study 15 different subjects each year, including two languages, with a third added in the middle grades. The focus was on rote memorization, preparing students poorly for higher levels of learning. To meet the urgent need for textbooks, foreign ones were imported, creating a widely varying mix of supporting materials in many different languages. Textbooks created by the state were full of patriotic and nationalist themes that highlighted the importance of respecting the monarchy, and were filled with illustrations of people in Western clothes living in Western-style houses, far from the experiences of the students. Despite the government's desire to make Pashto the country's official language, it failed at implementing this in state schools. There were few textbooks available in Pashto, native Pashto speakers had very low rates of enrollment compared to their Persian-speaking peers, and Pashto lacked the modern technical terms needed to teach the new curriculum.

There were also issues with the quality of the teachers, many of whom were not well educated themselves. In the 1960s nearly half of the primary and elementary teachers in rural schools had not themselves studied beyond the ninth grade. Even among secondary school teachers, nearly one in five had not studied beyond the ninth grade. Student-to-teacher ratios were also poor, with a national average in 1968 of 56 to 1 in village schools, only improving to 27 to 1 in secondary schools. By the mid-1960s, the literacy rate in Afghanistan was estimated by the United Nations to be about 10 percent, compared to 17.6 percent in Pakistan and 24 percent in India. This was an improvement over the estimated 2 percent literacy rate earlier in the century, but was hardly a mark of success.

These ratios were partially driven by the large strides made over the 1960s to increase the number of students in school. This rose from about 10,000 students in state-run schools across the country in 1950 to 193,000 in 1960, and 664,000 in 1970. Even the latest figure still only represented less than 20 percent of the total school-age population, but it was a massive achievement. Girls were still enrolled at a much lower rate than boys nationally, but there were large regional discrepancies.

In the capital, and in the north and west where the majority of people were Persian-speaking, girls' enrollment was nearly on a par with that of boys. In the Pashto-speaking east and south, few girls went to state-run schools at all.

Despite all the efforts of the Afghan government, the quality of education, where it was being accessed, was poor. But the government's pursuit of a policy of mass education to drive modernization, without an equal amount of economic modernization to provide jobs for graduating students, also created a conundrum. Most people had no reason to seek a higher education because there was no way to put it to use. Little in the new curriculum was useful to the majority of Afghans who lived isolated, rural lives. And for those lucky Afghans who did receive a higher education, it often also came with growing aspirations to participate in politics and achieve progress. A greater awareness of the modern world made Afghanistan's conservative monarchy appear like a relic of earlier centuries. These aspirations found their outlet in the political parties formed in the capital, and particularly around Kabul University, in the 1960s. Students also brought these new ideas back with them to their homes outside the capital, spreading new ideologies beyond the limited intellectual circles where they had remained previously.

Zahir Shah hoped to liberalize the country by passing a new constitution. While the 1931 constitution was a facade for continuing control by the Musahiban clan, Zahir Shah wanted a charter that would be progressive enough to inspire the support of the new intelligentsia, while still keeping enough of the old system to appeal to traditionalists. In 1963 he appointed a seven-man committee to draft the document. Each member of the committee was a reformist, and one had even been jailed in the 1950s for opposing the government. For the first time in Afghan history, the constitution was being drafted by people outside the royal family.

After a year their draft was submitted to an advisory commission appointed by the king from across all walks of life, including for the first time two women. They made few changes to the document, which was then presented in September 1964 to a loya jirga for ratification. As before, this loya jirga was summoned by the amir, though the membership was different than previous ones. Zahir Shah was anxious that the group reflect sentiment from across the country, and so created as diverse a group as possible. It was composed of all the elected members of parliament, as well as an equal number of new representatives elected for the loya jirga. The amir then appointed a further one hundred representatives from interest groups (including four women), the previous senate, the cabinet, the supreme court, the original drafters, and the advisory committee. The jirga debated the draft constitution and made a number of modifications before finally ratifying it on September 20.

This new constitution, rather than simply justifying the current political order, spoke of the need to continue to evolve. Its preamble committed the Afghan state to "form, ultimately, a prosperous and progressive society based on social cooperation and preservation of human dignity." A great deal of effort was made to define the rights of individual Afghan citizens, including free expression, peaceful assembly, and free association. It also defined the citizen's obligations to participate in government by obeying the law, respecting the amir, complying with conscription, and paying taxes.

While the role of the amir was retained, the royal family's role in government was greatly reduced. Members were barred from cabinet and political parties. While the amir was "not accountable and must be respected by all," and wielded power such as the appointment of cabinet and the supreme court as well as a veto over legislation, the document was framed to imply that his involvement in day-to-day politics was to be limited.

The duty to govern was vested in the cabinet, and in a new Afghan parliament, composed of an upper house known as the Meshrano Jirga and a lower house known as the Wolesi Jirga. The 215 members of the Wolesi Jirga were elected to a four-year term, with all adults, male and female, given the vote. The Meshrano Jirga was composed of three equal-sized groups: one-third to be appointed by the amir, one-third elected by the provinces, and one-third composed of the members of the elected provincial councils. While past parliaments convened at the request of the amir, the new parliament was mandated to sit for seven months of the year. In the past, laws were made by royal decree or cabinet orders; in the future, laws would originate in either of the two houses. Once the cabinet was appointed by the amir, the appointments would be ratified by the Wolesi Jirga.

The 1931 constitution had been vague on the function of the judiciary, essentially allowing the customary system to continue under the direction of Islamic scholars. This was a necessary compromise to win the support of the ulema, but it did little to promote reform or support the recognition of individual human rights. The drafters of the new constitution saw the traditional judges as too independent and unaccountable, and so tried to bring the judiciary to heel. Many details were left to the Ministry of Justice to determine, but critically, the Jamiat-e Ulema that had dominated the judicial process by deciding what was compliant with shari'a would now report to the Ministry of Islamic Affairs. This greatly reduced its influence.

Provision was also made for the election of provincial governors and provincial councils, an attempt to make government relevant to citizens even in areas far removed from the capital. This reform was slow to be implemented, with varying forms of "democracy" put in play by provincial power brokers. At the same time, it was a radical attempt to decentralize power in hopes of sparking broader interest and participation in government.

The system envisioned by the drafters vested a great deal of power in parliament, while giving the amir the power to rein it in should its members become too radical or oppose his desires. Zahir Shah likely saw this as a necessary precaution to ensure that modernization proceeded in an orderly fashion, as well as to preserve his role as head of government. But including these strong powers for the amir to use *in extremis* created a potential conflict between king and parliament that would be difficult to resolve. It could easily result in deadlock and disillusionment.

The new constitution permitted the formation of political parties, but the details were to be covered in a separate law implemented by the amir directly. Zahir Shah worried that parties would challenge his power. If they formed along ethnic lines, they would deepen divisions that he was trying to erase. He also worried that radical elements in Kabul University would be the fastest and most effective at organizing, outmanoeuvring more conservative political elements. One of his closest advisers, his nephew and son-in-law Abdul Wali, advised him against signing the political parties bill, as it might provide a way for Daoud Khan to exercise power indirectly.

For these reasons, Zahir Shah hesitated to sign the bill into law. The 1965 parliamentary elections, the first under the new constitution, took place with the legality of political parties unclear. This did not prevent opposition groups from forming under names that avoided using the word *party*. The groups that were hindered in organizing for the election were those that supported the amir and did not wish to defy him by mobilizing as formal parties.

A number of the *mahfels* (discussion groups) around the university joined together in 1965 to form the Hezb-e Demokratik Khalq-e Afghanistan (the People's Democratic Party of Afghanistan, or PDPA). A socialist party with links to Soviet advisers, it organized into secretive cells to prevent the government from being able to easily extinguish it. The PDPA elected its leadership from among the influential members of the mahfels, choosing Nur Mohammed Taraki as leader and Babrak Karmal as his deputy.

Though both men had been members of Wish Zalmiyan, they could not have been more different. Taraki came from a lower-class background and was a dreamer. Though he had little sense of how to achieve or exercise power, he was a charismatic talker and writer who gained many followers in the university. Karmal was also a charismatic and fiery speaker. He came from a wealthy family, but his political views were tempered by his time spent in jail as a political prisoner, and he was eminently practical when it came to politics. Under their leadership, the PDPA sought to remake Afghanistan into a modern socialist republic. It advocated equal rights for women, a 42-hour work week, paid sick and maternity leave, and a ban on child labour. While there were other communist-inspired parties within Afghanistan (including at least one that espoused Maoism, and represented the competing side of the Sino-Soviet ideological split), the PDPA was the largest and most influential.

Initially organized in reaction to communist activities on campus, the Islamist parties made up the other major faction. Unlike earlier versions of these parties, the groups formed in the 1960s showed a growing understanding of political Islam. Even though they were much smaller than the leftist parties on campus, they can be credited with moving discussion of Islamic issues out of the mosque and into the streets, creating a public understanding of Islam as a political force. The Jawanan-e Musalman

(Muslim Youth) were formed with the intention of creating a theocratic government, and many early members — such as Burhanuddin Rabbani, Ahmed Shah Massoud, and Gulbuddin Hekmatyar — would go on to play major political roles over the next 50 years or longer.

The leaders of this movement, students or faculty at the School of Theology, were well educated and often had spent time at Al-Azhar University in Cairo, where they were influenced by the Muslim Brotherhood. They were able to translate and use religious and political tracts published by the Brotherhood, often printing them outside the country with the support of international Islamist groups. Until the 1970s Jawanan-e Musalman included both Sunni and Shi'a members, though over time it became more orthodox from the Sunni point of view, and the Shi'a were expelled to form their own organizations.

The parties that had the most trouble organizing were those that supported the current regime. Wahdat-e Melli (National Unity) was a monarchist party formed in 1965 by Khalilullah Khalili, a member of parliament and famous poet who had been the press adviser to the amir. He was able to attract conservative landowners and tribal leaders, but gained little support in urban areas where the radical parties won more followers. The amir quickly suppressed the party and sent Khalilullah to Saudi Arabia as ambassador. Leaderless, and rudderless as a monarchist party without the support of the monarchy, the party collapsed.

The results of the 1965 election were not as groundbreaking as the radicals hoped. Of the 216 members elected to the Wolesi Jirga, 68 percent were tribal or ethnic leaders. Of 16 different professions ascribed to the new parliamentarians, the most common was "mullah." But 4 PDPA candidates were elected, as well as 16 others who could be described as "opposing" the government. For the first time, three women were elected to parliament, all members of the first women's political party, the Sazman-e Demokratik-e Zanan-e Afghanistan (Democratic Organization of Afghan Women). Their platform focused on equal rights for women, improving women's literacy and access to education, and abolishing practices such as forced marriage and the bride price.

Recognizing its limited power in parliament, the PDPA flexed its muscles in a different way. It brought hundreds of student protesters to disrupt the first session of parliament and hold mass protests in the street. The issue the PDPA chose to contest was the amir's selection of cabinet ministers and reappointment of Yusuf Khan as prime minister. The protests turned violent and were suppressed by the army under the command of Abdul Wali, leading to the deaths of as many as 40 students. Until 1973 the anniversary of this date, Seyum-e Aqrab, was commemorated by students at the university. Yusuf Khan resigned and was replaced by former diplomat Mohammed Hashim Maiwandal.

Maiwandal was more charismatic than his predecessor, and quickly established good relations with students at the university. In 1966 he formed his own royalist party, Demokrat-e Motaraqi (Democratic Progressive Party), in hopes of capturing some of the students' loyalty and energy. But neither nationalism nor loyalty to the monarchy appealed to educated Afghans.

A story circulating at the time explains the lack of monarchist sentiment among intellectuals. Zahir Shah was invited to the home of his uncle, Hashim Khan, who took him out back and showed him a group of starving chickens. As soon as the men appeared, the chickens began to follow them. Zahir Shah was invited back the next day and again shown the chickens, who had since been fed. Now they ignored the two men. Hashim Khan's lesson for the amir was that men are like chickens — they will follow a leader if they are starved, but if well fed will not care. Many intellectuals blamed the amirs for deliberately keeping the country backward and in poverty in order to maintain their own power, and so looked beyond the monarchy for a better future. Maiwandal tried to include elements of the two major strains of political thought popular in Afghanistan in his party platform, socialism and Islamism, but they were largely irreconcilable, and his party never gained much popularity.

Zahir Shah and Maiwandal were wary of the growing popularity of the PDPA and of the newspapers that supported them. As part of Zahir Shah's turn toward democracy, he had liberalized the press laws before the 1965 election, but he now banned many leftist publications, with the full support of parliament.

Although Afghan socialists were convinced that their ideological approach was the right one, the Soviets were less certain. After a decade of investment in the Afghan economy, there was little to show for it. All the major donors — the United States, the Soviet Union, the United Nations, and Germany — had worked with the Afghan government to create economic plans to ensure that their investments were effective. The focus was often on large-scale projects, which typically did little to assist the lives of the rural poor who were still 90 percent of the population. Village communities were bypassed by road projects that served the needs of traders and transport entrepreneurs, as well as the strategic needs of the donor. Large-scale irrigation projects did create more arable land, but without cheap and easily accessible credit for small farmers, much of it was consolidated into the holdings of feudal landlords. Soviet efforts to create collectivized state farms, such as two formed around Jalalabad to grow citrus fruit, were not popular with the rural communities from a cultural point of view, and the fruit produced was almost entirely exported to the Soviet Union, creating income for the state but no betterment of the standard of living in their surrounding communities.

From the mid-1960s onward, Soviet aid changed focus from making Afghanistan self-sufficient to finding niche areas in the system of world trade where the country could be successful. This meant less industrialization and greater exploitation of natural resources such as coal, copper, and natural gas. Massive natural gas fields had been discovered in Afghanistan's north around Sheberghan, and a Soviet project to tap it for export to the Soviet Union by pipeline was completed in 1967.

Soviet development assistance was largely loans rather than grants, albeit on generous terms that allowed the Afghan government to pay in goods rather than in cash. American assistance was likewise a mix of loans and grants, but required repayment in cash. By 1969 Afghanistan was spending 20 percent of its national budget on debt repayment, a heavy burden compared to the economic benefit resulting from the loans. In response, the government doubled the land tax and increased the taxes on livestock. Many small landowners, who farmed at a subsistence level, suffered the loss of their land under this new system.

Other rural initiatives were also having unintended effects. The Directorate of Economic Development began to sell 135-horsepower tractors in 1966, intended to be purchased collectively by groups of farmers. In Pashtun areas, the idea of collectively owning such a large investment was unpopular, as culturally people preferred to be seen as independent. The cost of these tractors was exorbitant — 700,000 afghanis, to be repaid in seven annual instalments of 100,000 afghanis. This was equivalent to the price of 20 brides or over 150,000 kilograms of bread. Purchasing a tractor was well beyond the means of anyone except for rich landowners, who tended to be khans.

Khans maintain their position by making "social investments," generously supporting the communities they lead. But the purchase of a tractor meant that they had to recoup the costs in cash in order to make the repayments. To do this, they took two different approaches. Some began to plough other landowners' fields for a fee, an arrangement that seemed greedy and mean, but which was very lucrative. Some khans even sent their tractors far to the south to plough, moving northward in the spring. Others chose to use the tractors for themselves, expanding what had previously been a marginal form of agriculture known as *lalmi*.

As opposed to planting in irrigated land, lalmi was typically wheat sowed by hand without ploughing on the dry plains that surrounded irrigated land. This land had previously been considered in the public domain, and was used by Kochi to graze animals and by everyone to collect firewood. Lalmi was always a gamble, as it could be destroyed by either too much or too little rain, and so was seen as supplemental income. But the owner of a tractor could quickly plant huge amounts of lalmi on land owned by no one, making what had been the practice of subsistence farmers into the business of already rich men. The cultivation of lalmi required little labour until the harvest, and that could be accomplished by paying day labourers to do the work. Lalmi wheat became so lucrative that in some cases existing fields were turned over to it as well, expelling sharecroppers who were needed only for more labour-intensive crops.

The introduction of tractors into farming practice in the mid-1960s contributed to the loosening of social bonds between khans and their kinsmen and tenants. The social connection between landowners and sharecroppers became more of an economic one, based on a cash economy that had not existed before. Firewood that had been close at hand had to be gathered from much farther away, in some cases turning it into a commodity that now had to be purchased. While the old system was seen by groups such as the PDPA as feudal, every indication is that the change further lowered the standard of living of the rural poor, whose status as sharecroppers within a fixed community became that of day labourers eking out a marginal existence.

The marginalized rural poor provided a growing base of support for PDPA. The party was composed of two major factions, popularly known by the names of the publications each produced. Poor farmers favoured the Khalq (Masses) wing of the party, with its ideology of revolutionary change. The urban intelligentsia in the party tended to support the Parcham (Banner, or Flag) wing, which was focused on an evolutionary and parliamentary path to power. When the PDPA split formally in 1967, the fault lines matched the original mahfels from which the group was formed. The split also reflected the ambitions of Karmal, who led Parcham, and was not content to work under Taraki, whose leadership continued in Khalq.

By 1968, Kabul University was enrolling 5,445 new students every year, creating a large pool of young and enthusiastic men and women who were a fertile recruiting ground for the radical parties. And with every graduating year the university produced thousands of educated Afghans who had few economic opportunities available to them, and little hope of creating change. The radicals in parliament could not enact reforms, but their opposition left the government increasingly gridlocked. Maiwandal was forced to go overseas for major surgery and resigned, but his successor after a brief interim period, Mohammed Nur Ahmed Etemadi, had no greater luck working with parliament. The louder the opposition groups became, the less able the government was to govern.

Afghanistan was also opening up to the world, particularly through a massive increase in tourism. While in 1965 there were only 8,000 visitors, by 1969 this had climbed to over 63,000. The country sat along what was known as the "hippie trail" running from Amsterdam or London through Turkey, Iran, Afghanistan, Pakistan, and India to Kathmandu or beyond. Afghanistan became famous along this route for high-quality and easily acquired hashish. Special teahouses, called *saqikhana*, catered to hashish smokers, with dozens of varieties on offer. Domestic production of hashish had to expand in order to meet the new demand, which was a welcome source of income to struggling farmers.

As the fame of Afghanistan's hashish spread back to Europe and North America, traffickers began to organize shipments, for the first time linking Afghanistan to the international market for drugs. California's "Brotherhood of Eternal Love" (dubbed the "hippie mafia") hoped to start a psychedelic revolution in the United States by distributing drugs. It became the principal exporter of Afghan hashish, putting an even greater strain on supply. Whereas hashish had been an artisanal product up to this point, methods now changed to those of mass production, using fertilizer and tractors supplied by international donors and distributed by the Directorate of Economic Development. Opium production also increased. The Shah of Iran rescinded the opium ban in 1969, and the voracious appetite of that market consumed 100 tonnes of it a year, nearly all that Afghanistan could supply.

As was the case in the West, 1968 and 1969 were marred by massive student protests that shut down Kabul University for months. The Afghan students declared that their protests were in solidarity with those in Paris and Prague, a remarkable statement from what had long been an insular and inward-looking society. The impact of the ongoing failure to absorb the newly educated into the economy, beyond the minority who found jobs in government, was beginning to be felt. The students became particularly incensed when the results of new parliamentary elections in 1969 were revealed. The gains made by progressive parties and candidates in 1965 had been reversed. No women were elected at all, and only two candidates from the PDPA, one of whom was Hafizullah Amin, a Ghilzai Pashtun who had studied in the United States. Government interference helped ensure that the vast majority of new parliamentarians were conservative, and the largest bloc were Durrani Pashtuns from the amir's extended tribe. Violence continued at the university, with increasingly common clashes between leftist and Islamist students.

In 1970 extremist members of Jawanan-e Musalman shot at women on campus wearing short dresses, and sprayed others with acid. The backlash to these attacks was massive, with over five thousand women and girls organized by Sazman-e Demokratik-e Zanan-e Afghanistan demonstrating in Kabul to demand that the government find and punish the perpetrators. Mass arrests of Islamists followed, and those deemed responsible for the attacks were imprisoned. In later years these attacks were attributed to students directed by Gulbuddin Hekmatyar, then a student in the department of theology and a member of Jawanan-e Musalman. He was also accused of murdering a leftist student leader, Saidal Sukhandan, during clashes at the university in 1972. While there had been many years of tension and conflict over the role of women in society, it is perhaps only with the increasing freedom and equality on display that this conflict took on the form of direct attacks on women. Bacha Khan had been able to rely on the cultural hesitancy to use violence against women in his protests; it now appeared that this taboo was broken.

Further strain was put on the Afghan nation in the early 1970s, when one of the worst droughts to ever strike the country occurred. Nine of the 12 years from 1966 onward experienced less than average rainfall across much of the country, with no rain or snow at all in 1970 and 1971. Estimates suggest that as many as five hundred thousand people died during the famine in these years, and as many as a million were displaced into Iran. As much as 70 percent of the karakul sheep population died, nearly eradicating that industry altogether. The government worked hard to deny that there were food shortages, even as the price of wheat tripled. Ironically, in 1972 when the rains returned for a season, and there were bumper crops of wheat to be had, remote pockets of the population still starved. The country's inadequate infrastructure made it difficult for food to be distributed to where it was needed. Massive amounts of international aid were delivered to Afghanistan only to rot in government warehouses or be sold by corrupt officials.

When on July, 17, 1973, Radio Kabul announced that Afghanistan had become a republic, the country heaved a sigh of relief. Zahir Shah heard the news that he had been deposed while vacationing in Europe. Rather than mounting any resistance, he simply abdicated.

CHAPTER 10 AN AMIR BY ANY OTHER NAME

THE COUP was the work of only a few hundred soldiers, who met almost no resistance. With Zahir Shah out of the country, becoming a republic required little more than the radio announcement itself. This time no one was willing to stand up for the amir. His rule had left the country in economic distress, and he was thought to be spending too much time abroad rather than focusing on his duty to his country. Abdul Wali exerted a tremendous amount of influence in his absence, and was equally disliked.

The two military units that executed the coup were led by an air force pilot, Abdul Qadir, and an armour officer, Mohammed Aslam Watanjar. Both men were leaders of the Afghan Armies' Revolutionary Council (AARC), a pro-Soviet organization that operated independently from the PDPA and likely had between six and eight hundred members. The day after the coup, a second announcement was made: a "central committee" had named Daoud Khan as president. It was never revealed who the members of the central committee were, and it never publicly met again. It was likely a fig leaf for Daoud Khan who, himself a former general, had quietly built up relations with the AARC over the years since his ouster as prime minister.

Daoud Khan made it clear that the monarchy was to be abolished, and the 1964 constitution as well. The population of Kabul demonstrated in favour of the new republic, so relieved were they at the ouster of the corrupt and ineffective amir. Even the Pashtun tribes of the east and south, traditional kingmakers, accepted the dramatic change in government without any sign of concern.

This seems strange, given Afghan history, until one considers how dramatic a change the new regime represented. For traditionalists, the switch from monarchy to republic was significant, but the new president was a familiar leader, and was part of the Musahiban who had ruled since 1929, as well as part of the larger Mohammedzai who had ruled Afghanistan since 1826. Daoud Khan quickly established that his rule would be tightly controlled and direct, more akin to a monarchy than a constitutional government. In many ways his rule most resembled that of Amanullah: secular and progressive, but not democratic. His ascension represented only a small change, with the potential for more effective rule than that of the weak Zahir Shah.

Modernists and reformers also saw great potential in the new government. They had long advocated for an end to the monarchy, which was achieved almost painlessly. Daoud Khan was himself a modernist, and around him he gathered many young militants from within the ranks of Parcham. His connection to this wing of the PDPA was through its leader Karmal, who was the son of one of Daoud Khan's trusted generals, and who moved in the circle of confidants around him. Although Daoud Khan did not declare himself to be a leftist, judging by the company he kept he seemed to lean in that direction. For this reason French newspaper *Le Monde* nicknamed him the "Red Prince" soon after he took power. His seizure of power gave hope to the leftists in the capital, who might otherwise have balked at the coup, that the country was headed in the right direction.

Outside of the capital and major cities, the change in government was greeted with indifference. Aside from the spread of education, the government's reach was still limited. Attempts at wholesale change, such as the Helmand Valley irrigation projects, met with some success but did not threaten the power of the traditional leaders. Had Daoud Khan seemed inclined to attempt to centralize power in the country again, he might have provoked a reaction, but his early rule was so focused on simply maintaining power that little attention was paid to the countryside. The Pashtun tribes did not rise up against Daoud Khan in favour of the Pashtun monarchy in part because he was himself of royal Pashtun blood, but also because it did not impact their lives in any meaningful way. If anything, the coup reinforced the perception of Kabul as an alien capital, far removed from the concerns of most of the population.

But the fact that no opportunistic tribal leaders formed a lashkar to fight for Zahir Shah, even if motivated more by loot than idealism, was also rooted in the changes that had occurred within Afghan society since Nadir Shah took power. The balance of military strength had tipped decidedly against the tribes, who did not have the ability to stand against the modern aircraft and armoured vehicles of the Afghan Army. Changes in rural society had also loosened the bonds between tribal leaders and tribesmen, making it harder for an influential man to form a lashkar as well. The switch from sharecropping to wage labour also had an impact on the availability of men, with the working population who were surplus to local needs migrating either to the cities or to neighbouring countries.

The government of Zahir Shah was so weak at the end of his reign that Daoud Khan was not the only prominent Afghan who had been planning a coup. Abdul Wali was also planning to seize power from his father-in-law, using military units led by Pashtun officers from Paktia Province who were personally loyal to him. Former prime ministers Maiwandwal and Musa Shafiq were also allegedly plotting separate coups. Daoud Khan had them, and hundreds of others, arrested. Musa Shafiq and Abdul Wali were eventually released, but the remaining alleged coup leaders were executed. Maiwandwal died in prison. A final plotter, Habibur Rahman, was said to be supported by Pakistan, but he was arrested and sentenced to death by a military tribunal. These were the first executions of political prisoners since the rule of Nadir Shah, and they set the tone for Daoud Khan's new government.

A more serious threat to the republic was a planned coup that was discovered in December 1973. Initially, the Islamist students at the university held out hope that they could co-operate with Daoud Khan's government, as he was careful to always demonstrate respect for Islam. The ulema had lost influence during the reign of Zahir Shah, and its members felt that it might be possible to regain some of it. Daoud Khan, however, saw the religious student groups as the main threat to his plans for modernization, and did nothing to bring them into the circle of power. When they were discovered trying to recruit army officers, much as Parcham had done for many years, his reaction was swift. Mass arrests of Islamists followed, and five persons connected directly to the recruitment efforts were executed. Dozens of student organizers fled to Pakistan, including Rabbani, Massoud, and Hekmatyar.

In the new government's first announcement, Daoud Khan's priority became clear. He stated that he was certain, given "mutual goodwill," that Afghanistan and Pakistan could find a "peaceful and honourable" solution to the problem of Pashtunistan. He also said that he supported the "hopes and aspirations" of another oppressed group in Pakistan, the Baluchi. Their traditional homeland also straddled the Durand Line, although they had had little to do with the powers that ruled Afghanistan, and were resentful of Daoud Khan taking up their cause without consulting them. Given the dire situation in his own country, this seems like an absurd cause for him to champion, and although he may have wished to distract the population with an external issue that could unite them, there was little public enthusiasm for pursuing it, on either side of the border. His interest in Pashtunistan has the appearance of being a real obsession, pursued against his better judgment.

Although the Soviet Union supported the idea of Pashtunistan, no other country did besides India. In both cases, the support was tied to their own interests — weakening an American ally or weakening an arch-foe. Neither country provided tangible support. Militarily, Afghanistan was no match for Pakistan, which was now an even stronger military power than when Daoud Khan had pursued the issue as prime minister. He was forced to tread carefully in case he provoked a military reaction from Pakistan that would have spelled the end of his regime.

Daoud Khan promised robust, decisive leadership, in contrast to the situation under Zahir Shah. The Wolesi Jirga, or lower house, which he abolished, had been paralyzed in the last months of Zahir Shah's reign, unable to form a quorum for 82 consecutive sessions from March to June, and therefore unable to pass or debate any legislation. But Daoud Khan was also wracked with indecision, his focus almost entirely on the survival of his new government. The brutal tactics used by the police were effective at preventing organized resistance to his rule, but also created a cycle of resentment and revenge that led to new threats. These threats were not political but personal, like the one that felled Nadir Shah.

The early policies proposed by Daoud Khan were drawn directly from the platform of the PDPA, and the many Parchamis brought into his government were eager to implement them. But on the geo-political stage, Daoud Khan did not lean to the left, and tried to re-establish the balance that he built as prime minister. To do that, he sought better relations with the United States, to counter the influence of the Soviet Union that had grown dramatically since he first invited its aid in the mid-1950s. As his personal relationship with the American ambassador Theodore L. Eliot Jr. strengthened, Eliot became an influential figure in the capital. When Secretary of State Henry Kissinger visited Afghanistan in 1974, Daoud made it clear that he was no "Russian stooge," and that an American presence was welcome.

In many senses, though, the new regime was not that different from the old. Although Daoud had abolished the monarchy, he continued to pay his cousin Zahir Shah a stipend so that he could live in relative luxury in Rome. Zahir Shah's last prime minister, Musa Shafiq, was released from prison and brought back into cabinet. Many of the key jobs within the government that did not go to Parchamis were given to Musahiban relatives, with the key qualification being loyalty to the president. The difference was the inclusion of leftists for the first time, although members of Khalq remained shut out from power.

The new government's most urgent task was to improve the economy, still reeling from the effects of the recent drought. By the mid-1970s, the average per capita income was about $150 a month, which provided a bare subsistence level of living. Of an estimated population of 17 million, approximately 2.5 million were still thought to be living a nomadic lifestyle. Average life expectancy stood at 35 years, compared to an average of 50 years in neighbouring Pakistan. Although agricultural productivity had risen slightly in the previous 40 years, the total area under cultivation had begun to shrink by the 1970s due to mismanagement. The fertile plains of the country's north had actually supported a much larger population in the early 13th century, before they were depopulated by the Mongol invasions, than they were capable of supporting in the 1970s.

Afghanistan had received $1.3 billion in foreign aid from the Soviet Union since 1954, focused on three areas of development — the construction of infrastructure, large-scale irrigation projects, and the establishment of state-run industries. In each case, the work done had tended to reinforce the unequal division of wealth in Afghan society.

The efforts at building infrastructure, particularly roads, were successful in linking the major cities with Kabul and to the Soviet Union. But even after several decades of building, the road networks still bypassed many of the district centres and did not extend to the many villages where the country's population was concentrated. The roads themselves did not produce any economic growth. What profits were made from the road networks accrued among the traders and trucking companies, rather than building wealth among the rural population. Joint Afghan-donor committees often planned or approved such projects, allowing the bias of donors to sway the selection of objectives. Soviet-built roads, for example, did a much better job of connecting the major Afghan cities with the Soviet network than they did at creating intra-Afghan trade. By 1977 the Soviet Union was Afghanistan's principal customer for all types of exports, accounting for half of all export earnings.

State industries were almost uniformly unprofitable, and with no money set aside for ongoing maintenance or renewal of equipment, many had ground to a halt. Their influence on the wider economy had been limited in the first place, as two-thirds of the country's factories had been built in Kabul. The one industry that had proven successful was the natural gas field in Sheberghan. Despite sending all of its production by pipeline to the Soviet Union at rates below the international average price, it was one of the few sources of foreign exchange other than aid available to the government. By the mid-1970s, natural gas accounted for nearly 20 percent of all export profits, second only to fruits, nuts, and animal skins, which provided 36 percent.

Major irrigation projects had been implemented through American and Soviet funding, each with a different approach. The Helmand Valley Authority project had been intended to create a large new number of small landowners, and the government used this opportunity to resettle Kochi who were ready to give up nomadism. Although the original plan was for a hydroelectric generator to be installed in the Kajaki dam, this had to wait until 1975. The scale of the project was such that the Afghan government could not fund its continuance without American money, and after nearly 30 years this had dried up. Few Kochi were truly willing to remain on the land, even after issues with soil quality and salinity were addressed, and so development in the Helmand Valley ended.

The major Soviet project was the irrigation of 30,000 hectares around Jalalabad to form two huge state-run farms, employing nine thousand people. Despite the intention that it would provide economies of scale and allow for the use of modern agricultural equipment and techniques, the project was massively inefficient and operated at a perennial loss. The government felt forced to continue running it, however, as it was a crucial source of employment in the region. Unemployment in the mid-1970s was officially just over 20 percent, but it was almost certainly much higher. There continued to be large-scale migration throughout the country, both to the major cities and throughout the countryside, timed with the harvest seasons.

To spur growth in the agricultural sector, Daoud Khan chose to focus his economic efforts on land reform. This was also seen as a means to stave off the potential for a popular insurrection among the rural population. In 1974 he established the Land Reform Bureau to undertake the country's first complete land survey. This was to conclude in 1976 and drive land redistribution. Land ownership was to be capped at 20 hectares per person (40 for "unproductive" land), with the surplus purchased by the government on a deferred payment plan at 2 percent interest. The surplus land was then sold to landless peasants, who paid for it over a period of 25 years, also at 2 percent interest. This was meant to be a "zero-cost" initiative that would radically improve the lives of farmers.

An estimated 32,000 individuals received land through the bureau, but the system did not bring about the expected social improvements. Bureau staff were so badly paid that they accepted bribes to record holdings as smaller than they were. Large landholders registered their holdings under the names of relatives to stay within the limits, preventing the reform from functioning as planned. Even after it was completed, land continued to be held by a relatively small number of wealthy owners, and the vast majority of the rural population remained landless.

The only other major initiative discussed by the Daoud Khan regime was the idea of a railroad running from Kabul to Meshad in Iran. This was first suggested by the shah, at the urging of the United States, who wanted to provide an alternative to the growing trade with the Soviet Union. Meshad is Iran's second largest city, located in the northeast, and had formerly been a major stop on the Silk Road. Iran offered $2 billion in credit to implement the project, and although Daoud Khan agreed, work was never begun.

There were two areas of economic growth in the 1970s that did not benefit government coffers, but were also not new industries. Smuggling had been a mainstay of the Pashtun tribes along the Durand Line for many years, but it now morphed into a new form. An Afghan Transit Trade Agreement, originally signed in the 1950s, allowed for many goods destined for Afghanistan to be moved from the Pakistani port of Karachi to Afghanistan duty free. These goods could then be smuggled back into Pakistan and sold for a hefty profit, undercutting legally imported goods. The smuggled goods ranged from tea to household appliances. Pashtun smugglers had traded their camel caravans for large cargo trucks, some provided as aid by Germany, causing great distress to Pakistani traders.

The second growth area was the production of opium. In 10 years it had changed from a niche product to one that was grown in over half of Afghanistan's provinces. On lands irrigated by the Helmand Valley Authority project, the introduction of high-yield wheat allowed cash crops such as opium to be grown on surplus land. From an estimated 100 tonnes of opium produced in 1950, by the early 1970s Afghanistan was producing 250 tonnes a year. While hashish continued to be used internally but also smuggled to Western markets, Iran's voracious appetite for opium continued to consume nearly all of Afghanistan's production. Although both hashish and opium were technically illegal in Afghanistan, no efforts were made to enforce the laws. Daoud Khan's government would not take the chance of antagonizing farmers or lowering their standard of living, having only passed the law prohibiting narcotics to appease America in the first place.

Education remained a serious concern in Afghanistan, although Daoud Khan made little change to the policies of Zahir Shah. Widespread literacy remained elusive — by 1977 the rate across the country remained somewhere between 5 and 10 percent, and only 17 percent of eligible school-age children were enrolled. Of this small number of students, only 11 percent were girls, and these were still concentrated in the major towns and cities. Under Daoud Khan science, English, and psychology were added to the school curriculum by extending the program by two years. This meant that students required 14 years of study to acquire a high-school diploma, putting it even further out of reach of most students. While obtaining an education had over time come to be seen as a means to obtain a lucrative job or a position in government, causing many influential families to send at least one son through school, by the late 1970s this was no longer true. Approximately 70 percent of all high-school graduates at this time were unemployed, making the pursuit of education seem fruitless to many.

The policy of providing a salary and a standard curriculum to mullahs running local schools continued, but began to provoke a backlash in some areas. No training was given to the mullahs to enable them to teach the new subjects, making the changes to the curriculum largely ineffective. The new curriculum was widely seen as being too heavily influenced by leftists in government. Some schools withdrew from the program and returned to teaching a curriculum driven by Islam and the traditional panj kitab. Others tried to implement the changes, but were loathed by Islamists for teaching "communism."

Society as a whole remained split between urban and rural communities, even as the number of people living in urban areas surged to 14 percent of the population due to large numbers of migrant workers. Almost all of these were single men supporting families in their original homes, and in Kabul in particular many of these migrants were Hazaras who formed a large underclass in the capital. This had been true for over a century, but the number of Hazaras in Kabul had grown dramatically. About 40 percent of all urban dwellers worked for the state apparatus, either directly or indirectly, but most migrant workers were excluded from this part of the economy because of their lack of education.

Women were another group who were excluded from the workforce to varying degrees across the country, although their treatment varied widely. In Kabul women were relatively free to pursue education or work, and women dominated the teaching and nursing professions. In 1972 "Miss Afghanistan" was crowned for the first time in a televised pageant held in Kabul. Women in the capital were free to wear Western clothing.

In poor families in rural areas, women were also relatively free because their families could not afford to keep them cloistered. It was only when they achieved a certain level of income that families could afford for their women to be strictly isolated by purdah, either confined to their homes or allowed out wearing a burkha and accompanied by a *maharam*, or male relative who acts as an escort. The burkha was also common in towns other than the capital, where it was a middle-class affectation demonstrating both a degree of wealth and piety. Earlier initiatives to encourage women across the country to enter the workforce were undercut by the large labour surpluses in rural areas caused by the decline in sharecropping. This limited opportunities for women to work outside the home if they were not well educated and able to secure a position ahead of the masses of uneducated men.

An area where women achieved a level of equality was within the PDPA, where ideologically women were seen as peers. One of the founding members of the PDPA was Anahita Ratebzad, who was elected to parliament in 1965. Her father was the nephew of Mahmud Tarzi, making her a cousin of Queen Soraya. Ratebzad studied to become a nurse in Chicago, and then attended medical school at Kabul University, becoming the first female doctor in Afghanistan. Within the PDPA she was part of the Parcham wing, and was known to be Babrak Karmal's lover.

Although Ratebzad came from the elite echelon of Afghan society, and from a notable reformist family as well, she was part of a growing number of Afghan women who embraced a more modern lifestyle. Unlike during the period of Amanullah's reforms, which were driven from the top down, there was now a nucleus of women advocating and acting for themselves. This activism still did not extend outside of the capital, but it was a growing force.

While Daoud Khan's liberal attitudes to women did not cause uprisings as in Amanullah's day, he was forced to contend with a number of challenges to his rule. The Islamist students who fled to Pakistan in 1973 received a warm welcome there from the Bhutto government. Frustrated by Afghan policy on Pashtunistan and support for Pashtun and Baluchi rebels, the Pakistani government began to train Afghan dissidents. Hekmatyar and Massoud were two of the notable members in the first three-month course run by the Inter-Services Intelligence Directorate (ISI) for commanders. In total, five thousand Afghans were trained under this program. In July 1975 these Islamists were armed and sent back into Afghanistan to attempt to start a popular uprising that would lead to the overthrow of the Afghan government. Much of the fighting occurred in the Panjshir Valley, located in Parwan Province to the north of Kabul.

The attempted uprising failed miserably, and hundreds of students and religious leaders were arrested and executed. The survivors retreated back to Pakistan, where they soon engaged in bitter infighting. The group split into two parties with a bitter hatred for each other. The first, Jamiat-e Islami (Islamic Society), was composed of the Afghan-educated, Persian-speaking members, many of whom came from the country's north. This group was led by Rabbani and Massoud, and argued for a broad-based coalition within Afghanistan that included liberal Muslims. The second group was a splinter of Jamiat known as Hezb-e Islami Afghanistan (Afghanistan Islamic Party), and was more radical. Led by Hekmatyar, it was largely Pashto-speaking and drew mainly from students who had studied outside of the theology department. His organization was highly disciplined and tightly run. Pakistani interest in either group waned as the two directed their efforts toward fighting each other.

A second threat emerged in August 1975, when militants began attacking police and army posts in Badakhshan. The attacks were conducted by a group named Settam-e Melli (National Oppression), formed in 1966 by Taher Badakhshi, a breakaway member of the original PDPA Central Committee. He saw the PDPA as too dominated by Pashtuns, and so denounced both the Khalq and Parchami factions. Seeing the logical conclusion to an analysis of the country's problems as a peasant uprising against the Mohammedzai regime, his party followed a Maoist ideological line. Settam-e Melli militants had received training in Pakistan, much as the Islamists had, and had begun their series of attacks at the urging of the Pakistani government.

Even though the attacks were conducted in a remote part of the country and led by someone with local knowledge, they were not successful. Within weeks the majority of the group's members had been captured by the army; many were executed without trial. Badakhshi himself managed to escape, and the remnants of the group went into hiding.

Although these uprisings did not pose the existential threat to the government that past risings had done, Daoud Khan sought a new understanding with Pakistan to reduce tensions. He made his first move in the United Nations General Assembly, asking Pakistan not to delay at resolving its human rights issues for Pashtuns and Baluchi. This was not a success. He also shut down the section of the border that was used by Baluchi rebels fighting the Pakistani government, denying them easy access to sanctuary in Afghanistan. In 1976 Daoud Khan visited President Bhutto in Islamabad. Their talks did not produce an agreement. Daoud Khan did not seem to realize that there was no "resolution" of the issue that would be acceptable to Pakistan.

At the same time he was also working hard to neutralize internal threats. As early as 1974 he began to distance himself from the PDPA and the army officers in the AARC, both of whom were responsible for putting him into power. That year he made a stridently nationalistic speech at Kabul Polytechnic Institute, where he said, "We have no connection with any group, and linking us to any group or movement is a sin." And although it was not included in the official transcript of the speech, he also allegedly threatened radical leftists with castration.

He began to slowly purge leftists from his cabinet, in some cases sending them abroad as ambassadors, in others giving them lesser jobs in remote parts of the country. In every case, he concealed his political motives, whether it was a promotion or a demotion. In their place, he put members of his family or other cronies from the old Kabul elite.

His approach to the military was the same. Abdul Qadir, a central figure in Daoud Khan's seizure of power, was removed from command after a public spat with him and put in charge of a military abattoir. He also arranged for fewer officers to be trained in the Soviet Union, sending them to India or Egypt instead. Along with this came a reduction in the number of Soviet advisers, from one thousand in 1972 to only two hundred in 1976, none of these employed within the lower echelons of the army. Over 80 percent of the army's officers, and many of its career soldiers, were Pashtun, and Daoud Khan worked to gain their loyalty by promulgating the idea that he was the "father of the modern army."

In 1975 he formed his own political faction, the National Revolutionary Party, and banned all others, including the PDPA, although he took no action against them. Parcham's policy had been to work with Daoud Khan under the assumption that eventually it would take power. His early implementation of socialist policies drawn from its own platform had been heartening, but the purge of members from key posts and then the party ban had dashed Parcham's hopes. It was this kind of pragmatism and willingness to work with non-socialists that had earned Parcham the derisive nickname "the Royal Communist Party." Khalq, lacking the social access that allowed this kind of alliance, was seemingly proved right.

Although the party ban led to discussions of the possibility of the two factions merging again, nothing concrete was done until 1977. Finally, at the urging of the Soviets, the two groups held a unification conference at which they named a new 30-person central committee, with the members drawn equally from the two groups. Taraki became general secretary again, and Karmal his deputy — the same positions they had occupied before the split. There remained a tremendous amount of distrust between the groups, highlighted by the fact that they both continued to recruit military officers to their cause separately. Khalqi military officers practised the execution of a coup, ready to strike if Taraki was arrested or Daoud Khan otherwise moved against the party.

That same year, Daoud Khan called a loya jirga to approve a new constitution, 15 percent of which were women, higher than any previous jirga. The assembly members were handpicked by him and his loyalists. Although still a Pashtun concept, the jirga had slowly changed through its use by Afghan rulers seeking a stamp of legitimacy. Far from its origins as an egalitarian domain for men, now it was at the same time more representative in terms of genders and ethnicities, and less in terms of the real interests of the people represented.

The new constitution instituted a single-party system for the country. It named Daoud Khan president for a term of six years, after which elections would be held. The powers vested in the amir in the 1964 constitution were transferred to the president, who also absorbed the powers and responsibilities of the prime minister, the foreign minister, and the minister of defence, as well as oversight of the judiciary. Islam was again affirmed as the religion of the state, although only in a general sense, without reference to the Hanafi school of law that had previously been dominant. It also codified gender equality more clearly than before, stating: "The entire people of Afghanistan, both men and women without discrimination and privileges, have equal rights and obligations before the law." The two houses of government under the 1964 constitution were to be replaced by a single elected chamber called the Melli Jirga (National Assembly).

Daoud Khan also sought to modernize the legal system, using legislation modelled on that of Egypt. It blended shari'a law with secular law, using the religious strictures for matters of family and inheritance, and a secular code for all other matters. Customary law, which was the most common type of regulation in use throughout the country even at this date, was not given any place in the new civil code. Yet the continuing importance of customary law can be seen in the fact that Daoud Khan sought legitimacy through the use of the jirga, a key component of customary law.

Apparently secure in his position, the next month he announced a new cabinet that omitted all its leftist members except one, who was an old friend. Some of the cabinet were even avowed anti-communists, creating concern for the PDPA. When Daoud Khan visited Moscow in April 1977, he had an angry confrontation with Leonid Brezhnev, the Communist Party's General Secretary. Brezhnev demanded that Daoud Khan eject all Western advisers, who from a Soviet perspective were little more than spies. Daoud Khan refused, telling Brezhnev, "We will never allow you to dictate to us how to run our country and whom to employ in Afghanistan," before storming out.

Daoud Khan was becoming increasingly dictatorial, as well increasingly paranoid. His police were quick to arrest anyone suspected of disloyalty, and their brutality was legendary. Not since the days of the Iron Amir had an Afghan ruler governed with such a heavy hand. He was also careful to keep a tight grip on the reins of power. By 1978 even cabinet ministers required his approval for expenditures over $150.

Against Moscow's wishes, the PDPA began to plan an uprising to overthrow Daoud Khan. The Soviets were worried that if it failed, it would give Daoud Khan the excuse he needed to brutally repress all known members of the party, much as had happened with the Islamists.

In contrast, the PDPA feared that repression would come eventually, whether it first stuck at the government or not.

On April, 17, 1978, a prominent leader within Parcham, Mir Akbar Khyber, was murdered in his home by two unknown assailants. Although Karmal was Parcham's leader, Khyber was its ideologue and key organizer. The PDPA accused the government of the murder. Khyber's funeral was attended by fifteen thousand people. This was a crowd of unprecedented size. Both Taraki and Karmal made speeches, blaming imperialists and Daoud Khan for the murder, and calling for his overthrow. The funeral procession ended outside the United States Embassy, laying blame for the murder at the Americans' doorstep. Daoud Khan reviewed police tapes of the speeches and then ordered the arrest of all the PDPA leaders.

Police arrested Taraki and four other key PDPA leaders shortly after midnight on April 26. By some accounts, the arrest of Taraki's protege Hafizullah Amin was delayed long enough to allow him to pass instructions to loyal military officers in the headquarters of the Afghan Air Force. Soon after, Amin was taken to prison with the other leaders, to await his fate.

CHAPTER 11 BLOODY APRIL

ALTHOUGH THE EVENT is known as the Great Saur (April) Revolution, this name reflects the PDPA's desire to put a popular gloss on what was a bloody coup. Even the idea that Amin passed on instructions to initiate the coup may be a falsehood added afterward to ensure that the PDPA were seen to be the ones behind it. Abdul Qadir and Watanjar were still the most prominent leftists within the armed forces and may have been acting in their own self-interest in executing the coup so quickly on the heels of the arrest of the PDPA leaders. Their connections to Taraki, Amin, Karmal, and others might quickly be beaten out of the arrested men.

On April 27 Watanjar led 60 tanks from the 4th Armoured Brigade, stationed just east of the capital at Pol-e Charki, in an attack on the Arg. Defended by the nearly two-thousand-strong Republican Guard, Daoud was inside holding a cabinet meeting to discuss the fate of those arrested. Fighting around the Arg continued throughout the day. Late in the afternoon, Abdul Qadir ordered jets from Bagram to bomb the Arg. It fell to Watanjar a few hours later. The military captured Radio Kabul around the same time, announcing that evening that the "power of the state rests fully with the Revolutionary Council of the Armed Forces," an organization that was previously unheard of. The spokesperson also said that the new government was in favour of the "preservation of the principles of the sacred teachings of Islam, the establishment of democracy, the freedom and security of the individual, and a foreign policy of positive active neutrality." There was no mention at all of any civilian leadership, or of the PDPA. In order to ensure that calm was maintained, the army also arrested four thousand Daoud loyalists.

Daoud Khan, the cabinet ministers, and their families were executed. Daoud Khan allegedly went down fighting, firing his pistol at the soldiers who entered the Arg to arrest him. In all, 73 people were killed during the coup. The city, and the country, remained calm throughout. No loyal elements of the army rose to defend Daoud Khan, nor did his tribe rise up against the plotters. This is a mark of both Daoud Khan's unpopularity and the irrelevance of the central government to most Afghans.

Once in control, the military released the PDPA leaders, along with ten thousand other political prisoners. For two days, Radio Kabul continued to repeat the message that the Revolutionary Council of the Armed Forces was in "complete control." It is unclear what unfolded in the back rooms of power over that time, but on April 29 the message changed. A new Revolutionary Council, not of the armed forces but formed of civilians, announced that Taraki had been elected president. In a speech just over a week later, Taraki spoke of overthrowing the regime put in place by Nadir Shah, equating Daoud's rule with that of his uncle and cousin. Taraki also made it clear that the country would belong to the "socialist camp" led by the Soviet Union. All formal authority would be retained by the state, as represented by the PDPA, with no role for the other traditional poles of power at all — the ulema and the traditional leaders.

The leading policy of the new government was land reform, including the creation of peasant collectives, but Taraki also announced the nationalization of industry and other measures meant to enforce the equality of all. Messes in the armed forces were combined, forcing officers and men to eat together. Similarly, government canteens would no longer have separate facilities for senior and junior bureaucrats. He also announced a long-overdue census, finally giving the government the data it would need to better control voting, collect taxes, and make economic plans. Taraki's policies intended to swing the balance of power decisively in favour of the state, leaving the ulema and traditional leaders out of the new structure entirely.

Taraki also moved to purge the ranks of the PDPA. Just six weeks after taking power, he arrested key Parchami leaders. Five Parchamis originally included in Taraki's cabinet were removed and sent abroad as ambassadors in a sort of semi-offical exile. Karmal fled. Many others were not so lucky. Two thousand Parchamis were arrested, and perhaps five hundred executed. When Karmal and the others in exile were later accused of plotting against Taraki and ordered to return to Afghanistan to face trial, they refused. Karmal went into hiding in Eastern Europe.

The government's first efforts were directed at combatting the economic stagnation of the past decade. There were no major private enterprises still functioning that could be nationalized, so the government seized medium and small ones instead, such as privately owned hotels, food-processing plants, and even handicraft workshops. None of these industries could provide the engine of the economy that the Taraki regime required, which it rightly assessed would come from agriculture.

Land reform had been a policy of previous governments, but none had implemented it successfully. This was in part due to the ineffectiveness of the government bureaucracy, the ability of large landowners (which included the Musahiban themselves) to circumvent the policy, and also the recognition that if it were ever implemented it would provoke an uprising. The PDPA government made the most credible attempt at implementing it, perhaps blinded to the consequences by ideology. The *Kabul Times* described the land reform decree as a "chain-breaking" law that struck a "stunning blow to feudalism." As with past attempts, the maximum individual holding was to be between one and five hectares per family, depending on the quality of the land. Party loyalty became a factor in the redistribution, and in many cases the government was forced to deploy police, the Sarandoy gendarmes, or the army to implement it.

What the policy ignored was that wiping out the large landholders affected the functioning of smaller farms as well. In addition to sustaining the sharecropping sector, the large landholders provided credit to buy seeds and handled the movement of crops to market for independent farmers. The government created an agricultural bank to provide credit, but its reach did not extend to remote areas, and it lacked funding.

A concurrent government policy wiped out all private loans and mortgages, without compensation to the lender. This was intended to break the "feudal bonds" that dominated the countryside, but instead it broke the system entirely. Given that business was conducted largely within extended families, it was wrong to think of the debt structures as exploitive, as at their best they could be seen as a form of joint venture between traditional leaders and their tribesmen. Credit given for seed was often repaid with a percentage of the resulting crops in a system known as *salaam*, which tied the interests of both parties to the harvest.

Taraki's policies were based on communist ideology, rather than on an attempt to co-opt the existing sources of political power in the country. He intended to establish the "correct" relationship between the "capitalist class" (composed of landowners and khans) and the "proletariat" (mostly landless sharecroppers). The unpopularity of this policy among the very people who were intended to benefit from it surprised the PDPA leadership. In essence, farmers were unwilling to trade their local leaders — khans or zamindars who were often kin of some sort, and also close by and understandable — for a distant, godless, and alien government with foreign ideas.

The very idea of class struggle made no sense to the egalitarian Pashtun. Although this policy would break the power base of the Durrani tribal leadership that had ruled Afghanistan for centuries, it required the rank and file of the Durranis to acquiesce, which by and large they did not. The effect of the land reform was mostly chaos. Agrarian production quickly dropped by 10 percent from an already very low degree of productivity, and within a year nearly 33 percent of arable land could not be cultivated due to growing armed conflict. The initiative also eroded the legitimacy of the state in the eyes of many Afghans, as the way the reform was implemented made it look simply like theft.

PDPA rule also saw a greatly increased role for women in Afghan society, largely again for ideological reasons, but also as a means of unlocking their economic potential. In October 1978 the government issued Decree Number 7, which explicitly gave equal rights to men and women, set the minimum age for marriage at 18 years for men and 16 years for women, and reduced what could be paid as a "bride price." The decree also paved the way for the creation of *mahakim-e famili* (family courts) to preside over family disputes, a system often run by female judges and similar in practice to that set up by Queen Soraya. The slogan promoting the decree said that it would "free the toiling women of Afghanistan from humiliating feudalistic relations and provide opportunities for their progress at all levels."

Seen as radical, these reforms had mixed results, even as they were enforced only in the towns and cities. By the middle of the decade, women were well integrated into many professions: 70 percent of all teachers, 50 percent of civil servants, and 40 percent of the doctors in Kabul were women. The Afghan Army got its first female paratrooper, Khatol Mohammadzai, in 1984 — she later became an army general in the post-Taliban era. The army also appointed its first female general, Sohaila Sediq, a Soviet-trained military doctor. In 1978 only 5,000 women had formal employment in the entire country, but by 1986 this had risen to 270,000, including 13,000 women in the military.

In 1982 a group of 10 Afghan women, drawn from the Democratic Women's Organization of Afghanistan and other government-sponsored organizations, were sent to Moscow to attend a conference on the status of women. Titled "Paths and Methods for Work Among Women in the First Years Following a Revolution," the conference brought together women from across the Soviet sphere of influence. Although these women were drawn from a particular segment of society and so did not represent the opinions of all Afghan women, their commentary is still revealing. While using the language of socialism, and advocating for greater freedoms, they did not share the concerns of other participants with the oppression "inherent" in Islam. They were much more concerned with the exclusion of women from public life due to extreme interpretations of purdah than with the practice of wearing the veil. In their conception of freedom, women can have an education and a job, even fight for the revolution, all while being Muslims and wearing a burkha. For many, loyalty to their family and to a moderate version of Islam outweighed the lure of "liberation." Their point of view was both practical and rooted in Afghan culture.

But the majority of Afghan women, living in rural areas, were untouched by these reforms. With few opportunities for work or education in rural areas even for men, there was little for women to strive for while still remaining near their families. Meanwhile, the changes to the law governing the "bride price" challenged the structure of families and in some ways diminished the status of women. In Afghanistan, "bride price" often refers to two different payments. The first, called a *walwar* (in Pashto) or *toyana* or *sherbaha* (in Dari), is paid by the family of the groom to the family of the bride, in recompense for its economic loss. This is an Afghan custom with no basis in shari'a, but it forms a major source of income for some families, as the sums demanded for a woman could be enormous.

Decree Number 7 set the walwar at 300 afghanis, which many saw as tremendously disrespectful to women, as it was less than many farmers would demand for an animal. The decree was also problematic in the sense that marriages were often used to cement relations or settle disputes between families, clans, or tribes. Under the new law, what had been a transaction between two groups become more the private decision of two individuals. Not only was this seen as an affront to traditional practice, it removed a culturally significant means of conflict resolution at a time when conflict was on the rise.

The second part of the bride price is the *mahr*, which does have a basis in shari'a and is paid from the groom directly to the bride herself. This money is for her own use, particularly should she become widowed or divorced, and it is greatly looked down upon should the groom or his family interfere with her use of this money. The new decree also set a low limit on what could be paid as mahr, which was seen as a *reduction* in the rights of women. In some regions, government officials began to coerce families to marry their daughters to them for what was seen as a nominal amount of money. As had happened before, the imposition of the state upon the affairs of families provoked a negative reaction.

The implementation of all of these policies after the coup created a groundswell of resistance across the country that had not been provoked by the coup itself. Unlike previous administrations, whose reforms were limited to the capital, Taraki and the PDPA made a genuine attempt to implement their reforms countrywide. Little was recorded about these spontaneous and uncoordinated uprisings, but they seem to have followed a pattern similar to that in the Pech Valley in Kunar Province. There a local jirga was called in response to the announcement of the redistribution of land to be implemented by officials seen to be corrupt, as well as the perception that the PDPA was disrespectful of Islam. This group went from village to village down the length of the valley, at each stop discussing the problem and persuading the local elders to pledge their support. In this case, that meant providing men for a lashkar, which grew with every village the jirga passed through.

The lashkar approached each successive village after the visit of the jirga, or otherwise the band of armed men would be seen as aggressors. This "rolling jirga" built up enough strength to attack pro-PDPA villages near the mouth of the valley (who likely benefitted most from the construction of roads, irrigation channels, and government schools), and even forced government officials and police to retreat. When the army counterattacked, many people from the rebellious villages were killed, both in combat and in reprisals, and villages were subjected to artillery bombardment. This set off a spiral of revenge in the Pech Valley that quickly consumed much of the country.

One of the earliest and most successful centres of resistance was the Hazarajat. All of the government officials in the region were killed or expelled, and replaced with a local administration called the Shura-e Inqelab-e Ittefaq-e Islam-e Afghanistan (Revolutionary Council of Islamic Unity of Afghanistan). Led by a religious figure, Sayyed Ali Behest, it created a parallel government, complete with schools and clinics, and even regulated working hours.

The early resistance in Helmand Province was also driven in large part by the planned land redistribution, even though the southern part of this province was the only area in southern Afghanistan where the communists were successful at recruiting party members and supporters. When the Helmand Valley Authority project was undertaken, new recipients of land all received six hectares, which was also the limit for individual holdings under the new scheme. They were settled into villages with no regard for the tribe from which they originated, creating mixed groups of Pashtuns not seen elsewhere. These two factors meant that their ownership of land was unaffected by the new policy, and they did not have traditional leaders to rally them against the government. In the remainder of the province were some of the largest estates in the country, often over 250 hectares, many granted to loyal followers by Nadir Shah, or by Ahmad Shah two centuries before when Pashtun hegemony was established. In these areas, resistance was fierce.

Land redistribution was implemented without careful consideration of its impact. In Helmand, the planned subdivision of land did not take into account access to water, which meant that the recipients of barren land were forced to either accept that their land was worthless or fight their neighbours over water rights. Land that was previously regarded as communal was not recognized as such, and was divided up among new owners, a further affront to tradition that eliminated common grazing land and the local source of firewood. The government set up Revolutionary Defence Committees at the provincial and district levels, and gave them responsibility for managing the land distribution and other policies. Dominated in Helmand by Khalqis, these committees favoured party members and their own families in their decisions, creating conflict with others that was not truly ideological, but based on old divisions of clan and tribe.

In order to implement its policy, the Revolutionary Defence Committee in Helmand had to rely upon force, using the local police and the *depaye khudai* militia. The depaye had been formed under Zahir Shah by arming high-school students under the leadership of their head teachers, and placing them at the disposal of the chief of police. Opponents of the reforms were accused of belonging to the Muslim Brotherhood and placed under arrest. Those arrested tended to be men of influence — khans, mullahs, or other traditional leaders, as well as rival Parchamis. In at least one instance, one hundred of these prisoners were thrown from an airplane into the Arghandab reservoir, starting a chain of revenge killings, and even pre-emptive murders, that were not based on ideology but on a struggle for political power and self-protection. Many villages, led by their khans, began to form self-defence militias to protect themselves from the government.

In January 1979 the district governor of Musa Qala, Zabit Aulleah (a Noorzai), and 300 depaye were preparing to supervise land distribution, when they were ambushed by a tribal leader named Nasim Akhundzada (from the Alizai or Hassanzai tribe). He drove the governor back into the *hukomat* (government offices) in Musa Qala, killing the head teacher and a hundred depaye —all local high-school students — where he besieged the survivors. Zabit Aulleah managed to negotiate his own escape, but 160 more depaye and government workers were slaughtered.

Nasim proclaimed himself the district governor, until an army detachment forced him out three days later. It installed as the new governor a Pashtun from eastern Afghanistan. But as soon as the army withdrew, Nasim attacked again and retook the hukomat. He executed 30 elders from his own tribe whom he accused of collaborating with the government, and buried them in a village square.

While Nasim's actions were driven by a desire for power rather than ideology, labelling his opponents as godless, alien interlopers into tribal affairs made a convincing narrative that influenced others to follow him. Coupled with the traditional means of persuasion used by the khans — the spending of physical capital to accrue social capital — he built a strong following. The fighting in Helmand continued for more than a decade, with the HAVA canal zone being largely pro-government and other areas opposed. Most of the fighting, however, was between opposition groups as they jockeyed for power in the province's hinterland.

A second motive driving the resistance groups that sprang up in the 1970s was simply filling a power vacuum left by the government. At the same time as unpopular policies were being created that required the coercive powers of government to implement, the military was weakened by other reforms.

The PDPA took steps immediately after the coup to purge the officer corps, removing perceived royalists and, later, Parchamis. Even though Khalq party members outnumbered Parchamis within the officer corps by four to one, these purges reduced the army's leadership from eight thousand officers to four thousand. Of approximately 80 generals, only one was retained. The Republican Guard was dissolved entirely, despite being one of the most effective units in the army. Perhaps as much as 40 percent of the army's enlisted strength deserted in the aftermath of the coup, unwilling to serve an openly communist government. The air force shrank by 50 percent owing to purges and desertions, and was grounded for many months due to concerns over its loyalty.

Even though the military relied on conscription to fill its ranks, it needed to find new methods to maintain its strength. The draftees' service was extended from three to four years. Press gangs roaming the capital and the countryside sometimes sparked a violent response from local militias. Deserters were offered an amnesty if they turned themselves in, rather than facing jail (or worse) if they were caught. Standards, already low, were lowered further, with the result that many soldiers and officers were functionally illiterate. Students in the 10th grade who volunteered to serve were awarded their 12th-grade diplomas upon finishing their service, despite not taking any further schooling. Volunteers in the 11th grade were admitted to the university or college of their choice, bypassing the rigorous competitive entrance exams. None of these approaches garnered many recruits, though by the early 1980s so many young men had either been conscripted or gone into hiding that there were almost no male students in the colleges and universities at all.

The army in 1978 was also not prepared to respond to the armed revolts that sprang up across the country. It was deployed in a wide arc stretching from Jalalabad in the east to Kandahar in the south, ready to repel an attack from Pakistan. There were no units or facilities to support it north of the Hindu Kush, as there had never been a reason to maintain troops there. This changed with the eruption of fighting all across the country, forcing units to scramble from their home stations into unfamiliar territory.

Outside the country the resistance was slowly organizing. Soon after the coup a number of groups announced themselves in Peshawar and Tehran, each attached to a charismatic leader rather than representing a part of the country or an ideology. In Peshawar the major parties formed the National Rescue Front in June 1978 to jointly resist the PDPA government. Together these parties claimed the allegiance of one hundred members of Daoud Khan's last parliament, creating a sense of continuity with the previous regime even though many of the Islamists within the Front had been persecuted by him. But at this point, thinking that the government would quickly fall, each of the constituent parties saw itself as a government-in-waiting. Because of this, none wanted to cede leadership to another. The Front collapsed after only six weeks.

The Pakistani authorities, who had been supporting Afghan opposition parties since 1975, tried to assemble another coalition in September 1978. Their focus was on working with parties and leaders they already knew well. The first of these was Jamiat-e Islami (the Islamic Society), led by Burhanuddin Rabbani, a Tajik religious scholar who had studied at Al-Azhar University in Cairo and was later a lecturer at Kabul University.

Rabbani had been heavily influenced by his contact with the Muslim Brotherhood in Egypt, but he sought to impose a relatively moderate theocracy in Afghanistan that was in keeping with its Sufi traditions.

The other prominent party supported by Pakistan was Hezb-e Islami (Party of Islam). It was perhaps the best organized party, with a hierarchical structure that placed the leader, Gulbuddin Hekmatyar, firmly in control. Arrested for murder under Daoud Khan's government, he had fled into exile in Peshawar years before the PDPA coup, and had broken with Rabbani's party when he saw that it was too moderate. Hekmatyar was an astute political operator but was personally disliked by many of the other groups' leaders.

Hizb-e Islami and Jamiat-e Islami agreed to together form a new organization, led by a neutral figure with no faction of his own, Mohammed Nabi Mohammadi. Mohammadi was a famous Islamic scholar and member of parliament who had preached against communism. Before long Hekmatyar and Rabbani left the coalition to resume the leadership of their own parties independently. The remainder of the group split further, with Mohammadi retaining control over his own party, Harakat-e Inqila-e Islami (the Islamic Revolutionary Movement), Sibghatullah Mojaddedi founding the Jebh-e Nejat-e Melli (the National Liberation Front), and Pir Sayyed Ahmad Gailani founding Mahaz-e Melli Islami (the National Islamic Front [of Afghanistan]). Hekmatyar's group also splintered, with a significant number of members choosing to follow Mohammed Yunus Khalis instead. His party was also named Hezb-e Islami. Confusing even for contemporaries, Hekmatyar's and Khalis's organizations were typically referred to as Hezb-e Islami Gulbuddin (HIG) and Hezb-e Islami Khalis (or simply Hezb-e Khalis) respectively.

HIG and Jamiat-e Islami were the largest of the six main parties; the third largest was Mahaz-e Melli Islami, described as traditionalist, moderate, or royalist. Its leader Gailani was a member of a prominent Sufi family who traced his ancestry back to the Prophet Mohammed, and supported the restoration of the monarchy as a means to create national unity. This put him at odds with the Islamist parties, who refused to allow Zahir Shah any influence in the resistance. Although formerly the owner of a car dealership in Kabul and not a religious or military leader, Gailani used his personal networks as a Sufi pir to expand his party.

While all the parties based in Peshawar espoused Sunni Islam (and all except Jamiat-e Islami were led by Ghilzai Pashtuns), the parties based in Iran were entirely Shi'ite and Hazara-led. Their influence in the conflict with the PDPA government was limited to the Hazarajat. They were backed exclusively by the Iranian government, which hoped to support their co-religionists even though Iranian national interest was more focused on the area around the Tajik-dominated city of Herat.

The Peshawar parties supported by Pakistan also began to receive aid from Saudi Arabia. The Carter administration in the United States took an interest in the resistance groups as well, and in early 1979 sent a special envoy to Peshawar. This led to a commitment to provide non-lethal equipment, primarily communications gear and medical supplies, to aid them in their struggle against the communist government, although at this point none of the parties was undertaking significant operations inside Afghanistan.

The U.S. decision to support the opposition groups followed an incident that had taken place in Kabul. The newly appointed ambassador Adolph "Spike" Dubs was abducted on February 14, 1979, with the kidnappers demanding the release of political prisoners in exchange for his freedom. The group responsible, Settam-e Melli, were Maoists from Badakhshan who had split from the PDPA on ideological lines. Although the events were not coordinated, this was the same morning that the U.S. Embassy in Tehran was attacked for the first time, in what became known as the "Valentine's Day Open House." Dubs was quickly located by authorities but was killed during the rescue operation. The death of the ambassador poisoned relations with the United States, which promptly cut development aid, leaving the Soviet Union and its satellites as Afghanistan's sole international sponsors.

While resistance to the government continued sporadically throughout the country, the towns and cities remained firmly under government control. In March 1979 this changed for the worse. Government officials in the western city of Herat had dealt with the local population in a brutal manner. A popular uprising began on March 15, either instigated or quickly joined by soldiers of the 17th Division. Khalqis were hunted down by vigilantes and killed. The chaos lasted for five days before troops from Kandahar arrived to restore order. It is likely that between three and five thousand people were killed, including up to one hundred Soviet advisers and their families. This was followed by further army mutinies in Jalalabad in April and May, and then in Kabul in June and August. In each case loyal units were found to quell the uprisings, but the situation was clearly worsening.

The policies put in place by the Taraki government were alienating a large part of the population and requiring increasing levels of violence to enforce. The prime minister, Hafizullah Amin, had come to play an increasing role in suppressing the growing discontent, in part because he had built close ties with military leaders while recruiting them for Khalq during Daoud Khan's presidency. Amin was a teacher with a graduate degree in Education from Columbia University, though he left the United States in disgrace after receiving a failing grade for his doctoral dissertation. Although he had been close to Taraki before the PDPA came to power, his bitterness toward Parchamis and his encouragement of a brutal response to unrest in the countryside caused Taraki to lose confidence in him.

Amin manipulated Taraki into attending a conference in Cuba, and while he was away, took control of the government. At the same time Amin accused four senior PDPA members loyal to Taraki of plotting a coup. On Taraki's return, he tried to convince the president to purge the men he referred to as the "Gang of Four." Instead Taraki advised them to go into hiding. They took shelter in the Soviet embassy in Kabul, and were later smuggled out of the country. Amin had also arranged for an anti-aircraft unit to shoot down Taraki's plane as it returned from abroad, but the plot was detected and the unit disarmed. In spite of these things, Taraki continued to try to placate Amin and accommodate him within the government.

On September 14 Amin arrived at the Arg to meet with Taraki and four Soviet representatives. A shootout erupted between Amin's and Taraki's bodyguards, which Amin interpreted as a bungled assassination attempt. He retreated to his office and ordered the air force to bomb the Arg, but the order was refused. The following day Amin called a meeting of the Central Committee and announced that Taraki had been deposed. Before the meeting was over, the army surrounded the Arg and arrested Taraki. That evening Kabul Television announced that the president had informed the Politburo that he would stand down due to illness. In his stead, Hafizullah Amin was appointed as the new president.

CHAPTER 12 A GODLESS AND ALIEN REGIME

AMIN'S RULE DIFFERED little from that of Taraki, though there was now no barrier to his use of military force to pursue the government's policies. It was announced on October 9 that Taraki had died after a "long illness," but later evidence suggests that he was smothered with a pillow in his prison cell on the order of Amin. Despite the obvious signs of Amin's violent takeover, there was no reaction other than whispers within the ruling party.

Although the PDPA officially welcomed all ethnicities, its leadership was dominated by Pashtuns, and it was seen by others as a Pashtun organization. Both Taraki and Amin were Pashtun, but more importantly they made all public speeches in Pashto and were the latest in a long line of Pashtun rulers. The first local uprisings against the regime were among the Persian-speakers in the country's north, while the Pashtun south was the last to rebel.

Most concerned by Amin's leadership was the Soviet Union. Surprised by the earlier coup that had brought Taraki to power, its advice had been to approach reform slowly. From a "scientific" Marxist point of view, Afghanistan was not yet ready for socialism. After decades of experience providing assistance to the country, the USSR had a clear-eyed assessment of what was and was not possible. Neither Taraki nor Amin accepted this advice.

Instead, both made repeated requests that the Soviet Union provide troops to support and protect the regime. During 1978 and 1979, 14 requests for the deployment of Soviet troops were made; every one was refused. The Politburo briefly considered sending a military contingent after the uprising in Herat, shocked by the death of civilian advisers and their families, but this mood did not last. Soviet Premier Alexei Kosygin told the Afghan president that "our troops would have to fight not only with foreign aggressors, but also with a certain number of your [Afghan] people. And people do not forgive such things. Besides, as soon as our troops cross the border, China, and all the other aggressors, will be vindicated."

The Soviets were also concerned that Amin might turn from the Soviet Union and seek to align Afghanistan with the United States. Amin's years studying at Columbia seemed suspect, and rumours swirled in the capital that he was a CIA asset. In fact, Amin disliked the United States because he had been failed by Columbia, and the United States had already decided to back the insurgents over the PDPA government. And with thousands of Soviet advisers assigned throughout the government and military, a change in allegiance was impractical, even though Amin's relationship with the advisers was becoming tense.

In late 1979 there were two more unsuccessful attempts on Amin's life. Fighting throughout the country intensified, and desertions from the army increased. As the country began to spiral out of control, sometime in October or November the Soviet Union began to make preparations to send troops into Afghanistan. Tens of thousands of reservists in Turkestan military district were recalled in order to bring two motorized infantry divisions up to strength, and eight thousand vehicles were commandeered from the civilian economy. The final decision to send a military contingent to Afghanistan was made in mid-December, and the first new units began to land in Kabul, Bagram, Shindand, and Kandahar airfields on December 24. As Amin had requested military assistance, the arrival of combat units did not cause him any alarm. On the advice of his Soviet advisers, he moved his personal residence from the indefensible Arg to the Tajbeg Palace just outside the city. He also ordered the 4th Armoured Brigade to move from Pol-e Charki to the palace to bolster its defences.

On December 27 Soviet troops and KGB commandos stormed the Tajbeg Palace and killed Amin. Unable to seize Radio Kabul, the Soviets broadcast on Radio Kabul's frequency from a transmitter in Termez instead. The Soviet troops were guided by the four Afghan ministers — Watanjar, Mazduriar, Sarwari, and Gulabzoy — who had fled only months earlier. The Termez message had been pre-recorded by Babrak Karmal in exile in the Soviet Union, announcing that the "bloody apparatus of Hafizullah Amin and his minions, these agents of American imperialism" had been broken. The following day, the radio announced that Karmal had been appointed President of the Democratic Republic of Afghanistan, and that Amin had been tried for his crimes and executed. Columns of motorized infantry entered the country from two locations in the north, spreading along the ring road that connected all the major towns and cities.

Although this is often described as a Soviet "invasion" of Afghanistan, the truth is more complex. Both Taraki and Amin requested Soviet troops to help quell the fighting across the country. Amin was betrayed by the Soviets, who did not trust him after his own betrayal of Taraki. But the imposition of Karmal changed neither the form of government nor its key policies. If anything, the replacement of Amin made the Afghan government *less radical* in its efforts to impose socialist reforms. Given that the Taraki and Amin regimes executed more than 17,000 people during their 20 months in power, this change was welcomed by many Afghans. Many reasons have been suggested for the Soviet decision to "invade" Afghanistan, all tinged by the biases of the Cold War era — to expand its empire, to take a step closer to seizing a warm-water port (in Pakistan or Iran), or to seize Afghanistan's oil or other natural resources. Declassified records suggest that, in accordance with the "Brezhnev doctrine," the real reason was simply to preserve Afghanistan as a country within the Soviet sphere of influence, and to support a socialist regime. Many within the PDPA welcomed the Soviet intervention, as the Afghan state seemed to be on the verge of collapse.

The "Limited Contingent of Soviet Forces in Afghanistan" (LCSFA) would rise to a strength of 120,000 soldiers, including the nearly 7,000 who were already stationed in the country before the force was committed. Although Afghanistan has been called the "Soviet Vietnam," the two conflicts are starkly different in terms of commitment. American military strength in Vietnam rose to over 500,000 troops, despite Vietnam being a fifth the size of Afghanistan. The initial intention was for Soviet troops to avoid combat entirely, focusing on supporting the Afghan Army by securing population centres and lines of communication. Military leaders were told to expect to redeploy by February 1980. From the Soviet perspective, this was to be a short, sharp intervention to strengthen the government's position, not entirely unlike those in East Germany (1953), Hungary (1956), and Czechoslovakia (1968).

The Afghan Army, however, was in poor condition and unable to take on the bulk of the fighting. By 1980 its strength had been reduced by desertions to 30,000 soldiers, many of them poorly trained and unreliable. The mobilization of Soviet reservists from Central Asia, many of them Muslims who spoke common languages with Afghans, was meant to create a good working relationship with the Afghan Army and the Afghan people. This effort backfired, as many of the Soviet soldiers sympathized with the rebels. The Central Asian divisions were quickly withdrawn and replaced by European ones. A degree of distrust existed between these new divisions and the Afghan Army, particularly where Afghan soldiers conspicuously practised Islam. As a security measure, all of the anti-tank and anti-aircraft weapons were withdrawn from the Afghan Army in 1980, in order to prevent them from being used against the Limited Contingent or turned over to the rebels. Security zones were also established on military bases where sensitive equipment was kept and Soviet troops were quartered, and Afghans were not permitted to enter.

The Soviet intervention also gave new impetus to the opposition groups based in Peshawar. Earlier in 1979 they had issued a call to jihad, making it a duty for all Muslims to respond and fight to protect the faith. This also gave the opposition the ability to describe themselves as mujahideen, meaning persons engaged in jihad, which wrapped their actions in religious sanction. The presence of Soviet soldiers in Afghanistan only amplified this message, creating a greater impetus for involvement. By the end of 1979 there was an ongoing insurgency in 18 of the country's 29 provinces, though this spread to all of them within months of the Soviet arrival. As a Hezb-e Islami spokesman is credited as saying, "Karmal may have the Russians behind him, but we have God."

Saudi Arabia attempted to entice the six major parties into a coalition by promising them aid money, and a Saudi representative was sent to Pakistan to negotiate with all the parties to this end. The person selected to lead this new front was Abdul Rasul Sayyaf, a graduate of Al-Azhar University and a former professor of theology in Kabul University. Fluent in Arabic, he retained strong ties to the Muslim Brotherhood in Egypt. He was a colleague of Rabbani and Hekmatyar in the 1975 Islamist uprising, and had returned to Afghanistan where he was arrested. The fact that he was a distant cousin of Amin may have influenced his release in 1979, after which he fled to Peshawar. Without involvement in the recent infighting between mujahideen parties, he was expected to show neutrality as their leader.

There were immediate problems in getting the groups to co-operate, as Hekmatyar insisted on a higher standing than the others within the coalition. This difference could not be resolved, and so in March 1980 the other five groups declared that they had united to form Ittihad-e Islami (the Islamic Union), with Sayyaf as their chairman. Their unity was short-lived, however. They quickly began to complain about Sayyaf's dictatorial style and his unwillingness to share money donated by the Saudis or the Gulf States equitably. They also disagreed on the form of government that they wished to create, with one of the major stumbling blocks being the role of the former amir.

Zahir Shah, still living in exile in Italy, had become something of a recluse supported by the Shah of Iran and then the Saudis. Surveys of Afghan refugees in Pakistan showed that a large majority wanted to see Zahir Shah return to the throne. But despite entreaties by Sibghatullah Mojaddedi, the grand-nephew of the Hazrat of Shor Bazaar who had supported Nadir Shah, the former amir remained aloof from the plight of his country. For his part, Hekmatyar publicly threatened to kill him if he came to Peshawar. When Zahir Shah had a change of heart in 1983 and wrote an open letter offering his support, he had become irrelevant and was largely ignored.

As aid and funding began to be sent to the mujahideen in increasing amounts, the Pakistani government moved to control it as well as the groups that were receiving it. All aid, even from the United States, was to be channelled through Pakistani authorities, specifically the ISI who were given responsibility for managing Afghan affairs. In early 1981, tired of the continuous intrigues and infighting, Pakistan decided on a policy of recognizing only the existing seven groups and allowing only these to receive arms or money. It also insisted that all refugees register with one of the groups in order to receive shelter, food aid, education, or other assistance. Dividing the aid this way served the Pakistani interest in not allowing any one party to grow too powerful and become the basis for a unified Pashtun movement that could encompass Pakistani Pashtuns as well. For the Afghan mujahideen, this policy created a new dynamic, with the parties vying against each other to "claim" a larger portion of refugees as their own. The rivalry led to bloodshed between Jamiat and Gulbuddin Hekmatyar's HIG.

By 1981 over two million Afghan refugees were living in Pakistan, and a million in Iran. These numbers continued to grow as the conflict worsened, creating the largest concentration of refugees in the world. Pakistan built 350 "refugee tented villages" (RTVs) to house them. Over time these became villages of mud-brick homes whose appearance was hardly distinguishable from other local communities. Women and children under 15 years old, however, made up 75 percent of the population in the RTVs; adult males were either off fighting or protecting their homes in Afghanistan.

Many families adopted a split-migration strategy, attempting to maximize security for themselves and their wealth, much of which was tied to their ancestral land. Families would migrate to safety in the RTVs, while the older men stayed to farm and protect their home, and the younger men fought as mujahideen. This strategy met the social and cultural obligations of protecting the family's women and children, maintaining a presence on the family's land, and fighting against the government and the foreign invaders.

Initially, both Pakistan and Iran welcomed the influx of displaced persons with open arms. Both countries officially referred to the migrants as *muhajireen*, a term with a deep religious connotation. The root of the word is *hijra*, which describes the flight of the Prophet Mohammed and his followers from Mecca to Medina, where they were welcomed. Those who welcomed them were also singled out as a special group, known as *ansar* (helpers). A passage in the Quran describes muhajireen in particular terms, saying , "As for those who emigrated for the sake of God after having been persecuted, We will provide them with a fine abode in this life; yet better still is the reward of the life to come, if they but knew it." Muhajireen were not just refugees, they were faithful Muslims forced to flee to maintain their faith, which was under threat from a godless regime.

Just as the Peshawar mujahideen parties vied for control of the migrant population, they also competed for the allegiance of the mujahideen active inside Afghanistan. During the initial years of the Soviet presence in Afghanistan, local mujahideen groups first arose to address local grievances, including the need for self-protection. Their access to weapons, ammunition, and funding were limited, the best source being defeated government troops. The most common weapon among the local mujahideen was the Lee-Enfield rifle, a Second World War weapon that was available in large numbers, as it had been the main armament of the Afghan Army in the 1940s and 1950s, and by the late 1970s had become standard among government militia units. It continued to be used even in the 21st century — Canadian soldiers captured at least one from insurgents that had originally been manufactured half a century before at Long Branch Arsenal outside of Toronto.

The Peshawar parties linked to the local mujahideen in a number of ways. Some connections were made through their extended families, who had to register with a party if they were housed in an RTV. Typically, however, they exploited *andiwal* (personal, or friend) networks, which came to matter more than tribal links given the displacement of the population. Connections between individuals that were made in schools, through business, or through close kinship decided political affiliation, rather than ideology or a vision for what a future Afghanistan would look like.

A connection with a Peshawar party was important in order to have a source of supplies, but the parties did not exert centralized control, and only on rare occasions did they have what might be termed a strategy. It was only later in the war that the parties began to appoint "amirs" of each province to better organize their efforts. In practical terms, this meant that as many as seven different parties might be represented among the mujahideen of each province and district, although typically the number was three or four. Approximately two hundred of these groups were active throughout the country. In many regions, particularly Helmand, the majority of fighting was not between the mujahideen and the government or Soviet troops, but between the mujahideen themselves. It was noted with bitterness that the party that received the lion's share of support from the ISI, Hekmatyar's HIG, was also the party that had the least number of affiliated groups fighting. It was also the party most likely to target other mujahideen parties over political disputes and control of territory and resources.

Despite all the international attention given to the Peshawar parties, they were not held in high esteem by the mujahideen who were actually doing the fighting in Afghanistan. A quotation from one guerrilla commander sums up their view well: "The ones who will decide the future of Afghanistan will not be the leaders sitting in Peshawar, it will be those fighting here in the countryside." He was correct: many of the mujahideen commanders would go on to occupy important positions in future governments.

By 1983 there were approximately eighty thousand full-time mujahideen fighters, with many more fighting seasonally, often sheltering in Pakistan with their families in the RTVs during the winter. A military term that has become popular during the most recent war in Afghanistan is "fighting-age male" or FAM, which describes men aged 18 to 35, believed to be the bulk of the insurgent forces. During the 1980s only 40 percent of the mujahideen fit this category, with the majority being either teenaged boys or older men. Early in the war deserters or even prisoners from the army were often welcomed into the mujahideen groups with open arms, particularly if they had roots in the local community. By 1982 attitudes had hardened enough, in large part due to the death and destruction wrought by the war, that prisoners were normally executed.

Faced with fierce opposition from the mujahideen and unable to overcome the anarchy in much of the country, Karmal was forced to rescind some of the government's earlier policies. He first sought to gain public sympathy by blaming Amin for the present situation, and to reconcile with Khalq by not publicly blaming Taraki. He released many political prisoners, some of whom returned to work for the government. Wary of creating new grievances, he also slowed the overall pace of reform, particularly the redistribution of land. He attempted to give the government an Islamic gloss as well, repairing mosques damaged in the fighting and trying to merge Islamic and Marxist principles. None of this was particularly effective.

The split between Parcham and Khalq had deepened. On taking power, Karmal purged or executed 76 percent of the Central Committee, and his appointment of a few token Khalqis afterward did little to increase confidence that he would not start a wider purge. Even within the committee there were long-standing conflicts. His first deputy prime minster was a Khalqi, the former security services chief who had fled the country under threat from Amin, Asadullah Sarwari. But his second deputy prime minister, Sultan Ali Keshtmand, was a Parchami who had been personally tortured by Sarwari after being arrested for allegedly plotting a coup in 1978.

Earlier purges, combined with arrests and executions, had hollowed out much of the government bureaucracy, leaving positions vacant or in the hands of young and inexperienced ideologues. Karmal sought to fill this gap in the government by enlisting even more Soviet advisers, an unpopular position that caused further resentment. Over time, even at the ministerial level, the advisers were no longer merely advising, but were in control. By the late 1980s there were likely more Soviet advisers in Afghanistan than members of the PDPA.

In 1980 Karmal proclaimed an interim constitution known as the "Basic Principles" by fiat, eschewing the tradition of holding a loya jirga to approve it. He hoped this would win the support of the rural population by directly representing their desires and interests. The short document, only six thousand words, declared the loya jirga as the highest organ of state power, but was silent on when it would be elected or consulted. In the interim, power would be wielded by the revolutionary council. The PDPA remained the "leading and guiding force of the state," although the constitution did not mention socialism or Marxism. There was a short section on the country's "special relationship" with the Soviet Union. Article 5 enshrined Islam as the sacred and true religion of the Afghan state, which was to be "respected, observed and protected."

In order to build more popular support, Karmal also created the National Fatherland Front, an umbrella organization for the PDPA and all the supporting groups that were created around it. The Front also included a "high jirga" of tribal representatives, in an attempt to draw in supporters from the countryside where the party had little reach. Karmal hoped that it would align all the progressive forces in the country, but when an inaugural assembly was planned, it had to be postponed four times due to lack of participation. When it did convene, it could not have been more farcical. In order to give the appearance of having widespread support, government officials were forced to wear "tribal dress" and impersonate members of the high jirga. Although scheduled to sit for four days, it ended after only one due to security threats made against the attendees. At least two delegates — a religious figure from Ghazni and a retired army general — were assassinated for attending. After this inauspicious start, the organization never fully began to function.

Karmal also worked to increase the coercive power of the state, beyond the capability of the military. The depaye became less and less relevant as a force over time, particularly as its main source of manpower, students, dried up. The Sarandoy gendarmerie was enlarged to one hundred thousand men and supplied with more heavy armaments. Many local armed groups were given government sanction and weapons as well, with over fifty thousand militiamen on the government payroll. The Afghan state had long had some form of secret police, but under Karmal a new organization was created, the Khedamat-e Atalat-e Dolati (State Information Service), often referred to simply by its initials, KhAD.

Mohammed Najibullah, a long-time associate of Karmal, was appointed to run this new secret police organization, which soon had a strength of over fifty thousand. A medical doctor training at Kabul University, his studies were twice delayed while he was jailed for his political activities. A burly man, he acted as Karmal's bodyguard for a number of years. As a Parchami, he was exiled by Taraki, forcing him to flee to Eastern Europe, where he reconnected with Karmal. KhAD itself was dominated by the Parcham faction, which allowed it to be used to settle old political scores as well.

Set up with advice from mentors from the KGB and the East German Stasi, KhAD quickly became highly effective and widely feared. Its staff were among the highest paid in the country, and received many privileges not afforded to ordinary citizens. One of its most effective tactics was paying local mujahideen groups to attack other groups, or co-opting them into becoming government militias. With a network of paid informants estimated to be over one hundred thousand strong, its tentacles reached into every part of the country. Kabul Province, as an example, was divided into 182 separate zones by KhAD, with as many as one hundred informants per zone, watching and reporting. KhAD quickly became a state within the state. Although Karmal had emptied the prisons upon taking power, KhAD quickly filled them up again.

While KhAD was taking a subversive approach to defeating the mujahideen, the soldiers of the Limited Contingent were being forced to take a much more active role than expected. The Afghan Army was largely incapable of undertaking the offensive operations the Soviets had envisioned. In time, the only offensive actions being taken were by the Soviet forces, typically with the Afghan Army supporting them. Historically, the Soviet Red Army had been successful at the sorts of operations needed in Afghanistan, as when it defeated the Basmachi in the Central Asian republics. But the institutional knowledge of those actions had not been retained, and the Red Army of the 1980s was not trained or structured for counterinsurgency. Contrary to the popular narrative that Soviet operations in Afghanistan were uniquely brutal and heavy-handed, the fact is they were much more nuanced. Many local commanders conducted their own "hearts and minds" campaigns even before this became the central strategy. As much as a third of the Soviet force in Afghanistan was engaged in building or repairing infrastructure, transporting humanitarian supplies, or demining populated areas at any given time.

The Red Army employed agitation and propaganda ("agitprop") units to try to influence popular opinion. These units, often staffed by Central Asian soldiers with knowledge of local languages and culture, broadcast messages via loudspeaker or through short films shown in villages, met with elders to try to convince them to support the government, provided medical assistance via mobile clinics, and distributed humanitarian aid.

Soviet combat operations were generally large sweeps by motorized troops to find and destroy mujahideen, which were generally ineffective given the mujahideen's skill in evasion and ambush. Over time, the Limited Contingent began to rely heavily on airborne mobile insertion of troops to catch the mujahideen by surprise, and increased use of *spetsnaz* (special purpose force) troops to conduct raids, targeted assassinations of mujahideen leaders, and ambushes. These new dynamic tactics were more effective, but did little to reduce the number of mujahideen opposing the government or to persuade Afghans to support the government.

Perhaps in frustration as their conventional forces struggled to come to grips with the *dukhi* (ghosts), as the Soviets nicknamed the mujahideen, aspects of their tactics became increasingly brutal. To ease the passage of convoys, they cleared fields of fire two metres wide on each side of the major roads, removing all the buildings, trees, walls, and other obstacles, without compensating their owners. While this made some tactical sense, it created new grievances that fuelled the conflict. They also made liberal use of aerial and artillery bombardment, with little regard for collateral damage, even in major built-up areas. The suppression of the uprisings in Herat and Jalalabad involved the bombing of both cities, causing widespread death and destruction.

Liberal use was also made of land mines. These were meant to impede the movement of the mujahideen, and so were employed to seal the mountain passes along the Pakistani border, but also around villages that were believed to support them. These tactics led to widespread civilian casualties and the depopulation of large parts of the country. Depopulating the countryside that supported the mujahideen was seen as an effective counterinsurgency strategy, but in terms of overcoming the insurgency it was self-defeating. Resistance to the PDPA government and the Soviet forces only grew.

The increasing ferocity of the fighting was exactly what Soviet leaders wished to avoid, as it undercut the message that the Limited Contingent was merely in Afghanistan to assist the Afghan government. In order to maintain this facade, the Soviet government did not admit to the death of a Soviet soldier in Afghanistan until September 1981, despite involvement in several years of combat operations. Soviet media only began to hint that the Limited Contingent was involved in combat in 1982, and by the end of 1983 had only reported the deaths of six soldiers. In reality, the Limited Contingent had suffered nearly twenty thousand killed and wounded.

Over time, in order to reduce the intensity of the resistance, the Limited Contingent began to negotiate local truces with mujahideen groups in areas of strategic need, essentially paying for peace. This was successful in Baghlan and Parwan Provinces, through which the highway ran that linked Kabul and the Soviet Union. Over time these truces evolved into alliances, with the mujahideen becoming paid government militias that were tasked to protect the highway.

These truces were crucial to stabilize the situation, as by 1983 the fighting had destroyed approximately half of the schools and more than half of the clinics and hospitals. It had also destroyed 14 percent of all state-owned vehicles, crucial for distributing food aid and getting officials out into the countryside to implement policy, as well as 75 percent of all communication lines. The destruction of a number of power plants led to intermittent blackouts throughout the country, even in Kabul.

The economic impact of this level of destruction was serious. The economy had already been shrinking since 1975, but by the end of 1983 overall economic output was what it had been in the 1940s. The overall figures, however, mask the real impact on areas whose output had increased over those four decades, largely the towns and cities. Kabul Province produced only 2 percent of the wheat in 1983 that it did in 1978, owing to fighting, depopulation, and destruction of agricultural land and equipment. In the remote rural countryside, where government and Soviet operations were infrequent, things continued much as before.

Kabul's population tripled in the early 1980s, rising to 1.8 million, as people sought safety within the city. Without policies in place to accommodate this influx, many found shelter in shanty towns that grew around the outskirts of the city and worked as day labourers. Poverty, always a problem in Afghanistan, became worse for many who were cut off from even their normal means of achieving a subsistence income.

The only bright spot in the Afghan economy was the production of natural gas in the fields developed with Soviet assistance in the north. Located only 20 kilometres from the Soviet border, nearly all of its production was shipped northward by pipeline. Even though the Soviet Union paid less than the standard international rate for the natural gas, by 1982 this resource provided 44 percent of state income and was vital for keeping the Afghan government on its feet.

Although the economy was struggling, smuggling continued unabated, and Soviet shoppers were amazed at the array of Western goods available in Kabul. A large black market grew as Soviet soldiers sold military equipment, petrol, food, spare parts, and even arms and ammunition in exchange for Western goods that were impossible to acquire back home, or for opium and hashish.

Although there had been a significant increase in opium production in parts of Afghanistan during the 1970s, with the loss of government control over wide swaths of the countryside, what limited barriers existed before disappeared. The HAVA, and even the areas around it that were not irrigated, soon became a hub for opium production that helped to indirectly bankroll local commanders such as Nasim Akhundzada. Nasim's brother Rasoul, a mullah, even provided religious justification for the production of opium: only its use was prohibited by Islam, while growing it to fund the jihad was a good deed that would be rewarded by God.

Rather than produce opium directly, commanders used the traditional salaam system to provide seeds in exchange for a share of the future crop. They also taxed production (typically at 10 percent), and as khans had done with all produce, organized transport to market. This system meant that the mujahideen did not have to force anyone to produce opium, as it was lucrative enough that farmers did so willingly. Commanders also encouraged production by spending some of the profits on building institutions such as schools and clinics. Agricultural equipment and expertise provided by the United States and the Soviet Union were turned to the production of opium. This increased production dramatically, despite the chaos that was disrupting so much else of the economy. Whereas in 1980 Afghanistan produced approximately 200 tonnes of opium, by 1989 this was estimated to have grown to over 800 tonnes, twice that of Iran and Pakistan combined.

The mujahideen parties quickly saw the benefits of the increased opium trade. Most if not all became involved by buying raw opium from commanders within Afghanistan and processing it into heroin for sale either in the traditional markets of Iran and Pakistan or in the West. The caravans carrying military supplies to mujahideen groups inside the country often returned laden with opium. Three mujahideen leaders in particular exploited drug production effectively: Hekmatyar, Gailani, and Ismat Muslim. Hekmatyar pioneered the creation of heroin labs to increase profits, whereas before Afghan traders had primarily dealt in raw opium. Hekmatyar's narcotics empire was facilitated by his close connections with the ISI. Its National Logistics Cell trucks would drive from Karachi to Peshawar laden with guns and ammunition, and would return carrying heroin and opium for sale on the world market. Mujahideen commanders in the north ran a similar system, but their market was further north in the Soviet Union. By 1981 Afghanistan accounted for approximately 54 percent of America's supply of heroin.

This upheaval had a major impact on those who wielded power in Afghan society. The role of the ulema was seriously challenged by the PDPA government, although much of their status and influence was regained within the structure of the mujahideen parties in Pakistan. Traditional leaders, particularly low-level khans, also lost power in many cases, as money from opium or through mujahideen networks allowed upstarts to act like tribal leaders. Mujahideen commanders used these resources to gain social capital, building followings not only in Afghanistan but within the refugee camps as well. The most successful of these commanders even supplanted the state entirely in "liberated zones," building schools and clinics, and establishing new versions of the traditional client-patron relationships. These successful commanders, particularly those whose military successes netted them supplies and whose control of opium production provided a steady income, became increasingly independent of even the mujahideen parties themselves.

This changing of the guard can be seen in the fact that nearly none of the people prominent in pre-1978 politics were involved in any significant way in the resistance. Most of these former power figures took advantage of their wealth and status to seek asylum elsewhere, far from the conflict destroying their homeland. Few former officers of the Afghan Army became involved in the mujahideen movement, despite the fact that the leadership of the army evaporated when Taraki came to power. Only perhaps a third of the officer corps that existed pre-1978 remained in the military through the 1980s, with many others fleeing into exile.

The balance of non-state military strength also shifted during this period, as it had long rested with the eastern Pashtun tribes. This often gave them the role of kingmakers in national politics, and allowed them to extract valuable concessions from the government. While Pashtuns led all but one of the mujahideen parties based in Pakistan, the party of

Rabbani, a Tajik, now came to possess a degree of military power that was sufficient to challenge Pashtun dominance.

Even in a non-military sense there was a shift in social structures, as displayed within the refugee camps themselves. Outside of the structure of khans and zamindars, power or at least influence often rested with the *spingiri*s (greybeards) within any particular group. But within the RTVs, young men who learned to game the system and therefore acquired more resources for their family and community came to be known as "ration maliks." Much as before, leadership was seen as stemming from the ability to dispense largesse, but in the bewildering world of the refugee camp, the spingiri and their traditional knowledge soon seemed irrelevant.

CHAPTER 13 WITH NEITHER THE SOVIETS NOR GOD

THE SOVIET ADVISERS in Afghanistan were deeply pessimistic about Karmal's ability to stabilize the political situation in the country, particularly given that he had ignored their pleas to heal the rift between Parcham and Khalq. As anti-government violence raged outside the capital, inside it the violence was almost all related to this feud, reaching as high at times as 12 political murders a night. The newly installed General Secretary of the Communist Party of the Soviet Union, Mikhail Gorbachev, believed that the Limited Contingent needed to be withdrawn. Shortly after taking power in March 1985, he told the Soviet military that it had one year to "win" the conflict in Afghanistan. This caused 1985 to be the bloodiest year yet in the conflict, as operations intensified in an all-out effort to crush the mujahideen. Even though these operations did not achieve anything approximating a victory, at the 27th Communist Party Congress in February 1986, Gorbachev announced:

> We would like, in the nearest future, to bring the Soviet forces — situated in Afghanistan at the request of its government — back to their homeland. The schedule has been worked out with the Afghan side for a step-by-step withdrawal, as soon as a political settlement has been achieved that will provide for a real end to, and reliably guarantee a non-renewal of, the outside armed interference in the internal affairs of the DRA.

This announcement was repeated in the government newspaper *Pravda*, making it well known both within the Soviet Union and abroad. What was needed was sufficient stability and calm so that a victory could be declared and the international press would not see the withdrawal as a rout.

Karmal was opposed to the withdrawal, fearing that it would spell the end of the PDPA regime. Of all the senior Afghan leaders, only one seemed to accept the need for the Soviet military contingent to withdraw, and that was Najibullah. Already running KhAD with ruthless efficiency, he was seen as much more flexible than the dogmatic Karmal, and so better able to reconcile the various factions and interests within Afghanistan. Karmal was summoned by Gorbachev and told that he was to resign. In November 1986 he duly did so, citing health reasons. He was succeeded by Najibullah. The first six regiments of Soviet troops had been withdrawn the month before in a sign of good faith, though they were air defence and tank units that were not necessarily needed for the kind of warfare the Limited Contingent was engaged in.

Najibullah, despite his reputation for brutality, quickly set out to bridge the differences between the government and the mujahideen. He created the National Reconciliation Program as a means to begin to co-opt groups within the resistance. Hard-line communist policies were softened or rescinded. He announced that the single-party system would be replaced by a multi-party one, with elections to follow in the near future. Shari'a was reintroduced for civil matters, and the cap on the size of individual landholdings was lifted entirely. Clandestinely, however, the government worked hard to buy off individual mujahideen groups, getting them to attack other groups in exchange for weapons and funding.

The competition between local mujahideen commanders, supported by the parties in Peshawar, became more complex as the government began to act as a sponsor as well.

In Helmand, for example, Nasim Akhundzada took the government's offer and broke from Harakat to form a pro-government militia. Funded by both the government and the narcotics trade, Nasim doubled the area under government control by 1987, though this also doubled the area under his own control that could be used for opium production. In 1987 a rival mujahid commander, Shah Nazar Khan, was appointed as the governor of Helmand in a deal negotiated by KhAD. The majority of Nazar Khan's family members continued their allegiance to the mujahideen, allowing the family to hedge their bets against what the future might bring, as well as doubling the resources available to them. An unaffiliated brother of Nazar Khan acted as a go-between to ensure that there was good communication between the halves of the family, and that no matter what distant leaders might order, they always acted in their own best interest.

Najibullah was not willing to pay for truces with all of the mujahideen commanders. Some were potential political opponents due to the fame that they had accrued fighting the government, with good connections with international media and donors. The best example of this kind of "superstar" local commander is Ahmed Shah Massoud, a Tajik from the Panjshir Valley who belonged to Jamiat-e Islami. The Panjshir Valley is easily defensible, allowing Massoud to defy Soviet attempts to defeat him. It also sits astride the southern end of the Salang Tunnel, allowing him to attack convoys travelling between the capital and the Soviet border. For this reason, the Soviets had negotiated local truces with him as early as 1983, without the agreement of the Afghan government, paying $350,000 for one year of peace. Najibullah saw Massoud as one of the few people with a reputation large enough to potentially replace him, and so he tried to forbid any further truces with the mujahideen of the Panjshir Valley, instead encouraging the Soviets to destroy them.

While many of the militias that were formed to support the government were unreliable, sometimes "taxing" mujahideen groups rather than fighting them, several stand out for their effectiveness. The natural gas fields around Sheberghan were a frequent target for the mujahideen.

They generated such a large percentage of government funding that they needed to be protected at all costs. A local defence unit was created among the gas workers, known first as the "Jowzjani militia" (after the district where it was formed), and later as the 53rd Militia Division. Its leader was a charismatic Uzbek with a fearsome reputation named Abdul Rashid Dostum, who personally recruited many of its members.

Forced to drop out of school at a young age, Dostum joined the Afghan Army in the 1970s, but left that as well during a purge of Parchamis. Despite only ever having been a private soldier, he quickly rose up the ranks of the militia, which he filled with personal loyalists from his home village. Although *Dostum* is a nickname that means "Our Friend," he built an imposing reputation that instilled fear in his followers and his enemies. Dostum's predominantly Uzbek militia not only defended the gas fields effectively, but was also flown around the country by the Afghan government, to be used whenever other units failed. The Jowzjani militia was not ideologically aligned with the communists, and insisted on being paid in American dollars — not rubles or afghanis — for any jobs they undertook. Despite this highly mercenary approach, they were in high demand as the situation in the country worsened. A similar militia was formed among ethnic Tajiks in a neighbouring province, known as the 80th Militia Division, and led by Sayyed Jaffar Naderi.

Elections were held in April 1988, although it was not possible to cast a ballot in much of the country. The PDPA won the majority of the seats in parliament, but Najibullah reserved a bloc of seats for the mujahideen parties should they decide to reconcile with the government. He even offered to share power with one or more of the mujahideen parties, but none were interested. They undoubtedly thought that they would be able to seize power entirely for themselves once the Soviets had withdrawn.

Despite Najibullah's open support for the withdrawal of the Limited Contingent, in practice he worked hard to delay the withdrawal, and to seek greater funding and security guarantees from the Soviet leadership. From 1986 to 1990 impoverished Afghanistan was the fifth largest importer of arms in the world — and this was at the height of the Cold War.

One area that suffered greatly during this period was education. As much as 80 percent of the pre-1979 university faculty were forcibly retired or executed, or fled the country, leaving few professors remaining. With

Soviet sponsorship, tens of thousands of Afghan students were sent to universities across the Soviet states. This program had an unintended consequence, as the students got to see the state of Soviet society, which fell far short of the communist utopia that they learned about in Afghanistan. They were also subject to varying degrees of racism, souring many of the exchange students on the Soviet Union and its political theories.

Government-run schools within Afghanistan also suffered, in part because they were a symbol of the government that could be easily attacked by the mujahideen. In 1982 alone, 1,812 schools were destroyed, approximately 86 percent of the total number in the country. In some provinces throughout the 1980s, the number of teachers and students assassinated was double that of government officials. This led to a crisis among teachers, requiring many unqualified people to be employed in that role. In 1986 only 0.2 percent of all teachers in the country had a post-secondary education, and nearly 5 percent had not even completed secondary school. It also led to the further militarization of teachers and students, who were armed in part to protect themselves. A famous pro-government militia in the ancient town of Balkh, one of several allied with Dostum known as the Gilam Jam ("the carpet is gathered up," an allusion to looting), were led by a man whose wife and children had been killed by the mujahideen because he was a teacher.

Although the number of students enrolled peaked in 1980 at over a million, this number fell dramatically throughout the decade. Female enrolment also peaked in government-controlled areas before dropping off sharply. While female education had always been controversial in many parts of the country, the PDPA added a new twist to the idea. In the past, children had always attended gender-segregated schools; the PDPA regime tried to enforce mixed classes. There was similar resistance to the government's literacy program, which was seen as humiliating for its adult participants, and even more so for the insistence of the young party members who ran the program that it be co-educational. In some cases, party members went door to door to round up students for night courses, increasing the sense of government overreach. The government claimed that by 1985 one million people had graduated from the programs of the National Agency for the Campaign Against Illiteracy, but this seems to be a better measure of the number of citizens provoked by the government than those whose lives were improved. Coeducational classes of any sort proved to be too provocative in many otherwise "modern" communities, creating a great deal of resistance where previously there had been little. This change was seen as another example of the government using education to indoctrinate the country's children.

For children growing up in refugee camps in Pakistan, schools provided an indoctrination of a different kind. Education was primarily provided by madrassas, either affiliated with Pakistani religious organizations or provided by the mujahideen parties with which refugees were forced to register. Although Western NGOs also provided education for Afghan refugees, their efforts were outweighed by the sheer number of madrassas. In Afghanistan, madrassas were run and funded locally, reflecting the morals and desires of the community around them. In Pakistan, many madrassas were part of larger networks, funded in part by wealthy patrons and pushing a centralized curriculum. Many of these were part of the Deobandi, which at its inception was similar to the Islam practised in Afghanistan, as it followed the Hanafi school of jurisprudence and included many elements of Sufism.

Funding from Saudi Arabia, both for the mujahideen groups in general and for the education of the Afghan refugees in particular, caused some changes to the form of Islam that was taught. The state-sponsored Sunni sect in Saudi Arabia is Wahhabism, which is much more conservative than Deobandism. Wahhabism and Salafism are sometimes used interchangeably, whereas Wahhabism is in fact a Saudi-specific form of Salafism. Many who are called Wahhabis reject this name for their faith, preferring either *Muwahhidun* (Unitarians, or believers in God's Oneness) or to simply be described as "Muslims" (though the implication in this case is that non-Wahhabis are not). A key aspect of Wahhabism is seeking to return society to how it was in the time of the Prophet Mohammed, or the first generations after him, rejecting nearly all established Islamic thought that has accrued since then. Wahhabis also attempt to live as closely as they can to the manner in which they believe the Prophet lived, leading them to shave the hair on their upper lips but not their beards, hem their pants above the ankle, and brush their teeth with a stick known as a *miswak*.

Wahhabis reject Sufism as a corrupted form of Islam, and many also adhere to *takfiri* beliefs. This idea reverses the mainstream Muslim idea that "to take one innocent life is as if to murder all mankind." Takfiris in many circumstances sanction the murder of non-believers and apostates, which is what they label any Muslims who do not follow their interpretation of the faith. This has led them to commit many acts of violence that would otherwise be prohibited within Islam.

The madrassas servicing the Afghan diaspora in Pakistan also radicalized many of them, both in religious terms and also as anti-Soviet fighters. Examples taken from mujahideen-era textbooks include such questions as "A mujahid is fighting five Russian soldiers. If he kills three of them, how many run away?" In this environment, it is little wonder that many young Afghans were eager to cross back into Afghanistan to fight. It is also interesting to note that in this environment, where there was ample opportunity for girls to go to school, they remained a minority among students. International aid agencies were strongly in favour of girls' education, but cultural feelings and a strong desire to reject anything similar to the PDPA's policies stood against it. This represents a lost opportunity for an entire generation of Afghan girls.

One of the Arab theologians who came to Pakistan during the 1980s was a Palestinian named Abdullah Yusuf Azzam. Azzam was a member of the Muslim Brotherhood who was educated in Damascus and Cairo, earning a PhD in Islamic jurisprudence from Al-Azhar University. He was expelled from Saudi Arabia following the seizure of the Grand Mosque in 1979, a revolt against the House of Saud that led to a brutal crackdown against fundamentalists. Azzam travelled to Pakistan, where he became involved in what he declared was a "jihad" against the Soviets in Afghanistan. Azzam first began to teach at a university in Islamabad, before moving to Peshawar and establishing a Maktab al-Khadamat (Services Office) for Arab volunteers coming to fight. This grew into a network of training camps, as well as a sophisticated worldwide fundraising network that even extended into North America, where Azzam had a recruiting office located in Tucson, Arizona.

Of the perhaps 35,000 foreign Muslim volunteers who came to Pakistan to fight the Soviets, the best known was a protege of Azzam, Osama bin Laden. Arriving with his wives and children in 1986, he quickly used his personal wealth to gain influence. Although he co-operated with his mentor on many things, he differed with Azzam on whether the "Afghan-Arab" volunteers should be dispersed among the Afghan groups (as Azzam thought) or formed together into an Arab Legion. Although much has been made of the presence of foreign fighters during the 1980s, in pure military terms they contributed little, as many were more interested in martyrdom than in achieving a political victory over the PDPA government and the Soviets. Even with training from the camps, their military skills were generally poor, and certainly far below the battle-hardened Afghan mujahideen. They were also unwelcome among many of the Afghans, who were culturally suspicious of outsiders regardless of their faith, and who deemed many of the Afghan-Arabs too radical.

The mujahideen party leaders most amenable to incorporating them were Abdul Rasul Sayyaf and Hekmatyar. These international recruits had their greatest influence not on the battlefield, but rather through connecting the Afghan parties with the greater Islamist movement outside of traditional channels, such as by studying and making contacts at Al-Azhar University. These low-level links between individuals would, in some cases, last for decades.

In January 1988 the educator and activist Bacha Khan died while under house arrest in Peshawar, his influence over the Pashtun tribes and his message of peaceful protest and resistance much diminished. The Indian government declared a five-day period of mourning, and Prime Minister Rajiv Gandhi made a visit to Peshawar to pay his respects. A ceasefire was arranged with the Afghan government to allow his body to be transported to Jalalabad, where tens of thousands of people attended his funeral, including President Najibullah himself. The procession through the Khyber Pass was marred by bombings in which 15 people were killed, despite the promises made by the mujahideen parties.

Violence in Afghan society had worsened to the point that by the late 1980s, political assassinations of even low-level officials, attacks on women, and small acts of terrorism against the Soviet population in the cities had become common. Many PDPA officials began to prevent women in their family from working or attending school, for fear that they would be targeted. Najibullah's wife, who was the principal of a girl's school in Kabul, was one of the many women who were forced to give up their jobs.

Negotiations for the withdrawal of the Limited Contingent had been dragging on since 1982, but they increased in urgency under Gorbachev. Although the Soviet forces were in a military stalemate in Afghanistan, the reasons for their withdrawal were primarily domestic. The Soviet economy had stagnated for many years, with a true accounting of the economic situation hidden from the people. Now it had become obvious that the economy was failing, that the standard of living was falling, and that the Soviet Union could not afford the "superpower" military that it required to compete with the United States around the world. Returning the Limited Contingent would not only cut costs and remove the irritant of national service in a morale-sapping war, but Gorbachev also hoped it would begin to normalize relations with the wider world so he could trim military expenses and revitalize the economy. The signing of the Geneva Accords on April, 14, 1988, allowed the Soviets just enough dignity to withdraw with neither a victory nor a defeat.

Facilitated by the United Nations, the accords were signed by the governments of Afghanistan and Pakistan, with the Soviet Union and the United States signing as guarantors. The accords were problematic for a number of reasons. Iran, which housed many Afghan refugees and supported the Shi'ite mujahideen parties, was excluded from the negotiations altogether. Intense pressure had to be put on Najibullah to persuade him to sign, with Soviet Foreign Minister Eduard Shevardnadze threatening to withhold all monetary and military aid. Pakistan signed the agreement without any intention of ending its support of the mujahideen parties. President Zia al-Huq allegedly told President Reagan that "Muslims have the right to lie for a good cause." Immediately after the signing, the United States Secretary of State George Schultz clarified the American position on non-interference: it would continue to support the mujahideen parties for as long as the Soviet Union provided support to the Afghan government. In reality, all that had been accomplished was the withdrawal of the Limited Contingent, leaving the Afghan government to fend for itself.

The mujahideen parties in Peshawar were also excluded from the negotiations. On the eve of signing the accord, they announced that they would not be bound by its terms because they had not been invited to participate, it contained no guarantees of Afghan self-determination, and it left

Najibullah in power. They urged refugees not to go home until the regime in Kabul had been defeated. For the most part this advice was heeded.

To ensure that its departure went smoothly, the Limited Contingent negotiated local ceasefires along the length of its withdrawal route. This was done without the involvement of the Afghan government, which in some cases objected. It was necessary to seek an understanding with the mujahideen led by Massoud, as his position in the Panjshir Valley could cut one of the two routes that the Soviets would use to withdraw. Najibullah was worried that this would only strengthen Masoud, whom he saw as a potential political rival. After a ceasefire had been agreed to, Najibullah insisted that the Soviets launch an attack against Massoud. Called Operation Typhoon, this attack involved over a thousand air sorties and massive amounts of artillery fire, and killed a large number of mujahideen.

The Soviet withdrawal was completed on February, 15, 1989, marked by Lieutenant General Boris Gromov crossing the Friendship Bridge over the Amu Darya River on foot as the "last Soviet soldier" to leave Afghanistan. Although the withdrawal was conducted in good order, the situation inside the country worsened. Attempting to seize a major Afghan town where they could proclaim an alternative government, the mujahideen parties tried and failed to take Jalalabad and Faizabad. The demoralized Afghan Army still fought fiercely when cornered, as capture or surrender likely meant torture and death. The four-month siege of Jalalabad caused the deaths of a thousand Afghan Army soldiers, four thousand mujahideen, and five hundred civilians. For a number of the mujahideen groups, this was more casualties than they had suffered through the previous 10 years of fighting, causing them to approach future conventional fighting with caution. The mujahideen did manage to seize Konduz in the country's north, but they were quickly ejected by the Afghan Army, heavily supported by Soviet bombers.

Discipline within the army had nonetheless begun to break down. When the Soviet 66th Separate Motorized Rifle Brigade handed over its garrison in Jalalabad to the Afghan 1st Corps, it left a three-month reserve of fuel, food, and ammunition. Soviet troops were ordered to make up their bunks with fresh linen, and then forced to sleep outdoors during their last night in garrison to ensure that the barracks were spotless when the Afghan Army took over. Immediately after the 66th departed, the garrison was looted by the Afghan troops who were meant to live there; everything of value was stolen, including the doors and windows. The commander of 1st Corps then pleaded with the government to be given more supplies, insisting that nothing had been left behind by the Soviets.

The Soviet intervention in Afghanistan did not stabilize the situation for the PDPA government as had been hoped. Figures for the number of Soviet soldiers killed vary from 14,000 to 26,000 over the 10-year period. In contrast, 1.5 million Afghans are believed to have been killed during the same period, and a further million wounded. A third of the population was forced to flee the country, primarily into Pakistan, and perhaps 2 million more were internally displaced out of a population of about 15 to 17 million. More importantly, the cohesion of Afghan society was badly damaged, if not broken, by the war. In the past, Afghan society had been fractious, but was still capable of being held loosely together by adroit leaders. The intense violence and resulting displacement of the past decade frayed the fabric of society and led to social incoherence unlike any other period in Afghan history.

Although the mujahideen parties continued to press for the defeat of the Najibullah regime, the withdrawal of the Limited Contingent caused many local mujahideen to stop fighting and return to their homes. Resisting the "foreign invaders" motivated these fighters, who in many parts of the country were willing to simply ignore the central government. Violence continued, but at a much lower level than before, and focused entirely on local conflicts over resources.

The Soviet Union was true to its word that it would continue to support Najibullah. Every week, a six-hundred-truck convoy provided supplies to the government in Kabul, and an air bridge was put into operation, carrying everything from flour to Scud missiles. The value of military aid to the regime jumped sharply from 1.6 billion rubles in 1988 to over 3.9 billion in 1989. This allowed Najibullah to continue the policy of co-opting local mujahideen. In return these pro-government militias received money and a wide array of weaponry, including tanks and artillery, with which to defend their communities.

In May 1990 Najibullah held another loya jirga to which he invited the local mujahideen commanders. Aside from using money and resources as bribes, he also tried to pit the traditionalist and the fundamentalist mujahideen against each other. By the end of 1990 approximately 25 percent of all local mujahideen groups had signed reconciliation agreements with the government, and approximately 40 percent more had signed ceasefires. In order to keep the peace, the government limited its presence in most of the country outside of the major towns, and enforced none of the progressive policies that the PDPA had introduced at the beginning of its rule. Some fighting in the provinces continued, but this tended to be between groups vying for local dominance, regardless of whether they were supported by the mujahideen parties or the government.

The mujahideen parties in Peshawar remained convinced that the Najibullah regime would soon fall without the Soviet military presence, and so they stepped up their operations against both the government and their rivals. Gulbuddin Hekmatyar's HIG, in particular, targeted rival leaders as it attempted to convert its predominance in Peshawar politics and Pakistani support into military and political power on the ground in Afghanistan. Nasim Akhundzada was one local leader assassinated by HIG, although he was quickly replaced by his brother Rasoul and his group remained a power in Helmand Province. While this violent intrigue continued, efforts were ongoing to create an interim government, heavily influenced by both Pakistan and Saudi Arabia. Formed in February 1989, the interim government excluded many interest groups — most non-Pashtun and non-Sunni groups, royalists, mujahideen commanders in Afghanistan, and the refugee population. The respected cleric Sibghatullah Mojaddedi was named as the president, based on a sham election by a small *shura* (meeting or assembly). He was seen as both honest and unthreatening, which made him broadly acceptable to the other party leaders, who also received roles in a government that only truly existed on paper. It did not take long for the leaders to resume fighting each other, both in the field and through waves of assassinations in Peshawar.

The ineffectiveness of the Peshawar parties as postwar political entities, only made more obvious by the ineffectiveness of the new interim government, did not sit well with many Afghans, particularly those mujahideen who had done the bulk of the fighting. Local mujahideen commanders began to organize themselves, meeting in a series of "commanders' shuras" where they discussed their own vision for the future of their country. More pragmatic and less influenced by foreign governments or their money, the commanders had begun meeting outside the auspices of the Peshawar parties as early as 1987. The first of these meetings was convened by the influential Tajik commander Ismail Khan in Ghor Province. A series of meetings in 1990 culminated with over three hundred commanders, representing groups from all 29 provinces, assembling in Paktia to try to agree on a joint military and political strategy. Unable to agree, and perhaps unwilling to definitively break with the parties that sponsored them, in the end the shuras had no lasting effect.

There was also jockeying among the mujahideen parties, as they sought to form alliances. The majority of these parties were led by Pashtuns, and the fact that Jamiat was a militarily and politically powerful group did not sit well with all of them. Jamiat's leading personalities, Ismail Khan, Rabbani, and Massoud, all Tajiks, had all gained international influence outside the regular channels in Pakistan. Not since Habibullah Kalakani had seized the throne in 1929 had a Tajik ruled the country. The desire for continued Pashtun hegemony was a strong motivator — even PDPA leaders Taraki, Amin, Karmal, and Najibullah were all Ghilzai Pashtuns — but they were not able to settle their differences and form a united Pashtun party. Abudullah Azzam and Osama bin Laden also fell out over the issue of how to deal with Jamiat. Azzam had met with Jamiat's pre-eminent commander, Massoud, several times and was on friendly terms with him. Azzam's son-in-law worked directly with Massoud as his chief organizer of Arab volunteers. He wanted to broker a truce between Jamiat and HIG, which would have united the bulk of the mujahideen's military power. Bin Laden, on the other hand, was friendlier with Hekmatyar, and like him saw no need to share power with another group, particularly one that was less fundamentalist. This dispute between the men almost certainly led to Azzam's assassination by a car bomb on November, 24, 1989, though no culprit has ever been found.

Although Hekmatyar was unwilling to co-operate with the other mujahideen groups unless they accepted his leadership, he did make an alliance of sorts with an unlikely partner. Shahnawaz Tanai was a Tani Pashtun from Paktia Province who had been a junior army officer before the Saur Revolution. A Khalqi, he was seen as a rising star within the military, and after two years as the chief of general staff, he was promoted into the cabinet as the minister of defence. A trial of soldiers associated with Tanai and accused of plotting a coup was soon to begin. Perhaps fearing that his own involvement with or knowledge of the plot would be revealed, he acted. On March 6, 1990, he led a coup attempt himself against Najibullah, with Hekmatyar's support. The fighting in the downtown area of the capital was fierce, as Tanai's troops both shelled the city with artillery and pounded it with bombs from the air. Approximately three hundred people were killed in the fighting. Tanai and his senior co-conspirators were forced to flee to Bagram. From there they took three military aircraft and a helicopter and escaped to Pakistan. Shortly thereafter they resurfaced, claiming both to be working with Hekmatyar and to still be loyal members of the PDPA. This alliance between Khalqis and Islamic fundamentalists shocked many Afghans, as it was an arrangement clearly made to seize power, rather than for any ideological purpose. If there had been any doubt about Hekmatyar's motivations, they were laid bare by this unsuccessful bid for power. The true dynamics of the Afghan conflict were also revealed, where fighting over ideological differences had given way to a scramble for power between increasingly fragmented groups.

Najibullah's grip on power was lessening by the day, and desperate acts such as a unilateral amendment of the constitution in 1990 did nothing to regain popular support. This version, agreed upon at a party congress, erased all mention of one-party rule. Najibullah publicly admitted that trying to implement Marxism had been a mistake, and promised that the PDPA (now renamed Watan, or Homeland) would share power. Despite these promises, he retained his position as president. Nothing really changed. The country's economy was a shambles, and inflation was soaring. Afghans were deserting government institutions, such as the police and army, in droves, leaving the highly paid militias led by Dostum and Naderi as the main instruments of government power.

A further blow to Najibullah was the Soviet Union's collapse in August 1991, cutting off the government's only major source of funding and support. The natural gas fields of the north had stopped producing, and the new republics to which the pipeline ran had no interest in buying natural gas that they also produced in abundance. Since the withdrawal of Soviet troops, the Soviet Union had been providing billions of dollars in military aid, and $480 million worth of food and other essentials. When this largesse ended the results were dire. Many government employees were let go, as they could no longer be paid. Food shortages, even in the capital, forced many to go hungry in the winter months. The entire Afghan Air Force was grounded due to a lack of fuel from January 1992 onward. This also had a knock-on effect on the large number of government-sponsored militias, who lost the government funding and supplies that had ensured their loyalty. This forced them to rely on other sources of income, largely criminality and looting, or otherwise taxation and control of the opium trade.

In the spring of 1992 the United Nations tried again to find a peaceful solution to the conflict. The United Nations Secretary General, Boutros Boutros-Ghali, sent an envoy, Benon Sevan, to try to implement a plan. A list of over a hundred leading Afghans who were broadly acceptable to all constituencies was compiled; these would in turn select a smaller working group to organize a loya jirga and another new interim government. This government would then organize elections. Despite the fact that Sevan announced that all parties had agreed to this plan, the leaders of the hard-line religious parties — Hekmatyar, Sayyaf, and Khalis — denounced it. Najibullah, however, was willing to step down, and so the process moved forward.

An unexpected twist to the plan for a transition of power occurred when Dostum and Naderi turned on Najibullah. No longer paid for their services by the government, the two militias they led had turned to other sources of income. One was the seizure of military supplies stockpiled by the Soviets at the key crossing between Hairaton and Termez. When Najibullah tried to replace Major General Abdul Momen (a Tajik) as commander of the garrison at Hairaton with a Pashtun general, Dostum and Naderi revolted. Massoud had long courted both commanders, and had long-standing local truce with them. The combined forces of Dostum, Naderi, Massoud, and Momen advanced on the capital, intending to seize power for themselves.

Not to be outmanoeuvred, the mujahideen parties in Peshawar also attempted to seize the capital. Hekmatyar advanced with his forces from the south, hoping to reach Kabul before the northerners. Across the country, what government garrisons remained surrendered or struck deals with local mujahideen, and the regime essentially evaporated. The

Afghan Army ceased to exist, with individual units choosing sides and aligning themselves with various mujahideen groups, often along ethnic lines. Najibullah tried to flee the country under the protection of the United Nations, but was barred from leaving by Republican Guard troops at the airport. He was forced to shelter in a United Nations compound, justifiably fearing for his life. Sevan, whose efforts had failed, was forced to return home.

While Massoud held his forces just outside of the capital in order not to spark an ethnic conflict, Hekmatyar struck. Although he had been named the prime minister of the new government, he was unwilling to wait for an agreement. His forces entered Kabul with the co-operation of Pashtun Khalqi former soldiers. Massoud responded by sending his troops into the capital to drive them out, and for several days chaotic fighting spread throughout the city between loosely aligned groups of the army, mujahideen, and militias. Hekmatyar was forced out of the centre of the city, which his forces pounded with artillery and rockets. Mojaddedi and the other party leaders not involved in the fighting arrived in Kabul, and assumed power in a brief ceremony. The absurdity of the situation was there for all to see: during the ceremony, the military forces of the prime minister fired rockets at those of the president.

Incredibly, the PDPA government had outlasted its superpower sponsor, though it ended by fading away. No government officials were present to hand power over to Mojaddedi, although some appeared later at the ceremony to congratulate him. Ideological differences were now much less important than ethnic ones, and despite the proclamation of a new government, the truth was that no government exercised power over the country, nor had one done so for a number of years.

CHAPTER 14 THE STUDENTS

RABBANI, THE LEADER of Jamiat-e Islami, replaced Mojaddedi as president in June 1992, placing his party in nominal control of the country. The truth was actually much more complex.

Jamiat controlled most of the capital, although the outskirts were contested and the city itself was subjected to rocket attacks by rival parties. Now the citizens of the capital no longer commonly wore Western dress: both men and women were admonished to dress conservatively. Although not as strict as future regimes, Jamiat still enforced an Islamist view of proper conduct and dress. It also controlled much of the northeast of the country, in particular the Panjshir Valley and the neighbouring provinces of Badakhshan and Takhar. Within this region, it ran a relatively progressive state apparatus that provided schools and hospitals to the population, protected by a well-trained and disciplined army of mujahideen *zarbati*s (professionals) as well as a second tier of village militia. Tension within the party was along regional lines, with a Panjsheri qawm (best represented by the party's pre-eminent military commander, Massoud) competing against a Badakhshani one (represented by Rabbani).

To the west of Jamiat's territory were the four provinces under the control of Dostum, who had remade his communist militia division into a political party, Jumbesh-e Melli-ye Islam-e Afghanistan (National Islamic Movement of Afghanistan). From his capital in Mazar-e Sharif, he maintained a level of peace and stability that was unsurpassed throughout the rest of the country. To achieve this he effectively managed an alliance of ethnic Uzbeks, Turkmen, and Tajiks, including former members of the mujahideen and many reconciled Parchamis. With easy access to the former Soviet states of Uzbekistan and Turkmenistan, Dostum was able to encourage a simple trading economy. He ran his fiefdom like a separate country, even issuing his own currency.

Farther west was the domain of Ismail Khan, the "Amir of Herat," who although supposedly a member of Jamiat, ran his affairs autonomously. Herat was an ancient city with a sophisticated culture, which Ismail Khan worked to foster. He too funded schools and hospitals, using the proceeds from taxing trade with Iran.

Control of the south of the country was divided between many petty warlords, most little more than bandits, who fought ferociously against each other while looting the civilian population. In Helmand the "provincial governor" was the militia commander Rasoul Akhundzada, who had allied himself with Ismail Khan, to depose a Jamiat commander, Akhwaendi. Nominally allied with the Rabbani government, like his sponsor Ismail Khan, Rasoul was in reality an independent player. Kandahar City, the country's second most populous and the capital of the Durrani Pashtuns, was split among numerous smaller commanders. Well-known mujahid Gul Agha Sherzai was the provincial governor, appointed by the government in Kabul, but although he lived in Kandahar he exerted little control. Criminality was present throughout the country during this period, but it was particularly rampant in the south, where checkpoints proliferated along the highway that leads from Pakistan to Iran, and connects the region to the rest of the country. At the height of the anarchy, there were 50 or more checkpoints, each controlled by a different bandit group, who extracted "tolls" equivalent to a half-day's pay for a labourer from every passing vehicle. This strangled much of the trade that had transited through Afghanistan, as well as emptying local markets of any goods that the common people could afford. The chaos of the region is sometimes described as *pshe pshe* fighting, meaning two table legs that fight each other, not realizing the inevitable result should one of them be destroyed.

The east of the country, dominated by the Ghilzai, was also split between many smaller commanders, although an alliance of former mujahideen had formed the Nangarhar Shura and ruled from the city of Jalalabad. The most prominent leaders in the shura were three brothers: Abdul Haq, Abdul Qadir, and Jalaludin Haqqani, all former members of Hezb-e Islami Khalis. Although many mujahideen in the eastern provinces had found ways to reach local agreements with the government over the course of the 1980s, these three men had refused, fighting the communists without mercy. The remote and mountainous province of Kunar, difficult to access even before the war, was ruled as a Wahhabist "amirate" by a mujahid commander named Jamil al Rahman. His forces clashed at times with more moderate Islamists to the south.

Hekmatyar, also a Ghilzai Pashtun, was fighting for control of the capital, but he did not have a large base of support among the civilian population. Pockets of supporters existed in a line from the northern city of Konduz to Jalalabad, but the political base of his support was in Pakistan, in Shamshatoo refugee camp, south of Peshawar.

The central region of the country, the Hazarajat, had been spared much of the destruction to which the rest of the country had been subjected, save ongoing fighting between the Hazara mujahideen parties themselves. By 1991, this fighting between traditionalists and Iranian-trained fundamentalists had subsided, and the parties formed Hezb-e Wahdat (the Unity Party). Wahdat formed a basic state structure and simple services such as schools and hospitals, partially subsidized by Iran. A degree of Hazara nationalism began to take root, with the public display of photos of religious leaders such as the Ayatollah Khomeini giving way to the display of "Hazara" figures such as Genghis Khan.

The desire to vanquish their opponents and rule the country drove the actions of Jamiat, Jumbesh, and Hezb-e Islami, with Wahdat seeking advantage by allying itself with one or more of the other parties when possible. In 1994 Hekmatyar convinced Dostum to betray his allies in Jamiat in an attempt to take control of the capital and establish a new national government. Jamiat found itself fighting against Jumbesh, Wahdat, and

Hezb-e Islami all at once, but still managed to retain control of Kabul. Within the parties, individual commanders emulated their leaders and cut deals with their enemies or switched sides as they saw an advantage to be gained. Any legitimacy that the party leaders had as protectors of the interests of Afghans quickly dissipated.

Perhaps a third of the pre-intervention population still lived outside the country at this point, but whereas they had been welcomed as mu-hajireen during the Soviet period, they were now seen as a burden by both Pakistan and Iran. New documentation issued to Afghans by the Iranian authorities labelled them not as muhajireen but as *panahande-gan* (refugees), a term that has a pejorative connotation of poverty rather than a positive religious one. Unlike in Pakistan where Afghan refugees had been concentrated and cared for by the state and international or-ganizations, with international funding, Iran had simply absorbed the Afghans into the economy. As domestic unemployment began to rise, the Iranians began to forcefully repatriate over a million Afghans be-tween 1992 and 1995.

Pakistan had nearly five million Afghan refugees within its borders in the early 1990s, although perhaps half this number had been born in Pakistan and had never been to Afghanistan at all. They had grown up in the densely packed urban refugee camps and had learned to navigate the bureaucracy of aid distribution in order to survive. This experience did little to prepare them to "return" to their sparsely populated rural homes, where the living was harsh and relied largely on their ability to farm marginally arable lands.

It was in this climate of anarchy that a new political force emerged from among the former mujahideen living in Helmand and Kandahar Provinces. A group of men who had returned to civilian life after the Soviets withdrew and had gone to study in madrassas began discussing what to do about the chaos engulfing their country. One of these men, Mullah Abdul Salaam Zaeef, had fought under the famous command-er Abdul Raziq, first in Harakat and later in Ittihad. He, along with 30 other former mujahideen who were now students or teachers, met in a mosque in Pashmul in 1994. They decided that they should take matters into their own hands and stop the looting and violence in their district. Groups of religious students had fought as mujahideen during the war, and so the idea was not new. The group from Pashmul had no formal name for themselves, not wanting to be seen as a new political party like those now fighting each other for power. They instead identified themselves using the same word that had been used for the groups of religious students: *taliban* (simply "students").

They approached former mujahideen in the area who were not engaged in banditry, other students, and members of the ulema, seeking support for this idea. In almost every case, they were rejected, as people assumed that they sought political power. The complicated local politics that resulted from years of fighting had fractured Afghan society, making it difficult for the community to rally behind any one leader. Because of this, the group sought out a neutral figure as their leader. The man they chose was Mullah Mohammed Omar Akhund, a man in his late thirties living in Sangisar. A former mujahid in Hezb-e Islami Khalis, he had distinguished himself under the famed commander Nek Mohammed through his bravery and piety, but not through his leadership. A provincial man, he was born into a Hotaki Ghilzai family of landless peasants near Kandahar. The civil war forced his family to move to Tirin Kot in Uruzgan, one of the most inhospitable and inaccessible parts of the country. Despite using the title mullah and running a small madrassa, he had not been educated in any of the famous madrassas of Afghanistan or Pakistan. He had studied in an informal religious school in Uruzgan under a teacher known as Haji Baba, who was a Sufi pir of the Naqshbandi order. When Mullah Zaeef first met him at his home, he was celebrating the birth of a son with a traditional recitation from the Quran. Mullah Omar agreed to meet with the group, bringing his friend and comrade from the jihad, Mullah Abdul Ghani Baradar, as well.

The next meeting, in late autumn of 1994, was twice as large as the previous one. A vote was taken, and Mullah Omar was confirmed as leader. The group lost no time in acting, starting by chasing the bandits out of their home district, and establishing their own checkpoint on the Herat-to-Kandahar highway at Hawz-e Mudat. Their focus at this point was entirely on protecting their own families, friends, and neighbours. Many legends have sprung up about the group's origins, all casting them as "Robin Hood" figures who fought to protect the common man. The best-known story is that Mullah Omar was asked by local villagers from

Srinesgar to rescue two young girls (sometimes young boys) who had been kidnapped and raped by bandits. With only 30 of his students, and half as many rifles, they freed the girls and hanged the bandit leader from the barrel of a tank. The truth behind this rumour is much more grim. Mullah Zaeef relates that when they took over a checkpoint abandoned by a bandit named Commander Saleh, they found the naked bodies of two Herati women in a ditch nearby.

The Taliban described their political aims in a very simple manner that did not change over the course of their development into a larger movement: to restore peace, disarm the population, enforce shari'a, and defend the integrity and Islamic character of Afghanistan. The Taliban movement from its inception was different from the mujahideen groups in southern Afghanistan that were largely homogenous, consisting of members of a single family, clan, or tribe. Although nearly all its members were Pashtun, they came from many different tribes that would otherwise be in conflict with each other. They were linked through andiwal networks, sometimes through membership of the mujahideen parties, but mostly through having studied together in religious schools. The Taliban sought to reduce the tribal and ethnic frictions that had long been present within Afghanistan, in favour of unity as Sunni co-religionists.

As word of the movement spread, it began to attract the attention of Pashtuns as far away as Quetta, some of whom came to meet with them to ascertain whether they were really the humble ghazis that they claimed to be. One of these curious visitors was Abdul Ahad Karzai, leader of the Popolzai tribe, who brought his sons Hamid and Ahmed Wali with him. The elder Karzai had been a member of the 1964 loya jirga and a member of parliament from 1964 to 1973, but was now living in exile in Pakistan. After speaking with the Taliban, he returned to Quetta without making any commitment of support.

The Taliban's fortunes turned as they began to expand their influence outside of their own district. On October 12, 1994, about two hundred Taliban captured the border town of Spin Boldak from men loyal to HIG. The town was strategically important as it controlled the road between Kandahar and Quetta, and was a major trucking route for goods entering and leaving the country. They also captured a massive arms depot belonging to HIG that had been moved across the border from Pakistan in 1990 to comply with international commitments to cease the supply of arms to Afghanistan. The depot contained eighteen thousand rifles, dozens of artillery pieces and armoured vehicles, and a veritable mountain of ammunition. The Taliban would no longer have to go into battle with fewer weapons than men.

A group to whom the Taliban seemed particularly appealing were the Pakistani "trucking mafia," who controlled the movement of goods throughout the region. The lucrative route through southern Afghanistan into Iran and Central Asia had long been closed, with the proliferation of bandits and checkpoints. Attempts to create a new route to Central Asia, via Peshawar, Kabul, Mazar-e Sharif, and Hairaton had failed due to the fighting between the mujahideen parties around Kabul. The value of this trade was important enough to Pakistan that President Benazir Bhutto became involved directly to try to negotiate with the Afghan power brokers to make it a reality. She secured the support of Ismail Khan and Dostum for the southern route, but could not get the fractious Pashtun bandit commanders to agree to it. The Taliban represented a force that could make the trade route feasible again.

A convoy of Pakistan Army trucks from the National Logistics Cell tried to run the route, thinking that even without the Taliban the Pashtun commanders would not stop them. Shortly after crossing the border, they were diverted and then held for ransom by an alliance of three bandit leaders — Amir Lalai, Mansur Achakzai, and Ustad (an honorific meaning "teacher") Halim. Hesitant to use their own forces to rescue them, the Pakistanis instead asked the Taliban for assistance. The group promptly routed the bandit forces and freed the Pakistani truckers, carrying on from there to capture Kandahar City in two days of fighting. Gul Agha Sherzai fled into exile as soon as the Taliban entered the city. Even more curiously, the most powerful commander in the city, Mullah Naqib Alikozai — also known as Mullah Naqibullah — made no effort to resist. Despite having 2,500 men under his command, he withdrew to his home in Arghandab district, a heavily fortified area that had resisted PDPA and Soviet control for many years. As the Taliban would do many times thereafter, they chose to bribe a powerful opponent instead of fighting him, making the Taliban seem more powerful than they were when the city fell to them so quickly.

Up to this point the ISI had primarily been backing HIG in its attempts to seize control of Afghanistan, much as it had favoured the party during the fight against the Soviets and the PDPA. The ISI had a tremendous amount of sway over the Pakistani government's foreign policy, and was filled with ethnic Pashtuns who insisted on backing a Pashtun faction in Afghanistan. It recognized that Hekmatyar had little remaining legitimacy among Afghans, and militarily he had rarely been successful. It began to shift its support from him to the Taliban.

Much like the mujahideen parties, the Taliban accepted the ISI's arms and money but refused its orders. Even as the Taliban granted Pakistan's wish to open up the southern route, they refused to allow Pakistani trucks to ply it. All goods would have to be transferred onto Afghan trucks at the border, and the Pakistanis were warned not to cut separate deals with the remaining bandit leaders or try to send a National Logistics Cell convoy again. The Pakistanis had little choice but to comply. The Taliban began to charge a single toll for use of the route, on the justification that they would protect all traffic, even though it only extended part way into Kandahar Province itself.

By December 1994 the Taliban had grown to a force of twelve thousand men and boys, largely drawn from the student bodies of the many madrassas that dotted the countryside. Perhaps a few hundred of these were Pakistani students from schools whose philosophy matched that of the Taliban. They had captured numerous tanks and heavy weapons from the stockpiles around Kandahar City, as well as MiG-21 fighter jets and helicopters from the military airfield nearby. They had quickly become the most powerful military force in the south, and a rival to the more established powers in the north.

The Taliban recruits gave their organization a different character than those descended from the mujahideen parties. Most were very young, too young to have fought against the Soviets or to remember Afghan society before the PDPA government. Growing up in madrassas located either in Afghanistan or in Pakistani refugee camps, they were disconnected from wider Afghan culture. While older Afghan men could recite their tribe's lineage and ancestral lands as a matter of course, these younger Afghans had often grown up with little knowledge of their origins. The traditional tribal structures had been broken by the years of fighting, with many villages or camps occupied by a jumble of tribes and ethnicities that bore no relation to historical norms.

Their knowledge of the world was almost entirely gained through the lens of the Quran and the hadith, as taught by often semi-literate and poorly educated teachers. Unlike the mujahideen parties, which included numerous highly educated Islamic scholars among their leaders and followers, the Taliban espoused a simple and austere view of Islam. As was the case with village mullahs for decades, if not centuries, they blended Islam with Pashtun traditions in a way that suggests they could not readily discern the difference between the two. The Taliban leadership sought to create a new society that was a combination of Islamic society as it existed during the time of the Prophet Mohammed, and an idealized version of rural Pashtun society that they believed had been destroyed by the PDPA. Most members had never experienced this idyllic rural life that they sought to re-establish, and perhaps it never existed as they imagined it. The harsh reality of rural life in Afghanistan had been forgotten.

The fact that most of the Taliban recruits were drawn from madrassas also had an impact on their views of women. Although Afghan society had long sought to control women in public, within the home the traditionalist view was that they must be respected. Women were included in family decision-making, even if outward appearances seemed to contradict this reality. Many rural families needed women's labour to subsist, so the women were commonly found outside the home. Many of the boys from the madrassas, however, had grown up in highly segregated spaces, with little knowledge or experience of women apart from their own mothers. For the many orphans educated in madrassas, even this was not true. Within the refugee camps, women were kept in purdah, for their own safety but also because their labour outside the home was not needed. Without first-hand knowledge of the important roles of women in traditional society, Taliban recruits often defaulted to what they themselves had seen and experienced — a society where women had no place in public.

The Taliban began to look outside of their home districts to impose their version of peace on the country. Within three months of forming they had captured 12 provinces in the country's south and east through the mix of fighting and bribery that would become their customary form of warfare. Afghan kings for many years had feared alliances between the ulema and tribal or traditional leaders. The Taliban organized itself through a twist on this pairing, combining the ulema with disaffected members of the rural population, tired of the predations of groups who pretended to represent some form of the state. While traditional leaders were co-opted into the group at various levels, they were largely supplanted at the top tier by religious leaders whose piety and honesty were seen as reasons to support them. In the eyes of many Afghans, the central government seemed to have brought nothing but destruction over the past decade, and traditional leadership structures had not been able to protect the local population.

As the Taliban's ambitions increased, Mullah Omar made no effort to change its structure. Even once they had taken control of nearly the entire country, the Taliban leadership made little effort to form anything resembling a functional government. In 1994 Mullah Omar moved into a mansion in Kandahar City from where he would rule. Living a reclusive life, he spent the better part of each day meeting with supplicants or Taliban leaders, listening to their requests and making decisions. Where these required orders to be given, they were written down on scraps of paper, cigarette packs, or pieces of wrapping paper. Subordinate commanders accepted these without question. Where money had to be dispensed, Mullah Omar did so from huge tin trunks that he sometimes sat on, which contained the country's treasury. Of all the previous governments in Afghanistan, the Taliban's most resembled that of Habibullah Kalakani in the way that it functioned, though the Taliban were much more serious about keeping the peace.

How the Taliban took control of Helmand Province, where former mujahideen bolstered by profits from the opium and heroin trade were well established, gives a clear idea of their methods. Rasoul Akhundzada had died of natural causes in September 1994, but had been replaced by his younger brother Ghaffar. Ghaffar had early contact with the Taliban, and had helped mediate between them and some of the commanders in Kandahar Province whom they ejected. This did not secure preferential treatment for him when they set their sights on Helmand: the Taliban negotiated with Ghaffar's subordinate commanders to turn them against him. They reached an agreement with Rais Baghrani, commander of the 93rd Division, a PDPA-era government militia whose loyalty to Ghaffar was limited. Other leaders were less pliable, and rejected the Taliban's narrative that they should side with the movement in order to be "good Muslims who would raise the Quran up high." As former jihadis who had fought the Soviets for 15 years, they did not accept the Taliban's supposed moral authority. But once Baghrani joined the Taliban along with his powerful 93rd Division, neither these minor leaders nor Ghaffar himself could resist them. Using their detailed knowledge of the politics of Helmand, the Taliban were able to manipulate individual commanders to get their way. With Baghrani's forces, they first cleared a number of checkpoints manned by HIG loyalists, and then turned on Ghaffar and forced him to flee the province with his family. Ghaffar, along with other minor Helmandi commanders defeated by the Taliban, took shelter with Ismail Khan in Herat.

The Taliban also pushed northward, capturing Zabul and Uruzgan without a shot through a mix of coercion, persuasion, and bribery. By February 1995 they had captured some of the smaller towns on the outskirts of Kabul, including the headquarters of HIG in Charasyab. The shattered remainder of HIG's field force retreated to Jalalabad. Whereas HIG had blockaded the capital in the past, the Taliban paused their offensive to allow convoys of much-needed food and medicine into the city. This gesture greatly improved the public perception of the Taliban among the civilian population of Kabul. At the same time, Taliban delegates met with the political leaders of Jamiat and also with officials from the United Nations, who were anxious to prevent another round of fighting in the city. The United Nations offered to broker a deal between Jamiat and the Taliban, bringing the newcomers into a power-sharing government with the more established party. The Taliban refused unless they were allowed to become the "neutral" guarantors of peace in the capital. No party would agree to this condition, and the fighting continued.

Massoud's forces launched an attack spearheaded by tanks against the Hazaras in the city's south, driving them out of their positions and into the countryside. As they fled, the Hazaras made a deal with the Taliban to surrender their heavy weapons in exchange for safe passage. The Taliban occupied positions in the city that had been abandoned by the Hazaras. Co-operation between the two groups was brief, however, as the Taliban were soon blamed for the death of the Hazaras' leader, Abdul Ali Mazari. Never again would the Taliban and the Hazaras work together.

On March 11 the Taliban lost their first battle, as Massoud pushed them out of the city with a force of tanks and infantry. The Taliban were no match for the battle-hardened and well-led soldiers of Jamiat, as their approach to military organization and tactics resembled their approach to governance. The ease with which they had defeated the bandit commanders of the south led them to think that their strong faith would be enough to overcome any obstacle. But while in the south they were often seen as saviours, outside the Pashtun heartland they were less welcome.

Blocked on the Kabul front, the Taliban then turned their attention westward to Herat. In March 1995 they crossed the Dasht-e Mango (Desert of Death) mounted in 1,500 Japanese pick-up trucks supplied by ISI. Although they covered the inhospitable lands between Helmand and Herat Provinces quickly, they failed to seize the airbase at Shindand, which had been built with Soviet assistance in the 1960s. An airlift of Jamiat troops from Kabul arrived to reinforce Ismail Khan's men, and the Taliban were forced to flee back eastward. They were harried by Jamiat airplanes as they went.

Ismail Khan had created a peaceful oasis in Herat since the Soviet withdrawal, but after the Taliban attack he realized that he had a problem. He had disarmed the population and replaced the many militias and mujahideen groups with a conscript army that was deeply unpopular, poorly trained, and low in morale. Without support from the Jamiat troops in other parts of the country, he would have difficulty repelling the Taliban again. At the same time, he was being goaded by the Helmandi commanders who had sought his protection to help recapture their homes and the lucrative poppy fields they had controlled. Hoping to snuff out the Taliban threat after their recent defeat, Ismail Khan launched an ill-advised offensive that nonetheless chased the Taliban all the way back to Kandahar.

On their back foot but not defeated, the Taliban looked to the ISI for assistance. The ISI was able to broker a deal with northern warlord Dostum, who sent technicians to repair the aircraft that the Taliban had captured in Kandahar, and mercenary pilots to fly them. Dostum used his own planes to bomb Ismail Khan's forces in Herat. In September 1995 the Taliban mobilized 25,000 new soldiers, drawn from madrassas in Afghanistan and Pakistan. With air support, they pushed Ismail Khan back to Herat. Ismail Khan and his senior followers fled to Iran, and the Taliban marched into the city. For the first time, they had captured a significant area that was not predominantly Pashtun.

This presented a problem for the soldiers of the Taliban. Most could not even speak Persian, the language of Herat and much of the rest of the country; they treated the city as if they were an alien army of occupation. They closed down schools, conducted mass arrests, and subjected the cultured Heratis to strict rules. The very idea of sophisticated Persians being ruled by uneducated, brutish Pashtuns was enough to create tremendous resentment toward the Taliban. Even as the Taliban edged closer to forming a national government, not a single Herati ever joined their administration.

Again drawing the wrong lessons from their experiences, the Taliban tried once more in October and November to seize Kabul, without carrying their tactics forward or refining their approach. Its agents tried, without success, to buy the loyalty of Rabbani's subordinates. This included Rabbani's deputy foreign minister, Hamid Karzai, who refused their offer to be made the Taliban representative at the United Nations. He later explained that he felt they were too heavily influenced by Pakistani intelligence.

Still halted at the gates of the capital, and retaining control of Herat only with difficulty, the Taliban were in crisis. The easy victories of the previous year seemed very distant. The movement's deputy leader, Mullah Mohammed Rabbani, was not related to Burhanuddin Rabbani but was considerd a moderate. He favoured opening peace negotiations with Jamiat, Jumbesh, Wahdat, and HIG. Others worried that this would make the Taliban no better than the mujahideen parties who had fought for years to take control of the country. Mullah Omar needed to take action to hold the movement together.

CHAPTER 15 THE COMMANDER
OF THE FAITHFUL

ON MARCH, 20, 1996, 1,200 Pashtun mullahs converged on the city of Kandahar from across the Taliban-controlled parts of the country. Kandahar City had long been the major city most associated with the Pashtun tribes. An oasis town in the middle of the desert, it was surrounded by lush gardens and farms, and was famous for its fruit orchards. For centuries, Kandahar had sent its grapes, melons, pomegranates, figs, peaches, and mulberries to markets in every direction. It had been settled for millennia. The "Old City" of Kandahar was laid out by and given its "modern" name by Alexander the Great, who chose a site beside an existing settlement dating to 500 BCE. An even more ancient city nearby, Mundigak, is believed to have been founded in 3,000 BCE.

The ancient city's famous orchards and the irrigation channels that fed them were used as cover by the mujahideen, so the PDPA government and the Soviets systematically destroyed them. Kandahar in 1996 was the most heavily mined city in the world, a shadow of its former self. To house the gathering of mullahs, the covered bazaar and the old citadel were converted into giant dormitories by rolling carpets out on the ground. Guests of Mullah Omar, the visitors were fed and sheltered at the Taliban's expense. This was the largest gathering of religious leaders in Afghanistan's history, though it was perhaps more notable for who was not invited: military or mujahideen commanders, tribal, clan or ethnic leaders, and political leaders from past or present governments. The Taliban saw the leadership of the country as consisting of the like-minded, largely Pashtun ulema, and ignored the tribal and political divisions that had long kept Afghans from achieving unity.

The Taliban's religious point of view did not necessarily coincide with the views of the majority of the Afghan ulema. Traditional Afghan Islam was heavily infused with Sufi thought and practice, and was extremely tolerant. The Taliban brand of Deobandism, in contrast, was very rigid. The Taliban leadership saw doubt as a sin, and debate, if left to go beyond acceptable bounds, could easily be seen as heresy. What they did have in common with the Pashtun ulema was that what they saw as shari'a was in fact a hybrid of shari'a and Pashtunwali. Although all Taliban leaders used the title "mullah," none could truly be considered Islamic scholars. Some had connections to the madrassas of Pakistan, but Mullah Omar did not. This gathering of the ulema allowed the Taliban to involve the broader ulema in deciding their policies on many matters, as the Taliban had no clear or comprehensive philosophy of their own.

Sub-shuras were created to discuss many topics of interest, including planned political structures, education for boys and girls, a system of Islamic courts, and military plans. The gathering lasted two weeks, with discussions extending late into the night. The meetings concluded without settling the main questions of how the country should be run. No institutions or structures were created, beyond the agreement that participants would adhere to shari'a as they saw it. The few decisions that were made generally reflected the strict Taliban interpretation rather than the traditionally tolerant one.

To cement the loyalty of the ulema to the movement, Mullah Omar did an extraordinary thing. Bringing the attendees to the Kherqa Sharif Ziarat, he stood on the roof of a nearby mosque and wrapped himself in the Cloak of the Prophet. This holy relic had been shown in public only twice in the last century, once in 1929 by Amanullah Amir when he sought to bolster his religious legitimacy after losing the throne, and again when the protectors of the shrine displayed it in hopes of countering a cholera epidemic in 1935. Now Mullah Omar sought to prove that he was the leader favoured by God, who would not have allowed an unrighteous leader to even lift the holy relic. To shouts of *Allah-u Akbar*, Mullah Omar was proclaimed the Amir al-Mumineen (Commander of the Faithful), leader of not just the Taliban but all Muslims worldwide. Everyone present swore a *baiat* to him, a formal oath of allegiance that would have evoked the relationship between the Prophet Mohammed and his followers. He ended the gathering by using his new authority to declare a jihad against the Rabbani government.

Although the gathering affirmed Mullah Omar as the Taliban's leader, its impact outside of the regions the movement controlled was negative. The idea that an uneducated village mullah would remove the relic from its shrine and declare himself Amir al-Mumineen was an affront to many. No Afghan had carried that title since Dost Mohammed Khan in 1834, when he declared jihad on the Sikh kingdom in Peshawar. The fact that Mullah Omar had used his authority to declare jihad on other Muslims only added to the insult.

Meanwhile, Rabbani was attempting to form a coalition against the Taliban with the other mujahideen parties. He sent an emissary to meet with Hekmatyar, Dostum, and the Wahdat leadership in Bamiyan, eventually convincing them to form a power-sharing government. Formally named the Jabha-ye Muttahid-e Islami-ye Melli-ye barayi Nijat-e Afghanistan (the United Islamic National Front for the Salvation of Afghanistan), its popular name was the "Northern Alliance." Dostum's agreement opened the road north from Kabul to the border at Hairaton, allowing trade to flow in and out of the capital for the first time in years. The newfound unity then allowed Rabbani to seek and receive material support from a number of countries that opposed either the Taliban themselves or their perceived role as Pakistani proxies. Soon, supplies were landing at Bagram airfield north of Kabul from Russia, Tajikistan, Uzbekistan, Turkmenistan, India, and Iran. That the mujahideen parties had previously fought against most of their sponsors mattered little. Iran even set up training camps near Meshad to train and equip fighters who had formerly been aligned with Ismail Khan.

The ISI also sent an emissary to meet with the mujahideen parties in an attempt to persuade them to ally with the Taliban. Its efforts were undercut by the Taliban's refusal to negotiate with their enemies. While the ISI hoped the Taliban would be its proxy, they never really fulfilled that role, though they were always willing to accept money and materiel. Saudi Arabia also began to fund the Taliban as an alternative to its previous favourite, Hekmatyar. Predictably, the influx of money and arms to both sides of the conflict caused the fighting to worsen.

The United States had largely lost interest in Afghanistan once the Soviets withdrew, although it now supported a United Nations Security Council resolution to place an arms embargo on the country. In the new politics of Afghanistan, the Americans were sympathetic to the Taliban, which they viewed as staunchly anti-Iranian, unlike the more politically flexible mujahideen parties. Nonetheless, the United States courted allies from across the political spectrum, and in June 1996 all the major factions were represented at a Congressional hearing on the country.

The unity government seemed to be holding together, and in June 1996 Hekmatyar entered Kabul for the first time in many years to take up his post as prime minister. Nine of his followers became cabinet ministers. He also brought soldiers to jointly defend the city with the other parties. The Taliban reaction was swift and brutal. It launched a massive rocket attack against the city, killing 61 people and injuring more than 100. The fact that this day of shelling stood out among all the others was remarkable, as the Taliban had been rocketing the capital mercilessly for months. In April 1996 alone they had fired 866 rockets. After years of such attacks, large parts of the city had been reduced to rubble.

But rather than attacking the capital again, in August 1996 the Taliban instead turned their sights onto Jalalabad and the three brothers who controlled it. All three brothers had fought as mujahideen under Hezb-e Islami Khalis, the same party as Mullah Omar. They had tried to remain neutral in the conflict between the Taliban and mujahideen parties, and had resisted overtures from Rabbani to join the unity government, even when he offered to step down as president to gain their loyalty. As the Taliban attacked, the brothers fled, allegedly having been paid $10 million to do so by the ISI. Abdul Haq and Abdul Qadir fled into exile, but Jalaluddin Haqqani reconciled with the Taliban, becoming their minister of frontier affairs.

After taking Jalalabad, the Taliban quickly captured the remainder of the surrounding province, Nangarhar, and then Laghman and Kunar Provinces as well. They then pushed toward the capital along the Jalalabad to Kabul highway, driving its defenders back to the outskirts of the city itself. In a much more sophisticated manoeuvre than they had attempted before, the Taliban also thrust a column northward and captured the airfield at Bagram, cutting the Rabbani government off from its source of foreign aid. With the Taliban once again at the gates of the city, and the speed of the attack creating panic, Massoud ordered a general withdrawal of his forces from the capital in an attempt to spare the inhabitants from suffering through intense urban fighting. The Taliban entered the capital unopposed.

One of their first acts was to seize former president Najibullah and his brother from the United Nations compound where they had sheltered for years. Although Massoud had offered to escort Najibullah out of the city to safety, he had refused — perhaps feeling that a Pashtun leader retreating from other Pashtuns under the protection of a Tajik would be too much shame to bear. A group of men led by Mullah Abdul Razaq, but under orders from Mullah Mohammed Rabbani, took Najibullah and his brother to the Arg where they were castrated, dragged around the compound behind a jeep, and then shot. Their bodies were hung from a set of traffic lights, cigarettes shoved between their fingers and money stuffed into their pockets as signs of their sinful behaviour and corruption.

Although initially the inhabitants of Kabul hoped that Taliban rule would provide safety and security, they were soon disappointed. Ruling the capital much as they did Herat, the Taliban imposed incredibly strict rules on the behaviour of everyone, but most especially women. All schools were closed; those for girls never reopened. Radio Kabul continued to broadcast, but now as Radio Shariat, used to announce new laws and the punishments for those who broke them. Men without beards were arrested and imprisoned, and women were forced to be completely covered and accompanied by a male relative at all times. While this was a cause of suffering for many, for the estimated 25,000 families headed by widows in the city it would prove to be catastrophic.

The essentially rural and Pashtun character of the Taliban movement was never more evident than when they gained control of a multi-ethnic city of 1.2 million people. Few of the Taliban footsoldiers had ever even visited a city before, and with the same language barrier they had experienced in Herat, they struggled to make sense of Kabul society. They again treated the city as if they were foreign occupiers rather than countrymen. When the Taliban set up a shura to govern the city, none of the six members were Kabulis. Even though many of the city's residents had been driven there by years of fighting, seeking safety and paid work, they were regarded as the cosmopolitan and decadent Kabulis who had been provoking uprisings among the pious Pashtuns since Amanullah's time. Mullah Omar showed his disdain and disinterest in the city by remaining in Kandahar.

Unlike Herat, the capital had a large contingent of international press who documented the Taliban's actions after the city's capture. This quickly led to an international outcry against their policies, although at first the focus was not on their treatment of women. Instead, the press focused on the many "bizarre" edicts issued by the Taliban. Flying a kite and keeping pigeons were banned, for example. There was also a complete ban on the use of recycled paper and toothpaste, playing marbles, taking photographs, listening to music, and watching television. Women were barred from wearing shoes that made a noise when they walked, or wearing shoes without socks, or wearing makeup (though how this could be discerned under a burkha is a mystery).

In order to enforce these rules, the Taliban reinvigorated the Amar bil Marouf wa Nahi an al-Munkar (the Department for the Promotion of Virtue and the Prevention of Vice), which already existed under the Rabbani government, but would now act with greater zeal. Similar organizations with the same name exist in other theocratic states such as Saudi Arabia. Maulvi Qalamuddin, a hard-line cleric even in Taliban circles, was appointed to run it. Young Taliban patrolled the streets with whips, clubs, and guns to ensure the rules were followed. They quickly became the most feared element of the Taliban regime in Kabul. Qalamuddin also formed a network of thousands of informants in workplaces across the city to report on their fellow citizens.

One of the most internationally publicized aspects of the Taliban's enforced morality was the requirement for women to wear the burkha. It is commonly understood that the burkha is a cultural practice rather than a religious one, as it is mentioned nowhere in the Quran or hadith. It is seen as a way for women to be "modest" in their dress (which is a Quranic requirement for men and women), but also as an element of Pashtunwali, ensuring that women guard their honour and maintain purdah by avoiding any sort of contact with male strangers. Although in the West the burkha is synonymous with the oppression of women, the reality is more complex. Even nearly 20 years after the fall of the Taliban, many women in Afghanistan continue to wear the burkha. Some women who have immigrated to the West from Afghanistan continue to wear it as well. It seems unlikely that in all cases they are being forced to do so by men.

Originally an affectation of rural middle-class Pashtuns, who were conservative enough to insist on maintaining strict purdah and who could afford for female family members to not have to do agricultural labour outside the confines of the home, it spread to other parts of society over the latter half of the 20th century. When universities in Afghanistan became ideological battlegrounds between leftists and Islamists, some women began to wear it even though they were educated and otherwise progressive. In Kabul and other cities, it spread as a form of grassroots protest against the policies of the PDPA, who were as focused on changing Afghan culture as the Taliban would be later on. In the countryside and in refugee camps, its spread was linked to a change to more conservative views of Islam than had predominated before.

The years of violence in Afghanistan meant that many families now confined women to their homes, to protect their family honour and ensure their physical security. For these women, the burkha was not an oppressive measure, but a liberating one as it allowed them a degree of free movement. In the refugee camps in Pakistan, it allowed them into the public sphere, where they could interact with other women and do mundane but necessary things such as shop in the bazaar. Given the years of ongoing anarchy, the burkha also gave a sense of security by allowing women to fade from view. What had long been a middle-class rural affectation became common across all social strata in Afghanistan.

Along with the imposition of the burkha, very early on the Taliban also banned women from working, citing concerns for their security and the requirement to maintain purdah. This had a major impact on society as a whole, as PDPA efforts to encourage the education of women meant that they formed a majority of all teachers, and nearly half of doctors and nurses. By banning women from the workplace, the country's education and health-care systems were damaged in a way that was not easily fixed.

By the time the Taliban established their rule over Kabul, the plight of women in Afghanistan was dire. Statistics gathered by the United Nations indicated that 1.7 percent of pregnant Afghan women died in childbirth, the highest rate in the world by a wide margin. And the disparity between men and women in life expectancy was staggering — an average of 61 years for Afghan men, but only 44 years for women. What is easily forgotten is that while the Taliban's policies exacerbated these problems, they long predated the Taliban regime. The plight of rural women, despite the machinations of various regimes in Kabul, had remained largely unchanged for decades.

Afghan women who opposed the bans on employment and the closure of schools found ways to work around the restrictions. Home-based classes, often run by former teachers, became common, especially for girls. Paid for by the parents of students, this model is not that different from the village madrassas that had been the norm throughout much of the country outside the major cities. Similarly, female doctors ran secret clinics for their women patients after the female-only hospitals initially permitted by the Taliban were closed. Both activities had the second-order effect of creating grassroots women's organizations, as well as bringing the idea of gender identity to the fore, whereas it had in the past been secondary to tribal or religious identities. Although the PDPA had tried for the better part of a decade to create similar organizations for women, none became as robust or effective as those that arose in opposition to the Taliban.

There has been a tremendous amount of scholarly work done in the West to examine the effects of the Taliban's policies on women, but little of it has expended much effort on understanding *why* they enacted the policies they did. It is not enough to simply accuse them of misogyny and assume that it drives their reasoning. Although Western criticism of the Taliban has focused heavily on their treatment of women, by contrast the Taliban themselves found this emphasis somewhat bizarre. They consistently told United Nations officials and others that their focus as an organization was, first and foremost, on fighting against their irreligious opponents until they had gained control of the country. Until that time, the majority of the government's revenues and attention would go to the war effort, with everything else to be worked out later on. The neglect of women reflected their attitude to every other aspect of governing as well: it was subordinate to achieving a military victory.

As much as the Taliban desired to create a just society that replicated the one that existed during the time of the Prophet Mohammed, their ability to do so — in terms of funding and the sheer ability to govern — was virtually nil. In everything other than military affairs, their focus was on the regulation of the outwardly visible signs of Islamic identity, for men and women. With no true policies of any kind to enact, nor the means to enact them, they remained focused on trivial things that nonetheless had a negative impact on many lives. But not all Afghans opposed the policies that they put in place, as in some areas they were merely reinforcing what were already common cultural beliefs and practices. In 1996 a hundred Herati women conducted an unprecedented protest outside the Taliban governor's office after he passed an edict closing the city's bathhouses, which for many were the only places to easily access hot water. They were arrested, and the bathhouses remained closed. But in predominantly Pashtun areas there was no groundswell of resistance to Taliban policies.

It was not until 1997 that the situation for Afghan women really caught the attention of the international community. In September of that year, Emma Bonino, the European commissioner for humanitarian affairs, was detained for a few hours by the Taliban along with two dozen journalists and aid workers while touring female hospitals in Kabul. They were accused of taking photographs of female patients, which the journalists admitted was true. Although the matter was quickly resolved and the Europeans released, the damage was done. From this point onward, the Taliban's treatment of women became a key issue for Western donors and institutions. What is unclear in all of this is what policies the Taliban would have put in place if they had consolidated control over the country and then turned their attention to social issues. It is possible that, once in power, they would have had to take into account a wider variety of views, and the new Afghan state's social structures would have come to resemble those seen in Saudi Arabia and the Gulf States. While not ideal from the perspective of Western gender politics, they are also not the focus of Western ire.

The Taliban themselves found the Western focus on issues such as gender equality to be puzzling. At times, though, they were able to see themselves through a Western lens. In perhaps a mocking way, they asked United Nations officials why they received no plaudits for their policies toward the physically disabled. On the central shura alone, Taliban leaders Mullah Omar, Nuruddin Tarabi, and Mohammed Ghaus each had only one eye. Mullah Mohammed Hassan Rehmadi and Mullah Abdul Majid had each lost a leg, and many of the shura were missing fingers. Injured during decades of fighting, with little or no access to health care, amputees were common in Afghan society. The Taliban argument that they could be seen as either progressive or conservative depending on the lens that was applied did little to endear them to the international aid community.

The Taliban's flexibility is best seen in the sphere of education. The Taliban are known for opposing girls' education, but this is not entirely true. What they opposed were mixed-gender classes with a Western curriculum. In practice this meant opposition to both the state schools set up under the PDPA and largely continued under the Rabbani government, as well as the schools run by international aid organizations. The ban on the employment of women caused the state school system to collapse, although this was likely not the intended effect. In places like Kabul and Herat, girls were eventually banned from going to school altogether, with an exception made for girls under the age of seven who attended madrassas.

In the Pashtun-dominated east, however, the Taliban did not ban girls' education at all, because culturally it was acceptable among the Ghilzai. To have closed the schools would have risked uprisings that the Taliban could ill afford. Like most actions of the Taliban government, implementation was patchy at best and subject to the whims of local administrators. It does appear, however, that had they turned their full attention to the issue of education they would have allowed education for girls in single-gender schools with an Islamic curriculum, much as they did in the east.

The Taliban government, although it included many of the same ministries as past governments, never progressed beyond being a hollow shell. There were no government functionaries to do the day-to-day work of the ministries; many who had done those jobs under several different regimes had fled. The Taliban never declared anyone as head of state, believing that the declaration of Mullah Omar as the Amir al-Mumineen was enough. Over time Mullah Omar became increasingly reclusive and autocratic, further limiting the ability of ministers to enact policies.

The only truly functional aspects of the Taliban government were the shuras that were set up in each city, district, and province, and the Islamic courts. The decisions made by shuras were enacted haphazardly, rather than through formal government procedures. In keeping with the Taliban's minimalist view of government, shuras were consistent with how society was governed during the time of the Prophet and no further structure was required.

Many government officials, including senior ministers, were also military leaders at the same time. The loose approach to governance was evident here as well, as when the military commander responsible for capturing a town or district would then be appointed its civil administrator. This meant that oftentimes civil government was at a standstill while decision makers were off "at the front." For example, Mullah Mohammed Abbas, the minister of health, was also second in command of the offensive against Mazar-e Sharif in 1997. For six months the ministry was completely inactive in his absence. Mullah Ehsanullah Ehsan, the governor of the National Bank, was killed in the same offensive. Leaders within the Taliban military and government were not appointed for their technical knowledge, but for their piety and loyalty, and were equally suited (or perhaps unsuited) for either role.

Like the mujahideen who fought the Soviets, the Taliban put little emphasis on military training beyond the technical aspects of operating specific weapons or equipment. Again, piety and loyalty were valued above tactical acumen, in sharp contrast to the professionalized soldiers led by Massoud and Dostum. The Taliban military never numbered more than thirty thousand soldiers at any given time, and these came and went almost at will. None of their soldiers were paid to fight, as this was seen as an affront to the belief that they were carrying out a religious duty. Military commanders were obligated to pay each soldier a sum of money whenever he returned home on leave, but this was meant to assist the soldiers' families rather than to represent pay for their service. With the constant flow of poorly trained soldiers in and out of units, the Taliban never achieved a level of military efficiency that approached that of their opponents.

While the Taliban consolidated their position in the capital, Mullah Omar remained in Kandahar. He had struck up an unlikely friendship with a foreigner whose presence during the jihad against the Soviets was controversial among many Afghans. Osama bin Laden had left the region in 1990 to return to Saudi Arabia, where he became disillusioned with Saudi politics and began to criticize the royal family as having failed in its duty as "Custodian of the Two Holy Mosques" in Mecca and Medina. Bin Laden left Saudi Arabia for Sudan in 1992, and his Saudi citizenship was revoked in 1994, leaving him stateless. In 1996 he returned to Afghanistan with his three wives and 13 children, living in Jalalabad under the protection of the mujahideen shura. He remained in the city after it was captured by the Taliban.

Mullah Omar had little contact with foreigners, even Muslim ones, and so it is unusual that he became friends with bin Laden. In some ways Mullah Omar looked up to the older and more worldly man, and they spent long hours talking about Islamic theology. In August 1996 bin Laden declared a jihad against the United States for the first time, though this language was not echoed by the Taliban, who remained parochial in their interests. In 1997 bin Laden and his family were moved to Kandahar as guests of the Taliban, and bin Laden swore a baiat to Mullah Omar as the Amir al-Mumineen. He kept in the Taliban's good graces by managing construction projects in the city that included houses for the Taliban leadership. In Kandahar he could be kept close at hand: many senior Taliban still harboured a deep-seated distrust of foreigners, even those with a long history in the country.

CHAPTER 16 GUILT BY ASSOCIATION

THE LAST TRUE stronghold that continued to defy the Taliban was Mazar-e Sharif, the capital of Balkh and principal town of the Jumbesh party. Dostum ruled the city from the nearby Qala-e Jangi (the Fort of War), a 19th-century fortress built to defend against the British. Although the city was connected to the former Soviet Union in the north, food and fuel were still in short supply during the winter months, and Dostum was often short of money. Nonetheless, despite his reputation for treachery, he was seen by many as the saviour of the northern Afghans.

The Taliban controlled most of the Afghan population, concentrated in the capital and the south and east of the country. By occupying the north, Dostum controlled 60 percent of the country's agricultural resources and 80 percent of its industry, gas, and mineral wealth. Even though it was outside the Pashtun heartland, the Taliban would need to capture the north to consolidate their rule over the country. But Dostum's soldiers, still wearing their communist-era uniforms, had a degree of experience and training that thoroughly outclassed the Taliban. So instead of confronting him head on, the Taliban found a different way to defeat him.

By the spring of 1997, Dostum's soldiers had not been paid in five months. Their leader was engaged in a bitter feud with his deputy, Malik Pahlawan, who accused him of murdering his brother Rasoul the previous year. The Taliban used their andiwal connections to approach Malik Pahlawan and strike a deal. He brought other key Jumbesh leaders into the rebellion, including his half-brothers Gul Mohammed and Ghaffar, and Majid Rouzi.

When the winter snows had disappeared from the mountain passes that separated the north from the rest of the country, the Taliban attacked on two fronts. Advancing directly north from the capital and from Herat in the west, they stretched Dostum's forces too thin to hold. When units under Malik Pahlawan's control stepped aside to allow the Taliban to advance unhindered, Dostum was forced to flee with his family to Uzbekistan and then to Turkey. The final insult was that in order to reach the Friendship Bridge over which the Soviets had also retreated nearly a decade before, he was forced to bribe his own troops.

The Taliban, led by Mullah Abdul Razaq, were able to roll into Mazar without a fight. They quickly subjected it, always one of the most open and liberal cities in the country, to their strict interpretation of shari'a. They took over the city's mosques and declared the Shi'a mosques closed. Schools were shut down and women driven off the streets. Burkhas had been almost unheard of in Mazar before the arrival of the Taliban, which now imposed them on any women who dared to venture outside. Even during the Soviet intervention, Mazar had suffered little disruption to its traditional ways. The arrival of the Taliban was a huge shock to the population.

As part of his deal with the Taliban, Malik Pahlawan not only betrayed Dostum but he also handed over Ismail Khan. He only realized that his treachery had not bought him a share of power in the north when the Taliban began to disarm his soldiers. Well accustomed to betrayals, he did not expect to betrayed by the Taliban.

But as the Taliban was disarming the Hazara soldiers, a dispute broke out that quickly became a general revolt. During 15 hours of intense fighting in the city, six hundred Taliban were killed and the remainder routed. A thousand more Taliban were captured at the airport, where they had concentrated in hopes of being extracted. Malik Pahlawan's men looted the city. When he regained control of his forces, he led them on an offensive against the Taliban that retook control of four northern provinces. Fighting was particularly heavy in the towns of Balkh, Samangan, and Konduz. Thousands more Taliban were captured, and most were executed.

In support of Malik Pahlawan, Massoud's forces launched an attack close to the southern end of the Salang Tunnel, blowing up the exit and trapping the Taliban forces in the north where they were prey to Jumbesh. Wahdat launched an attack against the Taliban who were besieging the Hazarajat, forcing them to retreat. This was the worst defeat that the Taliban had ever suffered, creating a crisis for their leadership. In 10 weeks, 3,000 soldiers had been killed and another 3,600 captured and likely executed. With nearly a third of their fighting force destroyed, morale within the movement plummeted. For the first time since becoming amir, Mullah Omar left Kandahar and visited the soldiers based around Kabul in a bid to raise morale.

He also made an urgent call to the Deobandi madrassas in Pakistan to send students to join the movement. Many closed down and sent their entire student bodies to Afghanistan, eventually numbering around five thousand. A summons also went out to the Ghilzai tribes to send their sons to fight. Many were reluctant to do so, however: although Mullah Omar himself was a Hotaki Ghilzai, the Taliban senior leadership was dominated by Durrani from Kandahar, and the eastern tribes felt shut out. Jalaluddin Haqqani paid tribal leaders to provide three thousand fresh troops, but their impact was limited. Dissatisfied with what they saw as the wasteful tactics of the Durrani leadership, most deserted over time and returned home. Traditional Afghan tactics valued the use of guile and the achievement of bloodless victories over hard-fought ones. Not surprisingly, the Taliban's penchant for martyrdom did not sit well with all of their recruits.

The Northern Alliance also took advantage of this pause in the fighting to reorganize. Malik Pahlawan was acclaimed as the new leader of Jumbesh. Rabbani was confirmed as president, with his capital as Mazar-e Sharif, and Massoud as minister of defence. In practice, however, neither Jumbesh nor Wahdat came under Rabbani's direct control, and Malik Pahlawan was treated with great suspicion. Although the alliance had held out against the Taliban in the spring, it was an even less cohesive group than before.

A pocket of Taliban had clung to the city of Konduz throughout the summer, and through the city's airport had been receiving supplies and reinforcements. In September they broke out of Konduz and attacked Mazar again. At the same time, Dostum returned to Afghanistan from exile and led his loyalists on a rampage. They burned down Malik Pahlawan's home and routed the forces loyal to him, causing him to flee the country. They then looted Mazar before the Taliban could reach it. When Dostum turned on the Taliban, he routed them as well. In the chaos, the retreating Taliban massacred 70 Hazaras in a village named Qadilabad, just south of Mazar. Regarding the Shi'a as infidels, they subjected them to savage cruelty.

With the Taliban defeated, Dostum attempted to recreate the administration that he had overseen before, but he was blocked from Mazar by Hazara militiamen. Instead, he set up his capital in Sheberghan, where he was among kinsmen. Incredibly, he then publicly accused Malik Pahlawan of having committed war crimes the previous spring. As many as two thousand Taliban prisoners had been brought to the Dasht-e Leili desert in shipping containers where many suffocated to death and others were shot. The dead were then deposited in mass graves. Although no one doubted that Malik Pahlawan was responsible, it was just as certain that Dostum would have done the same had he retained the upper hand.

The fighting in the north displaced an estimated three-quarters of a million people, many for the second or third time. There was little infrastructure available to assist these refugees, particularly if they remained in Afghanistan. A new tactic the Taliban was now using against the people living in the Hazarajat created even more large-scale distress. Rather than defeating them in battle, the Taliban instead blockaded the passes on all sides of the region and tried to starve them out. A million Hazaras suffered terribly over the winter, reduced to eating grass and seeds saved for the next year's planting. The Taliban refused the United Nations' request for humanitarian access to the Hazarajat, and in fact forced many humanitarian agencies out of the country, claiming that they were not working impartially for all Afghans.

For years the Taliban had been able to operate with little outside interest or scrutiny. This changed after their seizure of Kabul. Now that they were in regular contact with outside organizations, they quickly alienated potential donors. When members of the international community confronted them with the suffering of the Afghan people, the Taliban responded coldly and made it clear that they did not hold themselves responsible.

The United States also became much more interested in events in Afghanistan, though not for humanitarian reasons. In 1997 Afghanistan produced a staggering 2,800 tonnes of raw opium, 14 times the amount only a decade before. Pressed by the Americans, the United Nations Office of Drug Control (UNODC) tried to persuade the Taliban to curb production. Popular wisdom suggested that this would be exceedingly difficult, as the Taliban were seen as an organization funded by drugs. The truth was much more complex.

All the major players in Afghanistan — Dostum, Ismail Khan, Hekmatyar, Massoud, and Rabbani — profited in some way from the trade in opium and heroin. Particularly once the United States cut off funding to the mujahideen parties, and the PDPA government could no longer pay the militias, other sources of funding had to step up. Also, at the level of the individual farmer, opium was an exceptionally important crop. Hardy and compact, it was an ideal cash crop that had a ready market in all the major towns across the country. More traditional cash crops, such as fruit, were difficult to get to market before they spoiled, given the many disruptions caused by conflict. Where opium was grown and traded, many other industries sprang up in support — tea houses, fuel stations, rest stops, and small stores that accepted opium in barter. Many farmers, either just returned to Afghanistan or having weathered years of conflict, began planting opium in the 1990s.

When the Taliban seized control of Helmand in 1994, they encountered the vast opium fields that had been created on the irrigated lands of the Helmand Valley Authority project. Initially, they denounced the production of opium and burned the fields wherever they found them. This was in keeping with their strict moral code, given that intoxicants of all kinds are considered *haram* in Islam (sinful, or forbidden), and the fact that the movement's key leaders had not been reliant on the trade during the anti-Soviet jihad. They quickly realized that imposing a ban on opium would turn much of the rural population against them, and so were forced to accommodate the trade to keep the peace. By clearing the roads for transnational truckers, they also unintentionally made the trade in opium safe and secure, lowering transaction costs and improving the welfare of farmers. Supporting the opium trade gave the Taliban legitimacy among the large rural population that had been denied to previous Afghan governments that had pursued policies of eradication.

Production rose as the Taliban took over more of the country, not because they encouraged it directly, but because it was the most viable crop available to farmers. The profitability only increased as the Taliban tightened control, creating further impetus for farmers to grow opium rather than staples such as wheat, which they could now buy from international markets with the money made from narcotics. American efforts at countering heroin production in Pakistan also had the unintended effect of causing many of those producers to move their facilities into Afghanistan, outside the reach of the Drug Enforcement Agency.

The Taliban did debate whether supporting the narcotics trade was the right thing to do, but in the end made a practical distinction: opium, which was not generally consumed in the country, would be allowed, but hashish, used by many Afghans, would be forbidden. The consumption of either drug was also forbidden. While opium production was ignored by the authorities, a highly effective campaign of eradication was conducted against marijuana growers, almost completely eliminating this once common crop. They also began to tax opium production, charging a 2.5 percent *zakat* on producers. This was a form of alms to support the poor that shari'a obligated all Muslims to pay if they could, giving a gloss of piety to the opium trade. They also charged a further 10 percent *ushr* on shipment, a tax that in Classical Islamic society was charged only to non-Muslim traders, but in this case was applied because the produce traded was haram. Over time, the rate of ushr climbed as high as 20 percent, but it did not stifle the lucrative trade.

While the Taliban senior leadership did not personally profit from the narcotics trade, some local commanders either became involved in the business themselves or had already been involved during the anti-Soviet jihad. And while the ushr and zakat did become an important part of their government revenues, totalling approximately $375 million in

1998, this was still less than the profits from the long-standing Afghan transit trade smuggling business.

Much as before, the boom in Afghan opium and heroin production fuelled climbing addiction rates in neighbouring countries. In the late 1990s Iran had an estimated three million heroin addicts, while Pakistan had nearly five million. Half of the drugs exported from Afghanistan to those countries was consumed locally rather than being pushed out into the international markets.

The Taliban agreed to a deal with the UNODC to prohibit production in 1997, in exchange for a paltry $25 million in aid for farmers who lost their crops. There were likely two reasons behind the Taliban agreement to this deal, neither truly related to UNODCs goals. The Taliban senior leadership had never been entirely comfortable with the trade, and must have felt that their control over the country was stable enough that they could weather the backlash against eradication. They were also looking for international recognition for their regime. But the deal fell apart the following year, and opium and heroin production continued unabated.

Foreign interest in Afghanistan also centred around the potential for oil and gas pipelines. Although its own gas fields had been shut down since before the Soviet withdrawal, just to the north of Afghanistan were vast oil and gas resources, only some of which had been tapped. The Central Asian states were either unstable or ruled by autocrats, and few Western companies were interested in doing business there. An exception was Argentina's Bridas, which signed a series of lucrative contracts with Turkmenistan. In order to create new markets, it then proposed to develop a 1,400-kilometre pipeline from Turkmenistan to Pakistan, crossing through Afghanistan. In the mid-1990s Bridas executives met with leaders of all the Afghan factions, including the Taliban, seeking their approval for the project. Dostum hoped that the gas fields in Sheberghan could also feed into this pipeline, bringing him much-needed revenue.

As the project gathered steam, Bridas was outflanked by the American company Unocal, who signed a deal with Turkmenistan to develop the pipeline Bridas had originally pitched. Unocal was backed by the Clinton administration, which hoped to cultivate closer relations with Turkmenistan to prevent it from falling into the orbit of Russia or Iran. What Unocal lacked was a deal with the Taliban. The two companies began to court the Taliban, who skilfully played them off of each other. Soon their offers included not just rent for the pipeline itself, but development projects that included roads, schools, clinics, and other infrastructure. Taliban officials were brought to Argentina and flown around the country to see Bridas's other operations. They were also flown to Washington, where State Department officials tried to persuade them to sign with Unocal. In March 1997 Bridas opened an office in Kabul, in order to better communicate with the Taliban. Unocal funded vocational training for electricians and pipefitters in Kandahar, and bought the Taliban leadership a generator and a fax machine.

The following year the whole project fell apart. Unocal was coming under increasing pressure from feminist protesters in the United States opposed to any business dealings with the Taliban; they even asked California's attorney general to dissolve Unocal for committing "crimes against humanity." When the State Department lost interest in co-operating with the Taliban, so did Unocal. Bridas quietly pursued its plans for several more years, but peace was a precondition for the project, and that remained elusive.

The Rabbani government had inherited the Afghan embassy in Washington from the Najibullah regime, and used it to maintain contact with members of Congress as well as the CIA. In 1997 the deputy ambassador announced that he was defecting to the Taliban, a diplomatic coup that he hoped would win the Taliban official recognition from the United States. For weeks the Taliban and Rabbani factions co-existed in the embassy. After mediation by the State Department failed, the United States closed it entirely.

In early 1998 the United Nations ceased operations in Kandahar after senior Taliban officials beat and threatened several staff members. The Taliban also made operations in other parts of the country more difficult when they ordered all female United Nations staff to be accompanied by their husband or a male blood relative whenever they left their homes. This was clearly impossible for the international staff. The restriction hit the mission especially heavily because the United Nations had greatly increased the proportion of female staff members in the country in order to better access the women of Afghanistan. This edict was closely followed by the Taliban order to close all offices of non-governmental organizations across the country, as the Taliban felt they were undermining their rule. This created a humanitarian crisis, as more than half of the 1.2 million people living in Kabul relied on food aid to survive.

Largely ignored by the Taliban government, the Afghan economy was a shambles. Average salaries, for those who found employment, were between one and three U.S. dollars per month. Surgeons at the government hospitals in Kabul were paid $5 per month, not enough to survive on. The World Food Program was importing 750,000 tonnes of wheat a year in 1998, which was still not enough to feed the population. Donors had begun to ask hard questions, worried that the aid that they were providing was sustaining the war rather than meeting humanitarian needs. Many wondered if the Taliban would be forced to reckon with the humanitarian situation and negotiate a peace settlement, if not for the support provided to the Afghan people by the international community.

Nonetheless, the Taliban retained their focus on defeating their enemies, attacking again from Herat in an effort to seize Mazar. Weakened by infighting, Dostum's soldiers were routed, and the Taliban captured eight hundred Uzbek militia whom they massacred near Maimana. They also captured nearly a hundred tanks, which they used to sustain their offensive. Once again, several of Dostum's key subordinates took bribes from the Taliban and betrayed their leader. Dostum again fled to Turkey.

The Taliban attacked Mazar on August, 8, 1998. The fighting was intense, as both sides knew that defeat meant certain death. Of the fifteen hundred Hazara defenders of the city, only one hundred survived to be captured. With the memory of their loss the previous year still fresh, the Taliban took brutal revenge on the city, looting and killing for days. Whereas before they had been chased and trapped in unfamiliar streets, this time they recruited guides from HIG who knew the city. Thousands of Hazara civilians were locked in sea containers and left in the Dasht-e Leili to die. Tens of thousands more fled the city on foot, and were attacked by the Taliban from the air.

In all, five or six thousand people were killed in Mazar, and perhaps as many more in the villages and towns along the route from Herat. Mullah Dost Mohammed entered the Iranian consulate with a group of Taliban soldiers and murdered 11 staff. The Taliban ignored Iranian government protests and took no action against the mullah, though he was later jailed after his wife complained that he had brought a Hazara concubine home with him to Kandahar. It is believed that four hundred Hazara women were taken by Taliban as sex slaves during the destruction of the city.

The Taliban had long considered the Shi'a not to be true Muslims, and in Mazar they put this theory into practice. They declared that all Shi'ites in the city had three choices: to convert to Sunni Islam, to immediately leave for Iran, or to be killed. The result was a massacre. Long-standing tensions between the Sunni and Shi'a communities in Afghanistan had subsided during the anti-Soviet jihad, as much of the rural population united against the foreigners and the government in Kabul. And for years before that, the PDPA had been promoting the equality of all ethnicities. The Taliban brand of Islam, however, borrowed from Salafists the idea that the Shi'a were not Muslims, leaving them open to horrible atrocities. While many previous Afghan governments had also targeted the Shi'a, this was often for practical reasons such as to seize land or other valuables. In the case of the Taliban, it was for ideological and religious reasons.

In August 1998 the United States embassies in Kenya and Tanzania were bombed in attacks that killed 224 people and wounded 4,500. Although bin Laden did not direct the attacks, they were perpetrated by alumni of his training camps, and he may have funded and encouraged them as well. The American response was swift. Dozens of cruise missiles were launched into Afghanistan, targeting six camps associated with al Qaeda. It was hoped that bin Laden might be among those killed, but he survived. Most of the dead were Pakistanis being trained for operations in Kashmir.

The American attacks raised the question of whether the Taliban should continue to shelter bin Laden. Doing so prevented them from gaining recognition from the United States, which they desperately wanted. Many Afghans opposed his presence in the country, seeing Wahhabism as an alien version of their religion, and the Afghan-Arabs as arrogant and difficult to work with. Bin Laden had provided a force of Afghan-Arabs to fight alongside the Taliban, known as 555 Brigade. They were unpopular for the way in which they treated Afghans, and were likely behind some of the more extreme behaviour exhibited on the battlefield, such as the torture and murder of Shi'ites. Bin Laden's ideas of a global jihad did not generally resonate among Afghans, whose interests largely lay within the borders of their own country. They had no interest in assisting the Kashmiris or the Palestinians or any other group fighting jihad.

Although bin Laden did have supporters among the Taliban leadership, such as Jalaluddin Haqqani, it was his friendship with Mullah Omar that mattered most. As the amir's personal guest, he was well-nigh untouchable. Within the Pashtunwali is the concept of *melmastia*, which obligates a host to protect and shelter a guest. Even when pressure on the regime mounted, Mullah Omar stubbornly cited this precept as the reason why bin Laden was allowed to remain.

In November the United States began to communicate directly with Mullah Omar via a satellite phone provided to him by the ISI. It offered a $5 million reward and international recognition if he would hand over bin Laden, but he refused. Prince Turki of Saudi Arabia flew to Kandahar to try to convince Mullah Omar to hand bin Laden to him, but to no avail. Mullah Omar insulted the prince so badly that the Saudis immediately suspended diplomatic relations with the Taliban, although they did not suspend their funding.

By early 1999 even Mullah Omar recognized that bin Laden had become a liability, and encouraged him to disappear discreetly from Kandahar to live elsewhere in the country. Mullah Omar wrote to President Clinton that year, saying: "whatever we are — even if we are as you say fundamentalists — we are far from you and we do not intend to harm you and cannot harm you either." The letter did little to change American perceptions of the Taliban. Yet the Taliban still hoped for international recognition. When the Hazarajat fell to a three-pronged Taliban attack that year, the Taliban largely refrained from massacring civilians, possibly fearing that to do so would strain relations with the United States even further.

In 2000 the economic situation in Afghanistan worsened even as the military situation improved. The southern provinces were stricken with drought, and plagues of locusts were reported in Baghlan. Food was in short supply across the country, and the international community was no longer willing to make up the shortfall. Donors were demanding a ceasefire as a precondition for providing aid. The United Nations received only $8 million from member states for Afghanistan drought relief, despite making an appeal for $67 million.

Ismail Khan escaped from prison by bribing his guards, but rather than leading Jamiat soldiers against the Taliban he went into exile in Iran. Massoud's forces withdrew into Badakhshan, an inhospitable province in the country's northeast and the last not under Taliban control. But rather than push hard to seize this last strip of land, the Taliban were forced to pause and consolidate their previous gains. Unhappiness among the Pashtun tribal leaders had grown as the Taliban sought to impose greater central control. In January 2000 a group of four hundred tribal leaders forced the Taliban to replace the local governors in four eastern provinces who were not from local tribes and who were seen as corrupt. Protests broke out against conscription and a sharp rise in taxes, with as many as two thousand people rallying against the Taliban in Khost.

Despite the unrest, in 2000 the Taliban decided to make a bold move. Gambling their thin domestic legitimacy against the possibility of gaining international recognition, they decided to unilaterally impose a ban on the production of opium. They had calculated that they could weather the farmers' opposition to eradication, and as a result the country would be allowed to re-enter the international system. By March 2001 production had dropped to virtually zero. The commanders who profited from the narcotics trade were likely placated by the tenfold rise in the price of opium within Afghanistan from the previous year, and the Taliban government benefitted from the increase in the value of the ushr. Yet although this was the most effective eradication program that the world had ever seen, recognition did not follow.

That year saw worsening food shortages that once again the international community would struggle to replace. The United Nations estimated that in 2001 there was 50 percent less land under cultivation than the year before, and that 70 percent of the country's livestock had died over the winter from lack of water and forage. The World Food Program estimated that it would have to feed five and a half million people over the coming winter, more than a million and a half more people than the year before. The Taliban had no solution to this problem, and so continued to focus on cultural and military objectives.

In March 2001 the Taliban ordered the destruction of the giant Buddhas carved into cliffs in Bamiyan Province. Believed to be 1,800 years old, they reflected a period when Afghanistan was a centre of

Buddhist learning, and Bamiyan was reputed to contain a thousand monasteries, each with a thousand monks. The destruction was meant to intimidate the Hazaras, who regarded the Buddhas as part of their cultural heritage. The man detailed to carry out this task, Mullah Dadullah Akhund, was the minister of construction. Dadullah had a fearsome reputation as a commander and was responsible for massacres of Hazaras in 1998. Using tank fire and dynamite, and in the face of massive international outrage, Dadullah ensured that the Buddhas were obliterated. Forty priceless statues held in the Kabul Museum and a giant reclining Buddha in Ghazni were destroyed at the same time. All of these treasures of world heritage were regarded by the Taliban as forms of idolatry, connected to the pre-Islamic past, that should be forgotten.

The most moderate leader within the Taliban regime, Mullah Mohammed Rabbani, was on his deathbed while the Buddhas were being destroyed. He succumbed to cancer the following month. He was an important voice on the Kandahar Shura who advocated for dialogue and compromise with Massoud and the United States. His death left no other moderate on the council who could persuade Mullah Omar.

In June 2001 the Taliban began a final offensive against Massoud with a rejuvenated force of 25,000 troops. Some reports indicate that this may have included as many as 10,000 foreign fighters, many from Pakistan, but also the Afghan-Arabs of 555 Brigade. Massoud's forces were fighting for their lives, and the difficult ground gave the advantage to the defenders. The Taliban assault gained no ground.

In hopes of reaching a deal with the Taliban on bin Laden, the new United States ambassador to Pakistan, Kabir Mohabat, met with Mullah Zaeef, the Taliban ambassador. Mohabat was an Afghan-American, a Pashtun from the Zadran sub-tribe in Paktia Province, and so hoped to be able to navigate Taliban sensitivities and Afghan cultural mores to find a solution. Zaeef was able to offer the United States three options: the United States could provide the Taliban evidence of bin Laden's involvement with the 1998 bombings and the Taliban would conduct a trial themselves; or a court could be formed with judges from three Islamic countries to do the same; or the Taliban would isolate bin Laden within Afghanistan and prevent his movement and prohibit any communications with the outside world. Mohabat rejected all three options, and the negotiations did not progress any further.

On September 9 two Moroccan journalists travelling on Belgian passports set up to interview Massoud. He had been very accessible to Western journalists for years, pleading for international assistance against first the Soviets and then the Taliban. Having done hundreds of interviews, he had no reason to suspect this one. The two Moroccans, agents of al Qaeda, detonated a bomb hidden in their camera, killing themselves and Massoud.

Why al Qaeda had chosen that date to kill Massoud, cementing their ties with the Taliban and removing the last effective leader in the Northern Alliance, only became apparent two days later.

CHAPTER 17 INFINITE JUSTICE

ALL INDICATIONS ARE that the Taliban, including Mullah Omar, were unaware of al Qaeda's plans to conduct the 9/11 attacks on the United States. Many in the rank and file of the organization were outraged that bin Laden and his followers would abuse their hospitality and draw the wrath of the world onto Afghanistan. While al Qaeda had dispersed into hiding as the attacks occurred, the Taliban were in no position to do so, and would bear the brunt of whatever response the United States would make.

The Taliban leadership initially made statements condemning the attacks, and casting doubt on the idea that al Qaeda were behind them. Their statements only became more belligerent as they were condemned by the United States, who quickly began to push the idea that the Taliban and al Qaeda were in essence the same organization. Members of the Kandahar Shura approached Mullah Omar and asked him to consider handing bin Laden over to the Americans, to spare their country from the consequences of the attacks. Mullah Omar refused, telling them that bin Laden had sworn to him that he was not personally involved. Many Afghans assumed that the United States would launch a rain of cruise missiles on targets associated with al Qaeda, much as it had in 1998. The Taliban braced for the expected attack.

This was not an effective option for the Americans, as all of their intelligence indicated that al Qaeda had dispersed and their known training camps were empty. The whereabouts of bin Laden himself were completely unknown, although it was assumed that he was still somewhere within Afghanistan. Without accurate intelligence, pinpoint strikes were impossible, and the failure of the 1998 strikes to cause al Qaeda any real harm was still a recent memory. But there was also no strong support for an invasion. The American combatant command responsible for that region, Central Command, is required to maintain contingency plans for major operations throughout its area of responsibility. It had no such plan "on the shelf" for Afghanistan, and given that it is a landlocked country with no neighbouring U.S. allies, an invasion would be difficult. Iran was hostile to the United States, and Pakistan would be, at the least, uncooperative. The Central Asian countries to the north were in the Russian sphere of influence, and even if a force could be deployed there, geographically they did not give easy access to the Taliban heartland in the south.

With the Defense Department not able to provide an immediate solution to the question of how the United States should respond to the 9/11 attacks, it was outflanked in Washington by the CIA. George Tenet, the CIA's director, briefed an audacious plan to President Bush at Camp David on September 15. Using a combination of CIA Special Activities Division operators and Special Operations forces, his plan was to link up with the Northern Alliance forces and, supporting them with money and air power, use them to defeat the Taliban. With no ready alternative, but also liking a plan that was inexpensive and risked few American soldiers, Bush gave his approval. The order for the initial phases of the operation was signed on September 17.

Originally named Operation Infinite Justice, it was seen as a follow-on to Operation Infinite Reach, the codename for the 1998 cruise missile strikes. This was changed to Operation Enduring Freedom when it was pointed out that in Islam, justice was the purview of Allah alone. The first hurdle to overcome in order to put the plan into action was that the CIA had no real links with the Northern Alliance, other than a tenuous association with the now-deceased Massoud. His replacement, General

Mohammed Fahim, was known to the CIA, but it did not have a relationship with him. All previous contacts with the potential Pashtun opposition in the south had been through the ISI, and the CIA was unwilling to tip its hand by asking to rejuvenate those contacts now.

The CIA was also hamstrung by the lack of relevant linguists on its staff. It had changed focus from developing human intelligence to using technical means such as satellites and data interception instead. The agency was forced to pull a veteran operative, Gary Schroen, out of retirement to head the first Afghanistan Liaison Team, codenamed JAWBREAKER, deployed just two weeks after 9/11. Schroen, at 59 years of age, was one of the agency's very few Persian speakers. The CIA had no one at all who spoke Pashto. Agents and Special Operations soldiers trained for the Cold War found that the only language they had in common with many of the Northern Alliance leaders was Russian.

Schroen and his operatives, supported by Special Forces teams as well, proceeded to pay off all the anti-Taliban warlords they could connect with. Dostum, certain that the Taliban would be the target of an American attack, reappeared in the country from exile and was almost immediately on the American payroll. Abdul Rasul Sayyaf, the only Pashtun commander openly fighting the Taliban, was also co-opted by the United States. The fact that he had been a close associate of bin Laden was either not recognized or ignored. The biggest beneficiary of these arrangements was Jamiat, as it was the largest of all the anti-Taliban forces. Fahim reputedly received $41 million as a payoff to support the Americans, and haggled for a further $5 million to agree that his forces would push the Taliban out of the north but stop short of entering the capital. How much of this money actually made it to the military forces it was intended to buy off is unclear, but the short war against the Taliban made Fahim the richest man in Afghanistan.

On September 13, NATO invoked Article 5, the clause in the organization's founding treaty that stated an attack on one member would be treated as an attack on them all. Members offered assistance against al Qaeda, but the United States declined. Its plan required no help from its allies. An offer of Russian support was accepted, though, and Russia helped the United States to arrange to use the Karshi-Khanabad airfield in Uzbekistan as a staging ground, known as "K2." American engineers improved the runway to accept an increase in long-range, strategic lift aircraft. The United States later negotiated with Kyrgyzstan for the use of Manas Air Base, just outside of Bishkek, as well.

Uzbekistan was hesitant to support the United States, as it feared that this would open it up to retaliation by the Islamic Movement of Uzbekistan (IMU). A militant group aligned with al Qaeda, and operating largely out of bases in Tajikistan and Afghanistan, it was sworn to overthrow the secular government of Uzbekistan. Initially the Uzbek leadership demanded $50 million, a defence treaty, and immediate admission into NATO as the price for use of K2. In the end, it settled for much less.

Russian assistance also included briefings for senior American commanders in Moscow by Soviet-era officers who had fought in Afghanistan. Confident that it would not repeat the mistakes of the Limited Contingent, by mid-October the United States had about two thousand soldiers of 10th Mountain Division in K2, ready to support the Northern Alliance in its attack as needed.

While military preparations were continuing, the United States also made political preparations to take control of the country once the Taliban were defeated. A group of Afghan exiles, known as the "Rome Group," had grown around Zahir Shah. Their principal activity was intriguing against each other, and they were largely dismissed as irrelevant schemers by the political and military leaders in Afghanistan and Pakistan. The Northern Alliance leaders, now sponsored by the CIA, were pressured into forming a Supreme Council with the Rome Group. Composed of 120 members, it was seen as a government-in-waiting. When news of this reached the Taliban, they responded by arresting anyone they perceived as being connected to the former king.

The ISI was also thinking about ensuring that Pakistan would retain influence should the Taliban be toppled, and so it threw its support behind former mujahid leader Pir Gailani. He gathered a conference of Pashtun leaders in Peshawar, paying many to attend. Gailani failed to convince any of this "Peshawar Group" to take up arms against the Taliban. Hamid Karzai, now the Popolzai leader after the murder of his father by the Taliban in July 1999, also tried to create a force of anti-Taliban Pashtuns. He received many tribal leaders at his home in Quetta, asking them to pledge allegiance to him and telling them that the trigger for action would be when Zahir Shah ordered an uprising.

The Americans hoped that the ISI could split a faction of moderates off of the Taliban who might then fight against Mullah Omar, or at least lay down their arms and decline to fight the Northern Alliance. For many years, the ISI had been proposing different people as potential moderates, including men such as Jalaluddin Haqqani, who was anything but. In fact, the ISI was trying to find a Taliban leader who would be acceptable to the United States, and whom it could control more tightly than Mullah Omar. The most prominent candidate to lead any moderate faction of the Taliban was Mullah Rabbani, but his recent death had left any such group within the organization leaderless, if it really existed at all.

Convinced that the ISI was not dealing straight with the United States, the CIA opened a secret channel to the Taliban. The station chief in Islamabad, Robert Grenier, travelled to Quetta to meet the Taliban's senior military commander, Mullah Akhtar Mohammed Usmani. Grenier tried to convince Usmani to surrender bin Laden to the United States for trial. Usmani refused, repeating the same three offers that the Taliban had made before 9/11. He was emboldened by a steady stream of convoys carrying military supplies sent by the ISI, along with a message to reject the United States' demands. The ISI convinced him that, whatever the Americans threatened, they would not invade. Nevertheless, the expectation of bombing and missile strikes by the United States caused millions of Afghans to flee their homes, primarily from the major towns and cities, either dispersing into the countryside or trying to enter Pakistan and Iran as refugees. Even the threat of attack created a humanitarian crisis that left aid agencies working on the periphery of Afghanistan at a loss.

On September 25, speaking in a news conference, George Bush made clear what he saw as the scope of the upcoming operation. He said: "We're not into nation-building. We're focused on justice, and we're going to get justice. It's going to take a while probably, but I'm a patient man. Nothing will diminish my will and my determination. Nothing." Experts in the State Department had convinced Colin Powell, the Secretary of State, that this was short-sighted. Even if nation-building was out of the question, there had to be a plan for what happened after the Taliban fell, including a transition to a new government. Powell was persuaded to commit to stabilization, rather than democratization, which became known as a policy of "nation-building lite." Of all the experts who were advising the State Department at this time, there were only two Afghans. Ashraf Ghani was an anthropologist who had left Afghanistan in the 1970s to study at Beirut University. He had taught at several American universities, and was then working for the World Bank. Daoud Yakub was much younger, but had been an adviser to a number of American Congressmen on Afghan issues before running Zahir Shah's office in Rome.

On October 2, Bush approved the final plan for Operation Enduring Freedom, which envisioned the defeat of the Taliban but included no plans for what would happen afterward. No funding had been allocated for the reconstruction of the country's infrastructure, despite the plan to target it when defeating the Taliban. On October 7, Bush addressed the nation, beginning with these words: "On my orders, the United States military has begun strikes against al Qaeda terrorist training camps and military installations of the Taliban regime in Afghanistan. These carefully targeted actions are designed to disrupt the use of Afghanistan as a terrorist base of operations, and to attack the military capability of the Taliban regime." Although the Taliban were not responsible for the 9/11 attacks, their role in harbouring al Qaeda, and their refusal to hand over bin Laden, was enough for them to be targeted equally.

The first strikes were by 50 cruise missiles and dozens of laser-guided bombs against 31 targets in Kabul. Almost all of these were related to the Taliban, rather than al Qaeda. The United States also dropped over 37,000 humanitarian food packages that first night, intended for the population of Afghanistan who it was assumed would flee the bombing. But most civilians, expecting a swifter American reaction, had left the cities weeks before.

That night in October is also significant as it saw the first use of an armed drone by the United States. Unarmed drones had been flying over Kandahar since September 7 the previous year, searching for bin Laden. A potential sighting caused the U.S. military to rush an armed version into prototype production and then into use. The Predator unmanned aerial vehicle was armed with a single Hellfire anti-tank missile, and at this point was controlled by the CIA. Although armed drones would later become ubiquitous in many conflict zones, in 2001 they were considered a "secret weapon."

The Predator operator, actually sitting in a hangar in Langley, Virginia, reported that he was "98 percent" sure that he had Mullah Omar in his sights, leaving his home in a convoy of vehicles. When the convoy stopped at another building and Mullah Omar went inside, the Predator fired. The missile struck one of the cars outside of the house, killing the men in the vehicle, but allowing Mullah Omar to escape. The first drone strike was a failure, but by mid-November the Americans had fired 40 more Hellfire missiles at targets across the country. (This Predator is now exhibited in the Smithsonian Air and Space Museum.) After the second night of bombing, the United States had exhausted its list of fixed targets, a symptom of its lack of detailed information on the country.

Although the United States had amassed 40,000 soldiers, and Britain 20,000, either on ships off the coast of Pakistan or in neighbouring countries to the north, the majority of the work of defeating the Taliban was done by just 115 CIA operatives and 300 Special Forces soldiers, along with the revitalized Northern Alliance. Facing them were 60,000 Taliban, including perhaps as many as 3,000 Afghan-Arabs, and 2,500 members of the IMU.

The obvious first move for the Northern Alliance was to recapture Mazar-e Sharif, which would provide access to the nearby crossing into Uzbekistan and secure a large concentration of people. The city was surrounded, however, by three Northern Alliance commanders who all hated each other: Dostum, Jamiat leader Ustad Atta Mohammed Nur, and Mohammed Mohaqeq. Taliban positions continued to be bombed for four weeks while the CIA and Special Forces tried to persuade Dostum and Atta to work together. When they finally joined forces, they quickly pushed 8,000 Taliban out of the city. Fleeing eastward to Konduz, all along their route they were targeted by American bombers.

Three days after the fall of Mazar, the Northern Alliance had captured most of the north of the country. Ismail Khan next attacked in the west, recapturing Herat on November 13 and again causing the Taliban to flee. Then came the turn of the Hazarajat to be liberated. Soon the Taliban were reduced to controlling the capital, a small pocket around Konduz in the northeast, and the Pashtun heartlands of the east and south. Fahim was impatient to move Jamiat south to seize the capital, ignoring the deal he had made with the Americans for fear that they would sell out

Afghanistan to Pakistani interests. At the same time, the United States was trying to manage the battle against the Taliban to prevent the regime from collapsing before a successor government could be formed. But to Fahim, all the Afghan pretenders to legitimacy that existed outside of the country, whether in Peshawar or Rome, were irrelevant. He exerted political control over whatever ground Jamiat seized.

In the south, Hamid Karzai entered Afghanistan when the American bombing began, with only a tiny entourage and without external support, hoping to rally his supporters in Uruzgan. The Taliban saw him as a threat and sent a sizable force to kill him. Using a personal satellite phone, he convinced the Americans to provide him with support, which they did in the form of a Special Operations team. As the only Pashtun leader fighting against the Taliban at the time, Tenet saw him as a valuable asset. He was protected by part of the Special Operations team in Helmand while the remainder helped his followers seize the town of Tirin Kot. This was a minor military action compared to those ongoing in the north and west, but at some point during this period Tenet decided to back Karzai as the next leader of Afghanistan. Regional interests made him almost the only possible choice. The Pakistanis would not accept a leader drawn from the Northern Alliance, which they saw as too closely aligned with India, and would insist on a Pashtun. Russia, on the other hand, would not accept a Taliban leader, even a "moderate."

A possible alternative to Karzai was another prominent Pashtun, Abdul Haq. He and his brothers had controlled Jalalabad until it was seized by the Taliban, and although his brother Jalaluddin Haqqani had ties to the Taliban, Haq did not. Wounded 16 times fighting the Soviets and having lost a foot, his credentials as a jihadi were impeccable. He was also charming and charismatic. Haq entered Afghanistan on October 21 with a similar mission to Karzai. He hoped to rally Pashtuns, in his case including disaffected Taliban, to seize control of the country. He was backed by neither the ISI nor the CIA, but by Chicago millionaires Joseph and James Ritchie. Only four days after entering the country, perhaps betrayed by the ISI, he was captured by the Taliban, tortured, and then hanged in Kabul. Karzai remained the American choice as leader.

On November 12 discipline within the Taliban in Kabul broke down, and they looted the capital. They emptied the National Bank and the city's money exchange, and abandoned the city the next day in a massive convoy of over eight hundred cars, heading south. The Northern Alliance captured the city without a shot fired. Kabul's joyous citizens greeted the victors: people played music and danced in the streets, children flew kites, men shaved off their beards, and women appeared unveiled for the first time in years. Fahim quickly moved six thousand of his solders into the city, seizing control of all the key buildings and routes and choosing not to chase the fleeing Taliban. His predominantly Uzbek and Tajik forces would not have any local support in the Pashtun regions of the country, putting them at risk of sparking a Pashtun uprising. As the Taliban withdrew toward Kandahar, local commanders began to emerge and take control of territory, reminiscent of the anarchy that the Taliban had emerged to end.

In the north, the eight thousand Taliban penned inside Konduz were in a conundrum. The Afghan-Arabs fighting with them insisted that they would fight to the death. The Taliban, however, preferred to negotiate their way out of the city. Hundreds of Pakistani officers and soldiers who had been advising the Taliban were also trapped, and their capture would prove highly embarrassing for Pakistan. President Musharraf telephoned Bush directly and negotiated a temporary pause of American operations around the city so that Pakistan could conduct an airlift of its own people. This was kept a secret, even from most members of Bush's administration. As many as a thousand people, including Pakistani officers but also key Taliban and al Qaeda leaders, were flown out of the city. American soldiers could only watch this "Operation Evil Airlift" in frustration. When Konduz fell, over three thousand Taliban were captured by the Northern Alliance. Many others bribed their way to freedom and escaped.

Those unlucky enough to be captured were brought to Dostum's old headquarters near Mazar, Qala-e Jangi. There they were interrogated by the CIA as part of their continuing search for key Taliban and al Qaeda leaders. That many of these had already been allowed to escape was seemingly ignored. The conditions inside the overcrowded fortress were appalling and also chaotic. On November 26, the prisoners revolted, using weapons that had not been found when they were searched. They killed a number of their Jumbesh guards, as well as CIA operative

Johnny "Mike" Spann, the United States' first casualty in the conflict. The uprising was only quelled when the United States bombed the inside of the fort, and Dostum sent in seven hundred soldiers to regain control.

Among the surviving prisoners was an American, John Walker Lindh, dubbed the "American Taliban," who was sent to stand trial in the United States. The remaining prisoners were packed into shipping containers and brought to Sheberghan. Few survived the trip, and the dead were buried in mass graves in the desert. Around the same time, Uzbek and Tajik soldiers within the Northern Alliance began committing atrocities against Pashtun civilians living in the north, driving many of them from their homes. Despite the presence of American advisers, nothing was done or said to stop them. The Northern Alliance fighters were "their" Afghans, and they were winning the war.

So far the ISI was having little luck retaining any forces within Afghanistan over whom it had influence. To improve this situation, it began to recruit former warlords based in Quetta who had been deposed by the Taliban to attack Kandahar before the Americans could get there. Principal among these commanders was Gul Agha Sherzai, son of a famous mujahid during the anti-Soviet jihad. A large, powerful man who instilled confidence by his demeanour, he had been ousted by the Taliban in 1994 and was eager for revenge. On November 25, the first American Marines were landed from ships off the coast of Pakistan, establishing Forward Operating Base Rhino about 100 kilometres southwest of Kandahar City. They were placed to interdict fleeing Taliban, of whom they saw few as the Taliban remnants were heading *southeast* from the city across the nearest border into Pakistan. Just over a week later, Sherzai captured the Kandahar airfield with the assistance of an American Special Operations team. The fall of the Taliban capital was imminent.

On December 5 Mullah Omar gathered his leadership shura in the basement of a Kandahari businessman, and asked them what they wanted to do. This was out of character for the Taliban leader, who over several years had become increasingly isolated and dictatorial. Most of the leadership were ready to stop fighting, but no one wanted to be the first to say it, not knowing how Mullah Omar would react. When one of them finally did broach the subject, Mullah Omar acquiesced. He told them that he was transferring power to Mullah Obaidullah Akhund, and absolving himself of responsibility for their actions. He wrote and signed a brief letter that made it official. He was no longer the leader of the Taliban.

Mullah Obaidullah was a Hotaki Pashtun from Dand district of Kandahar, and had been the movement's minister of defence. Like Mullah Omar, he had been a mujahid with Harakat, and since 1996 had become close with bin Laden. The next day, Mullah Obaidullah arranged to meet Karzai, driving north to meet him in Shah Wali Kot district of Kandahar and handing him a letter of surrender. They arranged, in what became known as the Shah Wali Kot Agreement, that the remaining Taliban would lay down their arms and either return to their homes or join with the new government. The senior Taliban leadership would not be arrested, and in exchange they would abstain from political life. When Mullah Obaidullah and the other key leaders physically surrendered themselves to either Karzai or Sherzai, even though many were on America's "most wanted" list, they were released in accordance with the agreement.

As this was going on, the United Nations was hosting a conference in Bonn that was meant to select an interim government for Afghanistan. Four major factions were invited to the meeting, and at the insistence of the United Nations, a number of Afghan women were included as well. The first of these factions was the Rome Group of exiles surrounding Zahir Shah. There was also the rival Cyprus Group, mostly intellectuals, some with political connections to Iran. Third was the Peshawar Group, who rather than being drawn from the breadth of the Afghan refugee community in that area, was entirely composed of family members of royalist mujahid leader Pir Gailani. He hoped that he might gain in negotiations what he could not win on the battlefield. Finally, there was a group representing the Northern Alliance, led by a Panjsheri Tajik named Yunus Qanuni. A protege of Massoud, he became Jamiat's political chief after its leader's death. Most of the delegation were also Panjsheris, which caused resentment from the other groups within the Northern Alliance who were not represented. The south of the country, where support for the Taliban remained strongest, was also not represented at the conference.

Before a new government could be appointed, several issues needed to be resolved. With Jamiat having seized the capital, Rabbani had resumed the title of president. Ensconced in the Arg, he had both the trappings of power and a legitimate claim to it under previous United Nations agreements. Jamiat also had the strongest military position on the ground, leaving the possibility open that it would fight to retain power. At the same time, there was support among the refugee community, and among the Rome, Cyprus, and Peshawar Groups, for Zahir Shah to return to power. Many people, willing to ignore the issues that had led to his downfall, remembered his reign with nostalgia.

The Americans put massive pressure on all involved to get their way in the conference, allegedly even threatening Rabbani with an airstrike if he didn't vacate the Arg. In the end, he agreed to leave the palace and renounce the title of president. The Northern Alliance was given four key cabinet posts in the new government: defence, interior, intelligence, and foreign affairs, all of which were occupied by Panjsheris. The Northern Alliance was also allotted three of the five deputy president positions. Zahir Shah was given no official role in the government, but was awarded the title "Father of the Nation." Karzai was conferenced into the meeting from his satellite phone, and gave a short speech before he was appointed president of Afghanistan. Thirty minutes later, the Taliban officially surrendered Kandahar City to Sherzai's men. Mullah Omar left the city on a motorcycle with a handful of bodyguards.

Sherzai's troops ran amok and looted Kandahar City. Hoping to restore order, Karzai wanted to appoint his own candidate as provincial governor, but Sherzai refused to relinquish control of the provincial capital as he wanted the job for himself. Backed by the United States, Sherzai had little reason to give in to Karzai's demands, and eventually the president agreed to let him stay on in the role.

As had been agreed in Shah Wali Kot, Karzai was willing to offer amnesty to the Taliban as a way to start to heal the fractured nation. This was at odds with the aims of the United States, which wanted to kill or capture as many Taliban and al Qaeda as it could. The American secretary of defence, Donald Rumsfeld, called Karzai directly and told him to rescind the amnesty that had been granted. Karzai had little choice in the matter, and soon directed Sherzai to arrest Taliban leaders and turn them over to the Americans. Many of those arrested would end up in Guantanamo Bay.

With the war lost, whatever remained of the Taliban military evaporated, as had so many Afghan armies before. The Taliban soldiers mostly just returned to their families and homes, either in villages within Afghanistan or to refugee camps in Pakistan. Those without families who went to Pakistan were welcomed by Pakistani Islamist groups.

Between eight and twelve thousand Taliban had been killed in the month-long war, and perhaps twice that many wounded. The only American casualty had been Johnny Spann. The United States had launched over six thousand airstrikes in support of the Northern Alliance and Karzai's small force. The war had cost America only $3.8 billion, which was considered a bargain. More than $100 million of that had been paid in bribes, to either the Northern Alliance to encourage them to fight, or to the Taliban to encourage them not to.

To America, this seemed like an easy and nearly bloodless victory. But this view ignored the perhaps eight thousand innocent civilians who had been killed or injured to achieve it.

CHAPTER 18 OPPORTUNITY LOST

NOT ONE SENIOR al Qaeda leader was killed or captured in 2001, even though the 9/11 attacks were the impetus for the invasion of Afghanistan. Very few of the Taliban leadership were captured either, except for those who turned themselves in or contacted the CIA themselves. Osama bin Laden, with his senior leaders, retreated to Tora Bora, about 40 kilometres south of Jalalabad. Close to the border with Pakistan, he had been active there during the anti-Soviet jihad and had built cave-like shelters into the side of the mountain where he now hid from the Americans.

Anti-Taliban fighters supported by the United States were ordered into the mountains to capture bin Laden, but there were few, if any, Americans with them. None of the al Qaeda leaders hiding there were captured, as they were able to bribe their way out of the cordon. Bin Laden fled into Pakistan, crossing back into Afghanistan and then again into Pakistan, to shake off any pursuers. He then took refuge in North Waziristan, under the protection of Abdul Haq's brother, Jalaluddin Haqqani. In December he released a video in which he taunted the United States for failing to capture him.

On December 13 Karzai was flown by the United States to Kabul to take control of the country. He was met at the airport by Marshal Fahim, now the minister of defence. A week later Karzai was sworn into office at a ceremony attended by two thousand tribal chiefs, warlords, and militia commanders, as well as diplomats and government leaders from around the world. The still perilous situation in much of the country was underlined by the death of 50 Karzai supporters, killed by American warplanes while travelling in a 15-car convoy through Paktia to attend his inauguration. They were targeted as they were connected to the Haqqani family, who at this point hoped to be included in the new political order in exchange for loyalty to Karzai. It is estimated that two hundred civilians were killed by American airstrikes in December alone, prophesying what would be a major problem for both Karzai and future Afghan governments.

The selection of Hamid Karzai as the interim president fit the political requirements of Pakistan and Russia, but did not reflect the reality of the power dynamics on the ground. Of all the men appointed to the new cabinet, he was the only whose power was not backed by a private militia. The four "security ministries" were held by Panjsheris whose private military power would outstrip that of the Afghan government for several years to come. Without strong backing from the United States and its restraining hand on the anti-Taliban militias, Karzai was unlikely to survive for long. What was not immediately recognized is that the decisions made in the Bonn Conference, apart from the selection of Karzai, in many cases put back in power the very rapacious bandit leaders and warlords whom the Taliban had been cheered for defeating in the 1990s. This too would come back to haunt both Karzai and the international coalition in Afghanistan.

Ismail Khan, re-established in Herat, had hardened during his two years of imprisonment under the Taliban. Although he was still a sponsor of the arts and culture for which the city was known, he insisted that women in the city be completely veiled, and he ran the government with ruthless discipline. He had the greatest income of all the country's warlords due to his control of the major border crossing into Iran, bringing in as much as $5 million a month in tariffs on licit and illicit goods. He maintained a personal militia of twenty thousand men, allowing him to defy the central government and retain all of the "taxes" he collected for his own use. Of all the warlords, he was also the most civic minded, running schools and hospitals with the money from the border crossing.

In the north Jamiat had begun to fall apart as a cohesive movement. Although Rabbani was ostensibly still its leader, the loss of Massoud caused its other military leaders to jockey with each other for power. Fahim had created a power base in the months since Massoud's death, but his popularity and control were largely restricted to the Panjsheri wing of the party. Two other Jamiat commanders, Atta Mohammed Nur in Mazar and General Daoud in Konduz, had military power to rival that of Fahim. Atta, in particular, had tremendous potential for wealth through his control of the border crossing into Uzbekistan through Hairaton. Ismail Khan was a member of Jamiat only in name, able and willing to act independently.

The east of the country was nominally controlled by Abdul Qadir, but banditry was rife. His power over the region was shared with Hazrat Ali, who had been a minor leader of the Pashai tribe until his partnership with the CIA elevated him to the status of warlord. Hazrat Ali was illiterate and had no great tribal status, but the wealth he gained by fighting the Taliban allowed him to quickly recruit a ragtag militia of eighteen thousand men. He had been the commander entrusted by the United States to capture bin Laden in Tora Bora.

In the south Sherzai had worked quickly to consolidate his power by placing fellow Barakzai tribesmen in positions of power. Through patronage, he rapidly built a power base that cemented his control of the region. By relying entirely on Barakzai, however, he alienated and excluded members of the many other tribes who also lived in the south. He added further injury when he muscled others out of the lucrative narcotics trade and established control himself. As much as he quickly became a powerful leader, in the process of establishing himself in Kandahar he made powerful (and plentiful) enemies as well.

In his new role as defence minister, Fahim should have begun the process of dismantling the militias that dominated the country in favour of building a national army. Instead, he did everything he could to resist this, as it did not suit his interests. The fact that he was now responsible for paying all the militias in the country, including his rivals, gave him a degree of power over them as well. Under Fahim, and at the behest of the CIA and the Special Operations forces still hunting for al Qaeda, the size of the militias began to grow. Officially known as the Afghan Militia

Force, and only nominally under the control of the Ministry of Defence, men continued to be recruited into what were essentially groups of Afghan mercenaries. By the summer of 2002 there were 45,000 men in these groups on the CIA payroll.

Compared to the strength of these groups, Karzai and the central government he led were irrelevant. His strategy to create stability and maintain power was to acknowledge the de facto powers throughout the country and bring them into the government in official roles. Of the first 32 provincial governors he appointed, 20 commanded private militias. The same strategy was followed by powerful men at the district level and in key security posts such as chiefs of police. This meant that not only did Karzai align the government with groups seen by many people as bandits, he built a government from them. In American parlance, these warlords became instead "regional leaders" in an attempt to make their inclusion in government more palatable.

To maintain their authority, these militia leaders used the same system that countless Afghan leaders had before them: patronage. They used their positions to reward their followers with subordinate positions of authority, money, and power. In exchange, they received the loyalty of their followers. This system of patronage, stretching from Karzai down to the district level, was likely the most stable system that Karzai could quickly implement. The bonds of loyalty were much stronger at the provincial and district levels than his own tenuous grip on power. The unintended effect of this system was to legitimize lower-level leaders, who acted like tribal khans, while delegitimizing the central government, which almost immediately was seen as weak and unable to exert control. From the perspective of the international community, it was also corrupt. Much of the authority of the provincial and district leaders also stemmed from their perceived (or actual) connection with the CIA and American military. This further impacted the authority and legitimacy of the central government.

It is a testimony to the hardships of the previous two decades that despite all of this the predominant feeling in the country at the time was one of optimism. With a fresh government and the full support of the international community, it seemed that there was a bright future for Afghanistan.

The arrival of foreign soldiers as part of the International Security Assistance Force (ISAF) was seen as a positive sign of the world's desire to help. Initially with a mandate only to secure the capital, it had difficulty even doing that. Arriving in December 2001, it was not until March 2002 that ISAF jockeyed Fahim's forces out of the way in Kabul, though he maintained garrisons within the city and to its north. ISAF was denied a mandate to operate outside the capital, as the United States felt that this would impinge on its own ability to hunt for al Qaeda. This may have been true, but in time the war in Iraq would be the focus of American forces, and many elements, including the CIA, would draw down their strength, leaving a vacuum outside the capital.

Under the Bonn agreement, Karzai was only the interim leader until a loya jirga was held to select an official one. This would be followed by a Constitutional Loya Jirga to confirm a new framework for government, and then elections. What was known as the Representative Loya Jirga was held in Kabul in June 2002. It was organized by Mohammed Ismail Qasimyar, a Qizilbash who had been a professor of constitutional law and was living in exile in Iran during the Taliban regime. He had been present for every loya jirga held in the country since 1964. Qasimyar was careful to ensure that all of the people of Afghanistan were represented among the 1,550 delegates, 10 percent of whom were women. The country's warlords attempted to influence who was selected to ensure that they controlled large blocs of voters, but they had mixed success. It is thought that as many as a third of the final roster of delegates were independent of any political party or group.

As there was no suitable building still standing in Kabul for a gathering of this size, Germany provided a massive tent that was normally used as a beer garden. While some of the delegates travelled to the loya jirga on United Nations planes, others arrived in Kabul with tremendous fanfare. Delegates marched through the streets in processions of camels, dancers, drummers, and armed guards. After years of oppression, the loya jirga seemed to offer hope.

The first sign that something was amiss was that the United Nations invited prominent governors and warlords to sit in the front row of the meeting, even though they were not official delegates. Many of the country's power brokers and strongmen had arrived for the meeting uninvited, keen to exert political influence over the process. Before it began, serious fighting had broken out in the north between Dostum and Atta, and there was no way for the central government to stop them. Fighting had also flared in the west, where a Pashtun rival to Ismail Khan, Amanullah Khan, had tried to oust him from Herat. Ismail Khan was also in conflict with Sherzai, primarily over control of the drug trade. Even worse, the meeting was broadcast live on radio and television, allowing the country to see all of the strongmen influencing political decisions, seemingly with the blessing of the international community.

Zahir Shah had returned to Afghanistan in the spring and opened the loya jirga with a short speech, for which he received a five-minute standing ovation. At 87 years old, he was frail and in ill health, but some Pashtun delegates saw him as a potential challenger for the presidency. It was only with great difficulty that the American special presidential envoy for Afghanistan, Zalmay Khalilzad, dissuaded him from standing for election.

Khalilzad was an Afghan-American who had been born in Mazar and had moved to Kabul where his father worked as a civil servant. As a teenager he was sent to California on exchange, and later studied on scholarship at the American University of Beirut. He took his doctorate at the University of Chicago, and later became a professor at Columbia University. He worked for Dick Cheney when he was Secretary of Defence, as well as at the RAND Corporation and at Unocal. As the special presidential envoy, Khalilzad was the most powerful man in Afghanistan, certainly more powerful than Karzai, creating a degree of friction between them.

After much discussion, the end result of the jirga was that the Americans got their way. Karzai was confirmed in his position as president until the next election with 83 percent of the votes. In second place was Mehsuda Jalal, a female medical professor who had been forced out of her job by the Taliban. Fahim had threatened her husband to try to make her withdraw, but she refused to do so and won 11 percent of the votes, which was seen as a sign of progress. Although the loya jirga had achieved its purpose, the optimism leading into it had been squandered. It was a positive step that delegates from across the country had come together to discuss political matters rather than fight over them, but nothing had been accomplished other than cementing the status quo. The fighting between warlords outside of the capital made it clear that this status quo was not markedly different than the situation before the Taliban.

Karzai used his new mandate to again confirm many of the warlords in cabinet positions. In a gesture toward greater diversity, he urged Fahim to replace at least some of the Panjsheris in key positions within the Ministry of Defence. Fahim acquiesced, though he retained a firm grip over the ministry.

One of the few exceptions to Karzai's usual appointees was his minister of finance, Ashraf Ghani. Ghani had been a university classmate of Khalilzad in Beirut, and had returned to Kabul as an adviser to the United Nations special representative to Afghanistan. In poor health after having part of his stomach removed due to cancer, Ghani was also short-tempered and arrogant. He was loathed by the other members of cabinet, who frequently complained about him to Karzai. If he had not also been brilliant and hard-working, he would not have lasted in the post.

Although friction between ministers was common, one dispute turned deadly. Abdul Qadir, who had been appointed as one of several vice presidents, was assassinated outside his office in July 2002. Popular opinion held that Fahim was behind the attack. Concerned for his own safety given that his bodyguard was controlled by Fahim's Ministry of Defence, Karzai accepted a 45-man guard of American Special Operations soldiers and later contracted the task to the American defence company DynCorps. The fact that the president could not rely on Afghans to provide his security reflected badly on Karzai. Fahim also took this new arrangement as a snub, and relations between the two men worsened as a result.

While the Afghan government was reorganizing, the Taliban were doing the same. In November 2002, the leadership council met in Pakistan, for the first time without Mullah Omar. They agreed that they would try to join the political process in Afghanistan, but were unable to receive any assurances from Karzai or the Americans that they would not immediately be arrested if they came out of hiding. A brother of Jalaluddin Haqqani was nominated to go to Kabul to speak to American and Afghan officials, but rather than being treated as a political envoy, he was arrested and mistreated. Although Karzai was open to including the

Taliban in Afghan politics, the United States saw them as a defeated force with whom it had no need to negotiate.

The next step in the political process was the creation and approval of a new constitution. A draft constitution prepared by experts from Afghanistan, France, Kenya, and the United States was unveiled in November 2003. The county's sixth constitution since the one drafted by Amanullah Amir, it resembled the constitution of 1964 in envisioning a multi-party democracy. The key difference between the two is that the new constitution did not include a role for the amir. The elected lower house, or Wolesi Jirga, was mandated to have a least one female representative from each province. The appointed upper house, the Meshrano Jirga, was to be gender-balanced.

A five-hundred-delegate Constitutional Loya Jirga was formed to amend and approve the new constitution. It sat for 22 days of debate beginning in mid-December 2003. Sibghatullah Mojaddedi was appointed to chair the meeting, as an Afghan elder statesman respected by many of the participants. To protect the gathering, eight thousand soldiers from ISAF and the nascent Afghan Army were deployed in multiple rings around the city.

Attendees were split over three key elements of the constitution that reflected long-standing differences in Afghan society. The first was the role of shari'a, as the constitution envisioned a secular code of laws rather than a religious one. Religious sensibilities were respected by stating that no law would be permitted that contravened shari'a. This was not enough for delegates such as Rabbani or Sayyaf, who argued that shari'a itself should be the supreme law of the land.

Centralization of power in the post of president also came up for debate. The Northern Alliance delegates wanted to create the post of prime minister with whom the president would share power, as was the case on paper under President Daoud. Their unspoken wish was to have one of their own appointed to this post, further weakening Karzai.

The Northern Alliance and other representatives speaking on behalf of the country's warlords also argued for a much less centralized state, with powers devolved to the provinces or regions. This model, largely rejected by the international community that watched the jirga with great interest, was a closer reflection of how power was actually divided at the time of the jirga, as opposed to the aspirational model outlined in the constitution.

As various delegates effectively argued for greater power for themselves, the former presidential candidate Malalai Joya publicly accused Sayyaf and others of being criminals, referring to the actions of their militias since the withdrawal of the Soviets. Jihadis among the delegates shouted her down, threatening to kill her. Mojaddedi restored order, only to remind Joya that under shari'a a woman's value was only half of that of a man, and that she should know her place. All of this was carried live on television. On January 4, with 29 amendments made, the constitution was approved. None of the three major concerns regarding shari'a and the centralization of power within the presidency or the state had been addressed.

Regardless of the form of government described in the constitution, Karzai's biggest problem remained that the balance of power favoured the many warlords spread across the country rather than the central government, limiting his ability to enact any policy with which the warlords disagreed. Although a new Afghan National Army (ANA) had been created by decree in December 2002, it still existed only on paper. The same decree also banned private militias and launched a program to disarm them, but this was slow to get underway.

Fahim initially wanted the ANA to be two hundred thousand strong, larger than the national army had ever been before. Foreign donors and advisers persuaded him that sixty thousand men was more realistic and affordable. The first battalions trained were made up of soldiers handpicked by Fahim, all Tajiks and many from existing Jamiat militias. Less than 10 percent of those selected appeared for the first day of training — perhaps from their perspective they were not truly joining a new army, but merely changing uniforms for the sake of convenience.

Despite this shaky start, the ANA slowly grew in size if not effectiveness. By 2006 there were 37,000 soldiers enrolled. Somewhere between 20 percent and 40 percent of all members, including officers, were illiterate. The ANA suffered a 25 percent annual desertion rate, not including soldiers who went on long periods of unauthorized leave but eventually returned. In many cases, soldiers were absent because they could not easily send their salaries home to their families other than by delivering the money themselves. Pay was initially fixed at $70 per month for soldiers, plus a hardship allowance where applicable.

The Afghan National Police (ANP) received much less attention than the army, despite the fact that it was crucial to re-establishing the rule of law. As before, poor administration meant that the police were effectively left to "live off the land," robbing and extorting the local population they were meant to protect in order to survive. At higher levels, the Ministry of the Interior became heavily involved in narcotics trafficking. Positions within the ANP were often auctioned off to the highest bidder, with jobs that paid less than $100 a month purchased for hundreds of thousands of dollars based on their potential for graft. Command of posts astride key roads in opium-growing areas, or along the border, fetched the highest prices.

Germany had agreed to take the lead in training the ANP, but the plan it developed would train only 3,500 police officers over three years, when 62,000 were needed. Combined with the apathy shown by Italy, the lead nation for justice reform, this undermined the legitimacy of the entire Afghan government. In 2003 the United States took the lead for police training from Germany, and awarded a contract for the work to DynCorp. The new trainers instituted only a three-week training program for new police officers, focused largely on tactical matters. There was no training on community policing, investigation, or any of the other hallmarks of a modern police force, nor was there any form of mentoring or follow-up to assist graduates in practising their new skills. The program cost $860 million from 2003 to 2005, and trained 40,000 police officers, but the results were largely useless. The police remained a poorly trained and predatory force with very low morale.

The hallmark program of the United Nations Assistance Mission in Afghanistan (UNAMA) during this period was the Disarmament, Demobilization, and Reintegration (DDR) of the Afghan Militia Forces. Operating under the umbrella of the Afghan New Beginnings Program (ANBP), UNAMA began in October 2003 by collecting all of the heavy weapons into cantonment sites, for eventual redistribution of the serviceable ones to the ANA. Fahim resisted this move for many months, with his forces the last to turn in their weapons. Next it focused on the demobilization of individual militiamen. After turning in his weapon, each demobilized soldier was given $200 in cash, a food package, and either agricultural tools for use on his own land or job retraining. Sixty-two thousand militiamen were processed through the program, which was considered complete by the end of 2005. Remarkably, one of the groups that initially was not affected by the ANBP was the Taliban, as it no longer existed as a formal military body.

Later assessment suggests that as many as 80 percent of the men who went through the DDR process were not combatants at all. The program was intended to undercut the power of the major militia leaders, the most powerful of whom were seen as potential rivals to Karzai, by eroding their military power bases. Hastily implemented with little understanding of the politics or players on the ground, the process was largely subverted by these same local commanders it was meant to undercut. They created "combatants" and gave them unserviceable weapons to turn in, extorted funds from those who had been demobilized, inflated the numbers of combatants in their militias in order to receive additional funding, and oftentimes simply "remobilized" soldiers back into their organizations once the process was finished. The focus of disarmament was on the individual soldiers, rather than on the command structures that employed them, which were left intact. At a cost of $141 million, the net effect of the DDR program was minimal.

In June 2005 the United Nations launched a second DDR process, also under the umbrella of the ANBP. Known as the Disbandment of Illegal Armed Groups (DIAG) program, it was intended for smaller armed groups that were not targeted by the first cycle — an estimated 1,800 of which existed. The focus was on reintegrating these groups back into their parent communities, looking at the issue from both sides: supporting the former combatants to become self-sufficient and productive civilians, and also building acceptance of the former combatants (who may have committed human rights abuses or preyed on civilians) among community members. Rather than providing funds directly to the former combatants, as was done under DDR, larger community-based projects were promised in exchange for demobilizing, such as rehabilitating marketplaces, irrigation systems, or road networks. The intention was to build a stake in the process among a wider swath of the population, and make it more difficult for local power brokers to subvert it.

Despite costing $36 million, the DIAG program was also a failure, as it presumed that the armed groups, once disarmed, would fall under the influence of community leaders. This was not the case, as the armed groups were politically more powerful than the community leaders, giving them little reason to give up their authority. As with the DDR program, the Taliban were excluded from the DIAG program, which created a clear incentive for anti-Taliban groups to remain armed. Few community projects were implemented as part of the program, even though it ran for seven years. In the rare places where it initially was successful, state security forces were often unable to fill the vacuum left by the disarmament of the groups. This led them to rearm, often simply to protect their community from other armed groups.

In 2005, in parallel with DIAG, a third DDR program was launched. Known as the Proceay Tahkim-e Solha (Strengthening Peace Program), or PTS, its focus was on disarming Taliban and other active anti-government insurgents. Although the individuals who went through PTS ended the process with highly publicized ceremonies of reconciliation in front of a provincial governor, their government assistance largely ended at that point. The focus of the process was more to encourage Taliban to surrender than to truly reintegrate them. This was remarkable given that DDR programs are typically implemented in a post-conflict environment, whereas in Afghanistan as many as a thousand civilians a year were still dying as fighting with insurgents continued. The program, headed by Sibghatullah Mojaddedi, was controversial from the outset when he made a public offer of amnesty to both Hekmatyar and Mullah Omar, if they accepted the Afghan constitution and recognized the leadership of President Karzai. While amnesties had been offered a number of times before, specifically naming these two individuals created an uproar, both within Afghanistan and internationally. The offer was quickly rescinded.

In six years of operation, 8,700 insurgents went through the PTS. Nearly all of these men were from the Taliban rank and file, rather than from the group's leadership. Where Taliban leaders did attempt to reconcile with the government, they did it through personal connections to government officials rather than through a structured process. Over time, it was determined that as many as 50 percent of those who went through the program were not actual insurgents. It had instead become a means to funnel international funding to Mojaddedi's political and tribal patronage networks.

The influence of foreign soldiers serving with ISAF in Kabul was seen as positive, particularly in terms of security, and in the summer of 2002 a decision was made to spread the "ISAF effect" further into the countryside. Small deployments of soldiers along with civilian and military reconstruction experts were created that became known as Provincial Reconstruction Teams (PRTs). The first was established in Gardez, followed by six more the following summer in Bamiyan, Mazar, Konduz, Herat, Jalalabad, and Kandahar. Based on their initial success, by 2005 there were 19 spread across the country, 14 composed of American personnel and the rest from other contributing countries to ISAF.

Despite their small size, the PRTs operated with a great deal of independence, each finding the best way to work in its local political context. Because they were small, often little more than a hundred people, they did not pose a serious military threat to local armed groups other than through their ability to reach back to ISAF for additional troops or air power. Because of this, they were often forced to reach accommodations with local warlords, who would be relied upon to create a secure environment. This had the unintended effect of enmeshing the teams in local politics, often creating the perception that they had taken sides. Many PRTs were provided an additional layer of security by local power brokers, which was initially welcome. The PRTs soon realized, however, that the local armed groups were limiting who among the population could access the teams, and using this control to increase their own perceived legitimacy.

Overall, the impact of the PRTs could best be described as mixed, depending on the nation that led the team and the region where it worked. The PRT in the relatively peaceful and ethnically homogenous province of Bamiyan was successful, as was the British-led PRT in the much more difficult security environment around Mazar-e Sharif. The American-led PRTs, in general, were not as successful as they stayed strictly within their mandates and did not act as mediators in local disputes (as the British did between Dostum and Atta) or work to directly create a secure environment. Humanitarian agencies were also vocal in their opposition to the PRTs as military organizations delivering development and emergency aid. This was seen as infringing on the role of these agencies, but also blurring the lines between military and civilian

actors in an active conflict zone. Some of the difficulty that humanitarian agencies experienced accessing insurgent-dominated areas of the
country was undoubtedly related to this.

The Afghan economy had been in disrepair for many years, as
under the Taliban government nothing more than a few mosques and
fuel stations needed by long-distance truckers had been rebuilt. Despite
tremendous need for humanitarian assistance immediately after the fall
of the Taliban, few agencies still had staff on the ground in Afghanistan,
and it took time for the international effort to begin in earnest. American
military forces had large sums of money earmarked for reconstruction,
but their focus was primarily on Quick Impact Projects (known as QIPs,
pronounced "kwips"). These were meant to be not only quick to implement but to also have an immediately positive impact on the community.
Typical QIPs were projects like digging a well, or repairing a structure
such as a bridge or school. What was needed instead were comprehensive projects to rebuild infrastructure or get the entire education system
back on its feet, which were beyond the PRTs' capabilities.

The Tokyo Conference in 2002 received pledges of $4.5 billion for
Afghanistan, although only $1.8 billion was received. This is still an ex-
traordinary sum of money, but it should be considered against estimates
that it would take between $12 and $20 billion to rebuild the country. The
funds pledged at the Tokyo Conference were also not allocated between
emergency and development aid, which led to most of the money being
spent on emergency projects that, while necessary, left Afghanistan without any improved infrastructure or industry. After over a billion dollars
had been spent, opinion was split on what had been achieved. While the
humanitarian agencies and their donors could point at the vast sums of
money expended as a sign of success, Afghans could equally complain
that nothing permanent had been built or repaired.

The expectation of international aid caused a huge influx of returnees,
over two million people in 2002 alone. The flow of returning refugees
peaked in the summer of 2002 at over 50,000 people a week, overwhelming the aid agencies that were in place to receive them. With limited aid
earmarked to invest in agriculture, and with rural infrastructure destroyed by the open conflict raging since 1979, many returnees chose to
settle in the cities. The population of Kabul ballooned from 1.7 million

people in 2001 to 3.6 million in 2005, without any major improvements in the city's infrastructure. Over 95 percent of Kabul was without electricity until as late as 2005, when the entire country was capable of generating about 260 megawatts, the same amount as the average small American town. Generators, and later solar panels, became ubiquitous for all who could afford them.

The influx of international agencies into Kabul drove the sudden inflation of prices for rent and other needs. A large house that could be used as an office or staff residence that might have been rented for $400 a month before the fall of the Taliban could suddenly command prices over $20,000 a month. There was also a brain drain of educated people out of Afghan institutions driven by the high salaries offered by the United Nations and other agencies. Civil servants were paid, on average, $50 a month, while many NGOs paid what they saw as a living wage, where even drivers might receive $1,000 a month.

Despite this influx of money, the Afghan government immediately had trouble raising revenues to operate. By the summer of 2002, it had only received about 10 percent of the money pledged for its annual operations, which in total was about $460 million. One of Ghani's signature projects as finance minister was to impose an income tax on the wealthy, which was deeply unpopular given that most Afghans had never paid any tax in their lives. He also butted heads with international donors by insisting that the Afghan government have a greater say in how they disbursed funds, and what projects they undertook. Ghani's relationship with both Afghan and foreign colleagues eventually became so poor that in 2004 he was forced to resign.

Not including the trade in narcotics, annual economic growth in Afghanistan from 2002 to 2004 was estimated to be about 15 percent a year, a phenomenal rate. It has to be considered against the fact that the country was starting from an exceptionally low point, and even with this rate of growth, poverty was endemic. International trade made up a large part of this growth, which could have provided customs revenue to the government. The value of taxes and tariffs was estimated to be $500 million a year in 2002, but the government managed to collect only $80 million, as the rest was retained by provincial governors and lesser warlords. In May 2003 Ghani convinced Karzai to summon the 12 worst offenders and threaten them to force increased remittances. Several days later Ismail Khan sent two heavily guarded pickup trucks directly to the Ministry of Finance with $20 million in cash. This was a mere drop in the bucket compared to what he was earning from the crossings into Iran.

Another of the men who benefitted heavily from the new regime was Marshal Fahim, whose annual income at this time was estimated to be about $1 billion a year. This was from a mix of activities, including tariffs on border trade, opium and heroin trafficking, graft and extortion, and illegal mining (particularly of gemstones). He also received a windfall in 2002 by intercepting a number of shipping containers sent from Russia that contained newly printed currency. He refused to hand the estimated $175 million over to the central government.

A large focus for the international community was kickstarting the Afghan education system. In March 2002, three million Afghan children went to school, many for the first time, and almost twice the number planned for. Funded by UNICEF and USAID, 4,600 schools across the country were reopened, albeit with many shortages of teachers, resources, and space. ISAF was involved in a massive effort to distribute textbooks, managing to deliver over eight million for the start of school. In Kabul, nearly 45 percent of the students were girls; nationwide they made up 25 percent of the student population. The total number of students in school grew quickly year on year, reaching 5.2 million in 2005 out of an estimated 7 million eligible children. But, because of the lack of schools for so many years, 60 percent of this total were in the first or second grade, creating a massive bulge that would take over a decade to work through the system, if they remained in school.

A second focus of the international community was the dire situation for women in Afghanistan. Although the new constitution guaranteed equal rights for women, this did not make it actually so. The lives of women were very different depending on where in the country one looked. Although there had always been an urban-rural divide, and this continued, there was also a cultural one. In the north and centre of the country, where the Uzbek, Tajik, Turkmen, and Hazara ethnicities tended to dominate, women were generally much freer. In the Hazarajat in particular, men and women were more or less considered equal. But in the Pashtun-dominated east and south, the public lives of women remained severely constrained.

And even though the Taliban no longer enforced the wearing of burkhas in public, the many years of their rule had caused a shift in culture such that many women wore it voluntarily, if only to not attract attention.

The conservative elements within society still existed. Only weeks after the Constitutional Loya Jirga, the supreme court sent a letter to Karzai complaining that women were allowed to be seen singing on television, and that this contravened Islam. The idea that nothing would be permitted in Afghanistan that was not allowed in shari'a was the promise that had gained Karzai the support of conservative clerics. The chief justice of the supreme court was a long-time ally of Sayyaf. As had often been the practice, Afghan religious figures included many non-shari'a practices in their interpretations, and claimed religious sanction for what were cultural or political desires. This was the case in the complaint against women singing, which has no clear basis in shari'a, but instead reflects conservative Afghan cultural mores, and those of Islamic hardliners like Sayyaf. Although Karzai did not ban women from singing on television, he did allow the Department for the Promotion of Virtue and the Prevention of Vice to begin operating again. Its agents no longer patrolled the streets looking for moral contraventions, but they did monitor society as a whole and advise the government where there were lapses. The ulema had lost much, but not all, of their power in society.

Presidential elections were scheduled for 2004, but due to insecurity across many regions of the country, the international community pressed for them to be delayed. Too many armed groups were still active who could sway voters, either in favour of particular candidates or not to vote at all. Excluded from the process, the Taliban vowed to disrupt the elections, threatening to attack election workers and polling stations, and to cut off the ink-stained fingers of voters. (Voters in Afghanistan have one finger dipped in ink to prevent them from voting a second time.) The United States, keen to show progress in Afghanistan before its own presidential election, insisted that the vote must occur on time. To accommodate the U.S. demand, the presidential and parliamentary elections were delinked and the parliamentary elections delayed for nearly a year so that the presidential vote could take place. It required monumental efforts to register voters in a country where there had been no national census since 1979, and where there was no national system of identification.

Each presidential candidate had two vice presidents as running mates. Karzai's two presumed running mates were Marshal Fahim and Karim Khalili, a popular Hazara mujahid leader. By this point Fahim had fallen out of favour with many due to his corruption and his interference with the DDR process. The United Nations and many European donors pressed Karzai to drop him as a partner. This was difficult given the outsized power that Fahim wielded. On July, 26, 2004, on the last possible day, Karzai registered officially as a candidate with his two running mates Karim Khalili and Ahmed Zia Massoud, younger brother of the deceased Jamiat leader. The capital was tense, but in the end Fahim accepted being dropped from the ticket. He encouraged the minister of education, fellow Jamiat leader Yunus Qanuni, to enter the race against Karzai. In all, there were 22 candidates running against Karzai for president.

After being twice postponed, on October, 9, 2004, the first direct election for a national leader was held in Afghanistan. Over 9 million of the 12 million registered voters cast a ballot, including 2 million living in Pakistan and Iran. Every vote was counted by hand. When the counting was finished, Karzai was declared the winner with 55.4 percent of the vote. Yunus Qanuni came second with 16 percent of the vote, followed by Mohammed Mohaqeq with 11 percent and Dostum with 10 percent. The single female candidate, Mehsuda Jalal, placed sixth with 1 percent of votes cast.

Even before all the ballots had been counted, it was clear that a tremendous amount of fraud had occurred, with some districts showing greater than 100 percent turnout. It was unclear which candidates benefitted the most from the fraud. There was little interest in trying to invalidate fraudulent ballots or bring the guilty parties to justice, as just holding the election was deemed a success. The election of Karzai and not one of the warlords suited the international community, which accepted the result without complaint.

Overall, the years between 2001 and 2005 represent a lost opportunity, a time when the nation of Afghanistan was largely united by hope for the future. Over time, the population became jaded as promises for aid and development were broken, dishonest leaders consolidated their hold on power in the new regime, and corruption became the norm. The central state was still seen as alien and predatory, with primarily coercive methods to interact with the population rather than assistive ones. It was in this environment of disappointment and corruption that the Taliban were able to stage their comeback, despite having been effectively shattered by the invasion in 2001.

While Karzai has been accused as himself being corrupt, this is only true from a purely Western perspective. He maintained his grip on power in the same way as all successful Afghan leaders before him, by creating a network of patronage in the same manner as a tribal leader. Rather than running a modern state, he tried to run an inclusive tribe, rewarding loyalty with resources and punishing disloyalty by exclusion from the benefits of the state. It is to his credit that, unlike his predecessors, he included many non-Pashtuns inside his tent.

CHAPTER 19 THE NEO-TALIBAN

AFGHANISTAN'S PARLIAMENTARY ELECTIONS took place on September, 8, 2005, though the final results were not released until mid-November. As in the previous year's presidential election, a tremendous amount of fraud marred the legitimacy of the government and the winning candidates. Encouragingly, women won 28 percent of the seats in the Wolesi Jirga. The two largest groups represented, however, were Jamiat and Jumbesh. Many of the successful candidates commanded armed militias.

After the election, Hezb-e Islami Gulbuddin (HIG) officials registered a new political party, Hezb-e Islami Afghanistan (HIA), as the political wing of Hekmatyar's armed mujahideen party. Forty members of parliament announced their membership in HIA, making it the largest faction in the Wolesi Jirga. Hekmatyar was still actively seeking power, using a two-pronged strategy of political participation and violence. He had left his exile in Iran and returned to Peshawar, where he went underground in the Shamshatoo refugee camp, his strongest base of support. HIG had concluded a truce of sorts with the Taliban, and in some cases even used their name and emblem. Hekmatyar released an audiotape in May 2006 in which he claimed to be ready to fight alongside Osama bin Laden against the United States and Karzai's "puppet government," even threatening the American commander in Afghanistan, Lieutenant General Karl Eikenberry, by name. While HIA was tolerated as a political party, American troops continued to fight against HIG and hunt for Hekmatyar himself.

A group of former and mid-level Taliban leaders had tried to register as a political party for September's parliamentary elections. They called their party Khuddam al-Furqan (Servants of Providence), after a mid-20th-century Islamist group that was later associated with the mujahideen party Harakat. Their application was rejected under pressure from the United States, and so the Taliban did not participate in the elections. Although no senior Taliban leader was involved in this initiative, it is likely that the attempt was a continuation of the leadership's desire to be included in the political process, perhaps hoping to adopt a similar strategy to Hekmatyar. The Afghan government was receptive. It showed its interest in including the Taliban in national politics when Karzai appointed the most prominent promoter of the initiative, Maulawi Arsala Rahmani, as a senator in the Meshrano Jirga later in 2005.

The Taliban leadership, now known as the Quetta or Rahbari Shura (Supreme Council), had spent the past few years regrouping and reestablishing itself within Afghanistan. Nearly all of the senior Taliban leadership had escaped capture in 2001, providing a strong base for reorganization. While it was widely believed at the time that Mullah Omar was also living in Quetta, or perhaps Karachi, he had never left Afghanistan and was actually living in isolation in rural Zabul. In an audiotape of an interview he gave in May 2002 that was meant to encourage the Taliban movement, he said that "the battle [in Afghanistan] has [just] started, and it will engulf the White House, seat of injustice and tyranny." Despite the heady rhetoric, he exercised no operational control over the movement he had led until 2001.

Using the andiwal networks that gave the Taliban their organizational strength, they made contact with their former fighters in Afghanistan and Pakistan. The initial message was for the movement's supporters to wait. Several splinter groups sought to take immediate action against the foreign soldiers and the Afghan government, but they attracted very few rank-and-file Taliban, who remained faithful to the baiat they had sworn to Mullah Omar.

The Rahbari Shura appointed four senior commanders — Mullah Baradar, Mullah Akhtar Mohammed Osmani, Mullah Dadullah, and Mullah Abdul Razzaq — to organize *mahaz*es (military fronts) in Uruzgan, Helmand, Kandahar, and Zabul, areas where the movement had enjoyed the greatest support. The mahaz system was a complex one of communication more than control. It resembled the coordination of the mujahideen parties in the 1980s, or the tribal system of patronage and loyalty, more than a military command structure. Thus, although these leaders were assigned specific territories, they maintained strong andiwal links with organizations in each other's areas. This created friction and competition between the mahaz commanders.

Although the Rahbari Shura is often treated in Western analysis as if it was a headquarters, this is not strictly true. It was merely a mechanism for making decisions, and equally as importantly, resolving conflict between the groups loosely aligned in the new Taliban movement. It had no fixed location, meeting in private homes, madrassas, or mosques. Not only did the mahaz commanders operate with a tremendous amount of autonomy from the Rahbari Shura, so did the groups within Afghanistan that were nominally under the authority of the mahaz.

In eastern Afghanistan, the Taliban reorganized independently of the Rahbari Shura, accepting Mullah Omar as their spiritual leader rather than their military one. Prominent regional leaders such as Saif ur-Rahman Mansur and Jalaluddin Haqqani, operating out of North Waziristan, created networks that blended their authority as jihadis with their roles as tribal leaders. Haqqani was the leader of the Zadran tribe, settled largely around the city of Khost. Mansur and Haqqani both had seats on the Rahbari Shura, though they did not generally take direction from it. The Haqqani and Mansur networks were more hierarchical than the mahazes, and also more firmly rooted in their local areas. They came to be known as the most professional organizations within the broad Taliban movement.

This new Taliban movement was even more loosely organized than it had been when it formed Afghanistan's government. For some local groups who opposed the Karzai government, it was simply a brand that could be adopted, or a name that was applied to them by their enemies. As the level of armed conflict in Afghanistan increased, local groups were increasingly forced to take sides. Foreign militaries, in particular, found it important to create a cohesive narrative of "good guys" and "bad guys." Individuals, villages, and whole tribes came to be branded as "Taliban" if they were seen to oppose the groups that supported the government, regardless of their actual motivations, histories, or ties to other groups. The simple Taliban political agenda of driving out foreigners, defeating the puppet government, and enforcing shari'a was broad enough to be accepted by many different people and groups within the country.

Confusingly for analysts trying to understand it, the new Taliban movement was simultaneously tribal and supra-national. At a local level, groups tended to be homogenous, based on local interests and blood ties. Vertically, however, these groups were integrated into the larger organization either by religious and ideological motivations, or for practical reasons such as accessing resources from the mahaz commanders. Although the Taliban have often been described as a Pashtun tribal movement opposing the central government, this is not true, even though Pashtuns make up the majority of the organization. This description ignores inconvenient facts, such as that many tribes and clans simultaneously support both "government" and "insurgent" organizations in order to access resources.

Afghans themselves differentiate between types of Taliban, and are able to do so because, like tribal lashkars, most are not a separate body from the people, but are simply that people in arms. Taliban who are operating as part of the formal movement are known as *aslee* (real) or *mahktabi* ("schooled") Taliban. The more common types are *majburi* or *na'raz* (forced) Taliban, who fight because they believe their treatment by others and the stain on their honour leave them no choice. An estimated 80–90 percent of "Taliban" fighters operate in or close to their home community, where the expectations created by the Pashtunwali can become powerful motivators, since in order to regain lost honour the only recourse is revenge.

Despite the efforts to reconcile former members of the Taliban, choosing the path of reconciliation is not simple. Particularly for those who were well known within the Islamic Emirate of Afghanistan administration, simply returning to "civilian" life has not been an option, as they continue to be subjected to a wide variety threats — from Western militaries that did not accept their reconciliation and sought to kill or incarcerate them, from rival tribes or other groups empowered within the new regime, or simply from local reprisals for old grievances. The same is true for members of the Taliban who have chosen to demobilize after fighting against the Karzai government, although to the list of threats above they can also add the threat from the Taliban itself, who have consistently targeted those who reconcile with the government.

The disenfranchisement of different groups (be they tribes, clans, or villages) by the empowerment of others is a natural result of the patronage politics used by the Karzai administration. It has created political winners and losers, often driving the losers to take up arms to regain access to resources or simply for protection. A similar result followed from the style of counterinsurgency practised by Western militaries in Afghanistan, which sought to leverage tribal dynamics for military purposes rather than reduce their negative impact overall. The crude "with us or against us" politics of military aid have sharpened tribal differences, as well as underlining the ineffectiveness of (and lack of Western trust for) Afghanistan's government. As a result, they have failed to create lasting support for Western goals among the population. Western militaries often could not identify what was motivating the people they were fighting, or who they were, leading to the over-application of the label "Taliban" and the use of euphemisms such as "armed opposition groups" to describe them. What was particularly difficult for foreign militaries to recognize was that their very presence was contributing to the level of violence in Afghanistan, which has increased every year since 2001.

By 2003 almost every day saw one or two attacks attributed to the Taliban somewhere in Afghanistan. At first these tended to be small, targeting weak links in the government's network of support. Aid workers, the poorly equipped ANP, and government officials were common targets. The thin deployment of military forces across most of the country created the conditions for the Taliban to organize and begin to exert control over the population. By the winter of 2003, the Afghan government estimated that the Taliban controlled 80 percent of Zabul Province, essentially everywhere outside of the capital and major settlements. Their increased presence was not just as a military force, but as a popular one that was more likely to look out for the interests of the local population than the government in Kabul.

Military intelligence in 2005 indicated that the Taliban were coming together in larger and larger groups to conduct operations. To counter this, international military forces began to expand their presence in 2006, when Canadian, British, and Dutch soldiers were deployed to the country's restive south in a combat role. In May 2006 British General Sir David Richards took command of ISAF. He supported using a strategy based on the classic "Malayan model," a pioneering and successful use of counterinsurgency warfare by the British in the 1950s. He had been quite critical, in private, of clumsy operations conducted by American troops who relied too heavily on firepower, without considering the effect on the civilian population. The Malayan model of counterinsurgency operations focuses on providing security to the civilian population, creating the environment for improvements to governance, the economy, health care, education, and the other features of a functioning society. This, in turn, would draw support away from the insurgents and toward the government. This was to be combined with a new focus on eradicating the poppy crop, hoping that this would cut off a vital source of insurgent funding. Despite his optimistic plans, operations in Afghanistan did not unfold as General Richards had hoped.

Part of the problem for the British in Helmand was that they had fundamentally misunderstood the situation that they were getting into. The governor of the province, Sher Mohammed Akhundzada, was seen by Western diplomats as corrupt. But, his connection to Karzai was strong as he had been one of the few supporters who accompanied him when he entered the country to fight the Taliban in 2001. As the son of Rasoul Ahkundzada, he had a political base of support with a long history in the province. He had attended school in Pakistan, where some of his classmates went on to become Taliban leaders, giving him access to a wide andiwal network. He was also well known as a mujahid commander in his own right, although it was also known that he had been on the payroll of KhAD. As governor, he had worked closely with the American Special Forces team deployed in the province, and had raised his own private militia to support their operations. The fact that most of the men in his militia were ex-Taliban from before 2001 did not raise eyebrows in Helmand, where the majority of the population had supported the Taliban as well. He deftly maintained power through use of his andiwal networks, and in doing so supported the central government and Special Forces operations, and protected the opium trade from which he profited. To help keep the peace, he maintained high-level contacts with the Rahbari Shura in Quetta as well. A Helmandi interviewed by British Army officer Mike Martin described this approach by saying, "With one bullet, he [Sher Mohammed Akhundzada] did many hunts."

The biggest source of conflict within the province before the British deployment was friction between Sher Mohammed's militia and the ANP. The chief of police for the province had little control over the ANP, which were split into five different factions in violent opposition to each other. All were involved in the opium trade, with some even operating heroin-processing labs. All five factions fought with Sher Mohammed as well, though their preferred method of conflict was fingering their rivals to the Americans as "Taliban," and letting the foreigners take them out.

British insistence that Sher Mohammed had to be removed from his post before British troops deployed to Helmand rankled Karzai, but there was little he could do to resist. He appointed a new governor, a technocrat named Mohammed Daoud who had no tribal base of power in the province. Sher Mohammed's brother, Amir Mohammed Akhundzada, was left as the deputy governor, despite his involvement in all the same family activities to which the British objected. When drug eradication programs were planned in the province, Amir Mohammed ensured that the only farmers affected were his rivals, or small landholders who had no means to respond. This was sufficient to meet the program's expectations without impacting his own operations. Sher Mohammed was appointed to the Meshrano Jirga in an attempt to maintain his loyalty, but the new political position in Kabul did not leave him sufficient power to protect his opium business. Not surprisingly, he defected to the Taliban along with his sizable militia and continued fighting against not only his old rivals, but now also the British as well. The security situation in the province worsened dramatically, almost completely halting reconstruction. The first half of 2006 was the most violent period the country had seen since the fall of the Taliban.

In this environment, versions of which were played out all across the south, the Taliban were able to portray themselves as a force for law and order, much as they had done in 1996. In order to protect themselves from the government, many local communities took up arms and were quickly labelled as "Taliban," whether they sought formal affiliation with the movement or not. The Taliban were also able to recruit demobilized soldiers from the 93rd Division who had previous links to Hezb-e Islami, as they were excluded from jobs in the security services that were given to the rest of their comrades. Nearly everything that the international community did in Helmand during this period strengthened the Taliban.

The Canadians deployed in neighbouring Kandahar Province had a less rocky experience. The governor, Asadullah Khalid, was formerly a director within the Northern Alliance–dominated Riasat-e Amniat-e Melli (National Directorate of Security, or NDS), the modern version of KhAD set up with the support of the CIA. A Ghilzai Pashtun, he had fought as a mujahid under Sayyaf and later against the Taliban within the Northern Alliance. He spoke fluent English and had connections to the CIA dating back to the 1990s. His closest ally in Kandahar was the chairman of the provincial council, President Karzai's half-brother Ahmed Wali Karzai. Both men have been accused of heavy involvement in the narcotics trade. Khalid's personal guard, Brigade 888, was raised from his home province of Ghazni and was notorious for its cruelty among the local population. Khalid himself has been widely accused of personal involvement in the torture of prisoners. Canadian authorities were aware of this, in part because they were monitoring the governor's cell phone conversations and processing them through their own intelligence centre. But unlike the British, they did not insist on his removal. When this became publicly known, it caused a political scandal in Canada.

Detecting a large concentration of Taliban in Panjwai district of the province in 2006, the Canadians, with the support of other ISAF nations, planned a deliberate attack to defeat them. Pashmul had been a mujahideen stronghold in the 1980s, relatively defensible due to the high concentration of villages, fields surrounded by mud walls, and irrigation channels. In a bloody 15-day fight in September 2006 dubbed Operation Medusa, in which 12 Canadian and 19 other soldiers were killed, the Taliban were forced out of Pashmul. Estimates of Taliban casualties vary widely, but were likely around 500. Yet the intense fighting, the largest combat operation NATO had ever executed, did not bring an increased level of security. The following day Taliban operations resumed, when four Canadian soldiers were killed by a suicide bomber. The degree of preparation that the Taliban were able to achieve is the most interesting aspect of the fighting in Panjwai. Only 35 kilometres from the provincial capital, they had managed to stockpile over a million rounds of ammunition, and thousands of rockets and mortar shells.

Rather than providing a heightened degree of security, the foreign military forces acted like a magnet for violence. The British forces in Helmand, who were deployed in isolated "platoon houses" to provide security and interact with the locals at the village level, were quickly subjected to heavy and ongoing assaults that, in some cases, lasted weeks and had to be repelled with heavy weapons and air power. In the last six months of 2006, American and NATO forces conducted over two thousand airstrikes, more than in the first four years of the conflict combined. Rather than protecting the population centres, they turned them into the front line between the Taliban and themselves, displacing the population away from wherever they were deployed. The Taliban had been given enough to time to reorganize that they were able to use conventional tactics again, trying to overrun ISAF positions to score political victories. When these tactics proved unsuccessful, after taking thousands of casualties, they changed their approach to rely more heavily on improvised explosive devices and suicide bombers instead.

They recognized that the strategic weakness of international military forces was an aversion to casualties among their domestic populations, particularly in a theatre where the Taliban had already been "defeated." Causing casualties to break the political will of the NATO population became the focus of Taliban operations against foreign militaries. In 2007 nine Canadian soldiers were killed in Kandahar in the 10 days preceding a vote in Canadian Parliament on whether to continue the mission in Afghanistan. Parliament voted narrowly in favour, 150 to 134.

The British in Helmand tried a different tack in September 2006, when they negotiated a ceasefire in Musa Qala. The town had been the scene of major battles between the British and the Taliban, to the detriment of the local population. With the agreement of the governor, President Karzai, and General Richards, a deal was struck with the local elders that both the British and the Taliban would withdraw from the area. The ANA and the ANP were also bound by this agreement, essentially leaving the town to its own devices. Lieutenant General Karl Eikenberry, commander of the American forces in Afghanistan, was furious when this truce was revealed, characterizing it as a surrender. The truce held until February 2007 when the Taliban returned, claiming that the British had killed the brother of a local leader in a nearby airstrike. They murdered the elder who had negotiated the truce and imprisoned the other tribal elders. When the British retook the town in December, they found a functioning heroin lab and 11 tonnes of opium. The relief provided by the truce to the civilian population was short-lived at best.

Although not all, and perhaps not even most, of the violence that wracked southern Afghanistan in the mid-2000s was attributable to insurgents fighting under the umbrella of one of the mahazes, this is not how the situation was viewed by ISAF. Their policy of identifying and targeting Taliban leaders created an intense focus on the most radical, and effective, of the mahaz commanders, Mullah Dadullah. Known by the nickname "The Lame Englishman," Mullah Dadullah was famous throughout Afghanistan. In this case, "English" is taken to mean "exceptionally devious," a stereotyped view common in Afghanistan. Originally from Uruzgan, he had fought under Nasir Akhundzada before joining the Taliban. Despite losing a leg to a land mine in 1995, he continued to be noted for his bravery and insistence on leading from the front. In the winter of 2005, intelligence estimates suggested that he controlled approximately three hundred soldiers. This was quickly shown to be wrong when he proved able to mass that many for a single attack, as when he captured the hukomat in Sangin. Mullah Dadullah himself claimed to control a network of twelve thousand insurgents.

Of the four mahaz commanders, he had the most public relationship with al Qaeda, including links to their organization in Iraq. He imported a number of tactics from there, especially the use of improvised explosive devices that included a shaped-charge variant that could pierce the hulls of armoured vehicles. He also imported the practice of filming the beheading of prisoners in propaganda videos, until Mullah Omar reportedly condemned the practice. Mullah Dadullah was also quick to state in his media that the Taliban and al Qaeda "are one," although this was at odds with statements from the Taliban's central media organization, which continued to insist that the Taliban "are one thing, and al Qaeda is another."

Mullah Dadullah was killed in a raid by the Special Boat Service in May 2007, and his younger brother Mansour Dadullah was appointed as his successor. This is a modern expression of the tribal khan khel, where a group's leaders are drawn from a single extended family. It is likely that the raid was the result of information given to the Americans by members of Mullah Osmani's tribe or mahaz, in revenge for Mullah Dadullah betraying Mullah Osmani to American forces in December 2006. The younger Dadullah's strident statements of support for al Qaeda and apparent unwillingness to be brought to heel by the Rahbari Shura led to his public dismissal from his post. Mansour did not have his older brother's standing as a jihadi that made his removal politically difficult, nor his reputation for military effectiveness that would make his removal undesirable.

As the number of potential al Qaeda targets had dried up in Afghanistan, the Special Forces operating there increasingly targeted the Taliban in "kill/capture" missions that Afghans call "night raids." These were meant to eliminate key leaders within the insurgency, and thus dismantle the movement without having to target every individual member. The pace of these raids increased as time went on, particularly under ISAF Commander General David Petraeus, who doubled the number of raids executed from the already high levels under his predecessor, General Stanley McChrystal. In the 12 months from June 2010 to June 2011 when Petraeus was in command, the Special Forces in Afghanistan killed three thousand insurgent leaders and fighters, and captured eight thousand more. This was less a tactic of counterinsurgency to protect the civilian population than it was an industrial-scale killing machine or a sustained campaign of assassinations.

Although the logic behind the massive effort to target the Taliban's leadership is clear, it was also problematic. The pace of these operations meant that there was little detailed understanding of how the Taliban movement intersected with local politics, as one individual often played multiple roles in society. By projecting a false organizational chart onto the disaggregated Taliban movement, the international coalition's forces consistently gave themselves the wrong impression of the people they were targeting. No thought was given to the impact of killing "insurgent commanders" who were amenable to (or engaged in) peace talks, were tribal leaders, or were otherwise associated with the government. This created unintended effects — enabling unexpected actors to fill power vacuums, some of them worse than the people they replaced, creating the perception that foreign forces had a tribal bias, or otherwise upsetting the balance of power in unpredictable ways.

The pressure to keep up the tempo of strikes meant that often it was simply the available targets who were struck. In practice this meant increasingly lower-level members of the insurgency, or people who had been sold out by their local rivals. In some areas, traditional tribal leaders were so badly attrited that decision-making and conflict-resolution processes such as the jirga broke down. Too often, the targets identified had no connection to the insurgency, but were betrayed by others due to local disputes. Even where actual insurgents were killed, the effect was that younger and often more radical individuals were promoted to take their place, undercutting efforts at finding a peace settlement. The raids also created a cycle of revenge, as the families of those killed or captured felt obligated to fight back as the only means to restore their honour. Finally, over time there was a heavy focus on targeting insurgents who were part of roadside bomb-making networks, which was more to protect ISAF and the international coalition from casualties than to influence Afghan society in a positive way.

The idea that killing any Taliban was a good thing is predicated on the belief that the movement is an external force that is oppressing society. This is untrue. Many insurgents were merely resisting what they saw as oppressive or exploitative "others," who might wear the label of "government," or might be rival insurgents. The impact of "kill/capture" missions on local communities was often not what was expected. For example, Shakir, a subordinate "Taliban commander" from the village of Shin Kalay in Helmand, was killed in an airstrike on his vehicle in 2009. That vehicle was turned into a martyr's shrine by the community he had allegedly "oppressed," and placed beside a main road, close to a bridge that had been built by the British. The shrine was undoubtedly a stronger symbol of the British presence than the bridge. Years of targeting insurgents did not have the desired effect. Rather than degrading the Taliban, it degraded the fabric of society as a whole.

In the face of this challenge, the Taliban began to shift the focus of its organization away from being a primarily military one to a hybrid civil/military structure. Infighting between the mahazes also forced the Rahbari Shura to attempt to assert a degree of centralized control. To supplant the mahaz system, in 2008 the Taliban began to establish *niza-mi* (military commissions) at the provincial and district levels that reported directly to the Rahbari or Peshawar Shuras. The nizami did not immediately replace the mahazes, but created a dual chain of command that it was hoped would do so eventually. Those who took direction from the nizami were rewarded with money, arms, and supplies. A code of conduct was published in 2006 that laid out 30 rules for the field force to follow, many emphasizing obedience to the chain of command and respect for the local population. The Taliban also attempted to rotate field commanders from province to province, to reduce corruption and increase the organization's control over field units. Both this and the ni-zami system were deeply unpopular, and broke down in 2010 or 2011, in part because of extremely high casualties among the nizami members.

The Taliban also formed civil government structures in areas under even nominal control, sometimes referred to as "shadow governments." These took the form of "shadow governors" operating at the provincial and district levels as well as mulki (political commissions) to support the governor in hearing complaints from locals. The most popular and successful element in the Taliban civil administration was its system of courts, which were able to respond to the increasing demands of Afghan society for dispute resolution and justice.

In this period the Taliban also greatly increased their capability to produce propaganda. When they had formed the government they had banned many forms of media, but as an insurgent force they embraced them instead. They developed a highly professional video production capability, as well as creating audio recordings of chants that were popular even among those who did not support the Taliban, especially as ring tones for mobile phones. From mid-2005 the Taliban maintained a website called Al Emirah (The Emirate) that published poetry and news articles in five languages: Pashto, Farsi, Urdu, Arabic, and English. While *shabnamah* or handwritten "night letters" delivered to homes or posted in public were a traditional means of delivering threats in Afghanistan, by 2007 it was becoming more common for the Taliban to deliver them by text message instead.

Their messages were simple, and aimed at the weak points in the Karzai government or supported by actions of their own in Afghanistan. The first video they produced in 2006 showed bandits being punished by a Taliban court. A key message that they drove home was: "Government courts are for the rich, Taliban justice is for the poor." This resonated with many Afghans, who, second only to peace, longed for justice.

Improved propaganda and an alternative form of civil governance gave the Taliban the ability to begin organizing in the north of the country, where they had not previously had support. They took a slow approach to expanding there, focusing first on communities where they could already find some sympathy. This included the Pashtun pockets in Faryab, Balkh, Konduz, and Baghlan, created by various governments through a century of social engineering and resettlement. They also looked for support among the region's Sunni clergy, no matter what their ethnicity. They used andiwal networks to find former mujahideen colleagues, particularly among former Hezb-e Islami. They built contacts with former Jumbesh and Jamiat commanders who had been disenfranchised by the new government. They also made inroads with the Turkmen community, who had been largely unmolested by the Taliban when they occupied the north because their elders quickly struck deals with them.

The Taliban first sent mullahs to spread their message northward, and then began to recruit small insurgent bands, eventually grouping these together into operational units. These included even non-Pashtuns, who were motivated by many of the same grievances as their Pashtun brethren. By late 2008 they completely controlled Chardara district in Konduz, an area that was predominately Pashtun and therefore had a history of neglect and social isolation in the Tajik-dominated province. They also expanded their control in Faryab in 2010, though by this time they included many Uzbeks, Aimaqs, and Turkmens in their ranks. The assumption that the Taliban are nothing more than a conservative Pashtun movement underrates their ability to influence others outside their own community. Recognizing that their movement is a response to legitimate grievances that affect nearly all Afghans makes their ability to extend their movement throughout Afghanistan apparent.

Besides this unexpected expansion, elements of the Taliban also adopted an unexpected tactic, the suicide attack. The first known instance in Afghanistan was the assassination of a Saudi-backed warlord named Maulvi Jamil-e Rehman in Kunar in 1992. The next known attack was against Massoud in 2001. But starting in 2004, insurgents in Afghanistan began to use the tactic with increasing frequency. There were only 6 that first year, but this climbed to 141 in 2006, causing over 1,100 casualties, mostly civilians. Concurrent with this was a large increase in the number of improvised explosive devices used against military and civilian targets. Although increasingly prevalent, the use of suicide bombers has remained the tactic of niche elements within the insurgency who are fighting for primarily ideological reasons. Suicide attacks have not entered mainstream thinking as an effective or necessary tactic.

Surveys suggest that only about 11 percent of Afghans believe that suicide attacks are justifiable or are sometimes justifiable if launched in defence of Islam. Unlike in other countries where suicide attacks are common, the bombers in Afghanistan are often recruited from vulnerable populations, such as orphans or the mentally ill. They were generally unsuccessful at creating any effect other than mass civilian casualties until 2009, when there was an increase in "complex attacks." In these attacks, the suicide bombers are used to breach security, while other attackers then strike at the target that has been made vulnerable, often a government office or military headquarters.

The issue of civilian casualties has become highly politicized in Afghanistan. Karzai often made public statements denouncing foreign military operations that killed civilians. In 2009 there were over 2,200 civilian casualties as a direct result of fighting, a quarter of them caused by either foreign or Afghan pro-government forces. The Taliban integrated the message that foreign militaries were causing civilian casualties into many of their media products, and published many news articles reporting on specific instances. They coupled this grievance with the issue of the treatment of prisoners to show ISAF and American forces in a bad light.

From the outset of the invasion, the United States did not treat captured insurgents in line with the Geneva Conventions, and instead built a system of prisons that were outside of normal laws. The detention facility at Guantanamo Bay, placed there because jurisdiction over that location is nebulous, is the most famous of these. But the United States also ran prisons within the military bases in Bagram and Kandahar, and used various secret detention centres run by the CIA (such as the infamous "Salt Pit" outside Kabul). It also tacitly accepted, and its personnel accessed, secret jails run by various Afghan warlords and the Afghan intelligence services. Many Afghan detainees were also subjected to rendition to other countries, such as Uzbekistan and Tajikistan, where they were often tortured. None of this remained secret for long. By 2005 the Afghan Human Rights Tribunal had registered eight hundred cases of prisoner abuse at more than 30 locations run by the United States in Afghanistan.

The substantial bounties that the United States was paying for al Qaeda members created a market for prisoners, and an incentive for both the ISI and the warlords to sell innocent men. American interrogators were hampered by a near complete lack of Pashto and Dari speakers, both in the army and the CIA, that made determining the true identity and value of any prisoner difficult. There were no current photos, or any photos at all, of many of the al Qaeda and Taliban leaders, further making identification difficult. The situation was confused enough that in the early days of the invasion the CIA bought fake photos of the leadership from Afghan con men for thousands of dollars.

The "gold rush" mentality toward selling prisoners created so much chaos that men like Jonathan "Jack" Idema, a disgraced former Special Forces sergeant, were able to operate in Afghanistan as private bounty hunters. Claiming to be part of "Task Force Saber 7," he and two other Americans, along with hired Afghan guns, conducted their own hunt for bin Laden, operating a private prison for those unfortunate enough to fall into their hands. They handed some prisoners over to American and Afghan forces, and seemed to enjoy some degree of official sanction. Idema, in reality, was a con man who simultaneously claimed to be running covert operations while also trying to charge journalists a fee to interview him. He sold faked footage of an al Qaeda training camp to CBS, and operated for three years before Afghan authorities finally arrested him.

The American approach to taking prisoners had multiple impacts. Firstly, little useful intelligence was generated despite the large number of people arrested. The United States simply lacked the capacity to process prisoners effectively and exploit the information that was extracted. Even worse, the widespread abuse of prisoners created grievances that fuelled the insurgency, as well as undermining the credibility of the international effort in Afghanistan as a whole, whether military or civilian. The men who had been held in Guantanamo Bay returned to Afghanistan as heroes, and many joined or rejoined the Taliban. For having suffered what they did, these men were accorded a great deal of respect in Afghan society, as they were living representations of the moral superiority of righteous Islam over American values.

Perceptions of ISAF and the American military were generally positive in 2001, but they soured over time. A watershed moment was an incident on May, 26, 2006, when the brakes failed on an American military truck driving through Kabul. It struck a number of cars, killing five people. When an angry crowd gathered, nervous American soldiers shot several people. This led to rioting across the capital that was allowed to unfold in many instances while the police stood by. It took the Afghan Army to reimpose order. After this incident came the first public calls from outside the insurgency for foreign forces to withdraw.

Opinion polls conducted in Helmand and Kandahar in July 2010 revealed that only 10 percent of respondents felt that "foreigners were present in Afghanistan to bring peace and security," while 47 percent felt that their intention was to "occupy Afghanistan or advance their own national interests." In a country where news often travels by word of mouth, there was a persistent rumour that the foreign militaries were working with the Taliban against ordinary Afghans. It was widely known that the West had funded the mujahideen through the ISI during the Soviet intervention, and it was assumed that it continued to fund the Taliban in the same way. The idea that a country as powerful as the United States could easily crush the Taliban if it really tried was also prevalent. The failure to destroy them in more than a decade of fighting was taken as evidence that it was not really trying. Even Karzai spread the rumour that the British were ferrying Taliban around Helmand in helicopters. Against these strong perceptions rooted in cultural narratives about the West, it was hard to convince many Afghans that the foreign military presence was intended for their betterment.

The combined military strength of ISAF and American forces in Afghanistan peaked in 2010 at one 138,000 soldiers, 15 percent more than the Soviet Limited Contingent at its peak. Conversely, the Taliban strength was much lower than that of the mujahideen when the whole country had been in armed rebellion. Nonetheless, the Western powers were having no more luck than the Soviets did in pacifying the country and creating a stable central government.

Part of the problem was that they were fighting an enemy who did not exist as they saw him. The centrally controlled, hierarchically structured organization of "others" invading Afghanistan from Pakistan and oppressing the people was not the Taliban they were fighting. It was hard for the U.S. and ISAF military to see that many of the policies they were enacting, such as the eradication of the poppy crop, were not undermining the Taliban, but were creating them in the form of farmers who took up arms to defend their land and families.

The high-intensity targeting of insurgent leaders at all levels did not reduce the intensity of the fighting, though oddly it may have prevented the Taliban from creating the hierarchical structures and central control mechanisms that the military thought they were targeting. It did create a tremendous amount of churn in the insurgent leadership, so much so that any potential for negotiating a peace settlement was nullified. It is unknown how many of the insurgents killed would have been willing to talk peace, or even how many were already doing so, as this was not part of the targeting calculus.

Rather than causing the insurgency to end, military operations in the 2000s merely caused the situation to disintegrate into armed chaos.

CHAPTER 20 LEFT TO STAND ALONE

DESPITE YEARS OF capacity building, the Afghan government remained highly dysfunctional. Staff in the various ministries were disconnected from what was going on in the country, but pushed forward with their programs nonetheless. Particularly in those ministries where there was opportunity for graft and corruption, buying and selling positions of authority was common. This was perhaps expected in sensitive portfolios such as counter-narcotics or customs, but also extended to the Ministry of the Hajj, which managed distribution of the limited opportunities to conduct the pilgrimage to Mecca each year.

There were also serious disconnects between the Afghan government and the international organizations operating in the country, as well as with the major donor nationsunderwriting the country's finances. Donors and others suspected their Afghan counterparts of corruption, while the Afghans suspected the foreigners of serving their own interests over that of Afghanistan. Afghans spoke dismissively of the cabinet as Karzai's *waraktun* (kindergarten), and called Karzai "the Mayor of Kabul" due to his inability to effectively extend government control beyond the capital. In addition, although Karzai was the American choice to lead Afghanistan in 2001, by 2009 his relationship with the United States was badly strained. The Obama administration, disenchanted by election fraud, strong allegations of corruption, and a record of inefficiency, had lost faith in him.

In 2010 Karzai angrily told American officials in a meeting that he had three main enemies: the United States, the international community, and the Taliban. Given a choice between the three, he said he would side first with the Taliban. Karzai's anger stemmed from being trapped between the competing elements of American foreign policy. One of the main examples of this was the pressure on him to disarm and disempower the country's warlords, many of whom he depended upon for support. He co-operated with this program under tremendous pressure from the United States, but at the same time his allies were being disarmed, the Americans were actively rearming other groups loyal to the United States.

Just as the Taliban imported tactics from the war in Iraq, so did the United States. Among its perceived successes in Iraq were the counter-insurgency methods used in Anbar Province in 2005 and 2006. In a series of operations sometimes referred to as the "Anbar Awakening," the province was secured by co-opting tribal leaders to provide men for local security organizations. The American military sometimes jokingly referred to them as "CLC" — "Concerned Local Citizens." They were in fact tribal militias who were armed and paid for by the United States to keep insurgents out of their home territory.

In Afghanistan the official programs to create local militias went by a number of names, such as the Afghan Social Outreach Program, the Afghan Public Protection Program, the Afghan Auxiliary Police Force, and the Afghan Local Police. The decision to arm local civilians to protect their communities from the Taliban suffered from the basic misunderstanding of who the Taliban were, typically locals themselves rather than an external force. Creating militias made local conflicts between communities, some identified as "government" and others identified as "Taliban," more violent. In many cases it also put arms into the hands of the Taliban, as many communities took resources from whoever would provide them. These initiatives were reminiscent of those of KhAD in the 1980s, with a similar, largely negative, result.

There were also many ad hoc efforts at creating militias, driven by Special Forces teams or the CIA. These were created to help protect American facilities, to accompany American forces on operations, or as proxies for operations in which the United States did not want to be directly involved. A prime example is the Kandahar Strike Force, whose members were handpicked from the ANA and trained by Special Forces soldiers based in Camp Gecko. Gecko was built around Mullah Omar's former residence in Kandahar City, which the Americans rented from Ahmed Wali Karzai. The Kandahar Strike Force acted with impunity for years until it stormed a Kandahar police station in 2009 and killed the police chief in revenge for the murder of one of its own men. Under immense international pressure, the unit's commander and 40 others were convicted of the murder.

A similar organization exists in Loya Paktia, known as the Afghan Security Guards. It exists primarily to protect Firebase Lilley, an army base close to the border with Pakistan that doubles as a CIA listening post and the training ground for the Counter Terror Pursuit Teams (CTPT). Allegedly three thousand strong, it conducts cross-border operations into the tribal areas of Pakistan under the control of the CIA. What is most problematic about these newly armed militias is that their chain of command is extremely murky, and does not extend to the Afghan government at all. When they commit crimes or other excesses, they often do so with impunity, unless as in Kandahar they spark a level of outrage that cannot be ignored.

Part of the impetus driving the creation of these local militias was the weakness of the ANP. In 2006 it suffered six times as many casualties as the ANA, despite not having a combat role. The ANP was significantly less professional than the ANA, as it had largely been created by absorbing anti-Taliban militias wholesale rather than being built from the ground up. While the ANA often operated far from the homes of its soldiers, ANP units were typically deployed in their own communities. While ideally this would give them local insights that would aid them in policing, in practice it created problems, as they were not seen as a neutral force.

From 2005 to 2007 a process of pay and rank reform was undertaken to try to professionalize the ANP. Senior officers were forced to take examinations to test their literacy and knowledge of the law. The number of generals in the ANP was reduced from over 300 to 120, and colonels from over 2,400 to just under 500. Their salaries were also increased to match those of the ANA. Despite these processes, political factors still intruded. In 2006 Karzai tried to appoint 14 ANP generals who had failed their exams or were flagged as having insurgent or criminal links. The international reaction was strong enough that he backtracked on most of the appointments.

As Karzai came to be increasingly at odds with the international community, he began to independently look to reconcile with former Taliban leaders. In August 2007 he held a seven-hundred-delegate Peace Jirga that included Pashtuns from Pakistan. This led to a second jirga in 2008 that ended with a call for peace talks with the Taliban. In mid-2008 the Taliban-associated party Khuddam al-Furqan published a seven-point plan for how peace negotiations might work. It envisioned a series of measures leading to a loya jirga to vote on a comprehensive agreement, shepherded by the United Nations and international Islamic organizations. The Rahbari Shura created a political committee that could engage in the proposed talks. It was headed by Mullah Agha Jan Mutassem, who represented the older generation of Taliban who were unhappy with the actions of the more radical younger generation, which included attacks on civilians.

While Karzai was unable to make meaningful contact with the Taliban, they did open a channel with the United States through former members now in the government. Initial talks were interrupted, though, when Pakistani authorities arrested Mullah Baradar, the Taliban leader most amenable to discussion. Without his moderate influence, the Taliban dropped the idea and chose to focus instead on continued military operations. Shortly thereafter, the tempo of American operations increased sharply as well.

This escalation was the result of a classified assessment of the situation written by General McChrystal in 2009, which was later leaked to the press. In it, he said that to win against the Taliban would require five hundred thousand troops and five years of time. This extremely large number of troops was based on his idea of how counterinsurgency should be fought, with a flood of soldiers spread out in every community. While his assessment was rejected by the White House as unrealistic, President

Obama eventually became convinced that a smaller surge of troops was necessary. By 2010 the number of American soldiers in Afghanistan had doubled from the level in 2009, though they were to be there for a limited time only, to help stabilize the situation.

In addition to seeking ways to reconcile with the insurgency, in 2009 Karzai also had to plan for elections. His patchwork coalition of technocrats and others within his patronage network would face the strongest challenge from former members of the Northern Alliance in a political party called the United National Front, with Dr. Abdullah Abdullah as its candidate. Abdullah was widely perceived as being a Tajik, despite being born in Kandahar to a Pashtun father and a Tajik mother, due to his close ties to the Northern Alliance over many years. He had obtained a medical degree from Kabul University and worked then as an ophthalmologist in Afghanistan and Pakistan. He joined Jamiat in 1983 and became a health adviser to Massoud, and later his chief of staff and spokesman. He had also been Karzai's foreign minister since 2001, before deciding to oppose him for the presidency.

Karzai again appointed Karim Khalili and Ahmed Zia Massoud as his running mates, to try to sap some Northern Alliance support from Abdullah. He directly targeted former warlords with offers of patronage positions in exchange for the votes of their supporters. Karzai made deals with Mohaqeq for the Hazara vote that Khalili could not deliver, as well as with Dostum, Fahim, Ismail Khan, Sher Mohammed Akhundzada, and Gul Agha Sherzai. To win Dostum's support he offered two ministerial posts, while Mohaqeq was offered five, as well as the creation of two new provinces in the Hazarajat. The campaign was light on policy, and focused instead on portraying Karzai as the symbol of national unity. His campaign slogans included "Afghanistan is for all Afghans," and "Our peace, our way."

Abdullah's major backers were General Atta, who had grown in power over the past decade, and Rabbani. He was not able to prevent Karzai from enticing senior members of the Northern Alliance away from his campaign, in part because of the advantage incumbency gave the president when doling out patronage. Abdullah campaigned on the ideas of change and hope, praising the jihadi martyrs of the past on one hand while highlighting Karzai's corruption and reliance on foreign powers for support on the other. Like Karzai, he had few substantive policies beyond buying blocs of votes from regional leaders. It is interesting, though, that the political fault lines in 2009 no longer matched those of the previous decades of conflict, but instead represented divisions that had grown out of the Bonn process and post-2001 politics.

Although 44 candidates and a hundred different political parties were registered for the 2009 election, few of these had a national presence. The best known of the other candidates was Ashraf Ghani, who improbably hired a Clinton-era American political strategist, James Carville, to help direct his campaign. Because of his extensive American ties and lack of a domestic power base, Ghani was derided in Afghanistan as one of *zana-e Bush*, or "Bush's wives." There were also two female candidates, Dr. Frozan Fana and Shahla Ata. Both had difficulty campaigning openly because of cultural expectations that they maintain purdah, and so not be seen in public or address men who were not relatives. Fana was particularly criticized for using campaign posters that featured her photo, and was reduced to campaigning primarily by inviting people to visit her in her home.

Although initially there was a positive feeling among observers about the high level of female voter registration in the south, these feelings turned sour when the total numbers went from good to improbable and then impossible. Women were typically registered in Pashtun communities by the men of their family, who collected and submitted their voting cards. This system was open to extensive fraud, an assertion supported by the fact that 72 percent of the registered voters in Kandahar were women. Further investigation found many suspect registrations, including one under the name "Britney Spears." Registration was also very high in districts where it was considered unsafe to run a polling station, again suggesting fraud. Without the census data that normally put limits on voter registration, problems were widespread.

Election day itself was the worst day of violence in 15 years. Thirty-one civilians were killed, including 11 election officials, as well as a number of ANA and ANP deployed to provide security. Turnout was low, between 30 and 35 percent, with some districts producing minuscule numbers of voters. In one area of Helmand, only five hundred people voted of the seventy thousand who were eligible. In the face of Taliban threats, Karzai put tremendous pressure on the Independent Electoral Commission (IEC) to open polling stations in parts of the country where even the ANA could not operate safely, and later audits suggested why. Fraud at remote polling stations in areas controlled by Karzai's supporters was rife. In Kandahar Province, for example, 14 times as many votes were reported as there were voters.

The results of this first ballot were audited by the United Nations, resulting in a reduction of votes cast for Karzai by 28 percent and for Abdullah by 18 percent. The adjusted results gave Karzai just under 50 percent of the vote, and Abdullah just over 30 percent. This meant that a run-off election between them would have to be conducted, which was problematic. The logistical and security demands of the first vote had been enormously taxing, and reports of widespread fraud had lessened the legitimacy of both candidates and the process as a whole. And so, under heavy American pressure to accept the adjusted results that necessitated a second round, Karzai announced that a run-off would be held three weeks later. IEC declared that 30 percent of polling stations from the previous round would be closed for security reasons, reducing the total number to seventeen thousand. It was at this point that Abdullah withdrew his candidacy, declaring the whole process illegitimate. This unexpected result made Karzai president again by default, but with considerably less legitimacy than before.

An ongoing source of friction between Karzai and the international community throughout his second term was counter-narcotics policy. Opium production increased dramatically while he was president, and he was seen as doing little to combat it. The American ambassador from 2007 to 2009, William Wood, had earlier served in Colombia and argued strongly for aerial spraying of defoliants to destroy the poppy crop, as had been done with coca plantations. Karzai adamantly refused, as the sure result would be a farmers' revolt. Despite the appearance that he was soft on the opium trade, it was in fact a problem that he inherited when he became interim president in December 2001, and which the Americans had long ignored.

The Taliban's eradication effort earlier in 2001 had been so effective that the farm-gate price of opium had skyrocketed from $28 per kilogram in 2000 to $301 per kilogram in 2001. The warlords and petty commanders who replaced the Taliban had no need initially to pander to Western interests, and so could profit by taxing opium and owning the means of producing heroin from it. By chance, the fall of the Taliban coincided with the planting season for opium poppies. Most of the farmers who had previously grown the crop planted poppies again, joined by many new growers. The initial lack of international aid in rural areas and the huge increase in the hardy crop's value made such a powerful argument that no one needed to coerce farmers into getting involved. The Taliban's prohibition, followed so closely by their fall, created a perfect storm that caused opium production to spiral out of control.

Western analysis often describes the narcotics trade as fuelling the insurgency, making counter-narcotics operations a key part of the battle against the Taliban, but this is a gross over-simplification. The opium trade is as profitable for government officials and police officers as it is for criminals and insurgents, providing funding for a diverse range of players across the political spectrum. There was de facto recognition of this immediately after the fall of the Taliban, when the United States refused to target heroin-processing facilities that belonged to its allies in the Northern Alliance. Many of Karzai's early supporters were also involved in the opium trade, such as Sher Mohammed Akhundzada in Helmand, and Arif Nurzai, the minister of tribal affairs whose sister married Karzai's younger brother. That brother, Ahmed Wali Karzai, was himself heavily involved in heroin trafficking, despite being considered a key American ally.

An early effort by the British in 2002 to eradicate the poppy crop focused on paying farmers compensation when they did not grow it. Approximately $80 million was given to Afghan officials to distribute to farmers, amounting to about $1,500 per hectare of poppies. This was insufficiently convincing compared to the $13,000 per hectare in profit to be gained from growing the poppies. To make matters worse, much of the money intended for farmers was pocketed by the officials. The size of the opium harvest instead increased.

By 2005 there were an estimated 2.3 million farmers, in every province of the country, growing opium poppies as their primary cash crop. The government established a Ministry of Counter-Narcotics and passed new anti-drug laws, but these measures did little to stem the opium trade.

The new ministry was tasked with monitoring the trade and coordinating the actions of the other ministries involved, but in Afghan political culture this was doomed to fail. Each ministry was run like a fiefdom, and no minister would accept being "coordinated" by another.

The size and value of the poppy crop continued to increase year on year, until by 2007 Afghanistan was producing 8,200 tonnes of opium annually. This represented 93 percent of the world's heroin, worth $3.4 billion.

Given how important opium had become to the general economy, eradication efforts could be seen as creating more instability than the insurgency. The instability created by the opium trade was primarily due to an increase in conflict between power brokers who sought to control it — some of whom were insurgents, and some of whom were in government.

From 2001 to 2007, all of the international organizations engaged in Afghanistan saw agriculture (aside from opium) as the engine of the Afghan economy. Despite the efforts that were eventually made to increase farm productivity, the expected growth failed to occur. This was in part because of a misunderstanding over how the rural economy worked. The assumption was that most people living in the countryside made their living as farmers, but this was not true, as many landholdings were small and families were heavily reliant on paid farm and non-farm work to make ends meet. The household economy in rural areas was not focused on maximizing profits as much as it was on survival of the group. Many aspects of local economies were not driven by pure market factors, but by social arrangements by which people accessed land, credit, and paid work. These were the traditional systems of patronage that had re-established themselves after years of turmoil, and which were invisible to many of the aid projects designed to boost the rural economy.

Trade was an area of growth in Afghanistan, with consumer demand driven in part by the influx of money from the narcotics trade. Bilateral trade with Pakistan leapt in value from $100 million a year in 2001 to $1.6 billion in 2006. This represented a resumption of important trade routes first disrupted by the Pashtunistan issue, but otherwise with very deep roots; it mostly benefitted the south and east of the country. These years also saw a slow resumption of Afghanistan's involvement in regional markets where it had been a major player pre-1979, such as in the trade of fruit and nuts, sugar beets, and cotton.

No matter what the market forces, all areas of the economy were hampered by high levels of corruption. Afghanistan sat at or near the bottom of Transparency International's Corruption Perceptions Index. The Afghan government did little to improve its standing, despite creating several bodies charged with tackling the problem. Apart from all the other problems that Afghans faced, over time corruption became a major driver of instability and insurrection that was not always clearly recognized as such. Government officials, at all levels and in all departments, came to be seen as so predatory that their actions undermined the argument for having a centralized state at all. In Karzai's second term there was perceived to be a major increase in government corruption, as officials rushed to line their pockets before being forced from power.

A major example of corruption was revealed when Kabul Bank, which had financed Karzai's re-election campaign, was revealed to be little more than a Ponzi scheme and collapsed. The government was forced to respond to the scandal with an investigation, but Karzai intervened to protect his brother and other well-connected personalities from prosecution. He also authorized an $835 million bailout, much to the outrage of foreign donors. Though their contributions to the Afghan government weren't used to pay for the bailout, they went to cover the hole in the Afghan budget the bailout created.

As had long been the case, foreign donations remained critical to the government's functioning. For many years the government had a net income of less than zero, as the cost of trying to collect taxes and customs exceeded the revenues raised. Its failure to be self-sufficient after over a decade of capacity building and assistance grated on many donors.

In this atmosphere of disappointment, Karzai came under strong pressure from the international community to again attempt to end the conflict through reconciliation. A new initiative was created, the Afghan Peace and Reconciliation Program (APRP), which had two streams, one aimed at low-level insurgents and another on engaging with insurgent leaders. Karzai also called a National Consultative Peace Jirga in June 2010, was presided over by Rabbani. Sixteen hundred people attended the meeting. The Taliban were invited to send a delegation, but refused to do so while foreign troops still "occupied" Afghanistan. Karzai's opening speech was interrupted by gunfire and rocket impacts. Police prevented suicide bombers from entering the tent, but only barely. The meeting was a failure, and both the head of the NDS and the minster of the interior resigned over the security breakdown.

Karzai pursued another peace initiative that year, creating the High Peace Council, a body of 70 members, most of whom had belonged to various armed groups in the 1980s and 1990s. Rabbani was again appointed to lead it. Twelve members were formerly officials in the Taliban government, and six were from Khuddam al-Furqan. The council was meant as a body that could negotiate with the insurgency because of its members' credentials as jihadis, but others in Afghan civil society saw it as a council of warlords and war criminals.

Many assumptions about the purpose of the continued American presence in Afghanistan were shaken in May 2011 when bin Laden's death was announced. Although the CIA later claimed that it had found bin Laden through meticulous intelligence, this was not true — a former ISI officer betrayed bin Laden in exchange for a reward. The reaction among Afghans was muted but generally positive, despite a growing trend of pan-Islamic feelings even among those who opposed the Taliban. Afghan society had typically been very insular, with little awareness of or interest in global issues. This was true even during the Soviet intervention, when the influx of Islamists from around the world provoked a greater sense of xenophobia than of comradeship. The change came after 2001, perhaps because of the impact that global issues have had on the country. Examples of the growing sense of pan-Islam were many. In 2005 there were protests and riots across Afghanistan in opposition to the alleged treatment of the Quran by Americans at Guantanamo Bay. In 2008 the Wolesi Jirga voted to condemn the Danish cartoons depicting the Prophet Mohammed. That same year and then in 2009 it also denounced the Israeli occupation of Palestine.

Nonetheless, bin Laden's death in 2011 did not create a major reaction. He was widely seen as the main reason behind the country's many years of suffering. The only serious concern was that with his death, perhaps the United States and other countries would lose interest in Afghanistan, and the funding needed to make so many parts of the government and economy work would dry up.

This appeared to be true when in June 2011 Obama announced that American forces would withdraw from the country, beginning with ten thousand troops who would return by the end of the year. All responsibility for security in the country would be handed over to the ANA by 2014, leaving only a small ongoing role for the United States. The announcement left Karzai in complete shock. Like Babrak Karmal's communist regime before him, he had not been consulted about this decision, only being told about it once it was made. As the number of foreign troops in the country began to draw down, their focus switched from conducting combat operations to building the capacity of Afghan forces to manage the conflict on their own. The American plan for the withdrawal — to reconcile with the Taliban, strengthen local security through militias, and build the ANA's capacity to operate independently — was essentially the same as the Soviet plan 26 years earlier.

Despite the United States' desire to end the conflict, the pace of insurgent operations had continued to increase, with no end in sight. Even with the additional pressure created by the American surge under General McChrystal, insurgent attacks increased by at least 40 percent annually from 2007 to 2011, with a sharp increase in the final two years. It is somewhat ironic that despite the Taliban also desiring the United States' withdrawal, it was the scale of the insurgency that was making it more difficult for the United States to do so.

Behind the scenes, peace talks continued to develop, including tentative meetings between the Taliban and members of the High Peace Council, which was seen as independent of the Afghan government. They reached a verbal agreement that the council would ask the Afghan government to request the United Nations Security Council to recognize the Taliban as an "independent political party to the Afghan conflict." This was significant, because up to this point the Taliban had been excluded from the political development of the country. This recognition would put them on an equal footing with the Afghan government and the United States, and therefore make them a negotiating partner with whom the conflict could be resolved. The inclusion of the term "independent" was likely meant to infer they were not a puppet of Pakistan, a criticism often levelled against them. The Taliban proposed joining an interim unity government, and a new discussion was scheduled for later in the year.

Whatever hope might have accrued from these talks, they ended abruptly in September 2011 when Rabbani was assassinated by a suicide bomber claiming to be a Taliban envoy. Although the Taliban never publicly claimed responsibility for the attack, and it may have been conducted by an element only nominally controlled by the Rahbari Shura, the Afghan government blamed them and ended the talks, reverting to the strategy of defeating the Taliban on the battlefield.

By 2012 both the ANA and the ANP had grown substantially in strength, with the ANA at 180,000 soldiers and the ANP at 150,000 police officers. Despite the imposing size of the ANA, outside of a few units it still required substantial amounts of international support and mentoring in order to operate effectively. The Taliban recognized this, and so found a means to strain relations between the ANA and its mentors. They conducted a series of insider attacks known as "green on blue" incidents, where Afghan soldiers killed foreign troops. In 2011 there were 24 green on blue attacks, and twice as many the following year. In 2014 Major General Harold J. Greene was the victim of an insider attack at Camp Qargha, located west of Kabul, becoming the first American general to be killed in combat since 1970.

These attacks created huge amounts of distrust between Afghan and foreign forces and forced new vetting procedures for the ANA and ANP that drastically slowed recruiting. The United States was forced to implement the Guardian Angel program, in which a few American soldiers monitored their Afghan colleagues and were prepared at all times to respond with deadly force if needed. It also meant that Afghans, even senior officers, were disarmed when meeting with their foreign counterparts, which many found insulting. Whereas before foreign mentors were encouraged to create close bonds with their Afghan units, they were now told to minimize the off-duty time they spent with Afghans. The mentoring program suffered badly as a result, as did joint operations in the field.

Despite worsening levels of mutual trust, an agreement between Afghanistan and the United States was reached that gave control of all special operations to the ANA, including conduct of the controversial night raids. Obama arrived in Kabul on the one-year anniversary of bin Laden's death to sign the Enduring Strategic Partnership Agreement designating Afghanistan as a "major non-NATO ally" and obliging the two countries to sign a more detailed Bilateral Security Agreement within a year. This process faltered when the White House publicly announced in

2013 that it was negotiating directly with the Taliban, who had opened an office in Doha as if they were a government-in-exile. Although it was only known inside a small circle of Taliban leaders at the time, one of the reasons that talks with the United States had begun again in 2013 was because Mullah Omar had died.

When he disappeared after the fall of the Taliban regime, even the $10 million bounty placed on his head did not help to locate him. It was common wisdom that Mullah Omar lived in Quetta, but it was not widely known that he had relinquished control of the movement, and the Taliban rank and file still saw him as their leader, even though most had never seen him, heard his voice, or read anything he wrote.

Deeply distrusting Pakistan and the ISI, Mullah Omar had in fact remained in Afghanistan throughout the remainder of his life. He first lived in a concealed room behind a cupboard in a house near Qalat belonging to a fellow Hotaki tribesman. Although the house was once searched by American troops, he was never found. When the United States built a base nearby, he moved to another house in southeast Zabul. While his neighbours knew that a former Taliban lived in the house, and offered food and clothing to support him, they did not know his true identity. By living in extreme isolation and only communicating infrequently with the Rahbari Shura, by sending audio cassettes by courier, he remained undetected. His only contact with the outside world was through the BBC's Pashtun news service, to which he listened regularly up until his death from illness on April, 23, 2013. On the day of his death, it is said that there was a freak hailstorm, a sign from Allah of his passing. He was buried almost immediately in a nondescript grave, leaving behind no will or any other instructions.

News of his death was relayed to just a few members of the Rahbari Shura. In order not to demoralize the movement, they kept the news of Mullah Omar's death a secret, and continued to issue proclamations in his name, much as they had done before. The unity of the Taliban was already being tested by the public announcement of talks with the Americans, and they did not want to create another reason for schism within their ranks. Mullah Obaidullah, placed in charge by Mullah Omar, had died in prison in 2010 and had been replaced by Mullah Akhtar Mansour. He now became the spiritual as well as temporal leader of the movement.

Even without news of Mullah Omar's death becoming public, for the first time in its history a viable splinter organization had broken away from the mainstream Taliban. Calling itself Fidai Mahaz (Sacrifice Front), the group was led by a man named Mullah Najibullah, who used the nom de guerre Omar Kitab. He was too young to have fought the Soviets, reportedly joining the Taliban at age 15 to fight under Mullah Dadullah against the Northern Alliance. He represented the younger, more radical generation of Taliban who were opposed to peace talks. From his perspective, the world was in a permanent state of jihad until all Muslims were freed from the atrocities committed by non-believers. Able to operate in both Afghanistan and Pakistan, the group must have enjoyed a degree of ISI support, perhaps to hedge against the risk that the Taliban would stop fighting before Pakistan's political aims were met.

Another round of presidential elections was scheduled for 2014, although Karzai was not eligible to run as he had served the constitutional limit of two terms. The main contenders were Abdullah Abdullah and Ashraf Ghani, who disliked each other despite many years working in close proximity. Twenty-five other candidates registered to run as well, but over half were disqualified by the IEC before voting began. Those remaining included Hamid Karzi's brother Qayum, and prominent warlords Sherzai and Sayyaf.

Since the last election, Abdullah had built a wider coalition of supporters, choosing Mohammed Mohaqeq and Khyal Mohammed Khyal Khan, a Pashtun from Ghazni who had been the head of finance for HIG, as his running mates. The addition of Khyal Khan allowed Abdullah to subtly shift his platform to one more focused on Islam, which would contrast with Ghani's Western, secular one.

Ghani's running mates were Dostum, who brought the Uzbek vote as well as a measure of jihadi credibility and military power, and Hazara politician Mohammed Sarwar Danish. Dostum was well known, if not liked, across the country, and Danish had been one of the experts tasked with crafting the constitution in 2002. Since then, he had been minister of higher education and justice, as well as governor of the newly created province of Daikundi.

As they had done before, the Taliban vowed to disrupt the election. For the first time the Afghan National Security Forces had the lead for protecting the process, which required major security operations across the country. The first round of voting showed Abdullah in the lead with 45 percent of the vote, followed by Ashraf Ghani with 31 percent. Voter turnout was around 30 percent, even though 8 million registered voters living outside of Afghanistan were added to the 12 million inside the country. After the second round of voting there were the normal delays in announcing the results, and in the atmosphere of uncertainty, each of the candidates declared victory and accused the other of cheating.

A million potentially fraudulent votes were discarded by IEC, which then announced that Ashraf Ghani had won by a margin of 10 percent. Abdullah disputed the count: even after the million discarded votes, there were still six hundred thousand more votes cast in the second round than the first, which seemed unlikely. "Unfortunately, the vote count process has lost its legitimacy," he said in a televised press conference. "We do not accept fraudulent election results and we will not accept a fraudulent government for a day."

The process had led to a crisis, as Abdullah would not concede defeat. It took intervention by the Americans to force a solution on both men. On September 19 a power-sharing agreement was signed between Ashraf Ghani and Abdullah, who was given the new role of chief executive officer. This role was remarkably similar to that of prime minister that Abdullah and others had demanded during the Constitutional Loya Jirga in 2002. Despite the bumpy process, for the first time in Afghan history power had been transferred between democratically elected governments.

Only a few months later, a ceremony was held to end the United States' and NATO's combat mission in Afghanistan. In 13 years of fighting, 3,458 foreign soldiers had been killed. Whether the impact of their intervention on the average Afghan citizen was positive or not was difficult to discern.

CHAPTER 21 FRAYING AT THE EDGES

WITHOUT QUESTION, 2014 was a watershed year for Afghanistan. It had been 10 years since the adoption of the latest constitution, its first president after Hamid Karzai, and the transition from one leader to another had occurred in an orderly and non-violent manner. But the decision to withdraw nearly all remaining foreign military forces had to be revised in the face of heightened insurgent attacks that Afghan forces remained ill-prepared to counter. Although Operation Enduring Freedom had ended, Operation Freedom's Sentinel would see just over ten thousand American troops, and two thousand NATO troops, remain in the country to train and assist the Afghan forces.

The National Unity Government of Ghani and Abdullah almost immediately found itself deadlocked. Lacking the legitimacy that would have stemmed from a clear electoral victory, neither man felt able to be magnanimous to the other, disagreeing over many relatively minor issues. Ghani's reputation as a micro-manager was borne out by his approach to governing, and he insisted on being involved in even insignificant decisions. More significantly, it took three months for the new government to form a cabinet, as the two men could not agree on who would take the key posts in the Defence and the Interior Ministries, and who would head the NDS.

Eventually, Ghani's pick for minister of defence — Sher Mohammed Karimi, the former Chief of Staff of the Afghan Army — was accepted, as was Abdullah's pick for the minister of the interior, Nur al-Haq Ulumi. Karimi was trained in the United States as a member of the pre-communist-era army, had fought with the mujahideen, and had strong links to the modern special forces community. Ulumi had been a lieutenant general in the communist-era Afghan Army, and was awarded the position of governor of Kandahar in recognition of his bravery. There he became known for turning a blind eye to the narcotics trade and negotiating local truces with the mujahideen, particularly those elements loyal to Pir Gailani (whose wife was related to Ulumi) and Gul Agha Sherzai (who was from the same Pashtun tribe).

Ghani also appointed three women to cabinet posts, as ministers for higher education, information and culture, and women's affairs. This was one less post than he had promised would be given to women, but was still notable progress toward gender equality if not balance. As much as the different appointments reflected the ongoing use of patronage as a means for both Ghani and Abdullah to retain power, they also demonstrated a degree of inclusivity that had not been seen before. Including a broad swath of Afghan society in the cabinet, a necessary step for the central government to be seen as representing all Afghans.

The continued ethnic element in politics was shown by another public squabble between the two men. The bodies of Daoud Khan and his family were discovered in 2008, and the government gave them a state funeral and reburied them on military land just outside the capital. Afterward, Tajik nationalists began to argue that Habibullah Kalakani should be given the same treatment. The issue was taken up by Tajik members of parliament, scholars, and warlords. Abdullah championed the issue as well, against Ghani's wishes. Although Habibullah Kalakani's portrait began to appear alongside those of Massoud in public spaces dominated by Tajiks, in the rest of the country he was remembered as a brute whose policies most resembled those of the Taliban.

Early in Ghani's term, the United States managed to negotiate a successful outcome with the Taliban as part of their ongoing low-key talks. It was agreed that the only American soldier captured during the war, Sergeant Bowe Bergdahl, would be exchanged for five senior Taliban officials held in Guantanamo. Two had surrendered to Dostum in 2001 and been handed directly to the Americans, and the remaining three had all actively offered or provided intelligence to the CIA before being arrested. Despite their unheroic pasts, their long captivity in Guantanamo gave them a degree of moral authority within the Taliban movement and Afghan society. All of the men returned to the Taliban movement after their release, perhaps hardened in their beliefs by their 12 years in prison, or perhaps seeing nowhere else to turn.

Despite this early success, the continuing talks were derailed the following year when news of Mullah Omar's death broke on the Fidai Mahaz website. Rumours had swirled for years within the Taliban, but this was the first time that any elements within the movement had stated categorically that he was dead. In addition, Fidai Mihaz accused Mullah Mansour of having murdered him in order to usurp the Taliban leadership. The NDS then released a statement also confirming his death, but stating that it had occurred in a Karachi hospital in April 2013. No one was certain what was true.

Mullah Mansour, forced to admit that Mullah Omar had died, could give no reasonable explanation for having concealed the information for so long. He also admitted that famed Taliban leader Jalaluddin Haqqani had died of an illness about a year before. There was outrage among the Taliban rank and file, and calls for Mullah Mansour to step down in favour of either Mullah Omar's son, Mullah Yaqub, or his brother, Mullah Abdul Manan. A video released by the Rahbari Shura showing clerics and tribal elders pledging baiat to Mullah Mansour and appointing him as the Amir al-Mumineen did little to calm the situation. The key issue for many was that Mullah Mansour had not been selected as leader by representatives of the whole movement, and so was illegitimate. In this atmosphere of confusion over the movement's leadership, the Taliban's negotiating team simply skipped the next scheduled meeting with the Americans, with no indication of when or if talks would resume.

Although the movement had remained mostly cohesive up to this point, the revelation that the leadership had concealed the death of Mullah Omar proved to be too much. Mullah Rasoul was a member of the Rahbari Shura who had been unaware of Mullah Omar's death until it became widely known. A Pashtun from Spin Boldak, he had been a close associate of Mullah Omar before 2001, and was the governor of Nimroz Province. In opposition to Mullah Mansour, he created a new organization called the High Council of the Islamic Emirate of Afghanistan, which saw itself as the legitimate Taliban carrying out Mullah Omar's original vision for the organization. It gained the most support in western Afghanistan, centred on Bakwa district of Farah, but with supporters stretching into Herat, Nimroz, Uruzgan, Helmand, and Zabul. Although still adhering to many of the same beliefs as the organization led by the Rahbari Shura, it differed on several key issues. While the High Council supported peace negotiations in principle, it rejected their legitimacy as long as Mullah Mansour or his representatives were involved. It also rejected the practice of suicide attacks, stating that Mullah Omar had opposed them. The High Council also professed a more liberal point of view than might be expected. The movement's deputy, Abdul Manan Niazi, told the BBC: "We have realized ... that under an Islamic system all rights of human beings — both men and women — need to be implemented 100 percent."

Mullah Rasoul garnered considerable support from other dissatisfied Taliban leaders, and was able to appoint four deputies, similar to the four mahaz commanders of the Rahbari Shura. These included Mansoor Dadullah and Sher Mohammed Akhundzada, who still retained a large power base in Helmand. Soon after the High Council's creation, fighting broke out between its partisans and groups still loyal to the Rahbari Shura. In November 2015 Mansour Dadullah was killed in Zabul during fighting between the Taliban groups.

Earlier in 2015 another rival to the Taliban had also announced its formation. Calling itself the Islamic State in Iraq and the Levant — Khorasan Province (ISKP), it was composed of defectors from the mainstream Taliban, the Islamic Movement of Uzbekistan, and various Pakistani extremist groups. "Khorasan" was the historical name of a region that incorporated parts of modern day Iran, Turkmenistan, and northern Afghanistan, harkening back to a pre-modern age. The group grew into a force of approximately three thousand fighters, primarily based in Nangarhar and Kunar. The Rahbari Shura and the High Council were both careful not to question the legitimacy of the Islamic State movement or its leader's competing claim to the title Amir al-Mumineen, which had support across parts of the Muslim world, although in both cases they stated that it was not welcome in Afghanistan as a competitor. ISKP was less conciliatory, and soon launched operations against the Taliban, the Afghan government, and the Shi'ite and Hazara communities. Although it gained little popular support, ISKP would grow over time into a hyper-violent organization that perfected the "complex attack" combining suicide bombers with armed gunmen to penetrate secure facilities, as well as attacks against purely civilian targets. In only 138 incidents in 2018, ISKP deliberately caused over two thousand civilian casualties. Its perception of the conflict is in absolute terms, pitting a narrowly defined set of "believers" against everyone else. Unlike the Taliban, it also sees the conflict in Afghanistan in global terms, connected to a struggle that encompasses the rest of the world.

Despite a growing number of rivals, Mullah Mansour's claim on the leadership of the Taliban was strengthened by the successful capture of Konduz in 2015. The Taliban had been consolidating their hold on the outlying districts around the city for several years, and had begun coordinated attacks against the city's garrison in the spring of 2015. The ANA unit within the city had been reinforced, but rather than attacking the Taliban in their strongholds, it merely manned a ring of security outposts on the city's outskirts. This allowed the Taliban to mass their forces in such numbers that they made propaganda videos of their strength in the region. They gained the support of many local people, especially in the formerly "pro-government district" of Khanabad, where pro-government militias fought each other for the right to impose "taxes" on local businesses and to conscript village youth. Much as was the case when the Taliban first began, they were seen as a bulwark against this kind of anarchy and corruption.

On September, 28, 2015, the Taliban stormed Konduz city from all sides and captured most of it in a matter of hours. Many police and military commanders abandoned their men and joined fleeing NGO staff and journalists at the city's airport. The last pocket of resistance in the city's Bala Hisar fortress held out for two days before surrendering. It took the Afghan government, with heavy support from American Special Operations forces and air power, two weeks to recapture the city, which was a major embarrassment. The country was in shock, not having seen such heavy urban fighting since the capture of Konduz in 2001. The loss of a major city shook confidence in the central government, especially in light of the impending withdrawal of foreign forces.

But despite the firepower that the United States and ISAF could bring to bear, there was a shocking lack of coordination between military and political aims. This is clearly demonstrated by the results of the drone strike in May 2016 that killed Taliban leader Mullah Mansour. Rather than weakening the Taliban, his death put an end to the High Council's challenge over the legitimate heir to Mullah Omar. In essence, the successful strike against Mullah Mansour left the movement more cohesive than before. His successor, chosen by a large and inclusive shura, was Maulvi Haibatullah Akhundzada, a religious scholar who headed the movement's court system. A Noorzai Pashtun from Panjwai district in Kandahar, he had also been responsible for devising the nizami system of military commissions. To broaden his base of support, he named two deputies, Mullah Yaqub and Jalaluddin Haqqani's son, Sirajuddin. As were his two predecessors, Maulvi Haibatullah was publicly named the Amir al-Mumineen. This was enough to calm most concerns about the legitimacy of the Rahbari Shura's leadership, leaving the High Council as a fringe group with limited appeal.

The Afghan government scored a political victory in September 2016 when it signed a peace agreement with HIG and Hekmatyar through the auspices of the High Peace Council that Karzai had created early in his second term. Under the terms of the deal, all members of HIG were removed from the United Nations sanctions list, imprisoned members were released, and they were integrated into the military or police and granted land. Hekmatyar moved back to Kabul in May 2017, entering the city for the first time since he was ousted by the Taliban in 1996 with little fanfare. Although his reconciliation with the government made for positive news stories, it had no impact on the increasing levels of violence in the country. HIG was no longer a real player on the battlefield, the most active or militant members having been absorbed by other insurgent groups. The most positive impact of the deal was that his credentials as a jihadi and his willingness to compromise undercut the Taliban argument that they would not negotiate with the Afghan government.

The Taliban's distrust of the central government was shared by many Afghans, even if they did not go so far as to see it as a puppet of American interests. Criminal behaviour and obvious corruption by powerful officials such as Vice President Dostum were largely ignored by the government, in his case because he could marshal large numbers of votes from his ethnic base. In late 2016 when Dostum was accused of kidnapping and raping a political rival, the government only reluctantly agreed to investigate. Even when Dostum fled into exile in Turkey to avoid prosecution, he remained in his post as vice president. Incidents like this highlight the high degree of corruption that remains the largest driver of insecurity in Afghanistan. The impunity with which government officials and their families can act makes it clear that the rule of law does not exist. It is no wonder that many Afghans distrust the central government, instead relying on local power structures they see as more reliable, formed from blood relations or through andiwal networks. A large part of the Taliban's success at growing as a movement has been through co-opting these existing relationships to form a loose conglomerate. The central government tried to do this as well, but poorly implemented policies created winners and losers at the local level. The inability of many Afghans to trust the central government or its representatives continues to drive cycles of violence.

In May 2017, Afghanistan's attorney general called the Ministry of the Interior "the heart of corruption in the security sector." This was rooted in the fact that, unlike the ANA, the various security organizations within the ministry were almost all built by rebadging existing anti-Taliban militia to provide local security. While this was expedient, it meant that the corrupt practices of these groups continued from inside the government. For example, there is a thriving market for the sale of appointments within the security services, where even minor jobs with a monthly salary of less than $100 are sold for five- or six-figure sums. These are positions with money-making potential — for example, oversight of a border crossing or of areas where opium poppies are grown. After having paid for a position, the person in it is forced to recoup the cost through racketeering, extortion, bribe-taking, smuggling, sale of government resources, or the enlistment of fictitious "ghost" employees, whose salary is kept by the official.

This differs from the practice of tribal patronage, which many Western analysts lump in with other forms of corruption. In a patronage system, money and resources flow downward from leader to followers in exchange for loyalty. Particularly within armed groups, this can resemble a loose feudal system. But in the system of corruption described above, the flow of money and resources is largely reversed. Lower officials funnel money upward in exchange for a licence to commit lucrative crimes. The first system creates tighter bonds within a community, while the latter destroys them.

This can be seen in the fact that while the ANA has a system of just over a thousand static security checkpoints across the country, the ANP has over seven thousand. Most of these serve no tactical purpose, and the isolation of these posts has been a driver of serious casualties among the police, as they are easily overwhelmed by insurgents. The ANP leadership insists on maintaining so many checkpoints because they are a source of income, largely through the extortion of travellers. It is no wonder that so many ANP members desert their posts, or negotiate local truces with the Taliban.

With the Ministry of the Interior deeply involved in narcotics trafficking, it is no surprise that eradication efforts have failed. In 2017, UNODC reported that there was more land under cultivation to produce opium in Afghanistan than at any other time since monitoring began in 1994, producing an incredible 9,000 tonnes of opium. This bumper crop drove the farm-gate price of opium as low as $45 a kilo, similar to what it had been in the 1990s. Combined with a sustained lack of rain and snow that created a severe drought in many parts of Afghanistan in 2018, this cut the opium output that year by as much as 40 percent. Farm-gate prices continued to fall in 2019, although many incentives remained for farmers to continue planting poppy in 2020 and beyond.

Poppy farming tends to be a high-risk, high-reward endeavour for farmers, which, besides creating incentives for them to seek protection from government eradication, has also pushed them to innovative farming methods. In 2009, the "Helmand Food Zone" was created to decrease the amount of poppy being farmed in the province's irrigated land through the use of aggressive eradication and crop substitution. It was unsuccessful in the longer term, but one of its immediate effects was to force large numbers of people, typically former sharecroppers or agricultural labourers, to move to land in the desert that had previously been considered unsuitable for agriculture. Distribution of this land was controlled by local power brokers, many of whom had a vested interest in the opium trade. In order to make this land tenable for farming, deep wells had to be dug to provide water for irrigation. This required diesel generators to pump the water, though the quality of fuel available was so poor that frequent maintenance or replacement of machinery became an additional burden.

To offset the high cost of diesel, in 2013 farmers began to switch to less costly and more reliable solar panels to provide power. This proved so successful that by 2019 satellite image analysis determined that there were 67,000 solar panels installed on farms across the province. Another innovation by the farmers in the region was the very intensive use of herbicides and chemical fertilizer to both improve yields and cut labour costs associated with manual weeding. Chinese-made herbicides with branding tailored to the local market have become ubiquitous, two popular brands being "Cruise [missile]" and "Zanmargai" (suicide bomber). While these innovations have provided livelihoods to over a million people on what was once marginal land, their environmental impact has been dire. The water table in Helmand has been falling by three metres a year, and will likely be completely depleted in the next decade. Groundwater has also become badly contaminated, creating health problems in new communities that lack access to government services such as health care. When these new farms in Helmand inevitably fail, roughly 1.4 million people will almost certainly be displaced, creating an economic and social crisis that Afghanistan is ill equipped to manage.

Given endemic poverty and a lack of opportunities for many Afghans, it was perhaps inevitable that there would be a large domestic market for opium. Although even basic census data regarding Afghanistan is suspect at best, in 2015 it was estimated that there were 2.9 to 3.5 million drug users in the country, out of a total population of perhaps 30 million. This would give Afghanistan one of the highest per capita rates of drug use in the world. While there has been increasing international support and funding for treatment programs, few Afghan addicts benefit from them due to the central government's limited authority in many areas of the country.

The 2017 opium income for farmers (not traders or traffickers) was estimated to be $1.4 billion, although it has dropped since with the reduction in production and falling prices. But with the value of opium and heroin exceeding that of all other licit exports combined, at this point any successful eradication program would be devastating for the Afghan economy, and in particular for the rural communities where it is cultivated — estimated in the south to be 93 percent of all villages. Regardless of international perceptions, poppy-growing in Afghanistan has become unquestionably normalized. One of the few market systems that functions well in Afghanistan is that for opium. Where previously many farmers sold their crop "at the farm gate," now local and regional markets exist that allow 70 percent of farmers to seek more competitive prices.

The narcotics trade in Afghanistan has also expanded beyond the traditional crops of opium and marijuana, to now include the production of methamphetamines known as *nakh* or *yakh*. First seized by authorities on the Iranian border in 2008, it is the lack of international focus on drugs other than opium and heroin that has created space for this trade to grow. When the government began to restrict access to cold remedies that were used as the main ingredient, Afghan producers switched to a local shrub called *oman,* a species of ephedra. Oman was previously considered worthless and used only as winter fuel, but in a repeat of how the opium industry began, traders now travel village to village to buy it from farmers who harvest it from public land in the highlands. The centre for the trade in oman, and consequently the production of nakh, is the Abdul Wadood Bazaar in Bakwa, which is also the epicentre of the High Council's support. Instead of being produced for export, most nakh is sold inside Afghanistan to users who are often addicted to heroin as well.

In addition to benefitting farmers and traffickers, widespread opium cultivation has also come to provide a tremendous amount of income for day labourers in rural areas. The best paid of these workers are the "lancers," whose job is to cut the opium pods with a small knife or razor to begin the days-long process of extracting the opium gum. As many as 16 percent of all farmers supplement their income in this way, which pays an average of $12 per day for 15 days a year. This compares favourably with the pay rate of a construction worker, for example, who receives an average of $4.80 a day. And with 20 percent of lancers taking payment in kind, opium becomes ever more firmly part of the rural economy. While the narcotics trade is often cited as driving the insurgency, it is in fact a symptom rather than a cause, and the "cure" of eradication is almost certain to kill the patient.

Other forms of criminality have also become more prevalent in the country in the past decade. Politically connected armed groups, particularly in the capital and surrounding regions, have grown in strength and become involved in lucrative activities such as robbery and extortion. A distinctly Afghan "gangster" culture has appeared among Kabuli youth who call themselves *bachaha-ye ba subut* (worthy men), with distinctive dress, manners, and language. Drawing from the large pools of unemployed and disaffected youth in the city, these groups are driving a spike in criminal incidents in the capital that surpass the rate at any other time in its history. Decades of conflict have eroded the social fabric that made the sprawling city an oasis of relative safety even as the countryside devolved into anarchy.

The Afghan government slowly started losing control of the countryside as foreign forces drew down beginning in 2014. The Taliban repeated the audacity of their offensive against Konduz again in 2016, and then against two other major population centres — Ghazni and Farah City — in 2018. For five days in August, the Taliban fought to retain control of Ghazni after having wrested it from government forces. Arriving in the city with lists of individuals to target, they also disabled the city's telecoms network and electrical power, leading to widespread water shortages as pumps could not function. Large parts of the bazaar area in the city were burned to the ground, and nearly three hundred civilian casualties were reported. Much as before, the inability of the government to protect Ghazni was a major blow to its credibility.

In January 2019, the United States' own estimates were that the Afghan government controlled only 53.8 percent of the country's districts, while 12.3 percent were under insurgent control. By August 2019 the situation had worsened, with the Taliban controlling more territory than at any point since 2001. In addition, they were active in over 70 percent of the country, ready to exploit government weakness and take control. Their military forces had swelled to an estimated sixty thousand men, larger than they had been when they were toppled nearly two decades before.

Although Taliban "control" of districts is often characterized as something akin to military occupation, the truth is more complex. Typically it involves a large degree of public support. An example that is well understood is that of Zurmat district in Paktia. The inhabitants of the district are 90 percent Pashtun and 10 percent "Tajik" — actually Pashtuns of the Musa Khel sub-tribe who speak Persian and relocated to Paktia from Ghor Province several generations ago. Even though they are Pashtun who have lived in the district for decades, they are considered outsiders by many. The Afghan government has only a limited presence in the district, controlling little more than the hukomat and some of the area around it where the ANA and ANP are stationed. There had been a unit of the Afghan Local Police in the district, but it was disbanded in 2018 after it was implicated in abusive behaviour toward the local population. Other pro-government forces, such as the Khost Protection Force and NDS-backed Uprising Forces, occasionally still operate there.

The population of the district have strong anti-government feelings for a number of reasons. The ulema in the district are conservative, and generally agree with the social policies of the Taliban. Corruption among local officials is high, creating conflict between the community and the government. The Khost Protection Force and the NDS both conducted a number of night raids in the district in 2018 and 2019, during which civilians were killed.

The Taliban in the district are almost all local men with specific grievances against the government; their enlistment is made easier by the lack of paying jobs. There is a Taliban shadow governor, as well as committees for health, education, development, and conflict resolution. The Taliban has also set up a Department for Prevention of Civilian Casualties, with a website where the public can make complaints. The website indicates that Taliban units are receiving training on how to protect civilians in areas they control. Because the Taliban have little money for aid or reconstruction, they allow the government to implement projects in exchange for a portion of the proceeds. For example, the Taliban let the government operate 63 schools in the district (half are located inside a school build-ing, and the rest are in tents or mosques). The government pays teacher salaries, but the Taliban approve the appointment of each teacher, mon-itor the curriculum, and check on the attendance of teachers, docking their pay if they are absent. There are no girls' schools open in the district, not because the Taliban have prevented them from operating, but because there is no demand for them from the conservative population.

The Taliban also influence the mobile phone companies who oper-ate in the district. One of the most popular means to communicate in Afghanistan is WhatsApp, second only to Facebook. The Taliban use it extensively to coordinate, as do the army and most Afghan politicians. Within both the government and the Taliban, most decisions are still made at very high levels, just as in years past. But now both sides of the conflict use WhatsApp to allow this to happen much more quickly. The Taliban charge the mobile phone companies a tax to operate, and also force them to shut down their service at night. This lets the Taliban con-duct military operations while preventing the government from coordi-nating a response. When one of the mobile phone companies refused to pay its taxes, the Taliban destroyed its communication towers.

Exuding legitimacy, the Taliban charge a 10 percent tax on all local farm produce. The only real public service that they provide in return is a justice system, but this is enough for most people to pay the tax without complaint. It costs the plaintiff nothing to bring a case to the court, and the courts make decisions quickly. Unlike the government courts, they are also not seen as corrupt. When a Taliban court sentenced three men to death for kidnapping a child who was then murdered when the ran-som was not paid, over a thousand people came to watch the execution. Taliban justice is not only swift, it is public.

Had the central government been able to demonstrate that it was effective and benefitted the people, it is possible that the population of Zurmat would have rejected the Taliban. But the predatory behaviour of government organizations forced people to find alternatives. Tribal lead-ers effectively negotiate between the government and the Taliban, trying to protect themselves from both while wresting the maximum possible benefit. The government's willingness to coexist in the district with the Taliban undercuts its legitimacy, putting the two on an equal footing.

Operations against the Taliban in Zurmat are operations against the people themselves, creating cycles of revenge and only further entrenching the insurgency in the community.

Civilian casualties in Afghanistan have been incredibly high throughout the conflict, trending upward as foreign forces withdrew and the Afghan security organizations demanded increased use of air power to support their operations. The United Nations determined that over eleven thousand civilians were killed in the conflict in 2018, more than in any year since 2009. In the first half of 2019, more civilians were killed by Afghan and American forces than by the Taliban. High-profile errors, such as the American air attack in October 2015 that struck a Médecins sans frontières hospital in Konduz and killed 42 people, create fear and uncertainty. The United States' threat to arrest or sanction International Criminal Court (ICC) officials if American soldiers are charged with war crimes gives the sense that they operate with impunity. This was reinforced by the ICC's decision not to investigate possible war crimes in Afghanistan, not because there was no reasonable basis to believe that crimes had been committed, but because they felt that the governments of Afghanistan and the United States would not co-operate. In this environment, it is no wonder that the civilian population has lost hope, even though the ICC reversed this decision in March 2020.

This sense of war-weariness that pervades Afghanistan was expressed in a positive way in 2018 by a small group of Helmandis who started what became known as the People's Peace Movement. Nine men from all walks of life — farmers, students, businessmen, and a blind poet — began a hunger strike to protest a suicide attack in Lashkar Gah. Their leader was Iqbal Khaibar, a pharmacist with no political connections. The protest developed into a barefoot walk to the capital, covering 700 kilometres in 40 days, gathering 41 other marchers as it went. The group presented the attorney general with a list of demands, and did the same with the Taliban. The People's Peace Movement has built a large social-media following in Afghanistan, and although it did not begin as a political entity, it is possible that it will develop into one in the future as more and more of the population demand peace.

Partially in response to this growing sentiment, Ghani held a four-day Peace Loya Jirga in April 2019, the sixth jirga held in the country since

2001. Unlike many of the government-sponsored jirgas of the past, this meeting was meant to give Ghani advice rather than make its own decisions, as tradition dictated. The key issue discussed was a framework for the government to use in negotiations with the Taliban. The meeting was chaired by Sayyaf, now more of an elder statesman than the firebrand mujahid he once was. He made a forceful argument for women's rights and against suicide bombing, and insisted that peace was the "order of Allah."

The government put this argument into action when it unilaterally declared a three-day truce over Eid al-Fitr, the holiday marking the end of the Ramadan fast. Although there was fighting between the Taliban and the government on the days preceding and following the truce, the three days of peace were broken only by two attacks by ISKP. The Taliban never formally approved the truce, but members across the country respected it, and a tremendous amount of fraternization occurred, with Taliban fighters openly walking the streets of towns they had not been able to enter for years. The country witnessed remarkable displays of mutual acceptance, such as when the governor and shadow governor of Logar Province publicly prayed together. Similarly, the governors of Nangarhar and Farah invited the Taliban to meet with them in the hukomat, permitting them to enter without being searched. Women in Helmand held a protest in favour of peace, handing out flowers to Taliban fighters observing the ceasefire. The grassroots response to the truce was genuine and largely spontaneous, showing the depth of feeling that existed in favour of peace.

But above the grassroots level, there was still a hard core of leaders on both sides who disapproved of the truce. Former NDS director-turned-politician Amrullah Saleh tweeted: "The anti-Taliban constituency which provide the bulk of troops to ANDSF [Afghan National Defence and Security Forces] feel betrayed, confused & sold out." He has long maintained that no peace deal with the Taliban would ever be acceptable. Mullah Yaqub, one of the Taliban's deputies, also spoke against the truce. It is possible that the fighting that took place the day after the truce was instigated by leaders on both sides who wished to regain control of their forces and the narrative surrounding the conflict.

Reconciliation continues to be hampered by the tempo of strikes against the insurgent leadership, and the consequent unintentional deaths of civilians, as well as the deliberate targeting of civilians by groups such as ISKP. The election of President Trump led to a loosening of restrictions on the use of air power in Afghanistan, permitting American forces to strike at insurgents not just when they posed a threat, but based merely on their assessed allegiance. This greatly increased the amount of ordinance dropped on Afghanistan, reaching levels even greater than the previous peak in 2010.

Although strikes against drug labs had been carried out since 2008 when authority was first granted, the loosening of restrictions created more potential targets of this kind. On May 5, 2019, American forces struck 60 drug labs in Farah and Nimroz Provinces, targeting mostly the production of yakh. Investigation by the United Nations raised an interesting concern regarding the 84 civilians killed and wounded in the attacks, as they appeared to all be criminals rather than true insurgents. Many of the buildings struck were private homes engaged in cottage-industry narcotics production, not branches of a larger criminal enterprise. The Taliban largely profit from the narcotics trade through taxation and charging protection money, rather than owning the means of production. This raises the questions of whether these strikes were legal, as those killed were not combatants but rather criminals and their families. Women and children made up 30 of the dead and seven of the wounded. For the reasons already discussed, the ICC declined to investigate these incidents as possible war crimes, stating that "The current circumstances ... in Afghanistan are such as to make the prospects for a successful investigation and prosecution extremely limited.... It is unlikely that pursuing an investigation would result in meeting the objectives listed by the victims favouring the investigation."

Against this backdrop of increasing violence, the United States appointed Zalmay Khalilzad as special representative for Afghan reconciliation in September 2018. More serious talks with the Taliban began that December in Qatar. Although the Taliban continued to refuse to negotiate with the Afghan government until a timetable for the withdrawal of foreign forces had been agreed upon, Khalilzad kept Ghani (a former classmate at the American University of Beirut) well informed of his intentions and progress. Representing the Taliban at the talks were prominent members of the movement thought to have the moral authority to make an agreement that the rank and file would accept. Mullah Baradar, released by Pakistan at the request of the United States, led the delegation.

Khairullah Khairkhwa, one of the five Taliban released from Guantanamo four years earlier, also had a prominent place within the group.

The key Taliban demand in the negotiations was the withdrawal of all foreign forces. This goal is supported by many prominent Afghans not aligned with the Taliban, such as Karzai and several members of parliament. In exchange, the United States wanted guarantees from the Taliban that no al Qaeda–like organization would be allowed to take root in Afghanistan and threaten a second 9/11. Conspicuously absent from this dialogue was what the Afghan government and its people so desperately want: peace.

That would instead form part of the eventual discussions between the Taliban and the Afghan government, but this prospect created a sense of dread in Kabul. After foreign forces had withdrawn, the Taliban would have the upper hand in many parts of the country. The process that the discussions followed was also problematic. Khalilzad was trying to get a peace agreement in place before the presidential elections scheduled for late 2019, so that the present government and the Taliban leadership could merge into a National Unity Government. But without a common stance on the issues that had been driving conflict in Afghanistan for the past century — the roles of the central government and the ulema, human rights, women's rights, and the protection of religious and ethnic minorities — peace would likely be short-lived.

Although the Taliban negotiators stated that they did not see human rights as being in conflict with their view of Islam, even admitting that they had not safeguarded those rights effectively when they were in power, many people doubted their sincerity. Women, in particular, were vocal in their opposition to any peace agreement that did not guarantee their rights at the outset. It was also an open question whether the Taliban movement as a whole would honour the agreement, or if it would splinter into factions with whom peace could not be negotiated. Although a tentative peace agreement was reached, the United States withdrew from the negotiations unilaterally on September 9, 2019, over the death of an American soldier in a car bomb attack in Kabul. The Taliban remained open to negotiations, but they also characterized the United States as a poor ally for the Afghan people. In an interview with the BBC, Khairkhwa said: "The U.S. follows its interests everywhere, and once it doesn't reach those interests, it leaves the area. The best example of that is the abandoning of the Kurds in Syria. It's clear the Kabul administration will face the same fate."

With the peace talks ending abruptly in failure, the Afghan presidential elections went ahead as originally planned. The two key rivals were again Ashraf Ghani and Abdullah Abdullah, followed by a number of well-known Afghan politicians: Hekmatyar, Ahmed Wali Massoud, Zalmay Rassoul, and Ghani's former national security adviser Mohammed Hanif Atmar. Unlike in the previous elections since 2004, this time there were no female candidates. Held on September 28, polling was as difficult as ever due to the poor security situation. As 50 percent of the polling stations were based in schools, the government cancelled classes for several days before and after the election. Nonetheless, over five hundred incidents were recorded on election day, resulting in nearly three hundred civilian casualties, half of whom were women and children.

The issue of fraud was meant to be tackled through the use of biometric voter verification (BVV) technology, which recorded a photo and fingerprint for each vote cast. Although workable in theory, many of the thousands of machines deployed malfunctioned, meaning that voters used many different forms of identification to vote. Combined with a lack of accurate voter rolls, there was a great deal of scope for both duplication and fraud. Of the roughly 15 million eligible voters, only 1.7 million biometrically verified votes were cast, and even many of these appeared to be fraudulent. The IEC took five months to declare the final results, eventually declaring Ghani the winner by the slimmest of margins — 50.62 percent of the popular vote. Hours later, Abdullah declared himself the winner, refusing to accept the "fraudulent" election result, and vowing to form a parallel government. Both men held inauguration ceremonies, although the international community recognized only Ghani's. While Ashraf Ghani does not personally control a large militia, as Abdullah does, both men have supporters who do, including factions within the national security forces. As was the case during the PDPA regime, the potential for intra-government violence was very real.

CHAPTER 22 FAINT HOPE FOR THE FUTURE

WHILE THE AFGHAN government stumbled, peace talks between the United States and the Taliban resumed, finally resulting in an agreement on February 28, 2020.

The "Agreement for Bringing Peace to Afghanistan" was signed by Khalilzad and Mullah Baradar, but not by any representative of the Afghan government. As part of the agreement, the United States pledged to withdraw thousands of soldiers from Afghanistan immediately, and that all foreign troops would withdraw within 14 months. The Taliban agreed to prevent al Qaeda or other extremists from using territory under their control to attack Western interests. The terms by which Taliban compliance will be judged were not released (though they may have been included in classified annexes to the agreement), leading to accusations that the United States will withdraw no matter what the Taliban do. It is a sad irony that these terms could have been agreed to at the outset of the conflict, without the need for 20 years of war.

A key element of the agreement from the Taliban perspective was that the Afghan government would release up to five thousand prisoners as a precursor to direct talks. The United States agreed to this without seeking concurrence from the Afghan government, and it has become a major point of tension between them. Since these prisoners could be a major source of leverage in future negotiations, Ghani initially stated that he would refuse to honour this part of the agreement. The Taliban also agreed to a ceasefire with the foreign forces in Afghanistan, to which the American negotiators felt they were committing the Afghan government, as well.

Ghani's response on the prisoner issue caused the Taliban to resume attacks against the government, perhaps in recognition of the fact that American withdrawal is inevitable, driven by domestic political pressure in a re-election year in the USA, rather than by the state of things in Afghanistan.

The agreement was a clear win for the Taliban, as it placed very few obligations on them, while allowing them to achieve their long-stated goal of ejecting foreign forces from the country. The Taliban leadership celebrated the signing as a "day of victory," and Maulvi Haibatullah Akhundzada issued a statement that "Anyone who partook in hostilities against the Islamic Emirate or anyone with reservations about the Islamic Emirate is forgiven and pardoned for all past actions." This offer of amnesty was taken as an insult by the many Afghans who opposed the Taliban. At the same time, Ghani issued a statement that he would not commit to honouring the commitment to release Taliban prisoners. Although intra-Afghan dialogue was scheduled to begin within weeks of the initial agreement, the process immediately stalled.

Exacerbating the issue was the fact that the Afghan government was in disarray. Although Ghani had been declared the winner by the IEC, Abdullah disputed the final result. While the international community recognized the IEC's decision, there were no enthusiastic congratulations extended to Ghani. The general perception was that a new version of the National Unity Government would be required, in order to create a functional, inclusive government. Abdullah, in the weaker position, was open to this possibility, but Ghani was not. Both men held inauguration ceremonies on March 9, interrupted by the sound of explosions from Taliban attacks within the city. Although the international community attended

Ghani's ceremony, giving him tacit support, from an Afghan perspective Ghani seemed isolated, with the majority of the country's power brokers supporting Abdullah.

Secretary of State Mike Pompeo publicly threatened that the United States would cut $1 billion in aid to Afghanistan, representing nearly 20 percent of the government's annual budget, if the two sides could not settle their differences, but this achieved little. It was only after many rounds of shuttle democracy by Khalilzad, and further pressure behind the scenes, that an agreement was reached. Although there was not a National Unity Government as before, Ghani agreed to appoint Abdullah the Chair of the High Council for National Reconciliation (HCNR), which would take the lead on peace negotiations with the Taliban. He would also accept nominations from Abdullah for half of the positions in Cabinet, thus allowing Abdullah to exercise his patronage network. Abdullah had less structural power than he had within the National Unity Government, but chances were increased that the government could function without deadlock.

This was never more necessary than with the appearance of the COVID-19 pandemic. Afghanistan had suffered for years from issues with access to health care, as well as the quality of it when available. Sharing a very porous border with Iran, which was stuck hard by the virus, exposed Afghanistan to a region with out-of-control infection rates very early on. Many Afghans in Iran fled home as the pandemic took hold, further spreading the virus into communities across Afghanistan. Herat, which sits astride the major trade route from Iran, was particularly hard hit and had the country's first confirmed case.

The government declared a lockdown countrywide in March, but this was impractical. Many Afghans were daily wage earners with no savings, and the government could not make good on their announcement that aid would be provided to allow people to remain at home. As in many other countries, panic buying of staples like bread and cooking oil led to massive shortages and price hikes. Government advice that eating fruit rich in vitamin C would counter the virus also caused the cost of fruit to skyrocket to the point of being unaffordable. It was not long before only schools and government offices remained in lockdown, while the rest of the country returned to normal life. The threat of the virus seemed abstract compared to the immediate problem of survival posed by poverty and insurgent attacks.

Although the Secretary General of the United Nations urged all the world's warring parties to declare ceasefires in order to jointly oppose the threat of the pandemic, the Taliban instead worked to use it to their advantage. In any insurgency, the government will lose if they are made to seem less competent than their opponents in meeting the needs of the people. The Taliban had done this effectively in a number of spheres, particularly the court systems, and tried to do the same with the pandemic response.

In late March, they produced a propaganda video that showed them distributing masks and hand sanitizer door to door, as well as conducting temperature checks. The video claimed that they were providing aid packages to families, and that they had established public-health teams and quarantine centres across the country. Taliban spokesperson Zabiullah Mujahid stated that during "coordination among the ulema, doctors and Taliban [it was decided] that medical instructions — taking precautions, quarantining when needed and avoiding gatherings — were obligatory for people to follow." The Taliban also famously recaptured a COVID-19-positive patient who escaped from an isolation ward in Balkh and returned him to the authorities.

At the same time that they conducted these benign activities, they also continued their attacks against the government, including its health facilities and medical teams, hampering the official response. The Taliban's self-projected image of competence stands in contrast to media reports of a lack of even basic preventative measures (such as masks) in government-run hospitals, scenes of families fighting over oxygen tanks for use by their loved ones, and accusations that officials were embezzling money from international donations. The fact that the Taliban's capacity to manage health issues across the country is extremely low was much less important to their strategy than simply looking less incompetent than the government.

Despite the pandemic and the agreement between the Taliban and the United States, the war in Afghanistan is just as violent and deadly in 2020 as it had been in 2019, if not more so. The Taliban launched their "Spring Offensive" as they had in previous years; although in this case they did not announce it, in order to maintain the fiction that they were ready for peace. Attacks on Afghan forces increased by 25 percent from the previous year, but the Taliban did hold back from launching major offensives to seize territory, likely reckoning that doing so might draw a response from the United States, who otherwise provided only limited air support to ANA operations. Many more civilians were killed in the fighting in 2020 than previously, and there was a sharp rise in the number of kidnappings, as well. The bulk of the fighting shifted from the south and east to the north and west, out of the Taliban strongholds and into territory that they would need to dominate if they were to again form a national government.

Against this backdrop of escalating violence, feelings about the peace process were not uniformly positive. Particularly amongst women, there was a sense that any deal reached with the Taliban risked having rights traded away for peace. This isn't just because of what the Taliban might demand, but also because women's rights are not strongly supported in many corners of Afghan society, including among supporters of the government.

A heartening development in recent years has been the number of grassroots campaigns started by women to advocate for their rights, despite strong societal pressure that the "best women" are those of whom you can say "neither the sun nor the moon has seen them." Laleh Osmany, a shari'a law graduate, started a social media campaign with the hashtag #WhereIsMyName in 2017. In very traditional families, the names of women are not uttered outside of their homes, as it is seen as bringing shame on the household. This practice carries over into civil law, so that the mother's name doesn't appear on a child's birth certificate, or even on a woman's death certificate (where it is replaced with "wife of" or "daughter of" a male relative). Osmany's campaign encouraged women to publicly share their names, and those of their female ancestors, often for the very first time. She also advocated for the Ghani government to change the practice within the state bureaucracy, which Ghani has ordered to be studied.

Well-known Afghan journalist Farahnaz Forotan founded an online campaign in 2019 called #MyRedLine, in which women state what personal freedoms they have that must not be compromised in the name of peace during negotiations with the Taliban. The phrase caught on quickly, and began to garner support from men as well, including from Ghani, who stated that his red line was the rights of women overall. As she told the BBC, "The Taliban have to accept the reality of today's Afghanistan. If they don't, these peace talks won't have a real result."

Laila Haidari is a woman who runs a restaurant in Kabul, Taj Begum, where, contrary to the norm, unmarried men and women can dine together. She uses the profits from the business to fund a drug-rehabilitation program. Despite coming from a conservative family who married her to a decades-older mullah when she was 12, she is a strong advocate for women's rights. She refuses to wear a headscarf, and drives her own car through the capital, often shocking other drivers when they realize that she is a woman. Opposed to any negotiations with the Taliban, she told an interviewer, "I'm not going to sit across from the Taliban wearing hijab begging for my rights." Her restaurant has been described disparagingly as a brothel in local media; she has received threats and has survived more than one attack.

In July of 2020 international media carried the story of a 15-year-old girl, Qamar Gul, who shot several Taliban attackers when they raided her house in Ghor and murdered her parents. A photo of her wielding a Kalashnikov rifle quickly became a popular poster in Afghanistan, and gave her folk-hero status. Ghani interceded to send a helicopter to whisk her and her younger brother to a safe house in the capital, lest the Taliban kill them in retaliation. Although this story played well into the idea of a "strong Afghan woman" opposing the Taliban, and drew comparisons with the women's units in the Kurdish army, the truth is more complicated. The men she killed were Taliban, but one was also her estranged husband Mohamed Naeem, who organized the raid to bring her back to his home. Her father was the leader of a local pro-government militia, but had also married Naeem's niece in an exchange of brides between families known as a *mohki* arrangement. There are few conflicts in Afghanistan that don't have a personal element that can be lost under such convenient labels as "government" and "insurgent."

The Taliban, and others, have increasingly been targeting prominent women in recent years. Politicians, journalists, activists, government negotiators, and actresses have all suffered from brazen attacks intended to cow or silence them. The result to date seems to have been the reverse, however, and has made some women even more outspoken. Although some Afghans have accused these women of attempting to derail the peace process over "unimportant" details, it is clear that to create a durable peace the needs of society as a whole have to be met. The idea that this includes women does not have wide currency in all parts of Afghanistan, on either side of the conflict.

Besides the individuals who oppose the idea of peace negotiations, several groups have also sought to derail them. There is reason to believe that ISKP, despite having a small footprint on the battlefield, has conducted attacks to try to cause the United States to re-enter the war in earnest. These have included rocket attacks on American installations, and possibly the shocking, unclaimed attack on the Dasht-e Barchi maternity hospital that killed eighteen people, including five women who were in labour. Weighing against these efforts is the strong pull of American domestic politics, in which there is much demand for ending that country's military commitment in Afghanistan.

It has also come to light that Russian military intelligence offered bounties to Taliban groups for killing coalition troops during the peace negotiations. While interrogations of captured militants have revealed that several bounties were paid, it's unclear which attacks they were for, and how much of an influence they had. Although it is ironic that the Russians would have strong links with the Taliban, they have been credibly accused of supplying them with modern weaponry and with funds. Russian intelligence links within Afghan society stretch back many decades, and appear to have been used to gain influence to counter the pro-Western post-2001 governments, and to create a quagmire for the United States by delaying or aborting the peace process.

The process of intra-Afghan talks had not begun as planned, largely because of Ghani's stance on the release of prisoners. He did not feel bound by the American agreement, and felt that the status of prisoners should be a subject of the intra-Afghan talks rather than being a precondition for them. For their part, the Taliban insisted that, though the text of the agreement states that the government would release "up to" five thousand prisoners, they should release exactly that, based on a list that they would provide. The Taliban also wanted to include the idea of forming an interim government, about which Abdullah appeared open to discussion and which Ghani rejected out of hand. During an interview with the Atlantic Council, he said:

> Any discussion of an interim government is premature.... I serve at the will of the Afghan people, not at the will of [the] Taliban.... Dr Najibullah made the mistake of his life

by announcing that he was going to resign. We have lived through a film — please don't ask us to replay a film that we know well.

Under immense pressure from the United States, Ghani eventually agreed to begin to release prisoners, starting in May with a hundred from Pol-e Charki prison.

The Taliban also began to release prisoners, although it has been suggested that the increase in kidnappings in 2020 may have been to provide sufficient numbers of detainees to allow them to meet their commitment. By late July, the government had released all but four hundred "especially dangerous" prisoners, but at that point Ghani again balked, suddenly claiming that the constitution did not give him the authority to continue. The only means to solve the problem, he insisted, was through a hastily convened "Consultative Loya Jirga."

Conducted over three days in early August, the gathering of 3,400 delegates met to decide whether the government should release the prisoners, and to give advice to the government for the coming negotiations. As Ghani opened the meeting, female Member of Parliament Belqis Roshan stood and displayed a banner that read "Concessions to the Brutal Taliban Are National Treason." Security bundled her out of the meeting so harshly that Ghani was forced to apologize to her later.

The jirga's appointed chair, Abdul Rasul Sayyaf, diplomatically asked Abdullah, who had no formal position in the group, to take his place. This ensured that the spirit of Ghani's agreement with Abdullah was kept, without Ghani's formally ceding any power.

American diplomats were worried that the jirga would give Ghani political cover to stop the transfer of prisoners, but in fact it did the opposite: it blessed the final release. The meeting allegedly produced a twenty-five-point resolution that appears to have been written in advance, despite protestations that the government did not interfere with the conduct or decisions of the jirga in any way. Although Afghan legal scholars have been clear that the President has the power to pardon only certain *convicted* criminals, and many of those being released were either still awaiting trial or had been convicted of crimes exempt from pardon, it was clear that the prisoner release was the price that had to be paid to get to the negotiating table. In a nod to international concerns, seven of the releasees who had been involved in attacks on foreign citizens (of France and Australia) were sent to Qatar, where they would live under constant surveillance. By early September, direct talks between the Taliban and government officials began for the first time.

While this is a positive step towards peace, success is far from guaranteed. Neither party to the talks is a strong, coherent group, and either could fracture if a splinter group senses an advantage to be gained. Another complication is that all sides have greatly reduced their reporting of their own actions, making it hard to truly know what is happening on the ground.

On the government side, Ghani's grip on power is tenuous despite tepid international support. The ongoing tension between him and Abdullah can be seen in his appointment of the members of the Leadership Committee for the High Council for National Reconciliation. Although the political agreement between the two men should have meant that this was Abdullah's role, Ghani appears unwilling to keep his word, seeking to reduce Abdullah's influence wherever possible. Ghani's nominees for the committee, whose role is to advise the negotiating team at the peace talks, were leaders from the tanzims and PDPA militias of the 1980s, senior government officials seen as in Ghani's camp, and eight women from civil society organizations, academia, and politics. Abdullah's response to these appointments was angry, although he waited until his Cabinet picks were confirmed before making a statement. He was also prevented from appointing the negotiating team itself, which is led by Masoom Stanekzai, a former head of the NDS, former head of the High Peace Council, and a Ghani supporter. Unlike his appointments to the Leadership Committee, Ghani's appointees to the negotiating team are mostly young and male: there are only five women. A number of the appointees have family connections to the country's major power brokers, including Bastur Dostum, Abdul Matin Bek (son of Abdul Mutaleb Bek), Khaled Nur (son of Ustad Atta), and Ghairat Bahir (son-in-law of Hekmatyar).

Abdullah's faction includes many ethnic groups — Uzbeks, Tajiks, and Hazaras — and militias who fought the Taliban for years and may not be willing to give much in negotiations with a foe against whom they harbour deep resentment. There has been little discussion of what process of disarmament, demobilization, and reintegration might be used to dismantle the Taliban's military organization, or if they would even be willing to undergo such a process. Suggestions that the Taliban might be integrated directly into the armed forces is almost certainly unworkable, and would be opposed by many within the security sector. It would more likely be a driver of further instability than a solution.

The Taliban are also far from monolithic, and might have difficulty "selling" a deal to their rank and file if they are seen as giving away too much. There are several noted skeptics within the Rahbari Shura, including Abdul Qayyum Zakir, Mullah Ibrahim Sadar, and Mullah Yaqub, who advocate for continuing the struggle until a military victory is achieved. It is even possible that the Taliban have agreed to negotiations in bad faith, and have no intention of ceasing military operations once the international military forces are out of the way. Even if the Taliban do sign an agreement, it is possible that there will be defections to more radical organizations such as ISKP or al Qaeda, or even a recusant Taliban splinter, as has been seen in the past. This sort of result, not unheard-of after peace agreements are signed, occurred in Northern Ireland and Colombia after the "end" of conflicts just as seemingly intractable as that in Afghanistan.

Even if an agreement is reached that satisfies the majority within both sides, it will be only the beginning of a difficult process. The hardest thing will be to reintegrate the many people involved in the conflict back into a unified civil society, and to create conditions such that they perceive that their interests are better met within it than by opposing it.

The continuing violence as direct negotiations begin creates uncertainty, and the potential for anarchy. In such a chaotic environment, it is little wonder that many Afghans no longer place great faith in the democratic system. It is hard to look at the present state of Afghanistan without being reminded of the dying days of the Soviet-backed government, when much of the population was in arms and the writ of the central government did not extend much beyond the capital itself.

These were the conditions that created the Taliban in the first place.

CONCLUSION

THE CONFLICT IN Afghanistan over the last hundred years has been about issues that chiefly concern the Afghan people alone, despite the involvement of foreign powers during certain periods. In essence, it has been about the balance between three poles of power in Afghan society: the state, the ulema, and traditional leaders. The struggle began when Amanullah Amir sought to swing the balance dramatically in favour of the state, creating a reaction among those in society with a vested interest in seeing the other poles exercise power. Wherever there has been conflict, it has been between opposing visions of how these three elements of Afghan society interact, and the type of society this creates.

While it has been argued elsewhere that the current conflict in Afghanistan began in September 2001, this is better described as the moment that the world again became interested in Afghanistan. That argument fails to recognize that the conflict is an internal one between elements of Afghan society, and that Western actors — military, humanitarian, and political — merely exacerbate the conflict rather than driving it or even truly being a party to it. A general misunderstanding of the roots of the Afghan conflict has meant that even the best of intentions and billions of dollars in aid and military expenditures have had little positive effect. If every Western organization withdrew from the country, there is no question that the conflict would continue in almost exactly the same form that it takes today. The West is little more than an interested bystander in the long-running conflict that has destroyed Afghan society.

We began our consideration of the conflict in Afghanistan with the reign of Amanullah, and his policy goals: access to education for girls as well as boys, the equality of men and women, bans on child marriage and slavery, abolition of restrictive religious dress such as the burkha, a secular constitution, and a centralized system of government and taxation. In response, tribesmen fought an insurgency against the national army to defend what they saw as their traditional way of life, free from government interference. The broad strokes of this conflict sound familiar because we recognize them in today's news. Similar attempts at changing the balance of power within Afghan society by later leaders — Habibullah Kalakani, Daoud Khan, Taraki, Amin, Najibullah, Mullah Omar, Karzai, and Ghani — all had similar results. We are fighting the latest incarnation of the same fight today, over the same issues, and often with descendants of the same actors on both sides of the conflict. The same disputes — modernism against traditionalism, centralism against regionalism, and Islamism against secularism — have defined the conflict within Afghan society since Amanullah Amir attempted his ambitious program of reforms. These are the issues that must be resolved for there to be reconciliation among the Afghan people and a lasting peace.

Although many Afghans desperately want peace, a number of aggravating factors that have arisen since 2001 have made reconciliation more difficult. The most significant of these is corruption. Many of the actors on both sides of the conflict today are the same as in 1996 or even earlier. In particular, those previously defeated warlords who now occupy places of power in the administration are widely seen as greedy, corrupt, and cruel, despite their perceived usefulness to Western powers. Many current insurgents point to grievances they have suffered at the hands of government officials — abuse of power, exclusion from power or resources, or the flouting of laws by the officials themselves — as their reason for fighting.

Although it seems counterintuitive, the need for personal safety has driven many to remain as active insurgents, as was also the case during the war to expel the Soviets. In a country as conflict-ridden as Afghanistan, it is difficult to survive without taking sides. For many who have participated in the insurgency at some point, simply returning to "civilian" life has not been an option. Demobilized insurgents continue to be subject to threats from Western militaries, the current government, previous victims, and their former comrades. Under these conditions, there is little incentive or opportunity for an individual fighter to leave the insurgency once he has become embroiled within it.

Loss of opportunity is another factor driving the insurgency today. The disenfranchisement of groups (be they tribes, clans, or villages) by the empowerment of others is a natural result of the patronage politics epitomized by the current Afghan administration, but also of counterinsurgency as practised by Western militaries in Afghanistan. Despite the vast sums spent on economic development and in other direct support to the government, the result has been increasing conflict between groups vying for a slice of the pie. This motivation is present even in arenas not seen as primarily economic, such as hiring for security forces or appointments to administrative posts. Heavy direct investment by foreign governments and non-governmental agencies, besides being unsustainable, also undercuts the very same Afghan government and economic structures that foreign militaries are ostensibly there to support.

It could also be argued that the presence of Western organizations itself adds to insecurity. A widely held cultural narrative in Afghanistan is that the country has long been the field for world powers to play out the "Great Game." This idea draws a line of continuity from Alexander the Great through Genghis Khan, the three wars with the British, the Soviet occupation, and the current conflict, casting doubt on the true motivations of any foreign presence. Polling has consistently shown that only a small minority of the population believe that foreigners come to the country to bring peace and security. This creates the paradox where the very presence of foreign military forces creates the insurgency they have been deployed to defeat.

Many analysts sidestep these issues by blaming Afghan "culture." An example of this misunderstanding stems from the idea incorporated in the famous Afghan maxim: "I against my brothers, I and my brothers against my cousins, I and my cousins against the world." This is often cited as "explaining" Afghan culture, as is the saying, "A Pashtun is never at peace unless he is at war." The idea that the insurgents in Afghanistan fight simply because that is what Afghans do (and have done for centuries), has surprising currency amidst what is otherwise good, nuanced analysis. It is an evasion, however, because to accept it means that no other explanation is required, and so it ignores the many addressable problems outlined above that motivate groups and individuals.

Similarly, the conflict in Afghanistan is misidentified as one primarily based on ethnicity or tribalism. While it is true that some conflicts in Afghanistan follow tribal or ethnic lines, the major insurgent groups clearly define themselves as supra-tribal. Western understanding of tribal structures is superficial and static, while in reality the "tribe" is a transient structure that reflects ideals and changing identities. Tribes and sub-tribes merge and divide over time for reasons of expediency, and their relations and standing remain in flux. These shifts are all the more common now that tribal structures have been weakened by years of targeting by all parties involved in the conflict.

Although it was the Taliban's decision to shelter al Qaeda that drew Western forces into Afghanistan in 2001, there is little to suggest that al Qaeda represents a reason for them to remain there now. The Taliban leadership have long since cut significant ties with al Qaeda, and have themselves conducted combat operations against more radical insurgents such as ISKP. The Taliban is unlikely to ever become a terrorist group with international ambitions, as it has never expressed any interest in widening the conflict outside of Afghanistan. The Taliban's grievances and desires remain entirely local.

American involvement in Afghanistan began in 2001 as primarily an act of vengeance, with no clear plan for what to achieve beyond toppling the Taliban and destroying al Qaeda. Continued involvement places the Americans in the same trap that has prevented Afghans from finding peace — the attempt to wash off blood with more blood, creating cycles of revenge and violence.

* * *

The conflict in Afghanistan is estimated to have cost the United States more than $2 trillion since 2001, including $49 billion in 2019 alone. Since 2002 American funding for reconstruction has amounted to only $133 billion, and 63 percent of this money was spent on creating national security forces, many of which have gone on to damage the stability of society, rather than on rebuilding infrastructure. For this massive expenditure, the return has been limited.

Since 2014, nearly sixty thousand Afghan security personnel have been killed fighting their own countrymen, including several thousand since the "peace agreement" was signed between the United States and the Taliban.

Two million Afghans remain as refugees in Pakistan, unable to return because of insecurity in their homeland.

After nearly 20 years, girls still have access to education in only 47 percent of the villages deemed to be under government control, with much lower rates elsewhere.

Afghanistan ranks 153rd out of 160 countries in a United Nations study on gender equality. Although the situation of women in urban areas has improved since 2001, 75 percent of Afghan women live outside of the towns and cities.

The immediate future for Afghanistan looks much as it did in 1993, when an isolated central government relied on external support to survive, while the countryside remained largely beyond its control. The refusal in late 2019 of two governors, in Balkh and Samangan, to comply with the president's order to step down from their posts does not bode well. If regional leaders were to turn on the government and defend their fiefdoms with armed force, it is unclear whether the national army could defeat them, or would even agree to try.

At the same time, there is a small glimmer of hope for Afghanistan in the grassroots peace movements that have begun to flourish. When foreign troops have left the country, it is possible that, as in 1989, large numbers of insurgents will feel that their fight is over, lay down their arms, and try to return to normal life.

The international community can support this by recognizing that the Bonn process is not truly complete until all Afghans feel that they have a place within the country. The solution cannot be one that is imposed from the outside, but must be devised by Afghans to create a society that balances power among the state, the ulema, and traditional leaders in a way that is broadly acceptable. The differences of opinion prevalent in Afghan society likely argue for a highly decentralized government that exercises power lightly. A process of truth and reconciliation is needed to allow former combatants to live in peace, while still recognizing the grave crimes that have been committed by all sides in decades of conflict. These solutions may not look like the ones that Western donors want to see, or match popular wisdom about how societies should function. Nonetheless, this is how it must be.

A commonly heard Afghan proverb is *Qatara, qatara, darya mesha:* "Drop by drop, a river is formed." This is how peace will be built by Afghans for themselves — by drops of trust and mutual interest, which over time will form a powerful current.

ACKNOWLEDGEMENTS

MANY PEOPLE HAD a hand in bringing this book to fruition, and no matter how expansive my acknowledgements are, I am certain that I will miss someone.

In my time in Afghanistan, I met many people who were eager to talk about their lives and their country. I spent many hours talking, and more importantly, listening, and learning about a part of the world that fascinates me. In particular, I want to thank my friends Doctor Wasif, Shawali Yusuffi, and Zamarey Faqiri for their patience in answering my questions, no matter how ill-informed or obvious they may have been.

Although he will never read this book, I would never have found myself in Afghanistan in the first place if not for the stories of my grandfather, a cockney lad whose time as a soldier in British India shaped his outlook on life forever after.

A number of people with deep knowledge of Afghanistan and some of the particular events in this book volunteered their time to read early versions of it and offer their advice. Their detailed feedback and the conversations that followed helped me shape this book in ways that I could not have done alone. My heartfelt thanks goes to Colonel Howard Coombs, Colonel Dwayne Hobbs, Lieutenant Colonel Kevin Doyle, Major Chris Wattie, Captain Rye Maybee, and Alyse Kennedy.

I think that often times librarians are the unsung heroes of many creative and scholarly works. The assistance and early encouragement of Jeanine Eakins, head of information services at the Canadian Forces College Library, launched this project in the right direction from the start.

It is no exaggeration that this book would not have happened without the hard work of my editor, Cy Strom. At points where I could not see a way forward, Cy was always ready with a calm and clear-eyed assessment of how to prune away the unnecessary and reveal the heart of the book. I owe him a debt that I cannot adequately repay.

When I first struck out as a full-time writer, there are only two people who believed in me without reservation — my children. They continue to be my biggest supporters, no matter what project I dream up.

GLOSSARY

AARC – Afghan Armies' Revolutionary Council.

amir – Arabic word for king. See also **shah**.

ANA – Afghan National Army.

ANBP – Afghan New Beginnings Program.

andiwal – a personal or friend network.

ANP – Afghan National Police.

badraga – literally "safeconduct." The "badraga business" means the practice of charging to protect caravans, a form of extortion.

baiat – a formal oath of allegiance in Islam. Its use is associated with the link between the Prophet Mohammed (PBUH) and his followers.

basmachi – a derogatory term used by the Soviets for insurgents in Central Asia, taken from the Turkish word for "bandit."

burkha – a head-to-toe covering worn by women to maintain their modesty. Vision is allowed by a fabric "grill," or lattice, over the eyes.

caliph – a successor of the Prophet Mohammed (PBUH) as the head of Islam. Used as a title. Also see **caliphate**.

caliphate – the office of **caliph** or the land the caliph rules.

Dari – a variety of the Persian language spoken in Afghanistan.

Darul Aman – literally the "Abode of Peace and Refuge" or the "Abode of Aman[ullah]." Modern 20th-century palace built by Amanullah Amin.

DDR – Disarmament, Demobilization, and Reintegration program.

Deobandism – a Sunni revivalist movement started in Deoband, India.

DIAG – Disbandment of Illegal Armed Groups program.

faqir – a Sufi ascetic.

fatwa – a non-binding religious opinion on a point of Islamic law made by a qualified jurist.

Fidai Mahaz – Sacrifice Front, a Taliban splinter group.

ghazi – the title given to a champion among Islamic warriors.

hadith – the collected second-hand accounts of the deeds, teachings, and sayings of the Prophet Mohammed (PBUH), used as a guide for behaviour.

Hanafi – one of four schools of Sunni religious jurisprudence.

haram – something that is forbidden by Islam.

hasht nefari – literally "one in eight." A system of conscription where one person is conscripted from a community, and seven others support the conscript's costs while enlisted.

HAVA – Helmand and Arghandab Valley Authority.

Hazarajat – the traditional lands of the Hazara people. A mountainous area located in central Afghanistan.

hukomat – literally "government," but refers to the government offices at the district and provincial level.

IEC – Independent Electoral Commission.

ISAF – International Security Assistance Force.

ISI – Inter-Services Intelligence (Pakistan).

ISKP – Islamic State in Iraq and the Levant – Khorasan Province.

jihad – literally "striving or "struggling." Islamic concept of making one's life accord with Allah's aim. The "greater" jihad is against one's own impulses, while the "lesser" jihad is waged either with the pen or the sword, to persuade others.

jirga – an ad hoc meeting of community members to resolve disputes or reach decisions through consensus. A key element of **Pashtunwali**. See also **shura**.

KhAD – the acronym for Khedamat-e Atalat-e Dolati, the State Information Service. The Soviet intervention–era secret police in Afghanistan.

Khalq – literally "masses." A faction of the **PDPA**.

khan – a leader or prominent person. Also used as a name.

khan khel – the clan from which a tribe's leader (or **khan**) is traditionally drawn.

Khedamat-e Atalat-e Dolati – see **KhAD**.

Khuddam al-Furqan – Servants of Providence, a 1950s Islamist party. The same name was used by the Taliban for a post-2001 political party.

Kochi – **Pashtun** nomads, primarily from the Ghilzai tribe, but also including some Durrani Pashtuns and Baloch tribespeople. Sometimes incorrectly considered an independent ethnicity, but in their own view see themselves as the most traditional of all the Pashtun.

Khudai Khidmatgar – Servants of God, an Indian political party founded by Abdul Ghaffar Khan. Also known as the Surkh Posh or Red Shirts.

lalmi – a grain crop, typically wheat, sowed by hand without ploughing on the dry plains that surround irrigated land.

lashkar – a posse formed by a community to protect itself or to enforce the decisions of a **jirga**.

LCSFA – Limited Contingent of Soviet Forces in Afghanistan.

loya jirga – a "grand" **jirga**, at the national or supra-tribal level.

madrassa – a school, typically with a religious curriculum.

mahfel – a discussion group, precursor to the Afghan political parties.

malik – a tribal leader, typically of less stature than a **khan**. In Afghanistan, a malik usually has the role of representing the government within his tribe. Also used as a name.

Melli Jirga – National Assembly, a single house of government created by the 1964 constitution to replace the upper and lower houses.

Meshrano Jirga – the upper house of parliament. See also **Wolesi Jirga**.

mujahideen – persons engaged in jihad. Often used to describe the guerrillas who fought the Russian invasion of Afghanistan, but also those who fought the NATO and American soldiers post-9/11. The singular form is mujahid.

mullah – a term of respect for an educated religious man. May refer to a local religious leader, although there is no set authority or required qualification for granting the title.

Musahiban – literally "courtier." Typically refers to a clan of the Mohammedzai sub-tribe of the Barakzai tribe.

nakh – an illegal narcotic produced from the **oman** shrub.

nang – honour, of a person or tribe. A key driver of decisions within **Pashtunwali**.

NDS – National Directorate of Security, the modern version of **KhAD**.

nezam-nama – literally "decree," the phrase selected by Amanullah Amir over qanun (law) for his government policies, as it implies that the man-made directives are lesser than the law of **shari'a**.

nizami – military commission.

nizami masul – military commissioner.

oman – a shrub used as winter fodder, now used to create the narcotic **nakh**.

panj kitab – literally "five books." Works of classic Persian literature that form the traditional school curriculum in Afghanistan.

Parcham – literally "banner" or "flag." A faction of the **PDPA**. See also **Khalq**.

Pashtunwali – the way and customs of the Pashtun people.

PDPA – People's Democratic Party of Afghanistan, or Hezb-e Demokratik Khalq-e Afghanistan.

pir – a saint or holy person, either living or dead. Used as an honorific for a Sufi teacher.

Proceay Tahkim-e Solha (PTS) – Strengthening Peace Program, a national reconciliation program.

PRT – Provincial Reconstruction Team.

purdah – the practice of separating men and women within a society.

al Qaeda – literally the Base." A support organization for the anti-Soviet **mujahideen** created by Osama bin Laden. Later, an international terrorist group.

qawm – often translated as tribe, it is an identity group that is based on many different factors, such as kinship, occupation, or residence. A low-level "in-group."

Qizilbash – literally "redhead." Shi'ites of Tajik descent, the Qizilbashi formed the bureaucracy of the Afghan court.

Quran – the holy book of Islam, believed to record the literal word of God as recited by the Prophet Mohammed (PBUH).

Rahbari Shura – "Supreme Council." Typically used to refer to the leadership council of the Taliban.

Sarandoy – the armed members of the Ministry of the Interior, similar to gendarmes or carabinieri.

shah – Persian term for king. See also **amir**.

shari'a – the body of Islamic law derived from the **Quran** and the hadith.

Shi'a – One of the two main branches of Islam. Adherents are referred to as Shi'ites.

shura – Arabic for a meeting. Differs from a **jirga** in that it suggests a regular membership and periodic meetings. The implication is also more religious than tribal.

spingiri – literally "greybeard." Used to refer to an elder.

Sufism – a mystic discipline of Islam that exists within both the Sunni and Shi'a branches.

taliban – students. The singular form is talib. The name given to the movement overthrown by the American-led invasion in 2001.

ulema – literally "learned ones." The body of Islamic scholars who both guard and transmit religious knowledge and practice.

UNAMA – United Nations Assistance Mission in Afghanistan.

ushr – a form of tax that typically was levied only against non-Muslim traders. In Afghanistan it was applied when the product being traded was **haram**, such as opium.

Wahhabism – an ultra-conservative religious movement within Sunni Islam.

walwar – the first part of the bride price paid by the groom's family to the bride's family to secure a marriage arrangement. It is a Pashtun cultural practice rather than one based in shari'a.

Wolesi Jirga – the lower house of parliament. See also **Meshrano Jirga**.

Ya chahar ya! – literally "O! Four Friends!" A Sunni war cry that refers to the four first **caliphs**.

zamindar – landowner.

SOURCE NOTES

CHAPTERS 1–3

I am highly indebted to a number of scholars whose work in the 1960s and 70s gives us a window into Afghan society in the early 20th century that was insightful and largely uncoloured by the pessimism of the present-day view of the country. Leon Poullada's *Reform and Rebellion in Afghanistan, 1919–1929* is of particular note, and is based on both historical documentation and interviews with contemporaries of Amanullah. Ludwig W. Adamec's work was also useful, particularly *Afghanistan, 1900–1923: A Diplomatic History.* Thomas Barfield has written many excellent articles, particularly "Shari'a in Afghanistan" and "Centralization/Decentralization in the Dynamics of Afghan History." Vartan Gregorian's work "Mahmud Tarzi and Saraj-ol-Akhbar: Ideology of Nationalism and Modernization in Afghanistan" is also an excellent source. No work on Afghanistan of this period could be complete without reference to some work of Louis Dupree as well, in this case "Mahmud Tarzi: Forgotten Nationalist," which furnished the Tarzi quotation in Chapter 3. I am also indebted to the social insights contained in the works of Mary Bradley Watkins ("Afghanistan: Land in Transition") and Donald Newton Wilber *(Afghanistan: Its People, Its Society, Its Culture)*. Also worthwhile is R.T. Stewart's book *Fire in Afghanistan, 1914–1929: Faith, Hope and the British Empire*. Excellent contemporary news sources and academic journals are the annual *Contemporary Review,* the *Annual Register,* the *Journal of the Royal United Service Institution,* as well as the London newspaper the *Spectator* and magazine the *New Statesman.* Edgar O'Ballance's more recent work, *Afghan Wars,* helps place the events surrounding the Third Afghan War in a broader military context. More recent scholarly work of note includes Murtazashvili and Murtazashvili, "Coercive Capacity, Land Reform and Political Order in Afghanistan," Sungur, "Early Modern State Formation in Afghanistan in Relation to Pashtun Tribalism," Bezhan, "Pan-Islamism in Afghanistan in the Early Twentieth Century: From Political Discourse to Government Policy, 1906–22," Chua, "The Promise and Failure of King Amanullah's Modernisation Program in Afghanistan," Amiri, Hunt, and Sova, "Transition Within Tradition: Women's Participation in Restoring Afghanistan," and Nawid, *Religious Response to Social Change in Afghanistan, 1919–1929.*

CHAPTER 4

Although covered by many of the general works already cited, particularly those of Leon Poullada, the rule of Amir Habibullah II, the Bacha-e Saqqao, is not as intensely studied as those of either his predecessor or his successor. Two primary sources for this period are of note: *Kabul Under Siege*, written by Afghan courtier Fayz Muhammad [Fayz Mohammed Kateb] and translated by Robert D. McChesney; and *My Life: From Brigand to King,* ostensibly written by Amir Habibullah II himself. Although Amir Habibullah's story is perhaps apocryphal, much of it accords with the known history and it is an engaging read. Vartan Gregorian's work *The Emergence of Modern Afghanistan: Politics of Reform and Modernization 1880–1946* remains the quintessential source on the entire period despite the decades since its publication. Sirdar Ikbal Ali Shah's works, *Afghanistan of the Afghans* and *Modern Afghanistan: The Rise of Afghanistan as a Modern State* are also key works by an academic with first-hand knowledge of the subject. Contemporary newspapers and journals such as the *Annual Register* are of great help establishing timelines for the often confusing and overlapping events.

CHAPTER 5

Vartan Gregorian's work remains one of the few comprehensive book-length works on this period of Afghan history. Many contemporary writers covered the events of the time. Good examples are Shah's "Nadir Shah and After," and Strickland's "The Economic Development of Afghanistan." The *Annual Register* was an invaluable source for creating a coherent timeline, as were contemporary newspaper the *Daily Telegraph* and magazine the *New Statesman*. Academics in the 1960s and 1970s conducted detailed investigation into the Afghan economy that is invaluable to understanding the period today. Of note are Guha's articles "The Rise of Capitalistic Enterprises in Afghanistan 1929–45," and "Economic Development of Afghanistan — 1929–1961." Marwat's *The Evolution and Growth of Communism in Afghanistan (1917–79): An Appraisal* is an excellent academic book on the political developments of the period. Many modern articles explore the topic as well, such as: Tripodi's "'Politicals', Tribes and Musahibans: The Indian Political Service and Anglo-Afghan Relations, 1929–39," Bakshi's "Afghanistan as a Rentier State Model: Lessons from the Collapse," Halliday's "Revolution in Afghanistan," Green's "The Trans-Border Traffic of Afghan Modernism: Afghanistan and the Indian 'Urdusphere,'" Holt's "Beyond the Tribe: Patron-Client Relations, Neopatrimonialism in Afghanistan," Choudhury's "The Localised Madrasas of Afghanistan: Their Political and Governance Entanglements," and Ritter's "The Final Phase in the Liquidation of Anti-Soviet Resistance in Tadzhikistan: Ibrahim Bek and the Basmachi, 1924–31."

CHAPTERS 6–7

For an alternative look at Pashtun thinking and culture, Abdul Ghaffar Khan's memoir *My Life and Struggle* is invaluable. Third-party works on his life include Eswaran's *Nonviolent Soldier of Islam*, and Banerjee's *The Pathan Unarmed: Opposition and Memory in the North West Frontier*. Richard Newell's seminal work *The Politics of Afghanistan* is also a key reference for this period. Older scholarly works are useful when looking at this period, such as Fox's *Agriculture in Afghanistan's Economy*, Alamyar's "Education in Afghanistan: A Historical Review and Diagnosis," Dupree's "Democracy and the Military Base of Power," Masannat's "Development and Diplomacy in Afghanistan," Franck's "Problems of Economic Development in Afghanistan," Newell's "The Dangers of Cold War Generosity," and Wilber's "The Structure and Position of Islam in Afghanistan." Modern scholarship of note includes Bezhan's "The Pashtunistan Issue and Politics in Afghanistan, 1947–1952," "The Emergence of Political Parties and Political Dynamics in Afghanistan, 1964–73," "Ethno-religious Dynamics and the Emergence of the Hezbe Seri Itehad (Secret Unity Party) in Afghanistan in the Late 1940s," and "The Rise and Fall of the Liberal Hezbe Watan or Homeland Party in Afghanistan, 1949–52," Goodhand's "Frontiers and Wars: the Opium Economy in Afghanistan," Ruttig's "How It All Began: A Short Look at the Pre-1979 Origins of Afghanistan's Conflicts," Emadi's "Radical Political Movements in Afghanistan and Their Politics of Peoples' Empowerment and Liberation," "The State and Rural-Based Rebellion in Afghanistan," and "The Hazaras and Their Role in the Process of Political Transformation in Afghanistan," Robinson and Dixon's "Soviet Development Theory and Economic and Technical Assistance to Afghanistan, 1954–1991," Rubinstein's "Soviet Imperialism in Afghanistan," Cronin's "Afghanistan's Armies, Past and Present," and Hauner's "One Man Against the Empire: The Faqir of Ipi and the British in Central Asia on the Eve of and During the Second World War." Of special note is the work of Doctor Antonio Giustozzi, whose academic writing on Afghanistan is nearly without parallel. His articles of note for these chapters include "March Towards Democracy? The Development of Political Movements in Afghanistan," "Nation-Building Is Not for All: The Politics of Education in Afghanistan," and "Between Patronage and Rebellion: Student Politics in Afghanistan."

CHAPTERS 8–9

The works of Newell, Bezhan, and Emadi remain invaluable for understanding this period. A deeper understanding of the politics of the opium and hashish economy in the region is very important, and a few academics have had a tremendous influence on research in this area. Alfred McCoy's *The Politics of Heroin* is a seminal work that provides the larger context. James Bradford's work, particularly *Poppies, Politics, and Power: Afghanistan and the Global History of Drugs and Diplomacy* is the authoritative source on the narcotics trade in Afghanistan. Of interest is Brodsky's *With All Our Strength: The Revolutionary Association of the Women of Afghanistan.* Also of note are Bradford's "Drug Control in Afghanistan: Culture, Politics, and Power During the 1958 Prohibition of Opium in Badakhshan," Charpentier's "The Use of Haschish and Opium in Afghanistan," and Bradford and Mansfield's "Known Unknowns and Unknown Knowns: What We Know About the Cannabis and the Hashish Trade in Afghanistan." Other articles of note are Leake's "The Great Game Anew: US Cold-War Policy and Pakistan's North-West Frontier, 1947–65," Schofield's "Diversionary Wars: Pashtun Unrest and the Sources of the Pakistan-Afghan Confrontation," Anderson's "There Are No *Khans* Anymore: Economic Development and Social Change in Tribal Afghanistan," and Ahmed-Ghosh's "A History of Women in Afghanistan: Lessons Learnt for the Future, or Yesterdays and Tomorrow: Women in Afghanistan."

CHAPTERS 10–13

The declassified cables from the American embassy in Kabul are available online and provide unparalleled insight into American thinking and perceptions at that time. A number of insightful books have been written on this period of Afghan history: Bradsher's *Afghan Communism and Soviet Intervention*, Amstutz's *Afghanistan: The First Five Years of Soviet Occupation* (which provided the quotation from the mujahid commander), Fenzel's *No Miracles: The Failure of Soviet Decision-Making in the Afghan War*, Kalinovsky's *A Long Goodbye: The Soviet Withdrawal from Afghanistan*, and Edwards's *Before Taliban: Genealogies of the Afghan Jihad*. Two remarkable books bear noting separately. Dr Aisha Ahmad's *Jihad & Co.* examines the connections between jihadist networks and conflict economies, including during the Soviet intervention in Afghanistan. Mike Martin's outstanding book *An Intimate War: An Oral History of the Helmand Conflict* captures narratives of the conflict in Afghanistan that are not typically understood. Useful articles on the period include Halliday's "Revolution in Afghanistan," Emadi's "The State and Rural-Based Rebellion in Afghanistan," and "Radical Political Movements in Afghanistan and Their Politics of Peoples' Empowerment and Liberation," Grau's "Breaking Contact Without Leaving Chaos: The Soviet Withdrawal from Afghanistan," Doohovskoy's "Soviet Counterinsurgency in the Soviet Afghan War Revisited: Analyzing the Effective Aspects of the Counterinsurgency Effort," Nawid's "Comparing the Regimes of Amanullah (1919–29) and the Afghan Marxists (1978–92)," Felbab-Brown's "Kicking the Opium Habit? Afghanistan's Drug Economy and Politics Since the 1980s," Barfield's "Problems in Establishing Legitimacy in Afghanistan," Gibbs's "Reassessing Soviet Motives for Invading Afghanistan: A Declassified History," Safri's "The Transformation of the Afghan Refugee: 1979–2009," and Muzhary's "The Bride Price: The Afghan Tradition of Paying for Wives."

CHAPTERS 14–17

The quintessential book on the Taliban before 9/11 remains Ahmed Rashid's *Taliban*, and few books on the aftermath of 9/11 in Afghanistan and Pakistan are as cogent and well informed as his *Descent into Chaos*. Also of note are Marsden's *The Taliban* and Matinuddin's *The Taliban Phenomenon*. More recent scholarship with important insight into this period includes Bradford's *Poppies, Politics and Power*, and Coll's *Ghost*

Wars. The autobiography of Taliban founding member Abdul Salam Zaeef, *My Life with the Taliban*, also provides tremendous insight into the movement without Western bias. Mullah Omar's letter to President Clinton is quoted from Murshed's *Afghanistan: The Taliban Years*. Useful articles on the period include Goodson's "Perverting Islam: Taliban Social Policy Toward Women," Ruttig's "The Great Talqaida Myth," and Zulfacar's "The Pendulum of Gender Politics in Afghanistan."

CHAPTERS 18–21

The most recent phase of the war in Afghanistan has created a renaissance of academic writing about many aspects of the conflict, the best of which includes Afghan voices and a nuanced understanding of the reality on the ground. Of particular note is the Afghanistan Analysts Network, an independent non-profit policy research organization founded in 2009. Sari Kouvo, Thomas Ruttig, Kate Clark, Martine van Bijlert, Ehsan Qaane, Obaid Ali, Fazl Muzhary, Jelena Bjelica, Fabrizio Foschini, and Ali Yawar Adili all deserve great credit for providing analysis of the conflict. Alex Strick van Linschoten and Felix Kuehn, founders of Afghanwire.com, also deserve tremendous credit for their contribution to the body of analysis of the country. Antonio Giustozzi is another academic whose writing on Afghanistan, and conflict in general, is deeply insightful: *Koran, Kalashnikov and Laptop*, and *Decoding the New Taliban*. Bette Dam's work to unveil the true story behind the death of the Taliban's leader, "The Secret Life of Mullah Omar," deserves to be better known. Other books of note are Strick van Linschoten and Kuehn's *Poetry of the Taliban*, Smith's *The Dogs Are Eating Them Now*, and Peters's *Seeds of Terror*.

Useful academic articles on this period include the Director of National Intelligence Open Source Center's "Master Narratives Country Report: Afghanistan," Waldman's "Golden Surrender: The Risks, Challenges, and Implications of Reintegration in Afghanistan" and "Dangerous Liaisons with the Afghan Taliban," Giustozzi and Reuter's "The Northern Front:

The Afghan Insurgency Spreading Beyond the Pashtuns," Farrell and Giustozzi's "The Taliban at War: Inside the Helmand Insurgency, 2004–2012," Huq and Ginsburg's "What Can Constitutions Do? The Afghan Case," Ruttig's "The Other Side" and "'Nothing Is Agreed Until Everything Is Agreed': First Steps in Afghan Peace Negotiations," Sajjad's "Peace at All Costs? Reintegration and Reconciliation in Afghanistan," Strick van Linschoten and Kuehn's "Separating the Taliban from al-Qaeda: The Core of Success in Afghanistan," Pain's "Growing Out of Poverty? Questioning Agricultural Policy in Afghanistan," Clark's "The Eid Ceasefire: Allowing Afghans to Imagine Their Country at Peace," "Filling the Power Ministries: Biographies of the Four Candidates," "Reforming the Afghan Ministry of Interior: A Way to 'Tilt' the War?" and "War Without Accountability: The CIA, Special Forces and Plans for Afghanistan's Future," Isaqzadeh and Giustozzi's "Senior Appointments and Corruption Within the Afghan MoI: Practices and Perceptions," Alamyar's "Education in Afghanistan: A Historical Review and Diagnosis," Sharan and Heathershaw's "Identity Politics and Statebuilding in Post-Bonn Afghanistan: The 2009 Presidential Election," Safi and Ruttig's "Understanding Hurdles to Afghan Peace Talks: Are the Taleban a Political Party?" Rashid's "How Obama Lost Karzai," Dale's "NATO in Afghanistan: A Test Case for Future Missions," and Kouvo and Qaane's "Will the ICC Start an Investigation in Afghanistan After All? What We Know So Far About the ICC Appeals Hearing."

Many publications by the United Nations and other international organizations provide the vital statistics on Afghanistan on which analysis must be based. Notable reports include UNODC's "Afghanistan Opium Survey 2018: Challenges to Sustainable Development, Peace and Security," UNAMA's "Afghanistan: Protection of Civilians in Armed Conflict" (Annual Reports 2017 and 2018), "Special Report: Airstrikes on Alleged Drug-Processing Facilities — Farah, 5 May 2019," and "Suicide Attacks in Afghanistan (2001–2007)," International Crisis Group's "Taliban Propaganda: Winning the War of Words?" and the Special Inspector General for Afghanistan Reconstruction's "Quarterly Report to the United States Congress," and "Reintegration of Ex-Combatants: Lessons from the U.S. Experience in Afghanistan."

* * *

News articles of interest include AP's "A Timeline of U.S. Troop Levels in Afghanistan Since 2001," BBC's "Afghan Conflict: US and Taliban Sign Deal to End 18-Year War," "Taliban to Resume Attacking Local Forces After Deal with US," and "Top Court Backs War Crimes Probe," Shah's "CIA Tactics to Trap Bin Laden Linked with Polio Crisis, Say Aid Groups," Smith's "House of Pain: Canada's Connection with Kandahar's Ruthless Palace Guard," Cavendish's "After the US Pulls Out, Will CIA Rely More on Afghan Mercenaries?" Yousafzai's "Mullah Najibullah: Too Radical for the Taliban" and "Inside the Mysterious 'Death' of Taliban Leader Mullah Omar," Ahmad's "Afghan Taliban Splinter Faction Picks Rival Leader," Mashal, Rahim, and Faizi's "Ghani Named Afghan Election Winner: His Opponent Claims Victory, Too," Mashal and Rahim's "Gunmen Kill Dozens at Event Attended by Afghan Politicians," Muñoz's "Drone Strike Takes Out Top Taliban Leader," Pannell's "Afghan Election Fraud Is Unearthed," Nordland's "After Rancor, Afghans Agree to Share Power," Kapur's "How Afghanistan's Peace Movement Is Winning Hearts and Minds," Tolson's "The Other Peace Talks: Afghan Women, Millennials, and Social Media," Bodetti's "From WhatsApp to Hawala, How the Taliban Moves Money Around," Woods's "The Story of America's Very First Drone Strike," Gibbons-Neff and Mashal's "U.S. Is Quietly Reducing Its Troop Force in Afghanistan," and Power's "Drug Lords Have Figured Out How to Make Meth from Plants."

CHAPTER 22

There continues to be excellent journalistic coverage of the conflict in Afghanistan, and, unlike in previous decades, when many of the correspondents were Western, there is now a large crop of Afghan journalists whose work appears around the world. The Afghan 24-hour television network TOLOnews also provides excellent coverage of everything going on in the country, often breaking stories ahead of Western media outlets.

* * *

Useful news articles on this period include Ansar's "Dostum's Continued Absence from Kabul Raises Questions"; Gibbons-Neff's "Taliban Violated Afghan Deal with Shelling of American Bases, U.S. Officials Say"; Koofi's "Afghan Negotiator and Campaigner Shot by Gunmen": Limaye's "The Sex Scandal at the Heart of the Afghan Government"; Nordland's "She's a Force of Nature, and She Just Declared War on Peace with the Taliban"; Nowrouzi's "Where Is My Name: Afghan Women Campaign for the Right to Reveal their Names"; Rowlatt's "What the Heroin Industry Can Teach Us About Solar Power"; Savage, Schmitt, and Schwirtz's "Russia Secretly Offered Afghan Militants Bounties to Kill U.S. Troops, Intelligence Says"; and Timory, Rahim, and Mashal's "In Afghan Attacks, Facts Are Murky. But It's Clear Deaths Are Piling Up," and "A Girl's Heroic Battle Against the Taliban Was Also a Family Feud."

From the Afghanistan Analysts Network, I recommend Adili's "Peace Leadership: Power Struggles, Division and an Incomplete Council," and "Still Preoccupied by 'Who Gets What': 100 Days of the New Government, but No Full Cabinet"; Clark's "War in Afghanistan in 2020: Just as Much Violence, but No One Wants to Talk About It," and her "New Special Report on Afghanistan's Newest Local Defence Force: Were 'All the Mistakes of the ALP' Turned into ANA-TF Safeguards?"; Clark, Adilo, and Qaane's "The End of the Jirga: Strong Words and Not Much Controversy"; Kazemi and Muzhary's "COVID-19 in Afghanistan (4): A Precarious Interplay Between War and Epidemic"; Ruttig's "From Doha to Peace? Obstacles Rising in the Way of Intra-Afghan Talks"; Ruttig, Adili, and Ali's "Doors Opened for Direct Talks with the Taleban: The Results of the Loya Jirga on Prisoners and Peace"; Qaane's "To Release, or Not to Release? Legal Questions Around Ghani's Consultative Loya Jirga on Taleban Prisoners."

* * *

Academic and think tank articles that provide good insight into this period include Jones's "A Failed Afghan Peace Deal"; Mansfield's "When the Water Runs Out: The Rise (and Inevitable Fall) of the Deserts of Southwest Afghanistan and Its Impact on Migration, Poppy and Stability" and "The Helmand Food Zone: The Illusion of Success"; Quilty's "Afghanistan's Unseen COVID Crisis"; and Jackson's "For the Taliban, the Pandemic is a Ladder."

The quote from Ashraf Ghani in this chapter was taken from a video produced by the Atlantic Council, *Afghanistan's Vision for Peace: A Conversation with H.E. President Mohammad Ashraf Ghani.*

SELECTED BIBLIOGRAPHY

Adamec, Ludwig W. *Afghanistan, 1900–1923: A Diplomatic History*. Berkeley: University of California Press, 1967.

———. *Historical Dictionary of Afghanistan*, 3rd ed. Lanham, MD: Scarecrow Press, 2003.

Adili, Ali Yawar. "Peace Leadership: Power Struggles, Division and an Incomplete Council." Afghanistan Analysts Network, September 6, 2020. Accessed September 10, 2020. afghanistan-analysts.org/en/reports/political -landscape/peace-leadership-power-struggles-division-and-an-incomplete -council/.

———. "Still Preoccupied by 'Who Gets What': 100 Days of the New Government, but No Full Cabinet." Afghanistan Analysts Network, August 5, 2020. Accessed September 10, 2020. afghanistan-analysts.org/en/reports/ political-landscape/still-preoccupied-by-who-gets-what-100-days-of-the- new-government-but-no-full-cabinet/.

Afghanistan. Office of the President. "Unofficial Translation of the Inaugural Speech by H.E. Hamid Karzai." Accessed March 5, 2020. president.gov.af/ Contents/72/Documents/960/President_Karzai_s_Inaugural_Speech_Nov.pdf.

Ahmad, Aisha. *Jihad & Co.: Black Markets and Islamist Power*. New York: Oxford University Press, 2017.

Ahmad, Jibran. "Afghan Taliban Splinter Faction Picks Rival Leader." Reuters World News, November 2, 2015. Accessed March 5, 2020. ca.reuters.com/article/topNews/idCAKCN0SR0Q220151102.

Ahmed, Akbar. *The Thistle and the Drone*. Washington, DC: Brookings Institute Press, 2013.

Ahmed-Ghosh, Huma. "A History of Women in Afghanistan: Lessons Learnt for the Future, or Yesterdays and Tomorrow: Women in Afghanistan." *Journal of International Women's Studies* 4, no. 3 (2003): 1–14.

Alamyar, Mariam. "Education in Afghanistan: A Historical Review and Diagnosis." *College and University* 93, no. 2 (Spring 2018): 55–60.

Amiri, Rina, Swanee Hunt, and Jennifer Sova. "Transition Within Tradition: Women's Participation in Restoring Afghanistan." *Sex Roles* 51, no. 5/6 (September 2004): 283–91.

Amstutz, J. Bruce. *Afghanistan: The First Five Years of Soviet Occupation*. Washington, DC: National Defense University, 1986.

Anderson, Jon W. "There Are No *Khans* Anymore: Economic Development and Social Change in Tribal Afghanistan." *Middle East Journal* 32, no. 2 (Spring 1978): 167–83.

Ansar, Massoud. "Dostum's Continued Absence from Kabul Raises Questions." TOLOnews, July 28, 2020. Accessed September 10, 2020. tolonews.com/afghanistan/dostums-continued-absence-kabul-raises-questions.

Baker, Robert L. "The Passing of an Afghan King." *Current History* 39, no. 4 (January 1, 1934): 505–06.

Bakshi, G.D. "Afghanistan as a Rentier State Model: Lessons from the Collapse." *Strategic Analysis* 22, no. 5 (1998): 783–97.

Banerjee, Mukulika. *The Pathan Unarmed: Opposition and Memory in the North West Frontier*. Oxford: Oxford University Press, 2000.

Barfield, Thomas J. "Centralization/Decentralization in the Dynamics of Afghan History." *Cliodynamics: The Journal of Theoretical and Mathematical History* 3, no. 1 (2012): 94–104.

———. "Problems in Establishing Legitimacy in Afghanistan." *Iranian Studies* 37, no. 2 (2004): 263–293.

———. "Shari'a in Afghanistan." *Review of Faith & International Affairs* 10, no. 4 (2012): 45–52.

BBC News. "Afghan Conflict: Taliban to Resume Attacking Local Forces After Deal with US." March 2, 2020. Accessed March 6, 2020. bbc.com/news/world-asia-51706126.

———. "Afghan Conflict: Top Court Backs War Crimes Probe." March 5, 2020. Accessed March 6, 2020. bbc.com/news/world-asia-51751717.

———. "Afghan Conflict: US and Taliban Sign Deal to End 18-Year War." February 29, 2020. Accessed March 6, 2020. bbc.co.uk/news/world-asia-51689443.

———. "Afghanistan War: UN Says More Civilians Killed by Allies than Insurgents." July 30, 2019. Accessed March 5, 2020. bbc.com/news/world-asia-49165676.

———. "CIA-Backed Afghan Troops 'Committed War Crimes': Report." October 31, 2019. Accessed March 5, 2020. bbc.com/news/world-asia-50236357.

———. "Kabul Bomb: Deadly Blast Targets Afghan Vice President Amrullah Saleh." September 9, 2020. Accessed September 10, 2020. bbc.com/news/world-asia-54084841.

———. "Saba Sahar: Afghan Actress and Film Director Shot in Kabul." August 25, 2020. Accessed September 10, 2020. bbc.com/news/world-asia-53901711.

Bezhan, Faridullah. "The Emergence of Political Parties and Political Dynamics in Afghanistan, 1964–73." *Iranian Studies* 46, no. 6 (2013): 921–41.

———. "Ethno-Religious Dynamics and the Emergence of the Hezbe Seri Itehad (Secret Unity Party) in Afghanistan in the Late 1940s." *Central Asian Survey* 31, no. 4 (2012): 445–64.

———. "Pan-Islamism in Afghanistan in the Early Twentieth Century: From Political Discourse to Government Policy, 1906–22." *Islam and Christian–Muslim Relations* 25, no. 2 (2014): 193–210.

———. "The Pashtunistan Issue and Politics in Afghanistan, 1947–1952." *Middle East Journal* 68, no. 2 (Spring 2014): 197–209.

———. "The Rise and Fall of the Liberal Hezbe Watan or Homeland Party in Afghanistan, 1949–52." *British Journal of Middle Eastern Studies* 42, no. 4 (2015): 401–26.

Bodetti, Austin. "From WhatsApp to Hawala, How the Taliban Moves Money Around." *VICE*, November 15, 2016. Accessed March 5, 2020. vice.com/en_us/article/bmv3g3/from-whatsapp-to-hawala-how-the-taliban-moves-money-around.

Bradford, James. "Drug Control in Afghanistan: Culture, Politics, and Power During the 1958 Prohibition of Opium in Badakhshan." *Iranian Studies* 48, no. 2 (2015): 223–48.

———. *Poppies, Politics and Power: Afghanistan and the Global History of Drugs and Diplomacy.* Ithaca, NY: Cornell University Press, 2019.

Bradford, James, and David Mansfield. "Known Unknowns and Unknown

Knowns: What We Know About the Cannabis and the Hashish Trade in Afghanistan." *EchoGéo* 48 (April/June 2019): 1–11.

Bradsher, Henry S. *Afghan Communism and Soviet Intervention*. Oxford: Oxford University Press, 1999.

Brodsky, Anne E. *With All Our Strength: The Revolutionary Association of the Women of Afghanistan*. London: Routledge, 2003.

Cavendish, Julius. "After the US Pulls Out, Will CIA Rely More on Afghan Mercenaries?" *Christian Science Monitor*, November 16, 2011. Accessed March 5, 2020. csmonitor.com/World/Asia-South-Central/2011/1116/After-the-US-pulls-out-will-CIA-rely-more-on-Afghan-mercenaries.

Charpentier, C.-J. "The Use of Haschish and Opium in Afghanistan." *Anthropos* 68, no. 3/4 (1973): 482–90.

Choudhury, Nafay. "The Localised Madrasas of Afghanistan: Their Political and Governance Entanglements." *Religion, State & Society* 45, no. 2 (2017): 120–40.

Chua, Andrew. "The Promise and Failure of King Amanullah's Modernisation Program in Afghanistan." *ANU Undergraduate Research Journal* 5 (2013): 35–49.

Clark, Kate. "The Eid Ceasefire: Allowing Afghans to Imagine Their Country at Peace." Afghanistan Analysts Network. Accessed March 5, 2020. afghanistan-analysts.org/en/reports/war-and-peace/theeid-ceasefire-allowing-afghans-to-imagine-their-country-at-peace.

———. "Filling the Power Ministries: Biographies of the Four Candidates." Afghanistan Analysts Network. Accessed March 5, 2020. afghanistan-analysts.org/en/reports/political-landscape/filling-the-power-ministries-biographies-of-the-four-candidates.

———. "New Special Report on Afghanistan's Newest Local Defence Force: Were "All the Mistakes of the ALP" Turned into ANA-TF Safeguards?" Afghanistan Analysts Network, August 20, 2020. Accessed September 10, 2020. afghanistan-analysts.org/en/special-reports/new-special-report-on-afghanistans-newest-local-defence-force-were-all-the-mistakes-of-the-alp-turned-into-ana-tf-safeguards/.

———. "Reforming the Afghan Ministry of Interior: A Way to 'Tilt' the War?" Afghanistan Analysts Network. Accessed March 5, 2020. afghanistan-analysts.org/en/reports/war-and-peace/reforming-the-afghan-ministry-of-interior-a-way-to-tilt-the-war.

———. "War in Afghanistan in 2020: Just as Much Violence, but No One Wants to Talk About It." Afghanistan Analysts Network, August 16, 2020.

Accessed September 10, 2020. afghanistan-analysts.org/en/reports/war-and
-peace/war-in-afghanistan-in-2020-just-as-much-violence-but-no-one
-wants-to-talk-about-it/.

———. "War Without Accountability: The CIA, Special Forces and Plans for
Afghanistan's Future." Afghanistan Analysts Network. Accessed March 5, 2020.
afghanistan-analysts.org/en/reports/international-engagement/war-without
-accountability-the-cia-special-forces-and-plans-for-afghanistans-future/.

Clark, Kate, Ali Yawar Adilo and Ehsan Qaane. "The End of the Jirga: Strong
Words and Not Much Controversy." Afghanistan Analysts Network, May 3,
2019. Accessed September 10, 2020. afghanistan-analysts.org/en/reports
/political-landscape/the-end-of-the-jirga-strong-words-and-not-much
-controversy/.

Coll, Steve. *Ghost Wars*. New York: Penguin, 2004.

Cronin, Stephanie. "Afghanistan's Armies, Past and Present." *Armies and
State-Building in the Modern Middle East: Politics, Nationalism and Military
Reform*. London: I.B. Tauris, 2014.

Dale, Helle. "NATO in Afghanistan: A Test Case for Future Missions."
Heritage Foundation. Accessed March 5, 2020. heritage.org/europe/report/
nato-afghanistan-test-case-future-missions.

Dam, Bette. "The Secret Life of Mullah Omar." Zomia Center. Accessed March
5, 2020. zomiacenter.org/projects/secrethistorymullahomar.

Director of National Intelligence Open Source Center. *Master Narratives Country
Report: Afghanistan*. Accessed August 18, 2011. publicintelligence.net/
ufouo-open-source-center-master-narratives-country-report-afghanistan.

Doohovskoy, Andrei A. *Soviet Counterinsurgency in the Soviet Afghan War
Revisited: Analyzing the Effective Aspects of the Counterinsurgency Effort*.
Cambridge, MA: Harvard University Press, 2009.

Dupree, Louis. "Democracy and the Military Base of Power." *Middle East
Journal* 22, no. 1 (Winter 1968): 29–44.

———. "Mahmud Tarzi: Forgotten Nationalist." *South Asia Series* 53, no. 1
(1964): 21–42.

Edwards, David B. *Before Taliban: Genealogies of the Afghan Jihad*. Berkeley:
University of California Press, 2002.

Emadi, Hafizullah. "The Hazaras and Their Role in the Process of Political
Transformation in Afghanistan." *Central Asian Survey* 16, no. 3 (1997): 363–87.

———. "Radical Political Movements in Afghanistan and Their Politics of
Peoples' Empowerment and Liberation." *Central Asian Survey* 20, no. 4
(2001): 437–50.

———. "The State and Rural-Based Rebellion in Afghanistan." *Central Asian Survey* 15, no. 2 (1996): 201–211.

Eswaran, Eknath. *Nonviolent Soldier of Islam: Badshah Khan, a Man to Match His Mountains.* Tomales, CA: Nilgiri Press, 1984.

Farrell, Theo, and Antonio Giustozzi. "The Taliban at War: Inside the Helmand Insurgency, 2004–2012." *International Affairs* 89, no. 4 (2013): 845–71.

Feifer, Gregory. *The Great Gamble.* New York: Harper Collins, 2009.

Felbab-Brown, Vanda. "Kicking the Opium Habit? Afghanistan's Drug Economy and Politics Since the 1980s." *Conflict, Security & Development* 6, no. 2 (2006): 127–49.

Fenzel, Michael R. *No Miracles: The Failure of Soviet Decision-Making in the Afghan War.* Stanford: Stanford Security Studies, 2017.

Finley, Mark. "Afghanistan." *Contemporary Review* 175 (January 1, 1949): 225–30.

Foschini, Fabrizio. "Kabul's Expanding Crime Scene (Part 1): The Roots of Today's Underworld." Afghanistan Analysts Network. Accessed March 5, 2020. afghanistan-analysts.org/en/reports/context-culture/kabuls-expanding-crime-scene-part-1-the-roots-of-todays-underworld.

Fox, Ray S. *Agriculture in Afghanistan's Economy.* Washington, DC: United States Department of Agriculture Economic Research Service, 1967.

Franck, Peter G. "Problems of Economic Development in Afghanistan." *Middle East Journal* 3, no. 3 (July 1949): 293–314.

Ghani, Mohammad Ashraf. "Afghanistan's Vision for Peace: A Conversation with H.E. President Mohammad Ashraf Ghani," YouTube video, 1:00:04. Posted by the Atlantic Council, June 11, 2020. youtube.com/watch?reload=9&v=gkQ78s1IC2g.

Gibbons-Neff, Thomas. "Taliban Violated Afghan Deal with Shelling of American Bases, U.S. Officials Say." *New York Times*, August 30, 2020. Accessed September 10, 2020. nytimes.com/2020/08/30/world/asia/taliban-afghanistan-peace-us-attacks.html.

Gibbons-Neff, Thomas, and Mujib Mashal. "U.S. Is Quietly Reducing Its Troop Force in Afghanistan." *New York Times*, October 21, 2019.

Gibbs, David N. "Reassessing Soviet Motives for Invading Afghanistan: A Declassified History." *Critical Asian Studies* 38, no. 2 (2006): 239–63.

Giustozzi, Antonio. "Between Patronage and Rebellion: Student Politics in Afghanistan." Kabul: Afghanistan Research and Evaluation Unit, February 2010. Accessed March 5, 2020. https://areu.org.af/publication/1004.

———. *Koran, Kalashnikov and Laptop.* New York: Columbia University Press, 2008.

———. "March Towards Democracy? The Development of Political Movements in Afghanistan." *Central Asian Survey* 32, no. 3 (2013): 318–35.

———. "Nation-Building Is Not for All: The Politics of Education in Afghanistan." Afghanistan Analysts Network. Accessed March 5, 2020. afghanistan-analysts.org/en/special-reports/nation-building-is-not-for -all-the-politics-of-education/.

———. "War and Peace Economies of Afghanistan's Strongmen." *International Peacekeeping* 14, no. 1 (2007): 75–89.

Giustozzi, Antonio, ed. *Decoding the New Taliban: Insights from the Afghan Field*. New York, Columbia University Press, 2009.

Giustozzi, Antonio, and Christophe Reuter. "The Northern Front: The Afghan Insurgency Spreading Beyond the Pashtuns." Afghanistan Analysts Network. Accessed March 5, 2020. afghanistan-analysts.org/en/special -reports/the-northern-front-the-afghan-insurgency-spreading-beyond -the-pashtuns.

Goodhand, Jonathan. "Frontiers and Wars: the Opium Economy in Afghanistan." *Journal of Agrarian Change* 5, no. 2 (April 2005): 191–216.

Goodson, Larry P. "Perverting Islam: Taliban Social Policy Toward Women." *Central Asian Survey* 20, no. 4 (2001): 415–26.

Grau, Lester. "Breaking Contact Without Leaving Chaos: The Soviet Withdrawal from Afghanistan." *Journal of Slavic Military Studies* 20, no. 2 (2007): 235–61.

Green, Nile. "The Trans-Border Traffic of Afghan Modernism: Afghanistan and the Indian 'Urdusphere.'" *Comparative Studies in Society and History* 53, no. 3 (July 2011): 479–508.

Gregorian, Vartan. *The Emergence of Modern Afghanistan: Politics of Reform and Modernization, 1880–1946*. Stanford: Stanford University Press, 1969.

———. "Mahmud Tarzi and Saraj-ol-Akhbar: Ideology of Nationalism and Modernization in Afghanistan." *Middle East Journal* 21, no. 3 (Summer 1967): 345–68.

Guha, Amalendu. "Economic Development of Afghanistan — 1929–1961." *International Studies* 6, no. 4 (1964): 421–39.

———. "The Rise of Capitalistic Enterprises in Afghanistan 1929–45." *Indian Economic & Social History Review* 1, no. 2, (1963): 143–76.

Habibullah, Amir. *My Life — From Brigand to King*. London: Octagon, 2010.

Halliday, Fred. "Revolution in Afghanistan." *New Left Review*, no. 112 (November 1, 1978): 3–44.

Hanifi, M. Jamil. "Editing the Past: Colonial Production of Hegemony Through the 'Loya-Jerga' in Afghanistan." *Iranian Studies* 37, no. 2 (2004): 295–322.

Hashimi, Sayed El. "Afghanistan on the Tightrope." *Contemporary Review* 193 (January–June, 1958): 95–98.

———. "Afghanistan Revisited." *Contemporary Review* 182 (July–December, 1952): 21–24.

Hauner, Milan. "One Man Against the Empire: The Faqir of Ipi and the British in Central Asia on the Eve of and During the Second World War." *Journal of Contemporary History* 16, no. 1. Special issue, *The Second World War: Part 1* (January 1981): 183–212.

Holt, Ron. "Beyond the Tribe: Patron-Client Relations, Neopatrimonialism in Afghanistan." *Military Intelligence Professional Bulletin* 38, no. 1 (January–March 2012): 27–31.

Huq, Aziz, and Tom Ginsburg. "What Can Constitutions Do? The Afghan Case." *Journal of Democracy* 116 (2014): 116–30.

International Crisis Group. "Taliban Propaganda: Winning the War of Words?" Kabul/Brussels: International Crisis Group, Asia Report no. 158 (July 24, 2008).

Isaqzadeh, Mohammad Razaq, and Antonio Giustozzi. "Senior Appointments and Corruption Within the Afghan MoI: Practices and Perceptions." Integrity Watch Afghanistan. Accessed March 5, 2020. iwaweb.org/wp-content/uploads/2014/12/moi_senior_appointments_and_corruption_english.pdf.

Jackson, Ashley. "For the Taliban, the Pandemic Is a Ladder." *Foreign Policy*, May 6, 2020. Accessed September 10, 2020. foreignpolicy.com/2020/05/06/taliban-afghanistan-coronavirus-pandemic/.

Jones, Seth G. "A Failed Afghan Peace Deal." Council on Foreign Relations, Contingency Planning Memorandum No. 37 (July 2020). cfr.org/report/failed-afghan-peace-deal.

Kalinovsky, Artemy M. *A Long Goodbye: The Soviet Withdrawal from Afghanistan*. Boston: Harvard University Press, 2011.

Kapur, Roshni. "How Afghanistan's Peace Movement Is Winning Hearts and Minds." *Truthout*. Accessed September 22, 2018. truthout.org/articles/how-afghanistans-peace-movement-is-winning-hearts-and-minds.

Kazemi, S. Reza, and Fazl Rahman Muzhary. "COVID-19 in Afghanistan (4): A Precarious Interplay Between War and Epidemic." Afghanistan Analysts Network, June 19, 2020. Accessed September 10, 2020. afghanistan-analysts.org/en/reports/war-and-peace/covid-19-in-afghanistan-4-a-precarious-interplay-between-war-and-epidemic/.

Khan, Abdul Ghaffar. *My Life and Struggle*. Delhi: Hind Pocket Books, 1969.

Khrushchev, Nikita. *Khrushchev Remembers*, vol. 1. Boston: Andre Deutsch, 1971.

Koofi, Fawzia. "Afghan Negotiator and Campaigner Shot by Gunmen." *BBC News*, August 16, 2020. Accessed September 10, 2020. bbc.com/news/world-asia-53795870.

Kouvo, Sari, and Ehsan Qaane. "Will the ICC Start an Investigation in Afghanistan After All? What We Know So Far About the ICC Appeals Hearing." Afghanistan Analysts Network. Accessed March 5, 2020. afghanistan-analysts.org/will-the-icc-start-an-investigation-in-afghanistan-after-all-what-we-know-so-far-about-the-icc-appeals-hearing.

Leake, Elisabeth. "The Great Game Anew: US Cold-War Policy and Pakistan's North-West Frontier, 1947–65." *The International History Review* 35, no. 4 (2013): 783–806.

Limaye, Yogita. "The Sex Scandal at the Heart of the Afghan Government." *BBC News*, July 11, 2019. Accessed September 10, 2020. bbc.com/news/world-asia-48882226.

Mansfield, David. "The Helmand Food Zone: The Illusion of Success." Kabul: Afghanistan Research and Evaluation Unit, November 2019. Accessed September 10, 2020. areu.org.af/wp-content/uploads/2020/01/1908E-The-Helmand-Food-Zone-The-Illusion-of-Success.pdf.

———. "Turning Deserts into Flowers: Settlement and Poppy Cultivation in Southwest Afghanistan." *Third World Quarterly* 39, no. 2 (2018): 331–49.

———. "When the Water Runs Out: The Rise (and Inevitable Fall) of the Deserts of Southwest Afghanistan and Its Impact on Migration, Poppy and Stability." Kabul: Afghanistan Research and Evaluation Unit, April 2020. Accessed September 10, 2020. areu.org.af/publication/2006/.

Marsden, Peter. *The Taliban*. Oxford: Oxford University Press, 1998.

Martin, Mike. *An Intimate War: An Oral History of the Helmand Conflict*. New York: Oxford University Press, 2014.

Marwat, Fazal-ur Rahim Khan. *The Evolution and Growth of Communism in Afghanistan (1917–79): An Appraisal*. Karachi: Royal Book, 1997.

Masannat, George S. "Development and Diplomacy in Afghanistan." *Journal of Asian and African Studies* 4, no. 1 (January 1969): 51–60.

Mashal, Mujib and Najim Rahim. "Gunmen Kill Dozens at Event Attended by Afghan Politicians." March 6, 2020. Accessed March 6, 2020. nytimes.com/2020/03/06/world/asia/afghanistan-kabul-abdullah-election-violence.html.

Mashal, Mujib, Najim Rahim, and Fatima Faizi. "Ghani Named Afghan Election Winner: His Opponent Claims Victory, Too." February 18, 2020. Accessed March 6, 2020. nytimes.com/2020/02/18/world/asia/afghanistan-election-ashraf-ghani.html.

Matinuddin, Kamal. *The Taliban Phenomenon: Afghanistan 1994–1997.* Oxford: Oxford University Press, 1999.

McChesney, Robert D., ed. *Kabul Under Siege: Fayz Muhammad's Account of the 1929 Uprising.* Princeton: Marcus Weiner, 1999.

McCoy, Alfred W. *The Politics of Heroin: CIA Complicity in the Global Drug Trade.* New York: Harper and Row, 1972.

Muñoz, Carlo. "Drone Strike Takes Out Top Taliban Leader." *Washington Times,* December 2, 2018.

Murshed, S. Iftikhar. *Afghanistan: The Taliban Years.* London: Bennett & Bloom, 2006.

Murtazashvili, Ilia, and Jennifer Murtazashvili. "Coercive Capacity, Land Reform and Political Order in Afghanistan." *Central Asian Survey* 36, no. 2 (2017): 212–30.

Muzhary, Fazal. "The Bride Price: The Afghan Tradition of Paying for Wives." Afghanistan Analysts Network. Accessed March 5, 2020. afghanistan-analysts .org/en/reports/context-culture/the-bride-price-the-afghan-tradition-of -paying-for-wives.

Nawid, Senzil. "Comparing the Regimes of Amanullah (1919–29) and the Afghan Marxists (1978–92): Similarities and Differences." *Journal of Critical Studies of Iran & the Middle East* 2, no. 2 (1993): 15–32.

———. *Religious Response to Social Change in Afghanistan, 1919–1929: King Aman-Allah and the Afghan Ulama.* Costa Mesa, CA: Mazda, 1999.

Newell, Richard S. "The Dangers of Cold War Generosity." *Middle East Journal* 23, no. 2 (Spring 1969): 168–76.

———. *The Politics of Afghanistan.* London: Cornell University Press, 1972.

Nordland, Rod. "After Rancor, Afghans Agree to Share Power." *New York Times,* September 21, 2014.

———. "She's a Force of Nature, and She Just Declared War on Peace with the Taliban." *New York Times,* February 15, 2019. Accessed September 10, 2020. nytimes.com/2019/02/15/world/asia/afghanistan-taliban-peace.html.

Nowrouzi, Mahjooba. "WhereIsMyName: Afghan Women Campaign for the Right to Reveal their Names." *BBC Afghan Service,* July 25, 2020. Accessed September 10, 2020. bbc.com/news/world-asia-53436335.

Nunan, Timothy. "Under a Red Veil: Staging Afghan Emancipation in Moscow." *The Soviet and Post-Soviet Review* 38, no. 1 (2011): 30–62.

O'Ballance, Edgar. *Afghan Wars: Battles in a Hostile Land, 1839 to the Present.* London: Brassey's, 1993.

Pain, Adam. "Growing Out of Poverty? Questioning Agricultural Policy in Afghanistan." Afghanistan Analysts Network. Accessed March 5, 2020.

afghanistan-analysts.org/en/special-reports/growing-out-of-poverty
-questioning-agricultural-policy-in-afghanistan.

Pannell, Ian. "Afghan Election Fraud Is Unearthed." *BBC News*, August
18, 2009. Accessed September 26, 2020. news.bbc.co.uk/2/hi/south_
asia/8207315.stm.

Peters, Gretchen. *Seeds of Terror: How Heroin Is Bankrolling the Taliban and
al-Qaeda*. New York: St. Martin's, 2009.

Poullada, Leon. *Reform and Rebellion in Afghanistan, 1919–1929*. London:
Cornell University Press, 1973.

Power, Mike. "Drug Lords Have Figured Out How to Make Meth from Plants."
VICE, October 2, 2019. Accessed March 5, 2020. vice.com/en_ca/article
/8xwv83/drug-lords-have-figured-out-how-to-make-meth-from-plants.

Qaane, Ehsan. "To Release, Or Not to Release? Legal Questions Around
Ghani's Consultative Loya Jirga on Taleban Prisoners." Afghanistan
Analysts Network, August 7, 2020. Accessed September 10, 2020. afghanistan
-analysts.org/en/reports/war-and-peace/to-release-or-not-to-release-legal-
questions-around-ghanis-consultative-loya-jirga-on-taleban-prisoners/.

Quilty, Andrew. "Afghanistan's Unseen COVID Crisis." *The Interpreter*, August
12, 2020. Accessed September 10, 2020. lowyinstitute.org/the-interpreter/
afghanistan-s-unseen-covid-crisis.

Rashid, Ahmed. *Descent into Chaos*. London: Penguin, 2009.

———. "How Obama Lost Karzai." *Foreign Policy* no. 185 (March/April
2011): 71–76.

———. *Taliban*. New Haven: Yale University Press, 2001.

Ritter, William S. "The Final Phase in the Liquidation of Anti-Soviet Resistance
in Tadzhikistan: Ibrahim Bek and the Basmachi, 1924–31." *Soviet Studies*
37, no. 4 (1985): 484–93.

Robinson, Paul, and Jay Dixon. "Soviet Development Theory and Economic
and Technical Assistance to Afghanistan, 1954–1991." *The Historian* 72, no.
3 (Fall 2010): 599–623.

Rowlatt, Justin. "What the Heroin Industry Can Teach Us About Solar Power."
BBC News, July 27 2020. bbc.com/news/science-environment-53450688.

Rubinstein, Alvin Z. "Soviet Imperialism in Afghanistan." *Current History* 79,
no. 459 (October 1980): 80–103.

Ruttig, Thomas. "From Doha to Peace? Obstacles Rising in the Way of Intra-
Afghan Talks." Afghanistan Analysts Network, March 3, 2020. Accessed
September 10, 2020. afghanistan-analysts.org/en/reports/war-and-peace/
from-doha-to-peace-obstacles-rising-in-the-way-of-intra-afghan-talks/.

———. "The Great Talqaida Myth." Afghanistan Analysts Network. Accessed March 5, 2020. afghanistan-analysts.org/en/reports/regional-relations/the-great-talqaida-myth.

———. "How It All Began: A Short Look at the Pre-1979 Origins of Afghanistan's Conflicts." Afghanistan Analysts Network. Accessed March 5, 2020. afghanistan-analysts.net/uploads/20130111Ruttig-How_It_All_Began_FINAL.pdf.

———. "'Nothing Is Agreed Until Everything Is Agreed': First Steps in Afghan Peace Negotiations." Afghanistan Analysts Network. Accessed March 5, 2020. afghanistan-analysts.org/en/reports/war-and-peace/nothing-is-agreed-until-everything-is-agreed-first-steps-in-afghan-peace-negotiations.

———. "The Other Side: Dimensions of the Afghan Insurgency: Causes, Actors — and Approaches to Talks." Afghanistan Analysts Network. Accessed March 5, 2020. afghanistan-analysts.org/en/special-reports/the-other-side-dimensions-of-the-afghan-insurgency-causes-actors-and-approaches-to-talks.

Ruttig, Thomas, Ali Yawar Adili, and Obaid Ali. "Doors Opened for Direct Talks with the Taleban: The Results of the Loya Jirga on Prisoners and Peace." Afghanistan Analysts Network, August 12, 2020. Accessed September 10, 2020. afghanistan-analysts.org/en/reports/war-and-peace/kabul-opens-door-for-peace-talks-the-results-of-the-loya-jirga-on-prisoners-and-peace/.

Safi, Khalilullah, and Thomas Ruttig. "Understanding Hurdles to Afghan Peace Talks: Are the Taleban a Political Party?" Afghanistan Analysts Network. Accessed March 5, 2020. afghanistan-analysts.org/en/reports/war-and-peace/understanding-hurdles-to-afghan-peace-talks-are-the-taleban-a-political-party/.

Safri, Maliha. "The Transformation of the Afghan Refugee: 1979–2009." *Middle East Journal* 65, no. 4 (Autumn 2011): 587–601.

Sajjad, Tazreena. "Peace at All Costs? Reintegration and Reconciliation in Afghanistan." Kabul: Afghanistan Research and Evaluation Unit, October 2010. Accessed March 5, 2020. areu.org.af/wp-content/uploads/2016/02/1035E-Peace-at-all-Costs-IP-2010-web.pdf.

———. "A Timeline of U.S. Troop Levels in Afghanistan Since 2001." Associated Press, July 6, 2016.

Salahuddin, Sayed, and Pamela Constable. "The Fight over a Shrine for a Tyrannical Afghan King." *Washington Post*, August 20, 2016.

Savage, Charlie, Eric Schmitt, and Michael Schwirtz. "Russia Secretly Offered Afghan Militants Bounties to Kill U.S. Troops, Intelligence Says." *New York Times*, June 26, 2020. Accessed September 10, 2020. nytimes.com/2020/06/26/us/politics/russia-afghanistan-bounties.html.

Schofield, Julian. "Diversionary Wars: Pashtun Unrest and the Sources of the Pakistan-Afghan Confrontation." *Canadian Foreign Policy Journal* 17, no. 1 (2011): 38–49.

Shah, Saeed. "CIA Tactics to Trap Bin Laden Linked with Polio Crisis, Say Aid Groups." *Guardian*, March 2, 2012.

Shah, Sirdar Ikbal Ali. *Afghanistan of the Afghans*. London: Octagon, 1982.

———. *Modern Afghanistan: The Rise of Afghanistan as a Modern State*. London: Sampson Low & Marston, 1938.

———. "Nadir Shah and After." *Contemporary Review* 145 (January–June, 1934): 337–42.

Sharan, Timor, and John Heathershaw. "Identity Politics and Statebuilding in Post-Bonn Afghanistan: The 2009 Presidential Election." *Ethnopolitics* 10, no. 3–4, 2011: 297–319.

Simon, M. "Chapter VI. The Middle East: Afghanistan." *Annual Register* 171 (1929): 272–77.

Smith, Graeme. *The Dogs Are Eating Them Now: Our War in Afghanistan*. Toronto: Alfred A. Knopf, 2013.

———. "House of Pain: Canada's Connection with Kandahar's Ruthless Palace Guard." *Globe and Mail*, April 10, 2010.

Special Inspector General for Afghanistan Reconstruction. "Quarterly Report to the United States Congress." Arlington, VA: Special Inspector General for Afghanistan Reconstruction, 2019.

———. "Reintegration of Ex-Combatants: Lessons from the U.S. Experience in Afghanistan." Arlington, VA: Special Inspector General for Afghanistan Reconstruction, 2019.

Stewart, R.T. *Fire in Afghanistan, 1914–1929: Faith, Hope, and the British Empire*. New York: Doubleday, 1973.

Strick van Linschoten, Alex, and Felix Kuehn. "Separating the Taliban from al-Qaeda: The Core of Success in Afghanistan." New York University Center on International Cooperation, February 2011. Accessed March 5, 2020. cic.es.its.nyu.edu/sites/default/files/gregg_sep_tal_alqaeda.pdf.

Strick van Linschoten, Alex, and Felix Kuehn, eds. *Poetry of the Taliban*. New York: Columbia University Press, 2012.

Strickland, C.F. "The Economic Development of Afghanistan." *Contemporary Review* 143 (January–June, 1933): 714–22.

Sungur, Zeynep Tuba. "Early Modern State Formation in Afghanistan in Relation to Pashtun Tribalism." *Studies in Ethnicity and Nationalism* 16, no. 3 (2016): 437–55.

Timory, Asadullah, and Mujib Mashal. "In Afghan Attacks, Facts Are Murky. But It's Clear Deaths Are Piling Up." *New York Times*, July 23, 2020. Accessed September 10, 2020. nytimes.com/2020/07/23/world/asia/afghan -taliban-violence-airstrikes.html.

Timory, Asadullah, Najim Rahim, and Mujib Mashal. "A Girl's Heroic Battle Against the Taliban Was Also a Family Feud." *New York Times*, July 22, 2020. Accessed September 10, 2020. nytimes.com/2020/07/22/world/asia/ afghan-hero-woman-taliban.html.

Tolson, Michelle. "The Other Peace Talks: Afghan Women, Millennials, and Social Media." Last modified February 27, 2019. thediplomat.com/2019/03/ the-other-peace-talks-afghan-women-millennials-and-social-media/.

Tripodi, Christian. "'Politicals,' Tribes and Musahibans: The Indian Political Service and Anglo-Afghan Relations, 1929–39." *International History Review* 34, no. 4 (2012): 865–86.

United Nations Assistance Mission to Afghanistan. "Afghanistan: Protection of Civilians in Armed Conflict, Annual Reports 2017 and 2018." Kabul: UNHCR, February 2019.

———. "Afghanistan: Protection of Civilians in Armed Conflict Special Report: Airstrikes on Alleged Drug-Processing Facilities — Farah, 5 May 2019." Kabul: UNHCR, October 2019.

———. "Suicide Attacks in Afghanistan (2001–2007)." Kabul: UNAMA, September 1, 2007.

United Nations Development Programme. "Afghanistan Disbandment of Illegal Armed Groups (DIAG), First Quarter Report, 2010." Kabul: UNDP, 2010.

United Nations Office on Drugs and Crime. "Afghanistan Opium Survey 2018: Challenges to Sustainable Development, Peace and Security." Kabul: UNODC, 2019.

———. "The Global Afghan Opium Trade: A Threat Assessment." Vienna: UNODC, July 2011.

———. "World Drug Report 2020" Vienna: UNODC, June 2020.

Waldman, Matt. "Dangerous Liaisons with the Afghan Taliban." United States Institute for Peace, Special Report 256, October 2010.

———. "Golden Surrender: The Risks, Challenges, and Implications of Reintegration in Afghanistan." Afghan Analysts Network. Accessed March 5, 2020. afghanistan-analysts.org/en/special-reports/golden-surrender -the-risks-challenges-and-implications-of-reintegration-in-afghanistan.

Watkins, Mary Bradley. *Afghanistan: Land in Transition*. Princeton, NJ: D. Van Nostrand, 1963.

White House Archives. "Selected Speeches of President George W. Bush 2001–2008." Accessed November 7, 2019. georgewbush-whitehouse.archives.gov/infocus/bushrecord/documents/Selected_Speeches_George_W_Bush.pdf

Wilber, Donald N. *Afghanistan: Its People, Its Society, Its Culture.* New Haven, CT: Graf, 1962.

———. "Constitution of Afghanistan." *Middle East Journal* 19, no. 2 (Spring 1965): 215–29.

———. "The Structure and Position of Islam in Afghanistan." *Middle East Journal* 6, no. 1 (Winter 1952): 41–48.

Williams, Brian Glyn. "Afghanistan After the Soviets: From Jihad to Tribalism." *Small Wars & Insurgencies* 25, no. 5–6 (2014): 924–56.

Woods, Chris. "The Story of America's Very First Drone Strike." *Atlantic*, May 30, 2015.

World Health Organization. "Global COVID-19 Update." Accessed September 10, 2020. covid19.who.int/region/emro/country/af.

Yousafzai, Sami. "Exclusive: Inside the Mysterious 'Death' of Taliban Leader Mullah Omar." *Newsweek,* August 14, 2015.

———. "Mullah Najibullah: Too Radical for the Taliban." *Newsweek,* August 30, 2013.

Zaeef, Abdul Salam. *My Life with the Taliban.* Edited by Alex Strick van Linschoten and Felix Kuehn. New York: Columbia University Press, 2010.

Zulfacar, Maliha. "The Pendulum of Gender Politics in Afghanistan." *Central Asian Survey* 25, no. 1–2 (2006): 27–59.

INDEX

ABOUT THE AUTHOR

PHIL HALTON has worked in conflict zones around the world as an officer in the Canadian Army and as a security consultant. His debut novel, *This Shall Be a House of Peace* (Dundurn Press, 2019), received a starred review from *Booklist*, and his most recent novel, *Every Arm Outstretched*, released in 2020. Phil holds a master's degree in defence studies from the Royal Military College of Canada and a graduate certificate in creative writing from Humber College.